Hawthorne, Melville,
and the American character

Cambridge Studies in American Literature and Culture

Editor

Albert Gelpi, Stanford University

Advisory board

Nina Baym, University of Illinois, Champaign-Urbana
Sacvan Bercovitch, Harvard University
Richard Bridgman, University of California, Berkeley
David Levin, University of Virginia
Kenneth Lynn, Johns Hopkins University
Joel Porte, Harvard University
Mike Weaver, Oxford University

Hawthorne, Melville, and the American character

A looking-glass business

JOHN P. McWILLIAMS JR.

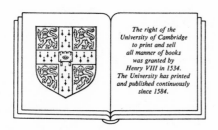

The right of the
University of Cambridge
to print and sell
all manner of books
was granted by
Henry VIII in 1534.
The University has printed
and published continuously
since 1584.

CAMBRIDGE UNIVERSITY PRESS

CAMBRIDGE

LONDON   NEW YORK   NEW ROCHELLE

MELBOURNE   SYDNEY

Published by the Press Syndicate of the University of Cambridge
The Pitt Building, Trumpington Street, Cambridge CB2 1RP
32 East 57th Street, New York, NY 10022, USA
296 Beaconsfield Parade, Middle Park, Melbourne 3206, Australia

First published 1984
First paperback edition 1985

Printed in the United States of America

Library of Congress Cataloging in Publication Data
McWilliams, John P., Jr.
Hawthorne, Melville, and the American character.
(Cambridge studies in American literature and
culture)
Includes index.
1. American literature – 19th century – History and
criticism. 2. National characteristics, American, in
literature. 3. United States in literature.
4. Hawthorne, Nathaniel, 1804–1864 – Knowledge – History.
5. Melville, Herman, 1819–1891 – Knowledge – History.
I. Title. II. Series.
PS217.N38M38   1984   813'.3'09   83-15235
ISBN 0 521 25900 2
ISBN 0 521 31146 2

For Andrew, Suzannah, Kirsten, and Elizabeth

The influence of Character, that is the Theocracy.

Emerson, *Journal* (1840)

CONTENTS

PREFACE

Like most inquiries into the past, this book has its origin in personal conviction as well as professional concern, both of which should be disclosed at the outset. My scholarly purpose can be stated with comparative ease. Although intellectual historians have recognized the importance of the concept of national character in defining and developing the American Republic during its formative years, literary scholars have yet to consider the portrayal of national character in the writings of the two great novelists of the period. In much of his best fiction, Hawthorne was deeply concerned with the development of New England character throughout historical time, and with its implications for the national future, yet there exists no thorough study of his New Englanders as he saw them changing from generation to generation, from colony to province to republic. We know that Melville once shared the heady national faith of America at midcentury, but the intellectual difficulties and literary consequences of sustaining that faith have not yet been explored in depth. This book attempts to remedy both deficiencies in our literary understanding.

To regard a gap as a deficiency amounts to tacit admission of an extraprofessional purpose. The years from 1820 to 1850 constitute the era when there developed a widely shared popular commitment to the values that were to build and sustain this nation until very recent years. Because of common family backgrounds, common political leanings, similar religious disaffiliations, and personal friendship, Nathaniel Hawthorne and Herman Melville perceived their culture's emerging values from a rare perspective of informed yet detached concern. To borrow a phrase from Larzer Ziff, they were "native-born outsiders," whose very selection of fiction as their medium shows us a preference for a historical rather than a prophetic vision.[1] Their portrayal of Americans can provide us windows, at once wide and many angled, for viewing lasting problems of mind and desire. I do not, however, contend that the identity of the

American or the future of the Republic was the central concern of either author, and I here explicitly say so. By exploring the national implications of their fiction, I imply no geographical restriction of its meaning, only a special pertinence to the culture of its origin.

The order of my chapters needs explanation. By citing well-known observations of the new republic, by Europeans as well as Americans, the introduction identifies recurrent conceptual problems in the many attempts to define the hypothetical "America" and "American" dear to mid-nineteenth-century nationalists. Later chapters study the ways in which the fictions of Hawthorne and Melville refine and question, deny or reaffirm, these same national models. Because of Hawthorne's heightened sensitivity to historical change, and to the particular temper of an era, his American fictions will be considered in chronological order of their place in New England and American history. Although this method risks ignoring possible changes of conviction during his writing career, Henry James was surely correct in claiming that Hawthorne's imagination remained very much of a piece, that "his mind proper – his mind in so far as it was a repository of opinions and articles of faith – had no development that it is of especial importance to look into."[2] The national implication of any of Melville's works depends heavily upon its particular context in a writing career of astonishing variety and change. Lacking Hawthorne's firm grounding in American history, Melville often treated issues of American character and destiny as moral imperatives only secondarily dependent upon societal causes and historical time. Younger and more volatile than Hawthorne, more impulsive in extending an idea to its limits, Melville was far more susceptible to the extremes of ecstatic national faith and disillusioned skepticism. The significance of his commitment to American values thus derives from altered assertions within his own writings, rather than observed changes within historical time. Whereas Hawthorne's imagined New England develops from past to present centuries, Melville's America changes with his own perceptions, thereby demanding a greater regard for the place of a work in the history of the author's imagination.

Michael Bell, Hennig Cohen, George Dekker, Albert Gelpi, Joel Porte, Roy Harvey Pearce, and Henry Nash Smith have been generous in offering helpful suggestions upon all or parts of this manuscript. The final draft has greatly benefited from David Levin's thorough and painstaking criticisms, especially with regard to the issue of Puritan decline, both in its seventeenth-century fact and in its nineteenth-century literary re-creation. I am grateful for research privileges and staff help at the following institutions: the Abernethy Library, the University of California at Berkeley, the Houghton Library, the University of Illinois at Chicago Circle, the

New York Public Library, and the Widener Library. The *American Quarterly* and *Studies in Romanticism* have granted permission to revise and reprint portions of published articles.[3] Cynthia Ketchum and Jennifer Nelson have brought accuracy and good humor to the typing of the manuscript. Liz Maguire of Cambridge University Press has brought the same to the editing of it. Margot McWilliams generously provided Time, Strength, and Patience, if not Cash. The greatest debt of anyone writing about Hawthorne and Melville is to the many who have gone before. I apologize for any omissions of scholarly indebtedness, all of which, like the other faults of this book, are quite unintended but wholly mine.

A word about my assumptions: I believe that a work of imaginative literature, even a prose romance, however otherworldly it may seem, is an individual's rendering of people, events, beliefs, or feelings that are rooted in personal and/or cultural experience. The written word is one means by which human beings attempt to convey their perceptions of life to others, and not a set of interreferential signs creating an autonomous world for decoding by academic critics. To those of the semiotic, structuralist, or deconstructionist persuasion, this book may therefore seem outmoded, even negligible. So be it. I ask them only to grant that the assumptions of historical criticism have proven to be no less valid, no less pertinent to the trials of living, than those of the new formalism. Throughout the many rewritings of this manuscript, I have tried to efface myself in my subject, to replace abstract words with concrete ones wherever possible, and to strive for clarity of statement.

INTRODUCTION: TOMORROW'S AMERICAN

We think our civilization near its meridian, but we are yet only at the cock-crowing and the morning star. In our barbarous society, the influence of character is in its infancy. As a political power, as the rightful lord who is to tumble all rulers from their chairs, its presence is hardly yet suspected.

Emerson, "Politics" (1844)

A nation, properly to boast itself, and to take and maintain its position with other States, must prove itself in possession of self-evolving attributes. Its character must be as individual as that of the noblest citizen that dwells within its limits.

William Gilmore Simms, "Americanism in Literature" (1845)

If one can ever justifiably use the term "consensus" in speaking of the values of an entire people, it is surely appropriate to Americans between 1828 and 1850. The consensus that intellectual historians have uncovered may have rested upon conveniently undefined abstractions, but it was nonetheless broad and intensely cherished. The very survival of the American Republic, together with its undeniable growth and visible if not universal prosperity, seemed to show that divine Providence was looking upon the Great Experiment with favor. Wherever one's private forebodings might have pointed, only a diehard Federalist or a temperamental croaker would have dared publicly to oppose any of the following desiderata: man's natural right to political liberty and equality, the Constitution as the Republic's palladium of collective freedom, equality of economic opportunity in a free marketplace, private property as a spur

1

to individual achievement, enlarging the domain of freedom, America as an asylum for oppressed peoples, and the treasured trinity of free schools, free religion, and free land. Loyalty to one's region was assumed somehow to complement loyalty to one's nation. Freedom of religion was expected to protect rather than discourage popular piety by permitting the egalitarian roots of democracy and Christianity to grow together more naturally.[1]

The building of institutions to encourage these values seemed to show that America was at least on the progressive rise of its historical cycle, if not bound for the Millennium, some form of secular utopia, or the best of all possible nation-states. Whenever these collective abstractions were brought to bear upon such vexingly particular issues as a national bank, tariffs, slavery, majority versus minority rights, qualifications for statehood, land-settlement policy, Indian removal, or libel, it quickly became apparent that the terms had different meanings depending on the values and interests of their users. Such variety of interpretation, however, served only to reaffirm the imaginative power and flexibility of the concepts themselves. The most reliable and well-trodden road to popular approval, for any political or social group, was to denounce one's opponent as an aristocrat, a usurper of power, a believer in big government, an atheist, or a defender of any kind of legal privilege.

Recurrent problems in affirming the national consensus surface in two of the age's most widely known documents, Andrew Jackson's "Farewell Address" of 1836 and George Bancroft's "Introduction" to his *History of the United States* (1834). By returning to Washington's ceremony of a presidential farewell, Jackson evidently sought to assure the nation that the founding fathers' dream had been realized:

> The progress of the United States under our free and happy institutions has surpassed the most sanguine hopes of the founders of the Republic. Our growth has been rapid beyond all former example in numbers, in wealth, in knowledge, and all the useful arts which contribute to the comforts and convenience of man, and from the earliest ages of history to the present day there never have been thirteen millions of people associated in one political body who enjoyed so much freedom and happiness as the people of these United States. You have no longer any cause to fear danger from abroad; your strength and power are well known throughout the civilized world, as well as the high and gallant bearing of your sons. It is from within, among yourselves – from cupidity, from corruption, from disappointed ambition and inordinate thirst for power – that factions will be formed and liberty endangered. It is against such designs, whatever disguise the actors may assume, that you have especially to guard yourselves. You have the highest of human trusts committed to your care. Providence has showered on this favored land blessings without number, and has chosen you as the

guardians of freedom, to preserve it for the benefit of the human race. May He who holds in His hands the destinies of nations make you worthy of the favors He has bestowed and enable you, with pure hearts and pure hands and sleepless vigilance, to guard and defend to the end of time the great charge He has committed to your keeping.[2]

The imperious mode of this exhortation surely led many Americans to believe, with Herman Melville, that Andrew Jackson had been the champion of a "great democratic God," selected from the "kingly commons" to be hurled upon a warhorse and thundered "higher than a throne."[3] Jackson's eloquence in the forum may now seem to be rhetoric in the study, but it is rhetoric of the sort that masks revealing problems. Twice in this passage Jackson couples the words "freedom" and "happiness," yet the only sign he provides of an American's happiness is the astonishing growth of the nation in size and prosperity. The sudden intrusive warning about the possibility of internal corruption thus suggests that Jackson's reliance upon external prosperity to illustrate internal happiness is perhaps an unconscious rationalization. By then assuring the nation that its prov- idential mission is for the benefit of the entire human race, he sidesteps the problems of Indian removal and emerging sectional conflict so that he can close with reassuring prophecy. The notion of providential mission ultimately serves Jackson much as the notion of sacred trust served Webster – as a goad to spur possibly unworthy sons into strenuous effort in a perplexingly unspecified direction.[4]

George Bancroft's "Introduction," which remained essentially unchanged in all the editions Bancroft supervised, offered similar assurances to gen- erations of American readers. Seemingly without a trace of doubt, Bancroft declares that the charge of America's historian is "to follow the steps by which a favoring Providence, calling our institutions into being, has conducted the country to its present happiness and glory." The introduction consists of a listing, almost a litany, which celebrates those qualities which are continuing to render the nation great: equality of political right, popular sovereignty, economic prosperity, domestic peace, cultivation of national resources, internal improvements, the complementary growth of farming and manufacturing, the Bill of Rights, and absorption of immigrant nationalities. Bancroft asserts that "the force of moral opinion is rapidly increasing," but he shows us only external conditions that might promote "happiness and glory." Although the narrative of the *History* acknowledges that the continued success of a libertarian policy depends on the internal virtues of its citizenry, Bancroft's introduction invokes the sheer power of America's transformative energy, while assuming that the people's inner and spiritual grace has already been achieved. Those readers who formed first conceptions of the country upon Bancroft's introduction rather than his text would not have known that slavery, sectional hostility, poverty, or political parties even existed in antebellum America.[5]

The reifying of these two cultural visions must ultimately depend upon the energetic and virtuous character of the American people. When Jackson declared, "No free government can stand without virtue in the people," he was reminding contemporaries of an unwelcome warning voiced by Washington, Jefferson, and John Adams before him: Liberty will last only as long as the people are worthy of it. The recognition that a republic presumes the virtue of its citizenry was to lead generations of cultural observers, European and American, to attempt a definitive account of the American character, partly out of intrinsic interest and partly to determine whether the Republic was to last. Even before the United States was recognized as an independent nation, Crèvecoeur's essay "What is an American?" endeavored to persuade prospective settlers that there was, indeed, one American character shaped by the conditions of a prosperous, agrarian, freeholding economy. Noah Webster compiled his dictionary in order "to inspire them [the people of this country] with the pride of national character." Although Washington Irving never completed his book on America, it was to begin with an essay titled "American Character." At the time Emerson was working on *Nature*, he was convinced that "history . . . ought to be written in a settled conviction that no event is casual or solitary, that all events proceed inevitably from peculiar qualities of the national character which are permanent or very slightly modified from age to age." The phrase "national character" served as one of the topics – and hence one of the lenses – through which the long procession of European observers, including Michel Chevalier, Francis Grund, Adam Gurowsky, Harriet Martineau, Phillip Schaff, and Alexis de Tocqueville, attempted to focus and organize their impressions.[6]

The attempt to render national character proved not to be readily transportable to the New World. It was comparatively easy to discover a national character in the substance of historical legends, the crises of history, the effects of long-standing institutions, the manners of fixed classes, or the customs of a single race. But how was one to define the national character of a people who, at least publicly, prided themselves upon being without a determining past, without constricting institutions, without fixed classes, and without homogeneity of race and region? Crèvecoeur provides the prototypical illustration of the problem:

> *He* is an American who, leaving behind him all his ancient prejudices and manners, receives new ones from the new mode of life he has embraced, the new government he obeys, and the new rank he holds. He becomes an American by being received in the broad lap of our great Alma Mater. Here individuals of all nations are melted into a new race of men, whose labours and posterity will one day cause great changes in the world.[7]

To be the new man, to be free, to be melted into a new race was not to have a describable national identity of one's own. It was merely to represent the promise of being freed from all that was Europe. Crèvecoeur's farmer is an American only through the power of a negative definition. Because he is so belligerently new and free, he cannot possess those positive traits which accrue through living commitments. Crèvecoeur does the best he can to endow James with both a character and local loyalties, but James's Americanness is defined largely by the autonomy of his agrarian household and by his political freedoms, rather than by any inner qualities.

It was logical to expect that, once the Republic had been firmly established, the inner character of the representative American would have begun to emerge. Later European visitors, however, showed even less certainty than Crèvecoeur in fleshing out the American. Tocqueville declared that the Americans' migratory habits and egalitarian laws were producing "one national character," but he did not specify what it was. After protesting that Parson Weems's glacial portrait of George Washington provided no model American for the 1830s, Harriet Martineau lamented that "the old world must have patience; for the Americans have no national character yet; nor can they have, for a length of years." Two decades later, the revolutionary Polish aristocrat Adam Gurowski, recognizing that his repeated insistence on American "elasticity" and "adaptability" was not gratifyingly specific, acknowledged that "hitherto the American mind has not reached the elevated standing of an absolute, intuitive individuality." Even Philip Schaff, who knew and admired Americans as thoroughly as any European, contended only that "in this chaos of peoples the traces of a specifically American national character may be found." "Though the main features of the American character may be already quite plainly discerned," Schaff concluded, "yet it is only in its formation state."[8]

One problem was that the political ideals which provided the seedbed for an American's virtues were often claimed to be the virtues themselves. Terms such as "democracy," "liberty," "equality" and "progress" not only constituted a political faith. For new men in a new world, these collective abstractions served as a way of defining their communal as well as individual character. In a typical patriotic oration, Williams Evans Arthur described a representative countryman as the embodiment of the nation's religion:

> The American is the ark of safety, the anointed civilizer, the only visible source of light and heat and repose to the dark and discordant and troubled World, which is heaving and groaning and livid in convulsions around him! He is Liberty's chosen apostle; he is a master workman and universal space is his workshop, and universal perfectibility his hallowed aim.[9]

Arthur may assert that the American is both the Christ and the master-workman of Liberty, but his mingling of religious and political terms serves to hide rather than reveal any individuating character. His metaphors describe how an American functions at the expense of what he intrinsically is.

Accustomed to such rhetoric, Tocqueville perceived the paradox it contained: All Americans would be individuals, yet all would be the same. Tocqueville could thus appreciate the novelty of the American term "individualism" while simultaneously insisting upon democratic conformity and the tyranny of majority opinion. Although the prospect of each citizen's unique identity is implicit in the individual's right to liberty, equality of political right encourages the hope that a democratic people will develop one character. Emerson, himself forever searching for traces of the true American character, was equally conscious that the very universality of American ideals worked against individualism. Although Emerson might write, in a public essay, "The appearance of character makes the State unnecessary. The wise man is the State," he also acknowledged in his journal that "character is scarcely allowed any rule at all. Everything governs but that. It is a force not yet known."[10] Forever trusting that America was evolving its national genius, and forever disgruntled at the paltry realities, he could assert that character is the only theocracy, write an essay on the subject, and yet include no American, not even Washington or Webster, among his *Representative Men.*[11]

Fully to appreciate the magnitude of this dilemma, we must recognize that the American character, like America itself, was not a present reality but a future prospect. In each of the preceding quotations, Tocqueville, Martineau, Gurowski, Schaff, and Emerson implied that the American character was yet to be. Because America and the American were becoming vacant mirror images of one another, no one was quite sure whether the individual should be defined through the nation, or the nation through the individual. Whichever way one perceived this reciprocal process, however, the search for the American demanded that one glimpse the future through an embryonic present.

Consider a number of the phrases by which even nonmillennialist Americans of these decades defined the merits of their new culture: the Genius of America, the Grand Experiment, the Sacred Trust, the American Scholar, the Universal Republic, the Open West, Young America, and Manifest Destiny. Each of these entities was a moral abstraction predicated upon an inadequate present and an almost certain future. Each contained a grand providential contract contingent upon Americans' remaining worthy of their democratic ideals, material advantages, and founding heritage. Rhetorically, such terms were admirably suited to adapting the mode of the American jeremiad to republican values.[12] Their cultural realization, however, had to remain unfulfilled. If developmental energies were to be released, such abstract goals could neither be attained nor abandoned. Even expansionists as unblushingly certain as William Gilpin insisted that America's destiny was still "untransacted." Within one paragraph, Walter Whitman would confidently predict a "holy millennium of liberty," only to fall into a doubt from which sheer reaffirmation provided the only exit: "If it should fail! O, dark were the horror and dreary beyond description the horror of such a failure – which we anticipate not at all."[13]

The people's contract with a progressive Providence, like the Puritans' covenant with their God, released both the exhilaration of a great promise and the anxiety of fulfilling it, thereby impelling Americans toward a future at once bright and vacant. This divided response pervaded writers of widely varying backgrounds and beliefs. Emerson's resolute will to believe led him to dedicate his 1822 notebook "to the Spirit of America. I dedicate it to that living soul, which *doth* exist somewhere beyond the Fancy." Even so settled a gentleman as Gulian Verplanck observed, "We are all pressing and hastening forward to some better future. The momentum of the whole, composed of myriads of living forces, is upon each individual, and he flies forward with accelerated velocity, without any other power over his own motion than that of the direction of its course." According to Harriet Martineau, energetic pursuit of an undefined future allowed Americans not to think about sectional conflict:

> With a dark and shifting near future, and a bright and fixed ultimate destiny, what is the true, the only wisdom? Not to pry into the fogs and thickets round about, or to stand still for fear of what may next occur in the path; but to look from Eden gate behind to heaven gate before, and press on to the certain future.[14]

Ascribing a different cause for the shapeless magnitude of the nation's quest, Tocqueville contended that the Americans' commitment to equality of right was impelling them "unceasingly toward that unmeasured greatness so distinctly visible at the end of the long track which humanity has yet to tread." As late as the mid-1850s, the man who had devoted himself to memorializing the nation's glorious past and happy present could assert that his generation's seeming failure could be no cause for lasting discontent. Writing to Evert Duyckinck, George Bancroft declared: "Happy man, that you are to be so young. You will live to see great things achieved in your country. The men of your day will go far beyond those of mine; America is destined to take the highest place in the empire of mind. I feel myself at most to be but a pioneer; and rest my hopes on those who come after me."[15]

A nation that will exist "in the empire of mind" is very like Emerson's anticipation of "a Columbia of thought and art which is the last and endless sequel of Columbus's adventure," or like Tocqueville's admission that "in America I saw more than America. I sought there the image of democracy itself, with its inclinations, its character, its prejudices, and its passions." Such futuristic image making evidently engrossed the populace for reasons that extend beyond Horace Bushnell's perception of "the remarkable power of abstractions in the American mind." "America," after all, had for decades retained a remarkable power of abstraction upon European imaginations. American citizens were engaging in a particular mode of defining self and country, a mode first recognized, as one might expect, by a European long resident in America. In his reflections on "National Character of the Americans," Francis Grund observed:

> An American does not love his country as a Frenchman loves France, or an Englishman England: America is to him but a physical means of establishing a moral power—the medium through which his mind operates—'the local habitation' of his political doctrines. His country is in his understanding; he carries it with him wherever he goes, whether he emigrates to the shores of the Pacific or the Gulf of Mexico; his home is wherever he finds minds congenial with his own.[16]

If home, as Melville would later imply, is any gathering of congenial democrats, then the West was not so much a place as a future wherein America might be realized. Following through the implications of these ideas, Grund arrived at the proposition that "America" is no more, but no less, than a future ideal created by its beholder:

> I will now add that the Americans *love* their country, not, indeed, *as it is*, but *as it will be*. They do not love the land of their fathers; but they are sincerely attached to that which their children are destined to inherit. They live in the future, and make their country as they go on.[17]

At this point Grund turned to other concerns, but his last sentence implies that an ever newly created ideal only draws one's eyes toward an ever-receding horizon.

For the journey to create America, the individual citizen was equipped, Tocqueville asserted, with a new and untried source of knowledge. Deprived of the institutions and hierarchies that gave men of the Old World their identity, yet contemptuous of the very idea of a past, Americans would be likely to extend individualism into the belief that all knowledge could be found within the self:

> To evade the bondage of system and habit, of family maxims, class opinions, and, in some degree, of national prejudices; to accept tradition only as a means of information, and existing facts only as a lesson to be used in doing otherwise and doing better; to seek the reason of things for oneself, and in oneself alone; to tend to results without being bound to means, and to strike through the form to the substance – such are the principal characteristics of what I shall call the philosophical method of the Americans.[18]

Tocqueville's belief that the American seeks the reason of things *in himself*[19] is no casual by-thought, but a conclusion based upon a group of logical propositions apparent elsewhere in his second volume. The Americans' belief in equality, he claims, renders them less likely to see distinctions among citizens: "In democratic communities, where men are all insignificant and very much alike, each man instantly sees all his fellows when he surveys himself." As a consequence, the American is prone to assume that "all the truths that are applicable to himself" must be "equally applicable to each of his fellow citizens and fellow men." Knowledge of self thus becomes knowledge of others; individual reflects nation; microcosm reflects macrocosm. Those Americans who believe the self to be divine may be exhilarated by the prospect of a pantheistic utopia, but all Americans must share in the discouraging process of self-enclosure: "Everyone shuts himself up tightly within himself and insists upon judging the world from there."[20]

Although the applicability of Tocqueville's ideas to Whitman's poetry has long been conceded,[21] we need to consider whether those ideas have a broader literary reach. To use more current terms, Tocqueville is asserting that the democratic American must be a solipsist who creates the world in his own self-image by projecting his self onto the world. When we consider that in the 1830s most Americans were living on the edge of at least twenty-five hundred miles of wilderness, under an experimental polity, without settled institutions or a visible history, but with real prospects of going ahead to some unknown and better future, is it not likely that they should have perceived their world as an extension of their selves? Faced with a bewildering variety of regional cultures that supposedly constituted one America, would not those citizens posit an America in the image of their own region? Under such conditions, the outside world, the Not Me, becomes a limitless void, the representative American becomes an extension of oneself, and America becomes one's unknowable future ascribed to all citizenry. Intending no exclusion, Northern white male Protestant writers would thus be led to write of the American character without recalling that the South, blacks, Indians, or women participated in America.

Assessments of Americans' responses to their environs unintentionally suggest that fear of vastness led many citizens to imagine the future of the wilderness in comfortingly personal terms. Tocqueville observed that most Americans were unable to perceive the natural beauty surrounding them because they loved to imagine themselves, in the aggregate, as subduers of the wilderness. Amazed at white settlers' indifference to an Indian dying in the streets of Buffalo, Tocqueville remarked, "In the heart of this society, so policed, so prudish, so sententiously moral and virtuous, one encounters a complete insensibility, a sort of cold and implacable egoism when it's a question of the American *indigenies*." While invoking the presumably inexhaustible resources of the continent, Whitman would note that "the mind becomes almost lost in tracing in imagination these hidden and boundless tracts of our territory." Francis Grund, who had observed businessmen in three Northern cities, remarked that "an American merchant is an enthusiast who seems to delight . . . to risk his capital and credit on some *terra incognita*, rather than follow the beaten tracks of others." Well aware that Americans regarded the sea as their second frontier, Verplanck gloomily concluded, "We are all of us as waves in the shoreless ocean of human existence."[22]

In all these passages recurs a haunted sense of inhabiting a void that one can reduce to order only by a strenuous imposition of the will. Either the other can be seen as an extension of self, or the other does not matter. An especially telling measure of this tendency is Frederick Merk's account of a common American explanation for the Mexicans' curious determination to continue resisting American Manifest Destiny by force of arms: American troops actually believed that "the Puros, or republican elements were . . . fighting our troops for no other purpose than to make sure those troops would not be called home. Nothing was so feared by the better elements as withdrawal of our forces, which would have the effect of delivering the people over to their native oppressors."[23]

No writer was more aware than Emerson of the American tendency to see one's own character in a void. Emerson's insistence that "it is the constant tendency of the mind to Unify all it beholds, or to reduce the remotest facts to a single law," closely resembles Tocqueville's contention that the American democrat needs "to explain a mass of facts by a single cause." Emerson's claim, "In man the perpetual progress is from the Individual to the Universal," reaffirms Tocqueville's belief that the democratic imagination sees all one's fellows in oneself.[24] In 1838, at the fullest tide of his hope, Emerson proudly wrote "Each man projects his character before him – praises it, worships it."[25] To engage in such projection is, quite literally, to make an icon of the self perceived in one's future.

If Tocqueville was correct, what Emerson perceived in himself he should also have perceived for his nation. And, in fact, shortly before writing the preceding entry, Emerson had declared America to be "a vase of fair outline but empty, which whoso seeth may fill with what wit & character is in him." During the late 1830s, he was so confident that the vase and the void could be admirably filled that he urged: "Every new mind ought to take the attitude of Columbus – launch out from the ignorant gaping World, & sail west for a new world." America, in sum, was the world of self-making, a state of mind in which, by sheer force of imagination, one could create oneself as the American Scholar or the

Poet. Aboard ship to the Old World in 1833, Emerson had suspected that "the creative efflux" evident in man's artifacts truly was "the America of America." By the time he gathered similar passages together for "The Over-Soul," he had arrived at a limitless confidence in every man's ability to create a self-sufficient universe out of himself: "The soul looketh steadily forwards, creating a world before her, leaving worlds behind her. She has no dates, nor rites, nor persons, nor specialties, nor men. The soul knows only the soul."[26]

For Emerson, then, as for many of his imaginative countrymen, everything that constituted America was yet to be, but whatever America was to become could only be a projection of unspecified, presumably admirable virtues in the individual's character. The phrase "self-made man," which Henry Clay introduced in an 1832 Senate speech,[27] enabled each citizen to see the American as the individual he was to make from himself. A few writers not only became aware of the psychological process, but found the perfect metaphor for it. In a typically unpursued flash of insight, Emerson confided to his journal the ironic predicament of any external search for one's future self: One would become "a pilgrim wandering in search of a man. This too will plainly be a looking-glass business." Charles Sumner opened his review of Grund's *The Americans* by picturing the dilemma of a people compelled to make their country as they go on: "The people of the United States are like persons surrounded by mirrors. They may catch their likeness from every quarter, and in every possible light . . . Turn we as we may, we catch our reflected features; the vista seems to lengthen at every sight." Herman Melville wrote *Moby-Dick* with the belief that the story of Narcissus was the key to it all, and Nathaniel Hawthorne, who explored the consequences of narcissistic self-projection in such tales as "Young Goodman Brown," also wrote a willfully whimsical sketch, etched in self-shadows, titled "Monsieur du Miroir."[28]

When Tocqueville imagined the thoughts of a future American author choosing a subject, he emphasized the American's mental proclivity for seeing outer world and inner self reflected in one another: "I need not traverse earth and sky to discover a wondrous object woven of contrasts, of infinite greatness and littleness, of intense gloom and amazing brightness, capable at once of exciting pity, admiration, terror, contempt. I have only to look at myself." The major American writers of the period illustrate the acuity of Tocqueville's prediction. While Tocqueville was writing his unsupported conjectures about the American imagination, Emerson was recreating the American Scholar in his own self-image, revealing that he often felt himself "part or parcel" of God, and declaring that "the Universe is the externization of the Soul." Throughout *Walden*, Thoreau attempted to wake the neighbors up to their own heroic potential by creating an exemplary rebellious self attuned to higher natural law, a self whom readers were meant to identify not only with the experiences but also with the self-created character of Henry David Thoreau. Whitman was to sing the divine equality of all Americans, therefore of all mankind, by singing of himself. By an act of will, Whitman wrote himself into being, making his self as he went along.[29]

Writers less convinced of the God within shared the same tendency to find types of the nation in themselves. *The American Democrat* proclaimed Cooper's political and social opinions as if all right-thinking Americans were at one with the title figure. Parkman projected his creed of unrelenting manly endurance into a succession of early American explorers. The poetic world of Emily Dickinson may have been rigidly restricted to the world of her soul's perceptions, but any reader was invited to share her emotions as if they were universal.

The temper of an age was clearly being intensified by the conditions of a country. While the romantic impulse granted new authority to in-dividual feeling, and democracy proclaimed the worth of the individual, antebellum American writers complained that they had no society to write novels or epics about, and turned to psychological romance, to romantic history, to voyage narratives, and to personal lyrics. Under such circumstances, their attempts to create a national heroic character were bound to be markedly solipsistic in origin and untainted in prospect. By the time the Leatherstocking Tales were completed, Cooper's hero was revealed to be a melancholy anachronism of the eighteenth-century frontier who had chosen to remain beyond civilization because he was more virtuous and competent than other pathfinders.[30] Many writers of the next generation, including Cooper in some of his later works, would seek a more representative hero for their promising future. Their need was to evoke a youthful, heroic self who could provide moral leadership for a community he had not forsaken. Sharing both of these responses, Hawthorne and Melville could perceive the possibly unhappy ends of the solipsistic imagination that their country cherished, and that even they could not wholly avoid.

O'SULLIVAN AND "THE YOUNG AMERICAN"

The influence of the nation's futuristic mentality upon the lives of Hawthorne and Melville was neither as tangential nor as impersonal as the preceding pages may suggest. The chief expression of a self-created future in literature was the Young American movement, whose founding spirit, John Louis O'Sullivan, had for years been a close associate of Hawthorne. O'Sullivan's designated successor, Evert Duyckink, was to be Melville's literary mentor for six crucial years. The most likely origin for the name of the movement is the title of a public address by Emerson concerning the definition of national character. Although the month-by-month details of the Young Americans' stratagems on behalf of a national literature now need no repetition,[31] their literary and political ideas form a crucial part of the cultural context in which Hawthorne and Melville were writing.

Because the age recognized no clear separation of literature from politics, the spirit of Young America can most clearly be perceived through its founder. John Louis O'Sullivan was Una Hawthorne's godfather, publisher of twenty-five of her father's short stories, one of Hawthorne's "very dear friends," an employer of Evert Duyckinck, champion of Young Hickory in politics, as well as of Young America in literature, editor of the *United States Magazine and Democratic Review*, and the influential editorialist who coined the term "Manifest Destiny." In 1843 and 1844, O'Sullivan tried repeatedly, through George Bancroft, to secure Hawthorne a needed political appointment; twelve years later O'Sullivan would receive a three-thousand-dollar loan from Hawthorne and stay for two weeks in the Hawthorne household.[32] The *Democratic Review*, in which O'Sullivan's best writing appeared, was at once a leading literary magazine and a forum for the most sanguine of Democratic political thinkers. During O'Sullivan's nine years as editor, the *Democratic Review* published writings by Bancroft, Bryant, Brownson, Emerson, Hawthorne, Longfellow, Lowell, Paulding, Poe, Simms, Thoreau, Whitman, and Whittier, thereby earning Frank Luther Mott's careful judgment that O'Sullivan had probably conducted "the most brilliant periodical of the time."[33]

In the opening statement of the first issue (1837), O'Sullivan pledges his periodical to advocacy of democracy and equal rights in politics, pacifism in international relations, Christianity in religion, philanthropy in social ethics, minimal government everywhere, and all of these desiderata in an independent national literature.[34] Proclaiming that America has all the external conditions of growth, prosperity, and boundless resources to build a utopia, O'Sullivan tries to resolve potential problems of national spirit. America's resolute devotion to liberty and democracy might turn its citizens into "floating atoms" (p. 7), but the principle of free association will enable the atoms to combine, so that "Democracy's faith in human nature . . . in its essential equality and fundamental goodness," can effectively prod citizens toward philanthropy (p. 11). Instead of considering sources for resentment between North and South, or even any "narrow prejudices of interest," readers should instead remember that "Democracy is the cause of Humanity" (p. 11). Like Melville in his review of Hawthorne's *Mosses from an Old Manse*, O'Sullivan is concerned to link Democracy and Christianity within a policy that has disestablished all churches. "Christianity's pervading spirit of democratic equality among men is its highest fact," he insists, and then he elaborates that "Democracy is the cause of Christianity, . . . a creed of high hope and universal love" (p.

11). Whatever apprehensions readers might have about the nation's present lethargy, they must remember that "every step in the onward march of improvement by the human race is an experiment; and the present is most emphatically an age of experiments. The eye of man looks naturally *forward*" (p. 9).

By 1839, when O'Sullivan wrote "The Great Nation of Futurity," his lingering doubts seem almost to have disappeared.[35] "Our national birth was the beginning of a new history, the formation and progress of an untried political system, which separates us from the past and connects us with the future only" (p. 426). Just as the past has become a vacancy, so has the future. O'Sullivan has arrived at the startling proposition that America is destined to inherit all space and all time: "The expansive future is our arena, and for our history. We are entering on its untrodden space, with the truths of God in our minds, beneficent objects in our hearts, and with a clear conscience unsullied by the past. We are the nation of human progress, and who will, what can, set limits to our onward march?" (p. 427). The only means by which O'Sullivan can conceive of Americans controlling so universal a republic is through a Melvillean process of federation along one keel. For O'Sullivan, however, the outcome will be harmonious and egalitarian: America will be "a Union of many republics, comprising hundreds of happy millions, calling, owning no man master, but governed by God's natural and moral law of equality" (p. 427). Men of all space and all time will choose to federate under the American temple, but their free choice has been predestined by the divine law that favors a republican policy.

When foreign observers tried to determine what might be the bond holding the expanding republic together, they often concluded that it could be nothing other than the idea of liberty itself. Francis Grund contended, "It was the genius of liberty which gave America a national elevation; and it is to this genius, therefore, we must look for national productions. It is the bond of union, the confession, the religion, the life of Americans." To Michel Chevalier, the drive for self-determination was so strong that Americans endured union primarily because the Republic was "indefinitely subdivided into independent republics of various classes," including states, towns, farms, banks, and the family, down to the ultimate subdivision in which "each individual is a republic by himself in the family." Only after careful reflection did Tocqueville advance his contentious belief that Americans would ultimately prefer equality above all else, even liberty. When writers insisted upon the bond of liberty, however, they skirted a perplexing problem: How could a national creed defined through gestures of separation continue to provide a bond of union?[36]

O'Sullivan's next major editorial, "Democracy" (1840), called for as extreme a degree of individual autonomy within a political system as one can imagine.[37] O'Sullivan had arrived at the astonishing proposition that "Man surrenders *none* of his rights on entrance into society" (p. 220, italics mine). Every man, he proclaimed, has the following natural rights: to gratify his sensual desires, to labor in whatever occupation he chooses, to live wherever he wishes, to cultivate all his mental and physical talents, and "to act according to that conscience which his God has given" (p. 218). Why could O'Sullivan not perceive that any government strong enough to guarantee such virtually unrestricted rights must be, by his own standards, detestably large and powerful? A possible answer is that patriots like O'Sullivan, while purportedly writing about a real, emerging polity, were unable to conceive of the American nation as anything other than a collection of wholly separate integers.

By the time O'Sullivan wrote the 1846 essay titled "Annexation,"[38] in which he urged "the fulfillment of our manifest destiny to overspread the continent," he had become equally unable to perceive territory outside America as anything more than a projection of America (p. 5). Texas, now included within "the sweep of our eagle's wing," "is no longer to us a mere country on the map. She comes within the dear and sacred designation of Our Country" (p. 5). Over the "detached wilderness" of California, "such a country as Mexico . . . imbecile and distracted, never can exert any real governmental authority" (p. 9). Without even a phrase acknowledging the existence of Mexicans or Indians, O'Sullivan exclaimed: "The Anglo-Saxon foot is already on its [California's] borders. Already the advance guard of the irresistable army of Anglo-Saxon emigration has begun to pour down upon it, armed with the plough and the rifle . . . Their [the Anglo-Saxons'] right to independence will be the natural right of self-government belonging to any community strong enough to maintain it" (p. 9).

To O'Sullivan, enlarging the area of freedom had become indistinguishable from the tread of the Anglo-Saxon foot. To force liberty upon retrogressive, or perhaps uninhabited, spots within the continent seemed no violation of the *Democratic Review*'s original commitment to international pacifism. Pledged to individual freedom, as well as to state freedom, O'Sullivan saw nothing inconsistent in the free federation of new slave states within a union dedicated to furthering universal humanity. Texas, Mexico, Oregon, and California had become the self writ large, the American future of space and time reserved for all democratic equals just like us. In O'Sullivan's editorials, projection has been extended from self to nation to continent to all of space and time.[39]

Although Emerson hoped that each American would project his character before him, he required plausible evidence before asserting that the Republic's gloriously unlimited future was assured. During the same year Duyckinck and O'Sullivan began to coedit the *Democratic Review*, Emerson delivered a lecture before the Boston Mercantile Library Association called "The Young American" (1844).[40] Not surprisingly, the most forceful passages of the speech are those in which he places demands upon his audience to embody the nation's energies:

> I call upon you, young men, to obey your heart and be the nobility of this land. In every age of the world there has been a leading nation, one of a more generous sentiment, whose eminent citizens were willing to stand for the interests of general justice and humanity, at the risk of being called, by the men of the moment, chimerical and fantastic. Which should be that nation but these States? Which should lead that movement, if not New England? Who should the leaders be, but the young American? [Pp. 387–8]

Except for the mention of New England and the flattering use of the term "nobility," this statement could have been written by any proponent of Young America. Nor would many have taken exception to Emerson's definition of the spirit that his country was to develop: "It seems so easy for America to inspire and express the most expansive and humane spirit; new-born, free, healthful, strong, the land of the laborer, of the democrat, of the philanthropist, of the believer, of the saint, she should speak for the human race. It is the country of the Future" (p. 371). Knowing that merely to be free, strong, and young is not sufficient to speak of a character, Emerson grants that Young America is yet to be formed by westward expansionism, and then asserts, "We shall yet have an American genius," because "the nervous, rocky West is intruding a new continental element into the national mind" (p. 370).

If we consider the argument of the whole essay, the reasons for Emerson's hedging the surety of his prophecy ("It *seems* so easy") clearly emerge. Although fertile lands may generate patriotism, providing "physic and food for our mind, as well as our body" (p. 365), America's growing cities drain the country of venturesome youth, leaving a poverty-stricken landscape with diminished prospects for democratic and natural arts. The commercial mentality, which once "planted America and destroyed Feudalism" (p. 378), has recently brought about inflation, bankruptcies, and urban congestion. A new spirit of community promises a turn toward "beneficent socialism," but the new reform associations and communities remain small, comparatively powerless, and intensely centripetal in their energies.

True to the American jeremiad's paradigm of futuristic reaffirmation, Emerson celebrates "the open future expanding here before the eye of every boy to vastness" (p. 393), while also admitting that "in America, out-of-doors all seems a market; in-doors an air-tight stove of conventionalism" (p. 388). He praises internal improvements and the advances of technology, yet can detect no motive for them beyond money: The young men who sit before him represent the beginnings of "a new and more excellent social state than history has recorded" (p. 395), yet he has earlier admitted, "I find no expression in our state papers or legislative debate, in our lyceums or churches, especially in our newspapers, of a high national feeling" (p. 388). Despite his call to general exertion, the only specific measure Emerson can urge upon his young men is "the more need of a withdrawal from the crowd, and a resort to the fountain of right" (p. 389). Young America shows its Americanness most truly by withdrawing from America.

It is a fully explicable irony that "The Young American" never describes the character of the Young American. His identity can be revealed only when the members of the audience, prompted by Emerson's urgings, will have created it. The present state of the nation may be so degraded that today's youth will never develop their divine potential: "It is easy to see," Emerson says, "that the existing generations are conspiring with a beneficence which, in its working for coming generations, sacrifices the passing one" (p. 374). The prospect of Young America being sacrificed, however, is not to be Emerson's final word. In his last paragraph, he exhorts his audience to believe "here stars, here woods, here hills, here animals, here men abound, and the vast tendencies concur of a new order" (p. 395). The agency of progress, however, is no longer the free will of the individual, but rather "the designs of the Spirit who led us hither and is leading us still" (p. 395). This spirit is surely the same as the one invoked earlier, the "sublime and friendly Destiny by which the human race is guided" (p. 371). Moreover, such a spirit is similar in its irresistible worldwide force, though not in political consequence, to O'Sullivan's Manifest Destiny. These similarities of kind suggest that the repeated use of the term "destiny," at the time of the nation's most expansive promise, contains an unspoken admission. America's irresistible destiny must now achieve the heroic task that the character of each individual seems too weak and incomplete to perform.

Michel Chevalier was among the few who tried to portray the existing American rather than to exhort him into being. Realizing that such hoary stereotypes as cunning Yankees and principled Virginia gentlemen were merely regional, Chevalier pictures a generic American in daily action:

> The American . . . has recourse to business for the strong emotions which he requires to make him feel life. He launches with delight into the ever-moving sea of speculation. One day, the wave raises him to the clouds; he enjoys in haste the moment of triumph. The next day he disappears between the crests of the billows; he is little troubled by the reverse, he bides his time coolly, and consoles himself with the hope of better fortune. In the midst of all this speculation, whilst some enrich and some ruin themselves, banks spring up and diffuse credit,

railroads and canals extend themselves over the country, steamboats are launched into the rivers, the lakes and the sea; the career of the speculators is ever enlarging, the field for railroads, canals, steamers, and banks goes on expanding. Some individuals lose, but the country is a gainer; the country is peopled, cleared, cultivated; its resources are unfolded, its wealth increased. *Go ahead*! If movement and the quick succession of sensations and ideas constitute life, here one lives a hundred fold more than elsewhere; all is here circulation, motion, and boiling agitation. Experiment follows experiment; enterprise succeeds to enterprise. Riches and poverty follow on each other's traces, and each in turn occupies the place of the other. Whilst the great men of one day dethrone those of the past, they are already half overturned themselves by those of the morrow. Fortunes last for a season; reputations, during the twinkling of an eye. An irresistible current sweeps away everything, grinds everything to powder, and deposits it again under new forms.[41]

This passage seems intended as a tribute to the italicized slogan of the era. One feels in it the freedom, energy, and hope of an entire people setting forward into a *terra incognita* of ever expanding opportunity. As its imagery accumulates, however, one also senses the emerging underside to Young America's spirit. The ever-moving sea may be a void awaiting the self's remaking, but constant waves seem to impede character formation. Enlargement, expansion, and freedom are real enough for the nation, but not necessarily for the single individual. "Going ahead" immerses one in boiling agitation; Progress demands that all be swept away, ground to nothing, and reformed. One begins to wonder whether the Americans' controlling emotion should be the exhilaration of liberty or what Harriet Martineau called "their universal servitude to worldly anxiety."[42] Familiar assurances about Young America building the happy republic here disappear into the vacant future from which it was to have been formed. In the face of such economic and environmental anarchy, Chevalier's American cannot evolve; he remains little more than a force of willful energy.

Hawthorne and Melville approached the configuration of "Young America" with complex and divided responses. The hazards of their various occupations led them to balance the exhilaration of going ahead against the inevitable return of worldly anxiety. The prospects held forth by Young America, however engaging, were postulated on views of human nature and causation that Hawthorne and Melville were predisposed, from their divided heritage, both to appreciate and to question. At a time when the Congregational and Presbyterian churches were proclaiming that sin was merely a willed act from which the individual could save himself, Hawthorne was developing an intense interest in Puritan forefathers and Melville was being baptized and raised in the Dutch Reformed Church, an enclave of Calvinistic orthodoxy. Despite all the rhetoric of self-making, sons growing to maturity in the Jacksonian era were expected to revere the fathers and forefathers who had made possible their prosperity and glorious prospects. Looking at General Peter Gansevoort, Major Thomas Melvill, Colonel William Hathorne, and Captain Daniel Hathorne, Herman Melville and Nathaniel Hawthorne had much ancestral virtue to revere, and some ancestral glory to envy, but little progressive prosperity to show. In the 1830s, while the nation sang of individual opportunity and declared that bankruptcy was no disgrace, Herman Melville's socially conscious, widowed mother remained deeply in debt, threatened with bankruptcy and the forced sale of her furniture. When Melville turned eighteen, the depression of 1837 struck. For seven directionless years he worked as a bank clerk and a schoolteacher, studied for a nonexistent position as a surveyor or engineer, shipped as a "boy" on a Liverpool packet, traveled to Illinois in fruitless pursuit of work with his uncle, resorted to the degraded job of a whaling seaman, jumped ship, vagabonded about the South Seas, and returned as an ordinary seaman to Lansingburgh, with absolutely no "going ahead" to show for his efforts.

Hawthorne's public acknowledgments of the faded condition of his family, and of his presumed status as the obscurest man of letters in America, were only in part a calculated authorial role. During his comparatively idyllic sojourn at the Old Manse, there were times when he could not afford writing paper or a trip from Concord to Boston. Being fired from the Custom House enabled him both to write *The Scarlet Letter* and to accept a collection of money gathered by George Hillard so that he could eat.[43] In post-Jacksonian America, the mingled pride, resentment, disgrace, and determination felt by these seemingly fallen sons of decayed patrician families must have been intense. At many moments, the national rhetoric of liberty, equality, and future self-creation must have seemed worse than incongruous, and their own positions less than noticed.

Responses so simple as cynicism or nostalgia would suffice for neither author. Having known the autocracy of the U.S. Navy, and the capabilities of the ordinary American seaman, White-Jacket nonetheless lands at Norfolk to kneel on "holy soil." Not long after writing the dispiriting final chapters of *The Blithedale Romance*, Hawthorne would write to Tickner, "We Americans are the best people in the world." Even though neither author cared sufficiently about politics to vote regularly or to refer to passing controversies, both were much concerned with their characters' political feeling. Seemingly indifferent to party, both men were nonetheless involved in party, and not simply because they were seeking employment. Their resentments of moneyed aristocracy, belief in local control, and preference for an agrarian economy made them decidedly of Democratic rather than Whig persuasion. One must not confuse their aloofness from ephemeral controversies with indifference to the condition of region or nation. An author who recognizes, as did Melville, that "the Republic's faith . . . holds that Man is naturally good" will consider whether the American people are worthy of the powers entrusted to them. To such minds, politics are paper products, but character is of the essence.[44]

The diverse qualities for which Melville valued Hawthorne show how intellectually enriching these inner contrarities can be. "Hawthorne and His Mosses" provides us with Melville's most explicit declaration of his literary creed as an American writer ("to carry republican progressiveness into Literature as well as into Life") and with his most explicit assertion about the source of literary excellence ("this great power of blackness"). To credit Hawthorne with a "Calvinistic sense of Innate Depravity and Original Sin" is hardly consistent, however, with praising Hawthorne because "the smell of your [America's] beeches and hemlocks is upon him; your own broad prairies are in his soul; and if you travel away inland into his deep and noble nature, you will hear the far roar of his Niagara." When blackness gains power, "republican progressiveness" is likely to suffer. And yet it is inadequate to conclude, as Perry Miller did, that Melville had distorted the darkened spirit of Hawthorne's writing in order to claim him for Young America. If one travels inward to the deepest cavern of the heart, Hawthorne wrote in a famous passage, one ultimately discovers a region of light, flowers, and "eternal beauty." Melville could respond to both aspects of Hawthorne's psychological chiaroscuro, because he knew the full range of those shadings himself.[45]

Atypical in heritage as well as in sheer complexity of mind, Hawthorne and Melville returned to fundamental cultural questions that many contemporary writers either did not perceive or believed had been answered. Placing Americans within the constricting settings of a New England town or a symbolic ship leads the reader to wonder how a culture that considers youthful innocence a virtue can ever grow to maturity. Are an American's political freedoms and his creed of self-reliance likely to end in heightened fellowship or worse loneliness? Will the virgin West encourage virtue and abundance, or a reversion to savagery? How can Americans create their better selves in the future, if they can do so only by mirroring fledgling souls into empty spaces?

Even among the finest American writers of the 1840s and 1850s, Hawthorne and Melville were unique in their willingness to treat such questions without losing sight of either the shadows of the self or the openness of the future. Emerson and, in lesser degree, Thoreau were reluctant to allow criticism of their nation, expressed in private journals, to surface in public lectures or writings. The world of Poe is so wholly solipsistic, so fundamentally dead, that it escapes political and social considerations almost entirely.[46] Cooper and Whitman were, to be sure, more explicitly and persistently concerned with national character than either Hawthorne or Melville. In differing ways, however, they adopted specific political and ideological principles that narrowed their vision. Cooper's commitment to a republic controlled by landed, highly educated gentlemen was no longer workable in Jacksonian America, and turned much of his later writing into special pleading. Until Walt Whitman published *Democratic Vistas* (1871), his barbaric yawp about the divine unity of American camerados, however compelling as poetry, often seems politically and socially naive, an example of the democratic (also Democratic) grasping after unlimited prophecy that Melville had worked through by 1851.

Unlike Melville, Hawthorne never once attempted to build a future with words, perhaps because he saw transmuted forms of past flaws living on within the present. To him, any American who would presume freely to project his self into all others, and all others into himself, was only ignoring distinctions created by region, time, family, and money. History might be dispiriting, but it was also an anchor in a void. And so, after the false start of *Fanshawe*, Hawthorne's artistic achievement would be repeatedly linked to his search for a usable New England past. Without exposing himself to the illogic of William Gilmore Simms's statement "To be national in literature, one must needs be sectional," Hawthorne simply assumed that New England's priority in historical influence lent it primacy in determinations of national identity. In a private letter he might confess that "New England is quite as large a lump of earth as my heart can really take in," but he approached the writing of New England historical fiction as a means of uncovering, in Sacvan Bercovitch's phrase, the Puritan origins of the American self.[47]

PART I

HAWTHORNE

The early history of New England has found no such genial and vivid illustration as his pages afford . . . It is as if we were baptized into the consciousness of Puritan life, of New England character in its elemental state; and knew, by experience, all its frigidity, its gloom, its intellectual enthusiasm, and its religious aspiration.

"Nathaniel Hawthorne," review by Henry L. Tuckerman,
Southern Literary Messenger (1851)

It [your review] gave me, I must confess, the pleasantest sensation I have ever experienced, from any cause connected with literature; not so much for the sake of the praise as because I felt that you saw into my books and understood what I meant.

Hawthorne to Tuckerman (1851)

1

JOHN ENDICOTT
AND THE FICTIONS
OF ORATORY

What brought the pilgrims here? One man says, civil liberty; another, the desire of founding a church; a third discovers that the motive force was plantation and trade. But if the Puritans could rise from the dust they could not answer. It is to be seen in what they were, and not in what they designed.

Emerson, "The Method of Nature" (1841)

Hawthorne's elated reply to Tuckerman's review, quoted in the epigraph for Part I, shows that he wished his historical fiction to be appreciated for its rendering of New England life and character above all else. Reordered in the sequence of historical event, his tales constitute a thorough study of New England's development between the time of first settlement ("The May-pole of Merry Mount") and the aftermath of the Revolution ("Old Esther Dudley"). Escaping all narrow authorial categories, Hawthorne wrote these tales as neither a historian bound by his sources, nor a moralist imposing ethics upon the past, nor a romancer seeking to escape historical specificity, but as a fifth-generation Hathorne who began, in the Salem of the 1820s, to search out the inner truths of regional legend as a means of cultural and personal discovery. From the outset, the New England past served him as a place where the Actual and the Imaginary might meet; his historical fictions contend, not for the literal truth of each detail, but for a much more important historical matter, "the authenticity of the outline."[1]

The shape Hawthorne gave to his region's past was not ultimately determined by annalists on the shelves of the Salem Athenaeum, by third-rate historical novels of New England contemporaries, or by any tradition of the American romance. As Nina Baym has argued, Hawthorne's career shows his desire to reach the widest possible audience for his writings, not in order to defer to its ethical or literary presumptions, but to meet that audience on its own terms.[2] If Baym's premise is correct, we should ascertain the precise sense of the New England past that Hawthorne's contemporaries were expected to share, especially between 1825 and 1837, when Hawthorne was most concerned with writing historical tales. Neither the purpose nor the import of his historical fiction can be determined apart from the context of popular beliefs that contemporary readers would have brought to it.

Because of a classical educational curriculum, early nineteenth-century New Englanders were trained to respect and practice a form of verbal art that Hawthorne apprehensively resented and that Melville called "that great American bulwark and bore"[3] – namely, the public speech. During the 1820s and 1830s a region needing to provide itself an identity through historic associations, and to justify a revolution, created the perfect medium for oratorical self-justification. Forefathers Day at Plymouth and the bicentennial celebrations of the founding of Massachusetts Bay communities offered annual occasions for calling forth the rhetorical talents of the most eminent academics, politicians, and jurists of the age. Their commemorative addresses, delivered before large, open-air crowds, usually on the spot of the settlers' landing, created a public legacy of Puritan history. Averaging nearly forty pages in length and two hours in delivery, these speeches were carefully prepared both in substance (quotations, footnotes, dates) and in form (Ciceronian structure, invocations, scenic tableaux). Based upon a conviction that filiopietism was a historically provable duty, the major speeches offer a remarkably uniform and progressive re-creation of the New England past. Like the romantic historians after them, the orators conceived of history as a linear sequence of events in which the virtues of the people, embodied in their leaders and favored by divine Providence, had impelled the progress of Western civilization.[4]

For these orators, to study the region's past was to uncover the origin of the two related triumphs of New World civilization: the American Revolution and the present condition of New England. After evoking the ordered prosperity of the town and the reason of its citizenry, the orator praised those Revolutionary fathers whose commitment to a constitutional republic had made the good life possible, and then proceeded to his essential concern: to perceive in the civilization of Puritan forefathers the source of the virtues and blessings of the present day. Metaphors that portrayed progress as a deterministic natural law proved especially appropriate. While asking his Plymouth audience "to detect in the acorn at our feet the germ of that majestic oak" which became Revolutionary New England, John Quincy Adams introduced the most workable – and overworked – of these images.[5] Later orators were to picture tides advancing to the full, streams evolving into rivers, seeds into flowers, and even hills rising into mountains. Whatever the variant, the kind of metaphor induced the audience to regard the centuries from 1630 to 1830 as a growth that was simultaneously slow, steady, natural, and inexorable.

The New England historical oration, like later encomiums on the American character, proclaimed that the pursuit of freedom was the moral force that had made Nature's nation grow. Rufus Choate shaped the centuries to make them represent "one long, glorious triumphant struggle for liberty." Edward Everett declared that the legacy of Plymouth was "an imperial patrimony of liberty." Ascribing Revolutionary ideals to the first settlers led Josiah Quincy to assure the citizens of Boston: "Their [the Puritans'] sufferings had created in their minds a vivid and inextinguishable love of civil and religious liberty, a fixed resolve, at every peril, to assert and maintain their natural rights."[6]

The most enduring passage in this commemorative tradition, the exordium of Daniel Webster's Plymouth speech, encouraged decades of classroom audiences to adopt a worshipful reverence for the settlers' libertarian purposes:

> We have come to this Rock, to record here our homage for our Pilgrim Fathers; our sympathy in their sufferings; our gratitude for their labors; our admiration of their virtues; our veneration for their piety; and our attachment to those principles of civil and religious liberty, which they encountered the dangers of the ocean, the storms of heaven, the violence of savages, disease, exile and famine, to enjoy and to establish.

The emphases within this single sentence mirror the rhetorical strategy of the commemorative address as a genre. Webster mentions religious piety among the forefathers' virtues, but does not define piety as a body of doctrine. Joseph Story, for example, declares that the Antinomian Controversy concerned "doctrines so mysterious and subtle as seem past all human comprehension." Instead, Webster considers how the political virtue of a liberal temper, applied to the divisible realms of civil conduct and religious belief, enabled the forefathers to suffer, and then to conquer, the immense dangers of the wilderness.[7]

An elaborate rationale was devised to define precisely what the "liberty" established by seventeenth-century Puritans truly signified. Orators listed the elements of Old World feudalism that the founders had simply abandoned: soccage, primogeniture, guilds, monarchy, titled nobility, and an established church. They then specified the institutions that the New World had developed to replace them: freehold, equality under the law, the franchise, an elected General Court, trial by jury, universal education, a representative legislature with powers of taxation, and separation of church and state. They then drew the predictable political conclusion about Massachusetts's origins: "The basis of [Salem's] institutions was from the first settlement republican. The people were the source of all power. They chose the magistrate and executive. They established a representative government."[8]

Even though most of the orators were lawyers and politicians, they did not inquire what the terms "equality," "franchise," "representation," or "republican" corresponded to in seventeenth-century political practice. Because their interest was in the character that would give rise to republicanism, the orators adopted the effective strategy of invoking Revolutionary principles as timeless realities present in New World voyagers, existing in embryonic spirit as the settlers approached the coast:

> There already – ay, in the Mayflower's cabin, before they set foot on shore – was representative, republican government. There were the congenial institutions and sentiments from which such government imbibes its power of life. There already, side by side, were the securities of conservatism and the germs of progress. There already were the congregational church and the free school; the trial by jury; the statutes of distributions, just so much of the written and unwritten reason of England as might fitly compose the jurisprudence of liberty. There already was the legalized and organized town, that seminary and central point and exemplification of elementary democracy. Silently adopted everywhere and in all things assumed, penetrating and tinging everything, – the church, the government, law, education, the very structure of the mind itself – was the grand doctrine, that all men are born equal and born free, that they are born to the same inheritance exactly of chances and of hopes.[9]

Such a coupling as "the securities of conservatism and the germs of progress" was neither atypical nor, in Choate's view, paradoxical. By tracing principles of 1776 back to 1620, these orators, Whig and Democrat alike, praised the Revolution as an essentially conservative reaction in which the fathers fought to preserve the progressive principles of the forefathers.[10] Their speeches enabled New Englanders to define themselves through the primacy of long-standing political ideals, rather than through traits of personality.

The commemorative orator not only asserted that the Puritan was America's ur-libertarian; he purported to show the growth of the libertarian, democratic spirit through time. His recasting of history, like all else, gradually became one extended convention. His audience was rarely asked to consider internal political developments and almost never to recall instances of internal dissent. Puritanism was seen as a progressive spirit developing through a century of external conflict with the dull-witted, Anglo-Catholic tyranny of the Old World symbolized by minions of the House of Stuart. The persecutions of the Puritans' English years entitled them to be regarded as "exiles of liberty and conscience,"[11] who could be appropriate types of America's growing revolutionary mission.

Most orators found the spirit of civil liberty in the same sequence of historical deeds. In the beginning was Winthrop's removal of the Massachusetts charter, an act likened to the civil compact created in the cabin of the *Mayflower*, because both peoples had covenanted to establish their own "republican, representative government." For Josiah Quincy, the resolution to remove the charter was the very type of the Revolution ("the first and original declaration of independence by Massachusetts"), in which the forefathers had shown their determination to govern and tax themselves.[12]

Lest the audience contemplate the possibility of Puritan decline after the Interregnum, their attention was focused upon Massachusetts's heroics during the Great Revolution of 1689. Even if an orator's subject was the settlement of Salem, Plymouth, or Charlestown, a paragraph on the expulsion of red-coated Andros was essential to the larger pattern of regional history. In account after account, "the people" were pictured rising en masse against the revocation of their old charter rights (franchise, self-taxation, town meetings) in order to enact, in Webster's phrase, "the first scene of that great Revolutionary drama which was to take place over a century afterwards!"[13]

The last essential episode, as important to Everett and Webster as to Salemites like Charles Upham and Joseph Story, required careful treatment of shameful matter. The Salem witch trials were introduced with admissions, often lengthy, of the Puritans' religious "fanaticism," "superstition," or "delusion." Admissions of fanaticism were introduced not for their own sake, but for their part in a greater whole. Instead of regarding the witch trials as a decline from the heroic days of the founding, the orators interpreted the prompt demise of the trials (the general pardon of suspected witches in 1693, the fast day of 1696, and the recantations of Sewall, Paris, and Anne Putnam) as signs of the Puritans' early entry into the Age of Reason. The witch trials were thus understood as an aberration of the forefathers' purpose, not as its representative expression. Because there had been no widespread decline in piety, there was no need for recovery. Among fourteen important commemorative addresses, there is no mention of the Great Awakening.

Enumerating the virtues of Puritan political morality led the orators to an equally important concern, the virtues of what Rufus Choate repeatedly called "the Puritan Character." The Puritan character, in turn, was quietly enlarged into a national type. Edward Everett, for example, showed how "that great word of 'Independence,' which, if first uttered in 1776, was most auspiciously anticipated in 1620 . . . implies not merely an American government but an American Character." Many of the virtues attributed to this generic American were a composite of possibly contradictory virtues of the Puritan, the farmer, and the Yankee. Joseph

Story saw the Calvinistic forefather as a saint: "In simplicity of life, in godly sincerity, in temperance, in humility, and in patience, as well as in zeal, they [the settlers of Salem] seemed to belong to the apostolical age." A bit later Story endowed Puritans and contemporaries with the virtues of a Revolutionary yeoman: "Such as we are, we have been from the beginning: simple, hardy, intelligent, accustomed to self-government and self-respect." Josiah Quincy, preferring to regard New Englanders in the Franklinian guise of a secularized Puritanism, praised his people's "frugality of disposition, temperance of habit, general diffusion of knowledge, pleasure in labor for oneself, success in enterprise."[14]

Whatever combination of yeoman, Yankee, or saint the Puritan character assumed, certain virtues had presumably remained constant. Above all, the American Puritan had steadily exhibited, in Choate's expressive phrase, "the iron quality of the higher heroism." Adapting Milton's notion of the higher argument, the orators repeatedly concluded that the Puritan, as a Christian hero, had progressed beyond the martial heroism of epics ("a nauseous compound of fanaticism and sensuality," noted John Quincy Adams, "whose only argument was the sword, and whose only paradise was a brothel") in order to bring the family, the home, and the arts of peace to the New World. And yet, the higher heroes remained men of iron, a term that for these orators bore no ironic connotations, as it did for Hawthorne. Josiah Quincy credited the Puritans with "a severe and masculine morality"; Rufus Choate complimented "the masculine, enthusiastic, austere, resolute character of this extraordinary body of men"; and Edward Everett exulted that "no effeminate nobility crowded into the dark and austere ranks of the pilgrims."[15]

At this point, the orator confronted the problem of determining which Puritan acts, setting aside the Puritans' reprehensible treatment of deviants, could best exhibit both iron masculinity and the higher heroism. The historical achievement that the orators chose to emphasize, one ideally suited to the age of Jackson, was the settling of coastal frontiers. In these orations, pages were spent evoking seventeenth-century Massachusetts as a land of "dreary wastes, cheerless climates and repulsive wildernesses, possessed by wild beasts and savages" in order then to praise the masculine courage necessary to subdue them. Listeners were reassured that iron masculinity had been a necessary trait in bringing republicanism and the family fireside to a promised land that "was indeed no Canaan flowing with milk and honey." Having established a controlling motive consistent with the higher heroism, the orator was then free to make such happy predictions as "Ere long the sons of the Pilgrims will stand on the shores of the Pacific."[16]

The commemorative orator was well aware that intolerance of religious dissent was the Achilles heel in his figure of the heroic Puritan. None tried to justify intolerance, though some tried to ignore it. Webster and Choate dismissed the problem with fleeting comments in order to fasten upon less treacherous topics, such as town democracy and the achievements of Puritan commercial enterprise. When Choate considered the literary use of Puritan materials, he openly urged that certain controversies, already significant to fellow townsman Hawthorne, be quietly forgotten. The loyal New England romancer would not perplex his reader, Choate said, with "the persecutions of the Quakers" or "the controversies with Roger Williams and Mrs. Hutchinson" or even "the disgrace of the Witch Trials." "He remembers that it is an heroic age to whose contemplation he would turn us back. . . . He tells the truth, to be sure, but he does not tell the whole truth, for that would be sometimes misplaced and discordant."[17]

The handy silence of Choate and Webster was not, however, the most common response to Puritan intolerance. Like Quincy and Story, Edward Everett discovered that there were advantages to admitting that "Quakers and Anabaptists and all other Dissenters from the Puritan creed had been unrelentingly persecuted."[18] A persistent difficulty in reverencing Puritan ancestors had been to keep the paradigm of historical progress credible while praising the statuesque perfection of the forefathers. If the Puritan had been tolerant as well as liberty-loving, a Christian civilizer as well as an iron man, what greater virtues could the Revolutionary father display to illustrate the progress of the American character through 150 intervening years?

The difficulty could be resolved by admitting that, with regard to the one virtue of tolerance, the Puritans' record might have been improved. Orators were careful, however, to point out that Puritan intolerance had been comparatively moderate. Seventeenth-century Massachusetts, Story observed, was far less intolerant than seventeenth-century England, Scotland, or France. Less frequently, intolerance was justified on grounds of necessity. What would have been the outcome, Josiah Quincy asked his audience, if in 1634 the Puritans had decided to tolerate Laud's Anglican agents in Boston? The most telling reply to the issue of intolerance, however, was promptly to offer listeners the exemplary figure of Roger Williams – libertarian, democrat, peaceful civilizer of savage lands, and tolerationist. By holding forth Roger Williams as the first Western man to proclaim "the doctrine of liberty of conscience," Joseph Story allowed Williams's singular commitment to toleration to expand into constitutional freedom of religion, while uncovering the germ of religious freedom among intolerant Puritans of the New World. By elevating Roger Williams to a position beside John Winthrop, the orators could offer complementary models of the American Puritan as wise statesman and tolerant individualist.[19]

Not all the commemorative orators agreed with Edward Everett that the settlement of Massachusetts Bay was "perhaps the greatest work on record in the annals of humanity." Many of them explicitly stated that this particular honor should be reserved for the fulfillment of Puritan liberalism in the American Revolution. But there was no disagreement regarding the immediate purpose of the commemorative oration itself. The principles of the forefathers, made permanent in the polity of the fathers, had to be transmitted to the present generation. Thus the commemorative speech characteristically began and ended with a direct appeal to the listeners to recognize the blessings of their heritage and to be worthy of its ideals. As early as 1802, John Quincy Adams, correctly anticipating a series of commemorative addresses like his own, trusted that such occasions would become communal rites, "at once testimonials of our gratitude, and schools of virtue to our children." Although the virtues of the forefathers might reappear in the sons, those virtues were not likely to be surpassed. The grand cadences of Webster's Plymouth "Discourse" serve a revealingly limited purpose: "to transmit the great inheritance unimpaired."[20]

On occasion, filiopietism even led orators to hope that the sons might turn back into the fathers. After twenty-two pages evoking "the iron quality of the higher heroism," Rufus Choate urged his audience to undergo a regression of character: "By gazing on these [Puritan virtues] long and intently and often, we may pass into the likeness of the departed, – may emulate their labors, and partake of their immortality." For a climactic end to his Charlestown address, Edward Everett pointed to two sets of tombstones in the Town Hill Burying Ground. After a dramatic pause, he exhorted his audience to be worthy both of "the sacred dust of the first great victims in the cause of liberty" (forefathers dead of disease in 1630) and of "the heroes who presented their dauntless foreheads to the God of battles" (father killed at Bunker Hill).[21]

The more common means of schooling the memory was to call the long roll of the audience's ancestors. No one provided a fuller or more wide-ranging list than Joseph Story in Salem:

> Where are Winthrop, and Endicott, and Higginson, and Dudley, and Saltonstall, and Bradstreet, and Pickering, and Sprague, and Pynchon, and Hathorne, and Conant, and Woodbury, and Palfrey, and Balch, and the other worthies? We are ready to exclaim, – they are here. This is their home. These are their children. They seem to live again in their offspring.

Lest any present descendant of these worthies forget the burden of the legacy being placed upon him, Story ended his ninety-page oration by declaiming, "I call upon you, young men, to remember whose sons you are; whose inheritance you possess."[22]

A listener who had carefully attended to an entire commemorative address should have been perplexed about a question even more pertinent to his legacy than toleration or the meaning of liberty. He should have wondered precisely who he was meant to be in history's providential scheme. Whenever the orator of the 1830s conceived of the Puritans in terms of familial bloodlines, he saw them as the forefathers, and his own generation as the children. Whenever he thought of the Puritans' place in national history and the march of progress, the forefathers represented the infancy of liberty that was finally to mature in the founding fathers of the Revolution. Although the prevailing assumption of the orators was that the child was not father of the man, and that the forefathers were the forefathers after all, there were revealing exceptions. Rufus Choate, for example, told the residents of Ipswich that "the Colonial Period . . . was the charmed, eventful infancy and youth of our national life. The revolutionary and constitutional age, from 1775 to 1789, was the beginning of its manhood."[23] The difference in rhetorical effect is of almost palpable significance. If the present generation were mature republicans, they might create new selves out of the old tradition. If they were merely the sons of heroes, their identity had largely been determined for them.

Even a listener who regarded himself as the mature embodiment of Puritan liberty must surely have felt a bit dispirited after the grandiloquent cadences had died away. He had been told that his forefathers and fathers were heroes, but that the great deeds had already been done. He had been asked to be endlessly grateful for blessings that had been provided him by his ancestors, not achieved by himself. At the outset he had been informed that, before he was born into his pastoral New England democracy, all major battles had been won, all great political issues solved. At the end he was urged to show himself worthy of the moral courage of his ancestors. The cumulative effect of the speech would surely have made a sensitive descendant doubt not only his worth, but the possibility of proving it. It is little wonder that Edward Everett, after thirty-five pages picturing the greatest work on record in the annals of humanity, felt a need to insert a disclaimer: "I deduce from this, not that they were highminded, and we base and degenerate; I will not so compliment the fathers at the expense of the sons."[24]

Although Everett may have recognized, like Emerson, that his age was building the sepulcher of the fathers, he sought no new revelation. Soon after denying any intent to denigrate the sons, Everett wistfully asserted that his generation could still be forefathers too, if only they might have a crisis. Under present circumstances, however, the most that the sons should realistically anticipate was not to disgrace their heritage. No matter how many republican virtues Webster might ascribe to his audience, he could only hope his generation might ultimately prove that "we are not altogether unworthy of our origin."[25] Unlike the Young American of the mid-1840s, a New England youth of 1830 was encouraged to view his heritage as a burden of greatness as well as a stimulus to individual fulfillment.

The first three volumes of Bancroft's *History*, which began to appear shortly after the climax of commemorative oratory, provide a history of pre-Revolutionary America that was prized for at least two generations. Bancroft shares the filiopietism of commemorative orators, but his regard for fact leads him to admit conflicting evidence, and his nationalism leads him to avoid parochial pride. New England nonetheless remains for him the model of American development. He assumes the plausible viewpoint that, no matter how harsh and intolerant, the Puritan provided the "germ" and "seedbed" of the American liberal faith. Among our Anglo-Saxon forefathers, Bancroft says, we first trace "the enfranchisement of the mind from religious despotism." Anticipating Weber and Tawney, Bancroft declares the Puritan spirit to have been "from the first, industrious and enterprising and frugal; and affluence followed of course." Connecting the founding with the Revolution, Bancroft regards the signing of the Mayflower Compact as "the birth of popular constitutional liberty"; the Pilgrims "scattered the seminal principles of republican freedom and national independence."[26] The imprisonment of Andros was a "popular insurrection on behalf of Protestant liberty," a "New England Revolution" that would "in less than a century . . . commence a revolution for humanity."[27] Bancroft's twenty-eight page account of the Salem witch trials, in which a sensible populace regains control from the credulous, power-hungry clergy, ends with a thankful prediction: "Cherishing religion as the source of courage and the fountain of freedom, the common mind in New England refused henceforward to separate belief and reason."[28]

Bancroft's desire to trace the growth of liberty sometimes leads him to assume that seventeenth-century seeds of individual rights carried their institutional fruition with them. Although he admits that Winthrop's charter "demonstrates that universal religious toleration was not designed," he places far more emphasis upon the moment of the Pilgrims' landing, when, presumably, "Democratic liberty and independent Christian worship at once existed in America." In his introductory account of the polity of Massachusetts Bay, Bancroft claims that "an entire separation was made between church and state," but twelve pages later he rightly defines "freeman" as a church member who alone possesses the franchise. Such a coupling as "purity of religion and civil liberty were the objects nearest the wishes of the emigrants" reveals Bancroft's will to believe that the Puritans somehow had built a godly society without sacrificing nineteenth-century liberties of citizenship. In his accounts of the Antinomian Controversy, Quaker persecutions, and witch trials, he grants the clergy an enormous influence over the General Court, the law, and the people. At the same time, however, he insists that Calvinistic Christianity brought popular liberty to the New World:

> Puritanism was Religion struggling for the People . . . Puritanism con-
> stituted not the Christian clergy, but the Christian people, the interpreter
> of the divine will. The voice of the majority was the voice of God; and
> the issue of Puritanism was therefore popular sovereignty . . . The
> fanatic for Calvinism was a fanatic for liberty.

Neither Winthrop nor Williams, in spite of their explicit commitments to civil liberty, would have seen any link between the individual's confrontation with God and the nineteenth-century ideal of "Vox Populi, Vox Dei." The degree of distortion in such a statement is not, however, as important as the fervor of its claims. Bancroft provides us perhaps the clearest expression of the Jacksonian desire to make libertarian politics into a national religion.[29]

Just as Bancroft uncovers the seeds of man's natural rights in the migrations of 1620 and 1630, so he uncovers a model of America's father in New England's forefather. The three qualities that Bostonian John Winthrop and Virginian George Washington had in common were personal generosity, prudential statesmanship, and abiding piety; all three contributed to making the American hero "in the strictest sense, a self-made man." Washington's "hand was liberal; giving quietly and without observation"; Winthrop's "lenient benevolence could temper, if not subdue, the bigotry of his times." By stressing Winthrop's devotion to civil liberties and Washington's belief in God, Bancroft establishes a continuum of character that links century to century, region to region. Winthrop was "averse to pure democracy, yet firm in his regard for existing popular liberties."[30] Believing that "divine wisdom not only illumines the spirit, it inspires the will," Bancroft defines the essential Washington as a pietist: "Belief in God and trust in His overruling spirit formed the essence of his character." John Winthrop's character thus shows us history at a turning point: "Disinterested, brave, and conscientious, his character marks the transition of the reformation into avowed republicanism."[31] The shift perceptible in Winthrop was to be realized in Washington, "the best type of America," a man whose "qualities were so faultlessly proportioned, that his whole country claimed him as its choicest representative, the most complete expression of all its attainments and aspirations."[32]

To Bancroft, Winthrop and Washington establish the poles of American character, but others define the path between them. The forming of the American thus is a process of massive accumulation; it does not depend, as in a twice-told tale, upon the moral character revealed in single episodes or controversies. All leaders and all events participate in the grand march of progress toward libertarian civilization. Because progress can arise only from the clash of contending forces, the apostles of liberty need an Old World despot to defeat. Therefore, although Bancroft may detest the Stuarts, he concludes his discussion of their tyrannies with the telling sentence: "Thus did despotism render benefits to freedom."[33] When offering summary judgments of controversies arising within the New World, however, Bancroft is careful to avoid suggesting villainy. Those in authority are praised together with those they exile. Endicott is a man of "dauntless courage," Roger Williams a saintly libertarian, Anne Hutchinson a woman of "admirable understanding" and "eloquence," and John Winthrop a charitable and moderate judge.[34] The second volume concludes with pages according unqualified praise to a series of figures who have only the general impulse of Protestantism in common: Luther, Calvin, Winthrop, Anne Hutchinson, John Cotton, Henry Vane, Mary Dyer, Roger Williams, and Jonathan Edwards. To charge Bancroft with evasiveness or inconsistency would be to miss his point completely. Because all forefathers laid the foundations of America's splendid republic, each of them contributed his several virtues to a greater whole of national character.

THE LIMITS OF HISTORICAL IMAGINING

Grandfather's Chair, Hawthorne's only general rendering of New England's historical development from 1620 to 1790, is also his only approximation of a narrative echoing the attitudes and conventions of commemorative oratory. While recounting "the eminent characters and remarkable events of our annals" to the grandchildren, Grandfather hopes to maintain "a distinct and unbroken thread of authentic history," a thread that contains nothing known to be "fictitious," but carefully avoids scenes or ideas unsuitable to the minds of youth.[35] Although this process may involve distortion by omitting incidents or by adding imaginative detail, Hawthorne asserts that Grandfather's account of the past is in essence reliable: "The author, it is true, has sometimes assumed the license of filling up the outline of history with details, for which he has none but imaginative authority, but which, he hopes, do not violate nor give a false coloring to the truth" (p. 6).

Believers in the commemorative version of the past would generally have been reassured by Grandfather's selection of seventeenth-century incidents and by his stated conclusions regarding the era. Elevated by religious sincerity and a sense of divine mission, the Puritans of 1630 were, quite simply, "the best men and women of their day" (p. 14). Like many a commemorative orator, Grandfather tacitly obviates any economic motives for emigration by identifying the Puritans as untitled gentlemen of middling prosperity who fled from religious persecution. Although the Puritans had no thirst for military glory, they nonetheless showed themselves a "rough and hardy people" (p. 16) by subduing the environment.

Near the beginning of his history, Grandfather affirms his generation's fundamental tenet about the forefathers: "Democracies were the natural growth of the new world" (p. 33). From this axiom reemerge many familiar conventions. Grandfather pictures Governor Winthrop with the charter, praises annual elections, recounts the popular uprising against Andros, and laments the passing insanity at Salem, all the while directing the children's attention forward to the presumed fulfillment of Puritan moral principles during the Revolution. Bancroft's work is recommended as the authoritative account of the nation's political history. Like Bancroft, Hawthorne admits that a minority of Puritans voted, and that "the clergy of those days had quite as much share in the government of the country, though indirectly, as the magistrates themselves" (pp. 27–8). When grandson Lawrence asks a pointed question about breadth of representation in his forefathers' polity, however, Grandfather simply reassures him that Massachusetts was America's first republic: "Under the first charter, the people had been the source of all power. Winthrop, Endicott, Bradstreet, and the rest of them, had been governors by the choice of the people, without any interference from the king" (p. 76).

Throughout *Grandfather's Chair*, Hawthorne's departures from the commemorative tradition are, with one exception, subtle modifications that might well have remained unnoticed. Although the orators were especially fond of concentrating on the Pilgrims, whose comparative lack of intolerance made them seem more plausible as democratic founders, Hawthorne restricts his history to Massachusetts Bay, and then allots Lady Arbella Johnson, John Endicott, John Hull, and John Eliot far greater space and importance than Winthrop or Williams. Unlike the orators, Hawthorne acknowledges that the significance of political incidents lies in their motivating force as symbols, rather than in the deeds themselves. The charter was a piece of paper important only because "the people *regarded* [it] as a holy thing, and as the foundation of their liberties" (p. 53, italics mine). These two changes affect Grandfather's rendering of the past. The standard by which he judges Puritans shifts from the quality of external political institutions and leading magistrates to the representative character of lesser-known figures described in unfamiliar ways. When Felt and other annalists lamented the death of Lady Arbella, they interpreted it as a necessary demise of the weak, feminine principle of aristocracy in the New World. Hawthorne's account, however, suggests that qualities of great value may have disappeared. Wary tribute is paid to John Endicott, whose virtues have their decidedly darker side. Because his "heart was as bold and resolute as iron," Endicott was "fit for the new world, and for the work he had to do." This very fitness, however, prevented him from extending the charity due from a Christian magistrate. Unable to understand how intimidating the New World could be, Endicott chidingly assured Lady Arbella, "In a little time, you will love this rude life of the wilderness as I do" (p. 17).

The prominence Hawthorne accords Hull and Eliot reveals untraditional purposes. By emphasizing the legendary wealth of mintmaster Hull, Hawthorne suggests that the Puritans had hardly been indifferent to money. Hawthorne's characterization of John Eliot attacks contemporary notions of the forefathers more directly. When considering the vexing issue of land ownership, the commemorative orator justified Puritan purchase or conquest of Indian lands through a combination of two arguments: What is common to all is proper to none; Providence designated the land for our Christian fathers because they alone could make it bear fruit.[36] Grandfather, however, introduces John Eliot as the "single man, among our forefathers, who realized that an Indian possesses a mind, and a heart, and an immortal soul" (p. 43). Because of Eliot's "disinterested zeal for his brother's good," he becomes "the Apostle Eliot" (p. 49), Hawthorne's substitute for the usual canonization of Winthrop, Williams, or Bradford.

The framing device of *Grandfather's Chair* allows Hawthorne to weaken the impact of Puritan intolerance. The reader is often invited to picture Grandfather's domestic circle, but he must accept Grandfather's abstractions regarding the past. The children never press Grandfather for a judgment on Roger Williams or Anne Hutchinson. Although Puritan intolerance toward religious heretics is condemned, the issue of Puritan severity toward moral offenders is never broached, nor are Puritan methods of legal sanction ever pictured. The sweep of 150 years allows Grandfather to view Puritan persecution of Quakers and witches as passing incidents of 1658 and 1692, rather than conflicts that reveal Puritan character. Like Bancroft, Grandfather is able to praise Winthrop and Williams, Endicott and the Quakers, by avoiding the particulars of conflict and dwelling upon virtues displayed elsewhere.

If we set aside Grandfather's attack on Puritan policies toward the Indian, his history's most important divergence from the commemorative tradition is a matter of authorial tone rather than specific attitude. The panegyric of the orators and the swelling periods of Bancroft are replaced by restrained sentences that convey a tempered view of cultural possibilities. Surfacing in descriptions of warfare and political suppression, Hawthorne's historical melancholy becomes memorably explicit at an appropriate moment. After acknowledging to the grandchildren that their forefathers had set King Philip's head upon a pole, Grandfather "almost regretted that it was necessary for them to know any thing of the past or to provide aught for the future" (p. 51).

Because Grandfather's response subverts the commemorative purpose of history, it must be kept momentary. In the main, *Grandfather's Chair* renders New England's past from within the tradition extending backward through bicentennial oratory and the New England histories of Jedediah Morse, Hannah Adams, and Thomas Prince, to Cotton Mather's *Magnalia*, and ultimately to Edward Johnson's *Wonder-Working Providence of Sion's Saviour in New England.*[37] Well before Hawthorne became deeply engaged in the matter of New England, however, ways of circumventing the attitudes of New England filiopietism had been discovered. Most obviously, a writer might not be of New England at all, but pass laughing or angry judgment upon the New England character from the vantage point of other regions, particularly New York. Secondly, a writer might choose to devise ostensibly historical fiction that would skirt or ignore the real achievements and virtues by which New England's glory had been defined. A third possibility was to write fictions that would reinterpret the crucial incidents and issues of commemorative history in historically credible terms. The most challenging and significant of all responses, this third possibility would be attempted only by native-born outsiders like Whittier and Motley, and would be realized in lasting literary form only by Hawthorne.

Although James Paulding's *The Puritan and His Daughter* (1849) criticized Puritanism vigorously, the essence of New York's viewpoint had been established by Irving and Cooper decades earlier. The seventeenth-century Puritans bordering on Irving's New Netherlands seem to be less Puritans than restless, selfish, nineteenth-century Yankees projected backward in time. Irving's summary judgment of them anticipates not only Jason Newcome's conduct at Satanstoe, but Hank Morgan's conduct in Camelot. Connecticut Yankees, Irving says, are "a crew of long limbed, lank-sided varlets, with axes on their shoulders and packs on their backs, resolutely bent on improving the country in despite of its proprietors." Irving's interest in the historical Puritan is limited to noting the hypocrisy that "having served a regular apprenticeship in the school of persecution, it behoved them [the Puritans] to show that they had become proficients in the art." Throughout the Knickerbocker *History*, seventeenth-century New Englanders are pictured as rustics, bundlers, squatters, gossips, and peddlers, men who, wandering like "the sons of Ishmael," and breeding children with names like "Determined Cock" and "Return Strong," are overrunning the blundering decency of Dutch civilization. The prying Puritan provides Irving an origin, outside old New York, for the vexing problem of the tyranny of the majority. The contemporary American's newspaper, Irving insists, has replaced the Puritan's whipping post: "The difference is merely circumstantial. Thus we denounce, instead of banishing – we libel, instead of scourging – we turn out of office, instead of hanging."[38]

Cooper's interest in the seventeenth-century Puritan was more historical than Irving's, but less condemnatory and less playful. *The Wept of Wish-ton-Wish* (1829) may satirize Mark Heathcote's biblical speech and his need to uncover a divine providence in every sparrow's fall, but it also portrays Heathcote's strength of will, patriarchal honor, and near-republican politics as virtues of the Puritan temper. Like Quaker Marmaduke Temple and Episcopalian Mark Woolston, Mark Heathcote has fashioned his isolated settlement into a symbol of the good life (his "Bethel") based on family harmony and agrarian prosperity. In one crucial quality, Mark emerges as the most admirable of these three settlers. His costly refusal to exact vengeance upon the Narragansetts is traceable to his abiding commitment to the governing Christian principle of his community: "No descendant of his should ever take life from a being unprepared to die, except in justifiable defence of his faith, his person, or his lawful rights." Rather than blaming the Puritans for their conduct in King Philip's War, Cooper has created a first-generation Puritan who worthily exemplifies Choate's notion of "the iron quality of the higher heroism." By novel's end, it is clear that Cooper's scorn is directed less at Puritanism than at the decline of Puritan integrity in Mark's son Content and in the Reverend Meek Wolfe, a second-generation minister.[39]

The New England women who first wrote historical fiction about the seventeenth century repeatedly devised marital plots that juxtaposed a rebellious daughter's heart against a father's overbearing pietism, thereby favoring female sensibility over male intellect, the humanitarian present over the Puritan past, and the promptings of nature over the repressions of Scripture.[40] Whatever psychic needs such juxtapositions served, they did not yield convincing renderings of seventeenth-century life. Although Hawthorne's opinion of these novels is unknown, we may infer it from the fact that, no matter how genuinely he valued the heart, his opinion of most women's fiction was decidedly low.

These early New England novels are not as "anti-Calvinist" as is often assumed. Lydia Child followed filiopietistic tradition in characterizing the Puritans as the "van-guard in the proud and rapid march of freedom," a community of men who, however "stern and unyielding, brought the pure flame of religion hither in their own bosom, and, amid desolation and poverty, kindled it on the shrine of Jevova [*sic*]". The most widely read of these fictions, Catharine Sedgwick's *Hope Leslie*, praises the Puritans as "an exiled and suffering people, who came forth in the dignity of the chosen servants of the Lord to open the forests to the sun-beam, and to the light of the Sun of Righteousness; to restore man – man, oppressed and trampled on by his fellow – to religious and civil liberty, and equal rights." Neither Webster nor Choate ever strikes a tone more unabashedly reverent. Rather than being anti-Calvinist or pro-Calvinist, these wildly improbable novels seem revealingly confused. The character of William Fletcher, Sedgwick's representative Puritan, is judged in strikingly contradictory ways within a very few pages. Child's and Sedgwick's readers can never be certain whether the Pequods and Narragansetts are noble savages betrayed by genocidal bigots or red devils subdued by civilized gentlemen.[41]

By the early 1830s, neither New York nor Massachusetts had produced convincing fiction that confronted the tenets of the commemorative tradition. Works like *Hobomok, Hope Leslie,* and *Rachel Dyer* were so filled with anachronisms, improbabilities, and overwriting that their criticisms could not be credited. *The Wept of Wish-ton-Wish* contained a convincing portrayal of Puritan character, but Cooper did not engage the historical axioms through which Massachusetts had laid claim to an American cultural heritage. Faced with inadequate fictions on the one hand and commemorative rhetoric on the other, Hawthorne was understandably cautious in his approach to the writing of historical fiction. Although he was to offer forthright defense of romance in "The Custom-House" twenty years later, Hawthorne began to write believing that successful historical fiction had best adhere to historical incidents plausibly rendered.

The frame that Hawthorne added to one of his earliest tales, "Alice Doane," shows us the audience he first expected for his historical fiction. The narrator's few listeners are women predisposed to be skeptical of the significance he attributes to any tale more concerned with witchcraft than with love. Like a commemorative orator, however, Hawthorne feels a duty to impress the formative significance of New England's past upon listeners who, surrounded by daylight prosperity, have presumably forgotten it. To build his own memorial for the forefathers, he concludes with the truly subversive suggestion that the appropriate monument to the Puritan heritage belongs atop Gallows Hill rather than Bunker Hill.

Hawthorne's desire to impress the formative power of the past upon the young women leads him to test the effects of two kinds of historical writing. He begins with a stagy gothic tale that nonetheless allows his audience to experience the psychological traits of the afflicted during the Salem witch trials: their distrust of venerated elders, their hysteria-inspired visions of universal evil, and their ready acceptance of spectral evidence. The young ladies promptly laugh at the crudity of his gothicism without pausing to consider that the inner soul of their forefathers might have been exposed through a fiction. At this point, however, the "piqued" narrator determines "to make a trial whether truth were more powerful than fiction."[42] By picturing innocent victims hanging on Gallows Hill in 1692, he readily evokes their tears. "Alice Doane's Appeal" thus resolves the problem of suiting genre to readers' expectations in a wry, antifictional way. Although Hawthorne might prefer to write imaginative fictions portraying actual qualities of the historical forefathers, only re-creations of well-known historical events (as in a commemorative oration) seem likely to affect the audience.

Hawthorne's most explicit statement about the desirable aims of historical writing, a little-known passage in "Sir William Phips," argues that controlled use of the imagination serves greater accuracy of historical characterization:

> The knowledge communicated by the historian and biographer is analogous to that which we acquire of a country by the map, – minute, perhaps, and accurate, and available for all necessary purposes, but cold and naked, and wholly destitute of the mimic charm produced by landscape-painting. These defects are partly remediable, and even without an absolute violation of literal truth, although by methods interdicted to professors of biographical exactness. A license must be assumed in brightening the materials which time has rusted, and in tracing out half-obliterated inscriptions on the columns of antiquity: fancy must throw her reviving light on the faded incidents that indicate character, whence a ray will be reflected, more or less vividly, on the person to be described.[43]

The essence of the past is not incident, but the historical "character" that an incident illustrates. The only license Hawthorne approves is the right to enliven the deadly coldness of annalists and biographers for purposes of restoring what now seem only the tombstones of history. The truly imaginative writer illuminates the past instead of appropriating it for the sake of universality. Even in later prefaces, Hawthorne's defense of the romance subsumes historical authenticity. Restoring Surveyor Pue's manuscript to public view is more than a hoary convention; it is a way of insisting that Hawthorne's words re-create seventeenth-century reality. The moonlight falling within the romancer's darkened chamber enables him to see his chair and table more distinctly, not less so.

Hawthorne's best-known comment on the purpose of historical writing should not continue to be interpreted as an attack on historical accuracy in fiction:

> [Mr. Simms's lectures] abound in brilliant paragraphs and appear to bring out, as by a skilfully applied varnish, all the lights and shades that lie upon the surface of our history; but yet, we cannot help feeling that the real treasures of his subject have escaped the author's notice. The themes suggested by him, viewed as he views them, would produce nothing but historical novels, cast in the same worn out mould that has been in use these thirty years, and which it is time to break up and fling away.

The first sentence of this passage, which is rarely quoted, is crucial to understanding its familiar second sentence. Hawthorne is not demanding that the historical novel be thrown away, but claiming that the form of historical novel now practiced by imitators of Scott and Cooper has become so hackneyed as to be no longer usable. His scorn is directed toward Simms's inability to discover the "real treasures" of his historical subjects. When Hawthorne contends that Simms "can merely elaborate what is already familiar," he infers that the higher art is to probe beneath accepted opinion to deeper historical truth. By attacking Simms's paradigm for a historical novel, Hawthorne reveals his preference for a form of romance more true to history because it isolates the inner psychological conditions of representative individuals.[44]

Although the writing of historical fiction rather than commemorative history did not permit Hawthorne to be less true to the past, it greatly altered his perspective upon it. Instead of absorbing a conflict within the long flow of political and historical developments, a twice-told tale dwells upon the signifying details of one episode. Historical abstractions are no longer an end, but merely the introduction to a picturing of controversy. The less-charted field of the historical tale frees Hawthorne from the self-imposed duties of selecting among his historical responses and ordering them within a form suitable for handing down the commemorative tradition to the next generation. Conflict between New World groups becomes the central concern, villainization of the Stuarts drops away, and the Puritans are seen as rulers rather than religious exiles. The social and psychological consequences of Puritan intolerance replace the democratization of Puritan institutions as the chief subject of historical narrative. Whereas the deviants and outcasts of Puritan society merit fuller consideration, portrayal of the sufferings of settlement and praise of the Protestant ethic recede. To summarize these changes is not to suggest that the history of *Grandfather's Chair* defers to known falsehoods, whereas Hawthorne's fiction releases his darker convictions. Rather, it suggests that writing a tale freed Hawthorne to express all of his sometimes contradictory responses. To write a series of discrete tales enabled him to test whether the conventional rendering of Puritan character was a historically defensible response to past controversies.

PURITAN OF PURITANS

Because Hawthorne was the first New England writer to grant Thomas Morton's community any merits in its losing struggle against the Puritans, "The May-pole of Merry Mount" acknowledges that complex issues of cultural value arose even before the settling of Massachusetts Bay.[45] Like a commemorative oration, Hawthorne's tale shows that the iron masculinity of the Puritan was necessary to subdue the wilderness. When John Endicott arrives to cut down the maypole, he emerges out of the "black surrounding woods" (p. 62) he has just mastered into the tiny clearing of the Merry Mounters. His summary of the virtues of Salem settlement – "valiant to fight, and sober to toil, and pious to pray" (p. 66) – precisely defines those qualities which enable him, sword in hand, plausibly to exhort Blackstone, "Now shall it be seen that the Lord hath sanctified this wilderness for his peculiar people" (p. 63). Hawthorne's tale, however, does not follow the commemorative tradition in celebrating Endicott's masculinity as the higher heroism. Instead, Hawthorne forces his reader to consider whether the necessary sacrifice of other virtues was a just price to pay for conquest.

Hawthorne ascribes to Merry Mount all the qualities that, in "The Gentle Boy" and *The Scarlet Letter*, he associates with Elizabethan England in particular and the Old World in general: sunshine, color, joy, festivity, art, and a free expression of passion. By symbolizing these qualities in the red roses of the Old World, which cannot flourish in the New, Hawthorne reverses the conventional metaphor according to which democratic Puritanism flowers in the New World. As a standard of value, immediacy of feeling assumes precedence over political principles. Accordingly, Hawthorne ignores the racial and economic causes of the Puritans' hostility to Morton's men in order to emphasize the larger significance of the conflict for "the future complexion of New England" (p. 62).

By the time Endicott's "grisly saints" conquer Morton's "gay sinners" (p. 62), Hawthorne's readers should no longer be content to celebrate or condemn the outcome. They should even question Hawthorne's first formulation of the meaning of the conflict: "Jollity and gloom were contending for an empire" (p. 54). Although the Merry Mounters initially seem natural and joyous, the narrator reveals them to be "sworn triflers of a lifetime" motivated by gay despair and a "wild philosophy of pleasure" (pp. 59–60). However vibrant their pageantry may be, they are acting out a daydream, trying to live in perpetual May even though it is Midsummer Eve, and attempting futilely to preserve Old England in New England. Conversely, the dour Puritans, introduced as "most dismal wretches" (p. 60), earn respect for their ability to adapt to the New World. When the heart of Salem's iron man is softened by the plight of the lord and lady of the May, the shallowness of Merry Mount is condemned by implication. The tale's ending suggests that, among the Merry Mounters, only Edith and Edgar are sufficiently mature to recognize that men are imperfect and then to abide the theocracy built upon that recognition.

Thirteen years after Hawthorne published his tale, John Lothrop Motley was to return to the Merry Mount conflict, redefining Hawthorne's study of cultural psychology within a more specifically social context. Placing his romance within the commemorative tradition, Motley announces his controlling purpose: "to awaken a spark of sympathy for the heroic souls who in sorrow and self-denial laid the foundation of this fair inheritance of ours."[46] An endeavor of such ancestral piety promises oversimplified characterization that Motley, like Hawthorne, is too good a historian to permit in a romance. Motley's Puritans no more qualify for sainthood than his Morton qualifies for villainy. As a class, the Puritans are judged to be "iron-handed, despotic, stern, truculent, bigoted religious enthusiasts" (II, p. 235), men with only minimal understanding of historical and moral complexity. By uncovering the questionable means used to suppress Morton, Motley exposes problems in long-standing assertions about the Puritans' commitment to man's civil rights.

Intolerant and oligarchic though the Puritans are, Motley grants spiteful Calvinists a progressive historical force that he denies to gay Merry Mounters. For Motley as for Hawthorne, Thomas Morton and his colony are to be regarded, somewhat regrettably, as anachronisms, as an embodiment of all those losing qualities summoned up by the word "cavalier." Whereas Merry Mount represents the English past, the Puritan represents the American future. The Puritan's narrowmindedness renders him active and purposeful; his intolerance provides the will necessary to settle a wilderness. After portraying Endicott as a theological bigot with a fast sword, Motley tells us: "Such a man of iron, rigid, incisive character was, perhaps, the true and only instrument by which the first foundations of the Puritan Commonwealth could have been hewn out in that stern and rocky wilderness" (II, p. 123).

By granting Endicott primacy as an embodiment of Puritan character, Motley was following Hawthorne's precedent, though probably unknowingly. In "The May-pole of Merry Mount," Hawthorne had called John Endicott, not Governor Winthrop or Roger Williams, "the Puritan of Puritans" (p. 63). For Hawthorne's vision of New England character, the significance of the substitution can hardly be overestimated. His readers were asked to stop imagining their representative forefather as a saintly statue of a governor and to begin to imagine him as a flawed man who had accepted the narrowing responsibilities of leadership. Hawthorne's desire to lend Endicott an importance equal to Winthrop's appears in as early a work as "Mrs. Hutchinson" (1830), written before most of the Puritan tales were conceived:

> Here are collected all those blessed fathers of the land, who rank in our veneration next to the evangelists of Holy Writ; and here, also, are many, unpurified from the fiercest errors of the age, and ready to propagate the religion of peace by violence. In the highest place sits Winthrop – a man by whom the innocent and guilty might alike be judged; the first confiding in his integrity and wisdom, the latter hoping in his mildness. Next is Endicott, who would stand with his drawn sword at the gate of heaven, and resist to the death all pilgrims thither, except they travelled his own path.

The wording of this comparison, usually quoted for its tribute to Winthrop, bears close examination. At the very moment Hawthorne offers us Endicott as an equally representative model of the forefather, he suggests that Endicott's intolerance was real, whereas Winthrop's virtues may be of our making. Although the Winthrops of the Puritan era "rank *in our veneration*" next to the evangelists, Puritans like Endicott "*are . . .* unpurified from the fiercest errors of the age." The accused are pictured "confiding" in Winthrop's integrity, or "hoping" in his mildness, but John Endicott "*would stand* with his drawn sword at the gate of heaven."[47]

"Mrs. Hutchinson" expresses but one of Hawthorne's many different responses to his representative Puritan. The six works in which Endicott is described fill in different aspects of a many-sided personality as it evolves through time. In *Grandfather's Chair*, Endicott is a conqueror of the wilderness who tolerates fear only because it is feminine; in "The May-pole of Merry Mount," he is a resolute exterminator of all frivolity who respects, and possibly yearns for, married love; in "Main-Street," he is the governor of Salem's early years, a "grave, and thoughtful . . . cheerful spirit" who joyfully builds a godly community; in "Endicott and the Red Cross," he is the religious intolerant who first asserts American independence; in "The Gentle Boy," he is the aged colonial governor, "a man of narrow mind and imperfect education," whose "uncompromising bigotry," fed by his "violent and hasty passions," has ended in the "brutal cruelty" of his policies toward Quakers.[48]

Although the figure of John Endicott offers a darker rendition of the Puritan than Hawthorne's contemporaries were asked to accept, it is nonetheless important to insist that Hawthorne's Endicott exhibits, like William Hathorne, "all the Puritanic traits, both good and evil."[49] Thus the single figure of Endicott demonstrates that the "good" and "evil" qualities of Puritanism are inseparable parts of a single character type evolved by Old World origins and New World conditions. Contemporaries who would admit Puritan self-reliance without Puritan intolerance, who would praise Puritan independence while slighting Puritan persecution, were trying to breathe literary life into half a man.

To charge Hawthorne with an inconsistent characterization of Puritans in "Endicott and the Red Cross" is to fall into precisely the same error. After introductory remarks condemning the "tyrannically violent measures" of Laud and Charles I,[50] Hawthorne opens his tale with a four-page description of newly settled Salem as it is reflected in Endicott's iron breastplate. Without mentioning any redeeming qualities, Hawthorne creates Salem as a brutally intolerant autocracy by a terse recounting of sharply drawn details: wolf's blood on the meetinghouse doorstep, an Anglican in the pillory, a royalist tippler in the stocks, a heterodox Puritan bearing the sign "Wanton Gospeller," a woman with a cleft stick on her tongue, and other permanently mutilated citizens bearing cropped ears, branded cheeks, or slit nostrils. Almost all of these details can be historically verified.[51] After Endicott cuts the red cross out of the flag, however, Hawthorne ends his tale with a paragraph of unqualified praise for the governor who has ordered the brutalities:

> With a cry of triumph, the people gave their sanction to one of the boldest exploits which our history records. And, for ever honored by the name of Endicott! We look back through the mist of ages, and recognize, in the rending of the Red Cross from New England's banner, the first omen of that deliverance which our fathers consummated, after the bones of the stern Puritan had lain more than a century in the dust. [P. 441]

Unlike any orator, Hawthorne here forces his reader to confront a paradox. The boldness, assurance, and self-reliance that prompt John Endicott to be the first to assert independence from England are the very qualities that lead him to wholly intolerant persecution of all deviants within Salem.[52]

By juxtaposing the end of his tale to its beginning, Hawthorne exposes the simplicity of contemporary accounts of New England's origins. Hawthorne is willing to slight neither the strength of Puritan self-reliance nor the narrow cruelty that is its consequence. The unfolding of the tale shows that the heroic will to independence and the hidden evil of intolerance were not only equally real, but interdependent qualities forming an American character. Endicott's rending of the red cross thus becomes Hawthorne's equivalent of Winthrop's removal of the charter, but Endicott's act is one of impulsive passion. Hawthorne emphasizes the difference between the sainted Puritan and the representative Puritan by having Endicott say contemptuously, "The Governor is a wise man, – a wise man, and a meek and moderate" (p. 438). Nor does the tale permit any confusion of independence with liberty. The rending of the red cross may be a glorious first omen of the Revolution, but it is explicitly a "deliverance," and not a defense of natural rights. In this tale, democracy does not seem to be, in Grandfather's phrase, "the natural growth of the new world." Instead, Hawthorne shows us that the strength needed to settle the wilderness entailed violence and the stifling of civil liberties.

The particulars of John Endicott's speeches challenge approved versions of history. Endicott's hectoring of Charles I as "son of a Scotch tyrant" and "grandson of a papistical and adulterous Scotch woman" (p. 439) echoes contemporary villainizing of the Stuarts. When Endicott praises "fellow exiles" for having proved themselves "Christian men . . . strong of hand, and stout of heart," who have civilized the "howling wilderness" and made "a new world unto ourselves," both his tone and his phrasing are remarkably similar to contemporary oratory (pp. 438–9). The three terse consecutive sentences in which Endicott denies any authority to "mitred prelate," "crowned king," and "England" (p. 440) resemble an orator's list of discarded Old World relics. Endicott rouses his audience by the same uses of parallel syntax and incremental repetition of phrase as a commemorative speaker.

Although Hawthorne never assesses the content of Endicott's rhetoric, he allows the Wanton Gospeller to refute one of Endicott's assertions, and then arranges for Roger Williams to sanction the refutation:

> "Wherefore, I say again, have we sought this country of a rugged soil and wintry sky? Was it not for the enjoyment of our civil rights? Was it not for liberty to worship God according to our conscience?"
>
> "Call you this liberty of conscience?" interrupted a voice on the steps of the meetinghouse. [P. 439]

Although John Endicott and Roger Williams did not regard "civil rights" and "liberty of conscience" as man's right by natural law, Choate and Story used the phrases in that sense when defining timeless Puritan principles. By characterizing Roger Williams as an "elderly gentleman" (p. 436) who counsels restraint yet opposes Endicott by standing for "liberty of conscience," Hawthorne uses one contemporary historical myth to subvert another.

It has been claimed that Hawthorne knowingly invented a political motive for Endicott's act in order to trace the origins of American independence back to his choice of a founding father.[53] It is true that all of Hawthorne's known sources follow Winthrop in arguing that Endicott was angered by popish idolatry; Endicott saw the red cross, Winthrop said, as a "superstitious thing and a relique of antichrist." No one, however, including John Winthrop, has ever known precisely why Endicott defaced the flag, because no eyewitness accounts or personal explanations are extant. Winthrop himself acknowledged, however, that, after Endicott's act, "much matter was made of this, as fearing it would be taken as an act of rebellion."[54] It is therefore at least plausible that Endicott had a rebellious purpose and that John Winthrop had good reason to deny it.

At the very least we must grant the sincerity of Hawthorne's surmise that Endicott had been driven by a retaliatory impulse into a political gesture. When portraying the incident in *Grandfather's Chair*, Hawthorne was to insist that "a sense of the independence of his adopted country, must have been in that bold man's heart" (p. 24). Hawthorne evidently believed the defacing of the flag to be "a very strong expression of Puritan character" (p. 25) precisely because it was inspired by mixed motives. By ranting against the pope, Hawthorne's Endicott asserts the right of home rule. Just as his gesture cuts redness as well as a cross from the flag, so his fierce assertion of independence stems from the narrow exclusions of his religion. The first stirring of national independence thus arises as a consequence of anti-Catholic bigotry and religious intolerance. From Endicott's inner rage, and not from Winthrop's stately piety, have our American origins been formed.

2

NARROWER SOULS

If our God will wrest *America* out of the Hands of its old Land-Lord, *Satan*, and give these *utmost ends of the earth* to our Lord Jesus, then our present conflicts will shortly be blown over, and something better than, *A Golden Age*, will arrive to this place, and this perhaps before all our *First Planters* are fallen asleep. Now, 'tis a dismal *Uncertainty* and *Ambiguity* we see ourselves placed in. And indeed our All is at the Stake; we are beset with a Thousand Perplexities and Entanglements.

Cotton Mather, "The Present State of New England" (1690)

In an age of trade and material prosperity, we have stood a little stupefied by the elevation of our ancestors . . . This praise was a concession of unworthiness in those who had so much to say of it . . . We shall no longer flatter them. Let us shame the fathers, by superior virtue in the sons.

Emerson, "Boston" (1861)

Although late seventeenth-century American Puritans were repeatedly told that their day of trouble was upon them, they could not have been sure how effective their own redemptive efforts might prove. The Half-Way Covenant, continuing incursions of Quakers and Anabaptists, King Philip's War, Boston's great fire, the smallpox epidemic, drought, crop failures, sudden deaths of the saints, the schemings of Edward Randolph, the revocation of the old charter, and the Salem witch trials – what did the near concurrence of such disastrous visitations portend? Were these events providential signs of inner moral decline from which the saints' lesser sons could never hope to recover? Were they, as the 1679 synod of churches publicly declared, God's warnings that the sons' recent back-sliding demanded *The Necessity of Reformation*? Or were they the last dire tests through which God was to steel his saints for the imminent Millennium? Whereas Perry Miller sees the jeremiads of the 1670s, 1680s, and 1690s as signs, however overstated, of real decline, Sacvan Bercovitch regards them as examples of a conventional rhetorical form through which providential disasters and human sins serve as goads to release millennial energies.[1] Because the sons of the saints could not have known whether they were permanently degenerating, temporarily falling away, or preparing for robes of glory, it is possible that both Miller and Bercovitch are correct, depending upon which sermon, or which part of a sermon, one chooses to emphasize.

To the early nineteenth-century commemorative orator, generational decline was an issue to be slighted, if not entirely avoided. The march of New England civilization into progressive republicanism could assimilate disgraceful episodes that merely proved the rule (the Salem witch trials), but not entire eras of degeneration in Puritan character. Whether progress moved in a linear or a spiral fashion, it moved steadily upward, rather than falling so that it might rise to a still higher state. The larger pattern of history demanded that, even though seventeenth-century troubles could be mentioned, the Puritan character had to be seen as sufficiently resilient to triumph over them. Accordingly, Choate, Story, and Webster search out political types for the Revolution, while ignoring the possibility of generational decline. Their presumption is that ancestral virtues, established during the founding, have reappeared and grown through crises. Even George Bancroft touches gently upon the problem of decline. His *History* provides unflattering details about King Philip's War, merchant luxury, and the loss of the charter, but the telling compromise of the Half-Way Covenant is mentioned fleetingly in order to emphasize the struggles of the independent Puritan spirit against Charles II: "It was still remembered," Bancroft declares, "that the people were led into the wilderness by Aaron, no less than by Moses; and in spite of the increasing spirit of inquiry and toleration, it was resolved to retain the Congregational Churches in their purest . . . Constitution."[2]

The Wept of Wish-ton-Wish is perhaps the first significant nineteenth-century work to reassert a late seventeenth-century decline in Puritan character. After the destruction of Mark Heathcote's Christian settlement by Narragansetts, Cooper reopens his narrative in 1676 by describing a larger settlement in which temporal and spiritual authority, formerly unified in Mark himself, have become dangerously divided between the Reverend Meek Wolfe, who cites Scripture to provoke Indian genocide, and Mark's son Content, whose wavering material values permit the unjust execution of Conanchet, a Narragansett who saved the lives of the Heathcote family. Purchasing his content at the price of his father's dearest principle, Mark's son represents a lesser, secular age when the Puritan readily yields to royal provincial authorities. At the tale's end, Cooper severs Puritan past from Yankee present by allowing Mark's quasi-utopian name for his settlement, Wish-ton-Wish, to pass from human memory. Mark's settlement has grown into just another reasonably prosperous village, but "the orchards, which in 1675 were young and thrifty, are now old and decaying."[3]

As a New Yorker, Cooper limits his interest in the issue of decline to portraying the waning of Puritan integrity in political and racial relationships. He makes little effort to render Content Heathcote's feelings toward his father's religion or toward his father's patriarchal stature. As a fifth-generation New Englander, Hawthorne has an utterly different perspective. The burden of filiopietism is an ever-present condition of life for his later-generation Puritans. Perhaps sensing an affinity between his own position and theirs, Hawthorne perceives that a slackening of faith and a resentment of saintly forefathers have been primary and complementary causes of generational decline. Without denying a steady growth in collective commitment to republican politics, Hawthorne accepts what the seventeenth-century Puritan had so worriedly debated – the decline in inner strength and integrity had been real, measurable, and perhaps irreversible.

For Hawthorne, the crux of decline had been a falling away of religious ardor. "Main-Street" specifies that the inability of the second generation to experience that "zeal of a recovered faith" which had kindled the lamps of the first generation inevitably rendered "the sons and grandchildren of the first settlers . . . a race of lower and narrower souls than their progenitors had been."[4] Because the gloom of the Calvinistic mentality descended upon half-believing children who had themselves achieved no founding, the sons developed greater need for outward marks of conformity in order to seem equal to their forefathers.

"Main-Street," "Dr. Bullivant," and The Scarlet Letter all portray ways in which, once the purposeful era of plantation was over, a sense of drudgery and routine fell upon Puritan communities, exacerbating the trend toward morbid introspection already present in the second generation. Whereas the representative Puritans of the age of founding (Endicott, Bellingham, Winthrop) had been accomplished magistrates of great "stability and dignity of character,"[5] the representative Puritans of later generations (Dimmesdale, Pearson, Brown, Doane, Hooper) were either inactive clerics or vacillating commoners. In the youthful Arthur Dimmesdale we see developing, as early as the 1640s, a crippling combination of new traits: veneration for the elders, a suppressed desire to deface their saintliness, outward conformity to sanctified behavior, and an unwillingness to test one's inner feelings in the world. The compulsive visions of Leonard Doane and Goodman Brown indicate that, by 1692, the new traits had become regrettably dominant.

These changes in generational temper are strikingly similar to the mixed feelings of inferiority, resentment, and relief with which the sons of the Saints acceded to the Half-Way Covenant.[6] The defensive conformity of Hawthorne's second generation reaffirms in fiction the change that led Perry Miller to write of "Declension in a Bible Commonwealth." Quoting William Adams, Miller rhetorically asked, "Could the founders have imagined a more ghastly mockery, than that their descendants should be carried to religious duties 'from external considerations only, by a kind of outward force without any spiritual life or vigour or delight in them?' "[7]

Hawthorne well understood the economic causes of decline that twentieth-century historians are likely to emphasize.[8] His early sketch of Anne Hutchinson contradicts the commemorative tradition by insisting that a sizable number of first-generation Puritans in fact had not been exiles of religious conscience, but economic failures seeking somehow to reaccumulate "the pomp of the Old World" in the New. Dr. Bullivant recalls how the ruling families of the theocracy had begun by the 1660s to become a threatened minority in an increasingly commercial world. The arrival of areligious merchants and adventurers after the Restoration formed a "new set of emigrants who followed unworthily in the track of the pure-hearted pilgrims." Having described the era's commercial freebootery, belligerent provincialism, and love of pomp, all symbolized in the figure of Governor Phips, Grandfather pointedly laments, "The old moral and religious character of New England was in danger of being utterly lost."[9]

These aspects of Puritan decline are contributing causes of the Quaker persecutions of 1656–61 as they are rendered in "The Gentle Boy." The Puritan elders, represented by John Endicott, have become so insistent upon religious forms that they identify Quakers by merely external signs, then punish them even if the inner voice has not yet led to explicit heresy. The second-generation Puritan children, "a brood of baby-fiends," trample upon Ilbrahim through sheer malice toward outsiders whose humanity they have been taught to deny.[10] Hawthorne accounts for the children's viciousness by assuming a degenerating inheritance: "The devil of their fathers entered into the unbreeched fanatics" (p. 92). Throughout "The Gentle Boy," as in The Scarlet Letter, the common people are united primarily in their zeal for persecution. To describe prudent elder statesmen as superior to the volatile folk is hardly a tribute to an emerging popular character.

Through the changing relationship of Tobias Pearson to the Puritan community, we see the destructive friction between the first and second generations. Pearson's late emigration to America was due to his tepid faith and the "more worldly consideration" of recouping hitherto "unprosperous fortunes" (p. 76). Having risen to be a representative to the General Court, Pearson possesses other self-made virtues integral to the nineteenth-century image of the Puritans. His home, built in the "western wilderness" but on the margin of the town, provides shelter for one family rather than a unit within a theocratic community (p. 74). His commitment to home and family proves unable, however, to withstand the combined pressures of New World conditions, his own weakness, and the relentless Puritan demand for conformity. He is even ashamed of adopting Ilbrahim, because he is made to feel a "consciousness of guilt" (p. 85) for such an act of compassion. When fellow Puritans ostracize him as a Quaker sympathizer and then harass the home he came to build, he has no inner resources by which to withstand them. Instead of confronting the community with its intolerance, Pearson adopts Quaker principles of which he is half ashamed, and then permits his inner confusion to lead to "neglect of temporal affairs" (p. 95). Although he knows that Quakers like Catharine have sacrificed their children to their religion, he nonetheless proceeds to do the same, allowing his love for Ilbrahim to become his cross, and Ilbrahim's newfound home to deteriorate. The final crushing of Pearson's soul ("Verily, I am an accursed man, and I will lay me down in the dust, and lift up my head no more" [p. 97]) shows the paralyzing self-divisions of any Bay Colony immigrant who, in times of energizing intolerance, could discard neither his human affection nor his Puritan upbringing.

Ilbrahim, symbol of the universal child, is victimized both by the religious sadism of the Puritans and by the religious masochism of the Quakers. At each stage of conflict – when Endicott hangs Ilbrahim's father, when Catharine vents her "flood of malignity" (p. 82) at the congregation, when the Puritans ostracize the Pearsons, and when the Quaker mentor urges Pearson to persevere to a glorious martyrdom – all are playing out anticipated parts in perversely satisfying hostilities.[11] During all confrontations, home, family, and children are sacrificed until Ilbrahim's death ends the devastation wrought upon the one Puritan family that seemed to retain the power of love.

On a moral level, the tale suggests the crucial priority of duty to family over duty to religious conscience. On a psychological level, it shows how, for Quakers as well as Puritans, "hatred and revenge . . . wrapped themselves in the garb of piety" (p. 81). But on a historical level, the tale's importance is its persistent repudiation of the conventional belief that Puritan intolerance was a wrong insofar as it violated the Quaker's right of conscience. Hawthorne's emphasis is on the ways in which the process of religious confrontation destroys the souls of Puritans as well as Quakers. The wearing intensity of conflict prevents the Puritans from ever, in Webster's terms, making a home of the wilderness. The most memorable line in the tale occurs when the gentle boy, sitting upon his father's grave, prophetically remarks, "My home is here" (p. 72).

Hawthorne challenges historical tradition by showing that neither Puritans nor Quakers could lay claim to moral rectitude or providential approval. The New England historians Hawthorne read adopt a uniformly critical view of the Quakers.[12] Their evidence for the disruptive force of Quaker religious mania is reflected in Hawthorne's characterizations of Catharine and Pearson's Quaker mentor. But Hawthorne also challenges regional tradition by explicitly citing only the Dutch Quaker historian William Sewel, and by then relying upon Sewel for accounts of Puritan persecution.[13] The result is a cross-weaving of sources through which Hawthorne implies a plague on both sectarian houses.

Hawthorne's belief that Puritan character had declined in the later seventeenth century conflicted with his desire, evident in *Grandfather's Chair*, to praise Puritans as the embodiment of American political independence. If the second and third generations lacked the religious courage and political sagacity of the first, how could they display their presumed spirit of independence in action? "The Gray Champion," usually regarded as an uncomplicated tribute to New England's democratic revolutionary spirit, attempts to resolve this problem. Because Hawthorne's re-creation of the revolt against Andros had to be faithful both to historical fact and to his own sense of generational decline, Hawthorne could only graft an unrelated legend upon history in order to explain how the moribund spirit of independence had led to an act of revolt.

No conflict of New England's past yielded so much unanimity of judgment among regional historians and commemorative orators as the revolt of 1689. Even pre-Revolutionary historians such as Mather, Neal, and Hutchinson had justified the revolt as a nearly unanimous uprising of the people to preserve their legal rights as Englishmen. In all these accounts, the factors that made Andros's regime a model of domestic tyranny are denounced in detail: a government appointed from England, a rich military nobleman as its governor, standing royal troops, imposition of new taxes, confirmation fees to validate land titles, and suspension of town meetings.[14] Hawthorne's introductory paragraphs reaffirm this tradition by enumerating the political sources of Andros's tyranny, and by pitting the aristocratic governor, his redcoats, and his few wine-warmed councillors against the gray mass of "the people." As in a commemorative oration, Andros and his government are seen as an insolent minority of aristocrats who represent "James II, the bigoted successor of Charles the Voluptuous." Surely, Hawthorne had well-considered reasons for selecting "The Gray Champion" to be the first story to be read in his first published volume of tales.[15]

One significant historical omission had been common among Hawthorne's post-Revolutionary sources. Neal and Hutchinson had followed Cotton Mather in acknowledging – quite correctly – the existence of differences in strategy among the colonists. The revolt had been prompted, Mather wrote, by "the country people," who had been prepared to use violence to regain charter privileges. Acts of civil disruption had been denounced, however, by the "principal gentlemen in Boston," who had agreed to "extinguish all essays in the people toward an insurrection" in order to await news of the Glorious Revolution from England. Mather's subsequent claim that, on the day of the revolt, "the whole town was immediately in arms, with the most *unanimous resolution* perhaps that ever was known to have inspired any people," minimizes the differences between the anger of the Country party and the needed restraint of gentlemen, clergy, and merchants.[16] When Bancroft and the commemorative orators re-created the event as a type for the Revolution, they ignored all differences among New Englanders, fastened upon Mather's italicized phrase "unanimous resolution," and produced sentences such as this one by Josiah Quincy: "In 1689, the tyranny of Andros having become insupportable to the country, Boston rose like one man." Hawthorne, however, restored the divisions that intervening commemorators had obscured. Facing the sullen anger of the massed people, Hawthorne's Bradstreet "besought them to submit to the constituted authorities" and to "do nothing rashly . . . but pray for the welfare of New England, and expect patiently what the Lord will do in this matter!" The crowd, deferring to its patriarch, accordingly does nothing.[17]

Hawthorne's insistence upon Bradstreet's moderating effect realigns the meaning of the historical conflict and prepares for the tale's fictive conclusion. The people massed in the square do not rise "like one man" to overthrow the minion of tyranny; they wait for the last of their patriarchs to lead them and then, when he declines, they wait upon the Lord. Their resemblance to the first generation is largely external: "There was the sober garb, the general severity of mien, the gloomy but undismayed expression, the scriptural forms of speech, and the confidence in Heaven's blessing on a righteous cause, which would have marked a band of the original Puritans" (pp. 10–11). Of the three voices from among the crowd, two express fears of a massacre and one expresses a longing for a champion, but none expresses confidence or resolution. Helpless to act for themselves, heeding their ministers, who "exerted their influence to quiet the people, but not to disperse them" (p. 11),

Boston's Puritans react to Andros's troops, not like an angered Country party, but by standing in silence, a mass of "sad visages and dark attire" (p. 13).

The Gray Champion thus serves as a needed device for maintaining continuity in Puritan political heroism while admitting the decline in Puritan character. As "the type of New-England's hereditary spirit" (p. 18), he represents a timeless will to independence that miraculously appears to reinspire those Puritans most mired in time. Historians and orators had never needed to posit a Gray Champion because the people had presumably done the champion's work. By adapting the legend of the Angel of Hadley to the revolt against Andros,[18] Hawthorne creates a symbolic embodiment of timeless Puritan virtues that he can no longer substantiate in history. To maintain the Puritan will to independence, Hawthorne resorts to providential history. Only the will of the Lord can account for the arrival of the champion, be he dead regicide or symbolic spirit, to deliver New England from tyranny.

However admirable Hawthorne's attempt to resolve the conflicting demands of decline and independence may be, the figure of the champion remains a lapse in historical logic, even as a symbolic device. On the eighteenth of April 1689, a Gray Champion who represents the "hereditary spirit" of the patriarchs has supposedly appeared to prevent the invader's step from polluting New England soil (p. 18). Before the champion appears, however, Hawthorne has shown us that the crowd does not possess such a spirit, that all the first-generation patriarchs save one are dead, and that the aged Bradstreet is in fact a moderate who counsels submission. After invoking a historically substanceless symbol to do the work of historical revolt, Hawthorne then ends his tale by asserting that the champion is a real spirit always present in the breasts of New Englanders.

Fortunately, the champion is Hawthorne's only attempt to make an imagined symbol into a historical being affecting a historical situation. The figure he hopes to render credible represents the legacy most dear to the commemorative orators of the preceding ten years. Just as Webster, Story, and Choate invoked the spirit of the forefathers in hopes of passing it on to the sons, so Hawthorne creates the Gray Champion to be not only "the type of New-England's hereditary spirit," but "the pledge, that New-England's sons will vindicate their ancestry" (p. 18). As in Webster's and Everett's orations, the great trials amid which the patriarchal spirit emerged in 1620, 1689, and 1775 only stimulate Hawthorne's desire to postpone the crisis by which his generation might have to prove itself: "Long, long, may it be, ere he comes again! His hour is one of darkness, and adversity, and peril" (p. 18). The most telling problem, however, is to achieve a historically convincing embodiment of a timeless popular spirit. Hawthorne's Gray Champion and Everett's Spirit of the Forefathers are personified abstractions from so distant and venerable a past that they seem beyond a contemporary's reach. The Gray Champion may emerge "from among the people" (p. 14), but he walks apart, commands the people with monosyllables, and exhibits a sadly deserved scorn for the sons of 1689.

FALSE SPECTERS AND UNWORTHY SONS

The popular revolt of 1689 was the only sure instance of heroic Puritanism Hawthorne detected in the century between the Restoration and the Seven Years' War. Following immediately upon the revolt against Andros, the Salem witch trials marked the unmistakable decline of Puritan character. Grandfather, who certainly does not search out the dark underside of his region's past, unequivocally calls the witch trials "the saddest and most humiliating passage in our history."[19] His short summary of the trials should be read by everyone who assumes that Hawthorne sought to lend credence to the dark visions Goodman Brown and Leonard Doane have of all-pervasive ancestral sin. "The Witchcraft delusion," Grandfather declares, was "a frenzy, which led to the death of many innocent persons" and which "originated in the wicked arts of a few children" (p. 77). The issue of the existence of witches is settled by three words: "There are none" (p. 79). The representative Puritan of the times, Cotton Mather, is unjustly described as the chief agent of the "delusion" – a divine of "dreamy" mind who wrote a disordered "pedantic history . . . in a queer, blind, crabbed, fantastical hand" (pp. 92–3). To Grandfather, Mather was an ingrown, third-generation Puritan who fell into credulity and superstition because of ancestor worship and untested religiosity. He is to be regarded as "an exaggeration of those pious and potent Divines, whom he reverenced as the great men of the preceding age" (p. 71). Although by 1692 "the ministers and wise men were more deluded than the illiterate people" (p. 78), the people nonetheless continued to defer to ministerial descendants of old families. It was the combination of ministerial authority, popular illiteracy, and universal delusion that made possible the tragedy of Gallows Hill.

As one should expect, Hawthorne's opinion of the trial procedures agrees with his historical sources. Neal, Hutchinson, Joseph Felt, and Abiel Abbot had all condemned the trials as a delusion in which everyone even charged with witchcraft had been innocent. In their view, the judges had become crazed with the superstitions of a benighted faith, while the people had been led astray by the clergy. The historical use of spectral evidence to obtain convictions, a procedure crucial to understanding "Young Goodman Brown," had explicitly been condemned by Hutchinson, Abbot, and Felt. The more recent accounts by Abbot and C. W. Upham, whose *Lectures on Witchcraft* (1831) Hawthorne had almost surely read, only increased the shrillness of the attack. Charging that the afflicted girls had been imposters seeking thrills or attention, Abbot and Upham anticipated Bancroft's view that the witch trials had been caused by a conspiracy of ministers who had used religious fear to regain political power.[20]

Accepting these opinions as historical truth, Hawthorne differed from his sources only in his refusal to append the customary progressive rationalization. After condemning the witch trials as an outrage against all New England and all humanity, Felt, Abbot, Upham, and Bancroft reassured their readers that by 1693 "the images and visions that had possessed the bewildered imaginations of the people flitted away and left them standing in the clear sunshine of reason and their senses."[21] Grandfather's summary of the witch trials ends in no such comforting conclusion. The children are led to consider the trials as a shameful sign of failing judgment, not the beginning of a new age. Nor, as far as we know, does Goodman Brown or Leonard Doane ever emerge from his bewildered visions into the "clear sunshine of reason." By adopting a point of view quite like a Jamesian reflector, Hawthorne frees the reader of his witchcraft tales to experience the psychological processes by which common people, not the ministers, saw specters. His fictions, however unfair to the clergy and the judges, restore the historical fact that popular credulity was an equally important cause of communal delusion. Denying his reader the comforts of progressive reassurance, Hawthorne gains an immediacy of experience that is more historical, not less so.

"Alice Doane's Appeal" has been viewed as an exploration of universal evil, a revelation of suppressed desires for parricide and incest, and a possible parody of gothic conventions.[22] Placed in its historical context, however, the tale portrays the psychological causes of Salem witchcraft in terms wholly consistent with "Young Goodman Brown" and *Grandfather's Chair*. Leonard Doane feels fears and desires similar to those which persuade Goodman Brown to be almost certain he saw the evil saints of Salem Village communing with the devil. At the tale's end, Hawthorne condemns the afflicted, the innocent, and Cotton Mather in even stronger words than those Grandfather uses, but the substance of the judgment remains the same.

Leonard Doane is the first of Hawthorne's New Englanders to project his repressed sense of self upon the void beyond him. Like Goodman Brown, Doane is a young Salemite confident of his own purity, yet "conscious of the germ of all the fierce and deep passions, and of all the many varieties of wickedness," that remain dormant within him.[23] Whether Goodman Brown projects his latent evil onto fantasized devils and witches must remain a matter for each reader's interpretation, but there can be no doubt that Leonard Doane does so. Hawthorne explicitly calls Doane "a young man . . . characterized by a diseased imagination and morbid feelings" (p. 270). The first expression of his diseased imagination is his loathing for Walter Brome, whom Doane imagines to be, not only the successful seducer of his beloved sister, but "my very counterpart" (p. 271). Although it is true that Walter Brome represents Doane's loathed longing for incest, Hawthorne directs our attention to the process of self-projection, not to incest itself. "Searching into the breast of Walter Brome," Leonard discovers "a resemblance from which I shrank with sickness, and loathing, and horror," one that inspires "a hateful sympathy in our secret souls" (p. 271). The advantage of transferring his own evil to another is that it allows him to continue to assure himself (perhaps, once more, like Goodman Brown) that his dark desires truly belong to a separate person: "[Walter Brome's education] in the cities of the old world, and mine in this rude wilderness, had wrought a superficial difference. The evil of his character, also, had been strengthened and rendered prominent by a reckless and ungoverned life, while mine had been softened and purified by the gentle and holy nature of Alice" (p. 271). By killing Brome, Doane attempts to exorcise his own evil, just as identifying and hanging a witch might exorcise a demon within a judge.[24]

Brown and Doane do not know whether their sense of self depends upon glorifying their ancestral heritage or denigrating it. Both young men revere dead fathers who killed Indians in self-defense, but both of them yearn, equally strongly, to expose their fathers' presumably tainted purity. When in the forest, Goodman Brown notes that the devil resembles his father, and then assures himself that "we have been a race of honest men and good Christians, since the days of the martyrs."[25] Looking at the body of Walter Brome, Doane is immobilized by his belief that the murdered face "wore a likeness of my father," until fear of the "fixed glare of the eyes" (his father's, not Brome's) finally drives him to try to bury the body (p. 273). For both young men, the presumed existence of devils and specters is inseparable from their desire to do away with the burden of noble fathers. However plausible the link between filiopietism and seeing devils may be historically, Hawthorne accepted a contemporary falsity when he fashioned Cotton Mather into the epitome of it. Mr. Mather, Grandfather was to assert, had not only been the greatest witch hunter of the age; he had consistently shown an undeserved reverence for forefathers.

Although the reader can never be sure that Brown is not a good man as well as a church member, Leonard Doane becomes an undoubted murderer. Because Doane's guilt is based on a criminal act rather than suspicions of universal sin, his need to posit an external source for evil cannot be questioned. Like Brown, Doane has a vision of the depravity of Salem's citizenry in which the "old defenders of the infant colony," "pastors of the church," and "old, illustrious . . . early settlers" are seen as gross sinners and hypocrites (pp. 275–6). Unlike Brown, Doane cannot possibly be experiencing a truthful revelation. The frozen moonlight setting, Hawthorne warns the reader, is one in which "a man might shudder at the *ghostly shape* of his old beloved dwelling" (p. 274, italics mine). Doane will not allow one exception to his belief in ancestral depravity: "None but souls accursed were there, and fiends counterfeiting the likeness of departed saints" (p. 276). In the final paragraph, Hawthorne draws a crucial distinction when he refers to "the whole miserable multitude, both sinful souls and *false spectres* of good men" (p. 276, italics mine). In the closing sentence, he even describes the procession as an "apparition" and an "unreal throng" (p. 277). Doane's midnight vigil can be regarded neither as a conclusive insight into universal evil nor as an authorial revenge against ancestors. It is quite clearly another historically authentic fictionalization of the dangers of accepting spectral evidence.

The tableau of historical events by which the narrator finally releases the "wellspring" of his listener's tears is a composite of separate incidents (p. 280). Rebecca Nurse, Sarah Good, John Proctor, Martha Carrier, and George Burroughs are all pictured dying on the same day beneath the triumphant gaze of Cotton Mather, "the one blood-thirsty man, in whom were concentrated those vices of spirit and errors of opinion, that sufficed to madden the whole surrounding multitude" (p. 279). Hawthorne's desire to expose the delusion of witchcraft here overreaches itself, resulting in distortion of fact and vilification of Mather.[26] To his credit, however, Hawthorne also insists, unlike Upham or Bancroft, that the people must have been as culpable as the ministers. Only because the "whole multitude" shares the maddened vision of their representative clergymen have the witch trials been able to grow into the event that "disgraced an age" (p. 279).

In his gothic tale, as in his historical tableau, Hawthorne has made every effort to show that Gallows Hill, where the forefathers' legacy should have its proper monument, has witnessed "the most execrable scene, that our history blushes to record" (p. 267). Because this judgment is defensible, it is all the more regrettable that Hawthorne's condemnation of Cotton Mather is simplistic history, whereas his overwritten gothic tale portrays accurate historical psychology.[27] We should recall, however, that the narrator's audience has displayed nothing but wrong responses. The young ladies laugh at Hawthorne's "fiction," weep over his "history," yet never understand the central point common to both: The acceptance of spectral evidence by commoners such as Leonard Doane has brought the accused – and the assumption of communal purity – to a shameful public end.

There is a tellingly depressing similarity among the major characters of Hawthorne's last generation of Puritans (1680–1710). Because Goodman Brown, Leonard Doane, Richard Digby, Father Hooper, and Reuben Bourne inherit accepted family names in established villages, they need not exert civic leadership or prove their regeneration through a confirmed faith. Seemingly untested until their maturity, they have had the leisure to brood over the central dogma of their cultural heritage, the universality of sin. They all become obsessed to the verge of monomania with sinfulness, whether it be real or imagined, their own or universal. Whereas the founding fathers acted with forthright public severity to root out sin, these sons of the third and fourth generation either hide their sins from themselves by projecting them onto others (Doane, Brown, Digby) or exaggerate their human imperfection into sin (Hooper, Malvin). Both groups fully exemplify a trait Hawthorne was to attribute in 1849 to the third generation of Puritans: "Nothing impresses them, except their own experience."[28]

Unlike Endicott or Bellingham, all five of these young men presume that sin is a forever irredeemable condition, and then fearfully seek to conceal it or to render it safely universal. Those who have committed a "sinful" act (Doane, Bourne) incur unrelieved guilt without the release of bearing public shame. Those who see sin in every heart except their own (Digby and possibly Brown) become ceaselessly distrustful because of the exclusions of their pride. The Puritan obsession with sin has grown so markedly that even an apparently blameless and compassionate young clergyman will fix upon himself a veil symbolic of mankind's blackness, and then wear it until eternity even though its meaning may be belied by his every act.

In differing ways, each of these men sees the world through a black veil of his own devising. The consequence for each is a crippling withdrawal from the community, a withdrawal quite unlike that of Hawthorne's first-generation Puritans. Richard Digby, convinced of "the horrible perversity of this generation,"[29] but sure that he alone is justified, withdraws to declaim jeremiads to an audience of trees. Tormented by excessive guilt for leaving Roger Malvin, Reuben Bourne fails to provide for his family's temporal welfare, and then withdraws, like Digby, to the forest. Although Leonard Doane and Goodman Brown remain in Salem, their visions of communal depravity isolate them from it, leaving them to brood over suspicions they can never prove. Even if the symbolism of Hooper's veil is a true rendering of man's state, the effect of the veil is to separate the community and its minister from one another, thereby allowing the townsfolk the smug pleasure of concluding that Father Hooper, unlike themselves, must feel guilt for a specific act. None of the five men is ostracized by an act of intolerance; each of their withdrawals is a self-initiated defense that excludes others from intimacy. By mirroring their own evils upon their fellows, Hawthorne's third-generation New Englanders isolate rather than aggrandize themselves.

These five men all belong among the "race of lower and narrower souls" who, as grandchildren of the patriarchs, inherited a life "sinister to the intellect, and sinister to the heart." Their several withdrawals also confirm one of Hawthorne's historical subtleties: "It was impossible for the succeeding race to grow up, in Heaven's freedom, beneath the discipline which their [the forefathers'] gloomy energy of character had established."[30] Confined by the rigidity of Puritan tradition, no third-generation youth proves capable of maturing. All five men embody their notions of innocence and virtue, not in religious principle, but in pure women who live in order to love them. And yet, by rejecting woman's appeal to rejoin marital or communal families, all choose to withdraw rather than to assume the responsibilities of adulthood. Unable to outgrow the notion that a man must be a black sinner or a white saint, Doane, Brown, and Digby can never understand that the devil uses truth for evil purposes, or that their forefathers might have been heroic and intolerant simultaneously. At this time in New England's history, to be the young son of illustrious forebears seems to preclude maturity.

The political prudence of the first generation, tainted though it was, possessed the merits of sanity and adaptation to circumstance. Without exception Hawthorne's third- and fourth-generation Puritans display some form of solitary madness ranging from the gently suggested derangement of Hooper to the insanity of Richard Digby. The lonely, embittered deaths of Brown, Digby, and Hooper contain no compensatory hint that their religious gloom has been justified. The imagery of shadows, caves, and sealed rooms with which these tales end exactly conveys the introverted Calvinism these men have inherited from the second generation and then aggravated. None save Brown leaves any progeny. Reuben Bourne, who had wished to be "the father of a race, the patriarch of a people," shoots his only child, Cyrus ("a future leader in the land"), in a perverse attempt to expiate his own guilt.[31] Quite evidently, Hawthorne believed that a widespread psychological condition had become a force in historical time. Considered together, these five characters suggest the deathbed of Puritanism as a social and religious order, a time when the spirit of the forefathers has reached an end without an exit. Ironically, however, they also constitute the first group of characters in which we can clearly identify the self-enclosed solipsism that Tocqueville would find characteristic of the American mind.

For ten years after publication of "Old Esther Dudley" (1839), Hawthorne wrote commemorative history (*Grandfather's Chair* and *Liberty Tree*), but no more historical tales. His return to the family home in Salem in 1846 – under conditions of financial necessity and after years of comparative independence in the Old Manse – must have brought feelings of a dispiriting return to the dead past, if not a measure of personal humiliation. Having recognized that New England custom did not respect mere storytellers, he accepted profitable labor that idled his pen and may have led him to attribute his own imaginative sluggishness to Salem and its Custom House. When in 1849 he wrote his fictionalized account of Salem's history titled "Main-Street," thirty years of New England's commemorative self-congratulation were drawing to a close. Under such circumstances, considerable shifts in Hawthorne's historical attitudes were bound to occur: a desire to summarize former beliefs, an even greater detachment from received opinion, a skepticism about the very process of re-creating history.[32]

"Main-Street" satirizes the conventions of New England historiography while inverting many of its conclusions. Salem's past is chronologically unrolled before us as if learning about history were like watching a traveling diorama promoted by a somewhat tedious hustler. Through the nasty comments of an "acidulous-looking gentleman" (p. 52), Hawthorne implies that this publicized past has been manufactured by the showman himself. Its succession of historical incidents, in which "miserable slips of painted pasteboard" (p. 63) pass for human beings, are jerkily cranked out of a machine. We are periodically reminded that the entire affair is an "exhibition," "puppet show," or "play" made up of fragments that gain credibility only through the haze of distance. Having found no new method for re-creating New England's past, Hawthorne ridicules linear, pictorial history, while simultaneously using it to suggest needed revisions.

The only important vestige of commemorative attitudes in "Main-Street" is the praise accorded to John Winthrop, John Endicott, and Roger Williams. Rather than justify a patriarchal civilization by condemning savagery, Hawthorne describes Squaw Sachem as "a majestic and queenly woman" whose matriarchy possessed dignity and order (p. 51). His accounts of the Quaker and witchcraft persecutions offer no extenuating circumstances for Puritan intolerance; if the arch-fiend came to Salem in 1692, he deceived an entire community into "Universal Madness" (p. 78). The racial priorities recently assumed by proponents of Manifest Destiny are mocked by sentences such as "The aforesaid Anglo-Saxon energy is now trampling along the street, and raising a positive cloud of dust beneath its sturdy footsteps" (p. 58).[33]

"Main-Street" thus subverts crucial assumptions of commemorative historiography. Instead of asserting the natural growth of Puritan virtues, Hawthorne expatiates at length upon their decline. Rather than praising the forefathers' will to independence, he exclaims, "How like an iron cage was that which they called Liberty" (p. 58). Customary assertions of material and political progress through time are upended. The showman abruptly concludes his history of Main Street with the great snow of 1717, thus returning Salem to seeming savagery: "It would seem as if the street, the growth of which we have noted so attentively . . . were all at once obliterated, and resolved into a drearier pathlessness than when the forest covered it" (p. 80). By claiming that neither Revolutionary nor contemporary Salem can be shown because "the scene will not move. A wire is broken" (p. 81), Hawthorne forces us to recognize that the glories of the future are merely predictions. He leaves his audience viewing Salem, not as a thriving part of America's Roman republic, but as a frozen reminder of "the fate of Herculaneum and Pompeii" (p. 81).

The detailed description of the great snow suggests that Hawthorne has not simply found a convenient terminus for an overlong sketch that might have been continued indefinitely. His intent is to hold forth an unexpected means to a new start. After Simon Bradstreet is buried and the great snow falls, the showman asserts: "Now, the traces of former times and hitherto accomplished deeds being done away, mankind shall be at liberty to enter on new paths, and guide themselves by other laws than heretofore" (p. 80). Whatever these new laws may be, progress seems to depend more on severance than linkage. Unlike the commemorative orator, who sought historical connections to bind his audience to imitate their forefathers, the showman dwells upon a cataclysm that seems to sweep the forefathers away, even though he knows that the dark main street must reemerge beneath the snow.

Such earlier showmen as Webster, Everett, Quincy, and Story had asked their audiences to join in expressing gratitude to the divine Father for sending the founding forefathers as models of character. The most famous passage in "Main-Street" ends with a subversive version of this conventional prayer. After the showman has finished explaining the sinister narrowness and growing rigidity of succeeding Puritan generations, he exclaims, "Let us thank God for having given us such ancestors; and let each successive generation thank him, not less fervently, for being one step further from them in the march of ages" (p. 68). Although both assertions of this sentence are equally sincere, "Main-Street" ends by truncating the linear sequence of history and questioning the idea of progress. While exposing the inevitable decline of Puritan virtue, the showman has been led to call – not too hopefully – for independence from the heritage he is recording.

THE CHARACTER OF DOOM

The Scarlet Letter is concerned less with Puritanism as a force in history than with the effect of Puritan society upon its four major characters, all of them outcasts, newcomers, or sinners. This change of perspective leads neither to less historical accuracy nor to vilifying the authorities of the first generation. Although the magistrates outlaw joyful Elizabethan pageantries, they retain the virtues of the patriarch: "They had a fortitude and self-reliance, and, in time of difficulty or peril, stood up for the welfare of the state like a line of cliffs against a tempestuous tide" (p. 224). And yet, because these magistrates must judge a moral failing without apparent political consequences, we see discouragingly everyday aspects of the founding fathers: a fondness for luxury, an inability to understand the caprice of children, and an imperviousness toward areligious or apolitical passions. Because "religion and law were almost identical" to the first generation (p. 50), the power of sanctioning religious commandments is exercised by elderly civil authorities – those members of the community who are least fit to "meddle with a question of human guilt, passion, and anguish" (p. 64).

Throughout the novel, the chief proponents of enforcing "the whole dismal severity of the Puritanic code of law" (p. 52) are not the magistracy and clergy, however, as has often been assumed, but the people. Although four of the five robust townswomen in the marketplace hope Hester will be punished to the fullest extent of the law, Bellingham and Wilson have reduced the sentence to three hours of public exposure. From the outset, the patriarchs know they can pass no final judgment on Hester's soul; they sentence her to wear her mark of shame only "for the remainder of her natural life" (p. 62). Before Hester's three hours on the scaffold are over, John Wilson offers to commute the sentence, telling Hester that sincere repentance and revelation of her seducer's name "may avail to take the scarlet letter off thy breast" (p. 67). Three years later, Hester pleads so successfully for her child that Wilson concludes, "Every good Christian man hath a title to show a father's kindness towards the poor, deserted babe" (p. 112). After more years have passed, the council seeks to relieve Hester of the shame of wearing the letter. Although the worst sinner may be the man who meddles in another's guilt, the meddler appears in the guise of an Old World scholar and Calvinistic leech, rather than an autocratic Puritan magistrate. The hesitant leniency of the magistrates raises a rarely asked question: If the patriarchs whom the people revere wish to release Hester from her stigma, who is responsible for her prolonged exclusion?

We have perhaps heard too much of Hester Prynne as a subversive dark lady of romance, as a suppressed feminist like the sainted Anne, or as a prophetess of a new order.[34] Although all these identities are real and important, they represent temporary qualities that emerge during the crises of Hester's estrangement. Hester looks and acts like a Lawrentian dark lady only during the forest scene. Her recovery of her sexuality, her belief that adultery has a "consecration of its own" (p. 185), and her decision to flee Boston for Europe express hidden desires that form but one side of her character. Similarly, Hester's identity as a prophetess of feminism is based entirely upon chapter thirteen, significantly titled "Another View of Hester," and upon one paragraph in the "Conclusion." If Hawthorne is as concerned with the historical accuracy of his characterizations as I have tried to show, we might expect Hester Prynne to be, of all things, a seventeenth-century Puritan woman whose one ineradicable response to her situation is that committing adultery is breaking the seventh commandment of God.

Hester Prynne was raised, Hawthorne tells us, as "the daughter of a pious home" (p. 107). There are nine separate passages in which Hester refers, either in thought or in discourse, to her adultery as a "sin," not a "consecration"; in none of these instances does the context suggest that she is using the word ironically.[35] During her long day of public ignominy, Wilson's proposal that the letter be removed prompts Hester to declare that it must be retained: "Never! . . . It is too deeply branded. Ye cannot take it off " (p. 67). Upon learning many years later that the council is considering removing the letter, Hester exclaims: "It lies not in the pleasure of the magistrates to take off this badge . . . Were I worthy to be quit of it, it would fall away of its own nature, or be transformed into something that should speak a different purport" (p. 161). Though Hester may have yearned to be a prophetess of the new order, she has raised Pearl with the primer and catechized her in the Westminster Confession when under no compulsion to do so. To contemporary readers accustomed to Sedgwick's and Child's Puritan heroines, Hester's theology must surely have seemed superstitious. She asks Chillingworth if he is not "like the Black Man that haunts the forest around us" (p. 75) and later tells Pearl, "Once in my life I met the Black Man! . . . This scarlet letter is his mark!"[36] Although Hester is always resentful of the civil power that has shamed her, she doubts the rectitude of the community's moral judgment of her only intermittently.

Both the credibility and the strength of Hester's character depend on her inability to resolve the clash between her theological heritage and her experience of human passion. She can discard neither the guilt she feels for committing a sin nor the fulfillment she has found in an act of love. Although she often feels guilt, she almost never feels shame, because she knows the patriarchs can never understand the creative aspects of her adultery. She must live her life on the margin of the community, resisting two opposite temptations. To yield to a belief in witchcraft, to believe that Pearl is the Devil's child, and the forest the only fitting place for Mistress Hibbins and herself, would be to deny that Pearl is her greatest treasure, her red flower inexplicably grown from a guilty passion. To return to Europe or to enter the forest, however, would be a futile attempt to discard the burden of her self-assumed guilt. Her fidelity to both her guilt and her passion forces her to develop strengthening but contradictory desires: to display her self-reliance, to minister to the sick and sinful, to flaunt the creative power of her love through her art.[37] Her return to her cottage to resume the scarlet letter, far from being an uncharacteristic or demeaning decision, is her greatest triumph. At a time when shame no longer has meaning, Hester chooses to return and to take up her own burden of guilt for a sin she can never wholly repent.

Whereas Hester, like Mrs. Hutchinson or Catharine, has committed an act that excludes her from the community, Dimmesdale remains a passive insider whose youth, orthodoxy, and reverence for patriarchal authority will be characteristic of later Puritan generations. Lacking the strength to acknowledge his adultery, he gains a reputation for spotless virtue by his eloquent sorrowing over the sins of others. Although his heightened ministerial powers never provide Dimmesdale the expiation he seeks, they suggest how the seemingly humbling creed of the Fall of Man would become, in later generations, a mask for hypocrisy and a source of pride.

Only through Hester can Dimmesdale summon the strength to act, confess, and bear shame. When he returns from the forest, his almost uncontrollable urge to blaspheme reflects his still unacknowledged guilt. Obsession with his own hidden sin has induced him, like Leonard Doane, to call up specters that satisfy his "gratuitous desire of ill, ridicule of whatever was good or holy" (p. 210). When Dimmesdale returns from the forest, he has descended to the condition Hawthorne had feared for Hester: "O Fiend, whose talisman was that fatal symbol, wouldst thou leave nothing, whether in youth or age, for this poor sinner to revere? – Such loss of faith is ever one of the saddest results of sin" (p. 84).

Because Dimmesdale delivers his election sermon shortly after loss of faith has released blasphemous desire, its vision of New England's future grandeur is delivered in an ironic context. Although Dimmesdale is glad that his "honorable" opportunity to deliver an address will precede revelation of his scarlet letter, he tells himself that his motive is public duty – a rationalization that Hawthorne calls "pitiably weak" (p. 203). He then composes his speech "with such an impulsive flow of thought and emotion, that he fancied himself inspired" (p. 212). The great effect of the sermon depends, Hawthorne notes, less on the meaning of the words than upon the people's premonition that their sorrow-laden minister is about to die.

After such a satiric description of the sermon's genesis, Hawthorne informs us of its content:

> His subject, it appeared, had been the relation between the Deity and the communities of mankind, with a specific reference to the New England which they were here planting in the wilderness. And, as he

drew towards the close, a spirit as of prophecy had come upon him, constraining him to its purpose as mightily as the old prophets of Israel were constrained; only with this difference, that, whereas the Jewish seers had denounced judgments and ruin on their country, it was his mission to foretell a high and glorious destiny for the newly gathered people of the Lord. [P. 234]

Although Dimmesdale's speech asserts the future greatness of the Lord's community in terms consonant with the nineteenth-century idea of progress, the circumstances turn his assertions into falsehoods. Not only is the speaker a regrettably weak-willed hypocrite; he is a forerunner of the generation that "wore the blackest shade of Puritanism, and so darkened the national visage with it, that all the subsequent years have not sufficed to clear it up" (p. 218). He prophesies a high and glorious destiny for New England on the one occasion most symbolic of the passing of patriarchal virtues, the proclamation of a successor to Governor John Winthrop. While the sinful, timid minister stands in the meetinghouse, "apotheosized by worshipping admirers" (p. 235) and honored by the greatest shout ever heard on New England soil, Hester Prynne remains in the marketplace, still within that "magic circle of ignominy" (p. 232) that good wives remain careful not to violate.

By such an amassing of ironies, Hawthorne suggests that, in 1649 and possibly in 1849, oratory about the progress of God's favored community is a lie that the people will continue to believe. A careful consideration of the ending shows how insistent Hawthorne has become upon the early failure of the Puritan experiment. Arthur Dimmesdale dies thankfully, rebuking Hester for suggesting that their woe could be ransomed in the afterlife, but convinced that he, at least, is saved. God, after all, has "proved his mercy, most of all, in my afflictions," brought him to confess, and thus allowed him "to die this death of triumphant ignominy before the people" (p. 241). Hester's return to resume the scarlet letter may be a tribute to her strength and honesty, but it cannot alter her marginal status in the community, or the "dusky grief" of her daily life (p. 247). Human fulfillment is granted only to Pearl, not by her mastery of the necessarily thin and rigid life of New England, but by her return to the Old World and marriage into the vibrant life of the English nobility.

The inscription on Hester's grave is the conclusive sign that the prevalence of the symbolic letter overwhelms any hope of progress. However creative the passion of Hester and Dimmesdale may have been, their perceiving that passion as the sin of adultery has brought burdens of guilt, shame, isolation, and hypocrisy that can end only in death. Because they are Puritans, Chillingworth, Dimmesdale, and Hester have to reorder their lives around the sin that has entered it. Neither Hester nor Dimmesdale is ever fully penitent for their act, nor should they be, yet Hawthorne forces us to recognize that their impenitence does not preclude their undergoing endless penance.[38] The dark power of the scarlet letter spreads through these characters' world because they project their sin everywhere. All have entered that "highly disordered mental state, when a man, rendered morbidly self-contemplative by long, intense, and secret pain, had extended his egotism upon the whole expanse of nature" (p. 148). Dimmesdale sees the letter in the sky, Chillingworth sees it on Dimmesdale's breast, and Hester sees it in her contemporaries. To delight in moments of rebellion, to foretell the glorious destiny of the Lord's people, can provide only momentary emotional relief from a growing knowledge of the dark self. The prophetic, utopian notions of generations of New Englanders, expressed in Dimmesdale's election-day rhetoric, are undermined by Hawthorne's sense of the way Puritan character develops through time: "And be the stern and sad truth spoken, that the breach which guilt has once made into the human soul is never, in this mortal state, repaired" (p. 190); "an evil deed invests itself with the character of doom" (p. 199). Set beside so irremediable a vision of the inner life, even the reevaluations of Puritan character demanded by a John Endicott or Goodman Brown seem limited.

In regrettable ways, Goodman Brown, Roger Malvin, Leonard Doane, Richard Digby, and Father Hooper share Arthur Dimmesdale's proclivity for expanding his egotism upon the face of nature. Whereas John Endicott showed how Americanness originated in self-reliant intolerance, later generations have become introspective to the verge of insanity. Reliance upon one's self, once a way to public achievement, has become reliance upon the tradition of self-reliance. The seeking of salvation for personal and communal good has increasingly been deflected into self-destructive brooding upon immutable sinfulness. Far back in pre-Revolutionary eras, Hawthorne had found the source of that intense absorption with self which would render it difficult for Americans to distinguish the Me from the Not Me.

We may wonder why Hawthorne, unlike most contemporary writers concerned with the Puritans, should have been so persistently interested in the era of decline? And why should his psychological fictions about later-generation Puritans – "Young Goodman Brown," "Roger Malvin's Burial," "The Minister's Black Veil," *The Scarlet Letter* – have a resonance, power, and literary finish unequaled among his works? May it not be because his own position, as native-born outsider and half-believing descendant, caught between presumably heroic forefathers and an increasingly commercial world, was so very like theirs? Whether a son confronts a Revolutionary father or a founding forefather, he inherits conflicting feelings of aggression and filiopietism, a conflict likely to end in an introspection from which, as an act of self-assertion, his egotism is extended upon the face of nature. Unlike a commemorative orator, however, be he an Arthur Dimmesdale or a Rufus Choate, Hawthorne understood the psychological process, and was therefore able to be both in and out of the game, to write critically of an imaginative response he knew he shared.

3

THE PURITAN
REVOLUTION
OF 1775?

Those Principles and Feelings [of national independence] ought to be traced back for Two Hundred Years, and sought in the history of the Country from the first Plantations in America . . . This produced, in 1760 and 1761, an AWAKENING and a REVIVAL of American Principles and Feelings, with an enthusiasm which went on increasing till in 1775 it burst out in open Violence.

John Adams to Hezekiah Niles (1818)

The race who fought the revolution out were obviously not of the same temper & manners as the first comers to the wilderness. They had dropped so much of the puritanism of their sires, that they would hardly have been acknowledged by them as sound members of their rigorous society.

Emerson, *Journal* (1824)

The year in which Hawthorne returned from Bowdoin to Salem to assume the risks of storytelling marked the fiftieth anniversary of the outbreak of the American Revolution. In June of 1825 Daniel Webster delivered "The Bunker Hill Monument" at Charlestown before the Marquis de Lafayette, two hundred aged veterans, forty survivors of Bunker Hill, the Masons, the Harvard faculty, and an audience proudly proclaimed by Richard Frothingham to be "as great a multitude as was ever perhaps assembled within the sound of the human voice." Edward Everett, orator at Concord on April 19, charged the heroes' sons with the need to maintain generational continuity. Acknowledging that the aged Revolutionary fathers were "dropping round us like the leaves of autumn,"

Everett urged his audience "to pass the torch of liberty, which we received in all the splendor of its first kindling, bright and flaming, to those who stand next us in the line." The regional commemoration was of such importance that it afforded a literary opportunity to "our national novelist" in New York. In 1825 Cooper published *Lionel Lincoln*, the first of his proposed "Legends of the Thirteen Republics," a historical novel that pictured the battle of Lexington, the retreat from Concord, and the battle of Bunker Hill.[1]

The War for Independence that the orators charged citizens to remember was less a violent revolution in the name of Man's Natural Rights than an unwilling resort to arms in defense of British constitutional rights. Lest any auditor confuse the principled sobriety of the American Revolution with the anarchic violence of the French, Daniel Webster clarified the distinction:

> The great wheel of political revolution began to move in America. Here its rotation was guarded, regular, and safe. Transferred to the other continent, from unfortunate but natural causes, it received an irregular and violent impulse; till at length, like the chariot-wheels in the races of antiquity, it took fire from the rapidity of its own motion and blazed onward, spreading conflagration and terror around.[2]

Whereas the chariot of the French Revolution had ultimately reenacted the horrific chaos of Rome, the self-control of America's revolutionaries prepared the way for the greater, less vulnerable Rome that was emerging in the New World. Taxation without representation, disbanding colonial legislatures, and quartering a standing army were the most suitable issues for a nineteenth-century orator to use in portraying the Revolution as a glorious defense undertaken by somber Christians who wished merely to preserve their own property. In Webster's words,

> The character of our countrymen was sober, moral, and religious; and there was little in the change [of parent state] to shock their feelings of justice and humanity, or even to disturb an honest prejudice. We had no domestic throne to overturn, no privileged orders to cast down, no violent changes of property to encounter. In the American Revolution, no man sought or wished for more than to defend and enjoy his own. None hoped for plunder or for spoil. Rapacity was unknown to it; the axe was not among the instruments of its accomplishment; and we all know that it could not have lived a single day under any well-founded imputation possessing a tendency adverse to the Christian religion.

By such statements the commemorative orator could reassure his audience that the Revolution, once achieved, neither could nor should come again. The Revolutionary era had been, in Michael Kammen's phrase, the national season of youth, a rite of maturity that, once passed through, need never be repeated.[3]

The horror of the French Revolution thus provided an additional impetus for viewing American whigs as neo-Puritan farmers led into battle by gentlemen of reason who had regretfully left their country estates. Tracing the origins of Revolutionary feeling back to the Puritan spririt of liberty separated the French and American Revolutions, while lending continuity to an American history in which native irruptions of violence had no place. Compare the climactic tributes to American Revolutionary character in Everett's oration and in Cooper's novel:

> The genius of America, on this the morning of her emancipation, had sounded her horn over the plains and upon the mountains; and the indignant yeomanry of the land, armed with the weapons which had done service in their father's hands, poured to the spot where this new and strange tragedy was acting.

> Ignorant of the glare of military show; in the simple and rude investments of their calling; armed with such weapons as they had seized from the hooks above their mantels; and without even a banner to wave its cheering folds above their heads, they stood, sustained only by the righteousness of their cause, and those deep moral principles which they had received from their fathers, and which they intended this day should show were to be transmitted to their children.[4]

It was important that such affirmations be reserved for acts like the gathering of patriots at Concord and Bunker Hill. Because the English had sent troops inland to Lexington and had surrounded Bunker Hill, Everett and Cooper could picture the patriots as defenders of their homeland rather than as instigators of rebellion. Exemplifying the virtues of self-reliance, these farmers gathered of their own will, instead of moving under group orders. Nonetheless, their weapons and their principles explicitly derived from their fathers. These farmers were the true "Sons of Liberty" – middle-class defenders of Protestant traditions of legalized liberties, and not theorists about the Rights of Man. All listeners and all readers were encouraged to see themselves in these embattled farmers; neither Cooper nor Everett allowed his audience to believe that there were any native-born Americans who were not, in spirit, still among them.

Webster, Everett, and Cooper were expressing a view of the fathers' heroism that had long preceded the commemorative year, and would long outlast it. Despite great differences in historical credibility and stylistic quality, the two accounts of the Revolution most widely read among antebellum readers, Weems's *Life of Washington* (1800) and Bancroft's *History of the United States*, agree in crucial assertions. Both books present the Revolution as the watershed of human history, an event in which divine Providence revealed the virtues of liberty and democracy by blessing a defensive rebellion with success and a nation with prosperity. Both justify the Revolution through praising the character of its adherents. More particularly, both writers view George Washington as the epitome of virtues observable in the common people. To prove that rifles were fired only to secure legal rights, Weems and Bancroft cast the Revolutionaries as two different but interdependent types of disinterested patriots: rational gentlemen reluctantly agreeing to public leadership for the sake of liberty and yeomen farmers bluntly asserting their right to property, legal equality, and self-determination.[5]

Writing two generations apart, Weems and Bancroft adopted entirely different strategies for dealing with pre-Revolutionary agitation and the shift in national character from American Puritan to American farmer. Although both anticipated a national readership in need of heroes, Weems skipped over the smoldering political and economic issues of the 1760s in order to create pseudo-Homeric battles replete with tributes to liberty, reasoned courage, and the character of George Washington. Bancroft, however, assumed that the God-willed triumph of Republicanism had emerged through 150 years of political and intellectual conflict. Believing like Weems that 1775 began "the political regeneration of the world," Bancroft needed to demonstrate that the Revolution, "prepared by glorious forerunners, grew naturally and necessarily out of the series of past events by the formative principle of a living belief." Because the signing of the Mayflower Compact had been "the birth of constitutional liberty," because Pilgrims and Puritans had "scattered the seminal principles of republican freedom and national independence," Washington and Jefferson had had their roots in Winthrop and Williams.[6]

For Bancroft, the spirit of Protestant liberty had been the essential link between the defiant independence shown by seventeenth-century Puritans and eighteenth-century farmers. By insisting upon individual freedom as the cause of independence, however, Bancroft understandably slighted the national importance of the millennialist impulse in the winning of the Revolution. The impact of the Edwardsian revival, of Jefferson's resumption of fast days in 1774, and of the ministerial "Black Regiment" that prophesied an American Israel[7] was of small concern to Bancroft. In his view, the effects of the Great Awakening had been solely religious, because the democratic thrust of Puritanism had never really been asleep. If liberty, equality, or toleration had not been the declared ideal of a Revolutionary, the Revolutionary's ideals were not of paramount importance. What results from this process is a curious kind of disembodiment: To Bancroft, the Revolutionary fathers possessed the independent republican energies of Puritan forefathers with hardly a trace of their harsh force or religious faith. The desired traits of the Puritan forefathers merged into a national type, while less-admired qualities silently fell away.

The foreground of Revolutionary history presented awkward factual obstacles to the commemorative impulse. Bancroft acknowledged the seizure of British goods and the burning of Governor Hutchinson's house, but viewed them as the necessary blemishes of libertarian zeal. The orators managed to be wholly affirmative by ignoring such troubling facts as the violence of popular crowds, the demagoguery of popular leaders, and the plight of American loyalists. They justified the deeds of the past by proclaiming the successes of the present. And they assumed that Americans had been motivated by the nobility of legal freedoms, not by profit, security, or a need to prove their manliness under trial.

For writers attempting to find the representative American in the era when America came to exist, there were problems in deciding how far into the past they should delve. Those who believed that Democracy, Liberty, and Toleration were timeless abstractions could readily uncover their origins in pre-Revolutionary times, as the orators did, but they ran the risk of resurrecting the whole figure of the intolerant Puritan. If they traced the American back only to Washington and the farmers, they foreshortened Massachusetts's history and diminished the power of the iron men's will to independence. A third alternative, increasingly common during the late 1830s and 1840s, was to "go ahead" historically and not worry about the antediluvian reaches of the past. In the age of Jackson, even such comparatively recent types as gentlemen of reason and libertarian yeomen represented historical forces receding before a new economic expansion based upon laissez-faire, town tradesmen, pioneering, and a religion of the self. In 1825 Webster had proudly proclaimed to the throng at Charlestown, "We are among the sepulchres of our fathers"; only eleven years later, Emerson was to open *Nature* by impatiently complaining, "Our age is retrospective. It builds the sepulchres of the fathers."[8]

SAM ADAMS AND OLD TORIES

Throughout his writings on the Revolutionary era, Hawthorne's interest was in the coming of war rather than the building of a republic, in conflicting loyalty rather than battlefield victory, in the foreground of violence rather than the future of liberty. Like Bancroft, Hawthorne assumed that national character developed through generational conflict and out of regional identities, but Hawthorne was not so willing to select among the Puritan traits that the Revolutionary fathers had inherited. Democrat though Hawthorne was, he brought to the Revolutionary era political sympathies that George Bancroft did not share. In addition to praising George Washington as the embodiment of his people's virtues, Hawthorne praised John Adams because "no base subserviency to the people, any more than to the government, could make him swerve from his own ideas of right." Such a judgment reflects not only regional loyalty but a complicating respect for aristocratic restraint. Hawthorne willingly printed under his own name, and probably wrote, that Alexander Hamilton had possessed those "high qualities that characterized the great men of that party [Federalist], and which should make even a democrat feel proud that his country had produced such a noble old band of aristocrats."[9]

In his journalism and sketches, Hawthorne affirmed the most familiar contemporary assertions about the character of Revolutionary leaders. His George Washington is cloaked in the customary impenetrable dignity, his General Lincoln is an American Cincinnatus, and his Boston Tea Party is an unpremeditated uprising of an entire folk against injustice.[10] To dismiss such writings as hackwork or pandering to clichés is not justifiable. The biographical and written record shows Hawthorne's desire to believe that these tenets of Revolutionary belief were historically accurate. Patriotic certitudes are, however, only one thread in a cross-woven web of responses. Hawthorne's disapproval of British political tyranny does not quell his fearful scorn for revolutionary mobs. Commendable ideals of political independence and individual liberty, he suspects, ended all too frequently in senseless violence. Nor does his approval of new republican political institutions preclude his fondness for the social graces of the old aristocratic province. When Hawthorne is most reverential toward Revolutionary fathers, he is likely to think of them, not as models assimilable to his own age, but as heroes transcending it. In "A Book of Autographs," he praises the Revolutionaries as "men of an heroic age" and then regrets that they are "now so utterly departed, as not even to touch upon the passing generation."[11]

The historical justification for declaring independence and casting off the British father poses for Hawthorne, as for the participants, a revealing choice of alternatives. Nowhere does he state that the laws of Nature's God entitle a people to political independence. Only occasionally does he mention John Adams's legalistic argument that the colonies had to fight merely to maintain rights guaranteed by the British Constitution. He draws no easy contrasts, as does Joel Barlow, between the supposed virtues of a republic (stability, peace, liberty) and the supposed evils of a monarch (instability, war, repression). Pragmatic arguments common to Paine and Burke (an island cannot forever control a continent; British trade acts hurt Britain by depressing American manufactures) simply do not interest him.[12] Although Hawthorne clearly prefers a republican form of government, he avoids justifying the Revolution because it fostered democracy. When he pictures battlefields, the hand of Providence never singles out the victor, nor does Hawthorne rehearse Webster's specious argument that the present prosperity of America proves the righteousness of a past rebellion.[13] In sum, Hawthorne shows little or no regard for the familiar justifications for the Revolution based upon political theory, political institutions, economics, moral law, or natural law.

To Hawthorne, no ideology per se could justify the agonies of revolution. Depending on one's motives and qualities, the same act undertaken in the name of liberty might have advanced the dignity of man, cloaked the license of an agitator, or encouraged a shallow dismissal of the past. Bloodletting to create a republic could be excused only if the character of the leaders and the people had been as admirable as their motivating ideals. Character, however, was no abstraction one could create with words; it had evolved through regional history and had been revealed in conduct. If readers of his fiction were to approve of their revolution, an admirable popular character must have emerged through conflict. But the belief that the origins of American character must have been in seventeenth-century New England posed for Hawthorne, as it did not for Bancroft, a vexing problem. Hawthorne was convinced that the inner character of the fathers had been declining up to the moment of its supposed fulfillment.

Because *Grandfather's Chair* is a history written without falsification but for children, Hawthorne's difficulties in justifying the Revolution appear more clearly here than in his fiction. By tracing "a distinct and unbroken thread of authentic history," he tries to show that an underlying continuity of character made the Revolution possible.[14] Unwilling to gloss over signs of Puritan degeneration, he argues that changes in character led, not to consistent upward progress, but to severe decline preceding recovery. Historical developments from 1690 to 1763 illustrate how "the iron race of Puritans . . . [has] now given place to quite a different set of men" (p. 71). While a virtually independent theocracy has devolved into an imperial province, stern simplicity has given way to aristocratic pomp. The new era, Hawthorne regrets, is dominated by "ambitious Politicians, Soldiers and Adventurers, having no pretension to that high religious and moral principle, which gave to our first Epoch a character of the truest and loftiest romance" (p. 72).

The great merit of the Revolution, Hawthorne insists, is that it brought about a rebirth of seventeenth-century Puritanism in the American character:

> No sooner did England offer wrong to the colonies, than the descendants of the early settlers proved that they had the same kind of temper as their forefathers. The moment before, New England appeared like a humble and loyal subject of the crown; the next instant, she showed the grim, dark features of an old king-resisting Puritan. [P. 151]

This definition of Revolutionary heroics is one that hardly any contemporary democrat or Democrat, let alone a Whig orator, could share. Superficially, Hawthorne may resemble Bancroft in portraying the Revolution as an expression of the Puritan temper, but where Bancroft detects progress, Hawthorne detects only restoration. Bancroft's Puritan Revolutionaries are heirs to British ideals of constitutional liberty and republicanism; they do not show the "grim, dark features" of old Puritan king killers. For Hawthorne, the revival of the Puritan spirit restricts the meaning of the term "liberty" to independence from the king and to representation of select freemen in legislative bodies. Liberty is not a divine abstraction or individual right; it is the same popular spirit of aggressive resistance, of rigid devotion to the principle of independence, that Hawthorne praises at the conclusions of "Endicott and the Red Cross" and "The Gray Champion." As in those stories, however, acts of king resisting can be valid types of the Revolution only if one acknowledges the underside of Puritan character. Because the implacable strength of John Endicott enables him both to defy a Stuart and to persecute Salem's deviants, generational continuity demands similar complexities in the Revolutionaries who carry on Endicott's spirit.

To substantiate the patriotic purpose of *Grandfather's Chair*, Hawthorne finds important events in Revolutionary history that can display the rebirth of king-resisting integrity without the taint of sadism or self-righteousness. Fidelity to the historical facts of three crucial incidents forces him to acknowledge, however, that the Puritan must be resurrected *in toto*. The sketches titled "The Hutchinson Mob," "The Boston Massacre," and "The Boston Tea Party" all suggest that great principles are being unwittingly acted out by thoughtless mobs. In none of the three incidents is Hawthorne able to dramatize his contention that the patriots displayed the self-control associated with Revolutionary yeomen, Revolutionary gentlemen, and the Puritans who bloodlessly resisted Andros. If any quality of Hawthorne's Puritans surfaces in the crowd, it is the sudden and decisive brutality of a John Endicott.

The spectacle of mob violence arouses Hawthorne's sympathy for the plight of the Loyalist official caught between monarchical loyalties, fondness for his colonial birthright, and an official obligation to serve both king and colonist. Hawthorne may exult over Hutchinson's complacent illusions about the coming of a landed nobility, but as soon as the mob gathers, Hutchinson is regarded as a principled gentleman who has refused to descend to demagoguery. When young Charlie exclaims that all Tories should have been tarred and feathered (like Major Molineux), Grandfather rebukes him by asking, "Can you not respect that principle of loyalty, which made the royalists give up country, friends, fortune, everything, rather than be false to their king?" (pp. 177–8). Hawthorne's three extensive treatments of the Revolution all conclude by concentrating on the dilemma of the Loyalist. The last sketch of *Grandfather's Chair* is "The Tory's Farewell"; the last sketch of "Old News" is "The Old Tory"; the last of the four "Legends of the Province-House" is "Old Esther Dudley." In all three sketches, Hawthorne's desire to arouse sympathy for the plight of the Loyalist stops just short of his explicitly adopting, in politics and in narrative technique, the Tory point of view.

Although Hawthorne's old Tories are engagingly humane and sympathetic in their victimization, they are never allowed to be models of political behavior. Grandfather finally manages a triumphant ending simply by informing us that Samuel Adams, "that stout old republican" (p. 207), was elected governor of Massachusetts in 1794. To Hawthorne, Sam Adams was the war's hero precisely because he was not a general, but an unswerving devotee of independence. Hawthorne will allow his reader no opportunity to view Adams as an agitator, propagandist, or demagogue:

> His character was such, that it seemed as if one of the ancient Puritans had been sent back to earth, to animate the people's hearts with the same abhorrence of tyranny, that had distinguished the earliest settlers. He was as religious as they, as stern and inflexible, and as deeply imbued with democratic principles. He, better than any one else, may be taken as representative of the people of New England, and of the spirit with which they engaged in the revolutionary struggle. [P. 173]

Unlike Bancroft, Cooper, or the orators, Hawthorne sometimes seems to feel that the revival of Puritan virtues is more important than the creation of the Republic. If we except the atypical mention of "democratic principles,"[15] the entire configuration of heroic Puritan Revolutionary traits is praised here: faith in one's rectitude, hatred of tyranny, inflexibility of principle, and an iron will to achievement.

When Sam Adams attains the governor's chair, the reader can almost, but not quite, forget such statements as "Mr. Oliver found but little liberty under Liberty Tree" (p. 160). Hawthorne's remarkable ability to render the violence of Revolutionary mobs is consistent with his inability to render Sam Adams by anything more than abstract adjectives. As one might expect, Hawthorne is aware of this disproportion of emphasis. Lest posterity associate the Revolution with mobocracy, Grandfather attempts a final, general defense:

> The world has seen no grander movement than that of our Revolution, from first to last . . . The people, to a man, were full of a great and noble sentiment. True, there may be fault to find with their mode of expressing this sentiment; but they knew no better – the necessity was upon them to act out their feelings, in the best manner they could. We must forgive what was wrong in their actions, and look into their hearts and minds for the honorable motive that impelled them. [P. 171]

Through smooth and assuring phrases, this passage induces us to believe that noble motives outweigh dishonorable acts, and worthy ends justify violent means. By no other logic could Hawthorne be true both to his understanding of the historical record and to his desire to justify the Revolution.

In historical sketches written for a solely adult audience, Hawthorne subtly challenges his age's assumptions about the Revolution. "Old News," a triptych of historical sketches drawn from newspaper columns, begins with a surprisingly accepting judgment of the province during the 1740s. Although "the rigid hand of Puritanism might yet be felt upon the reins of government," the representative figure of the era is a prosperous merchant whose mind is confined to velvet cloaks, silver buckles, his rum trade, and entertainments to impress the governor.[16] Hawthorne does not, however, belabor the merchant for losing his faith or toadying to aristocracy, as he does in *Grandfather's Chair*. Instead, he creates the merchant as a decent, limited man fond of his household and sure of his worldly place.

The next sketch, "The Old French War," views colonial Massachusetts with more affection than Grandfather permits; its diction reveals Hawthorne's fondness for an ordered society about to be rent asunder. As late as 1763 there was not yet "any disaffection to British supremacy, nor democratic prejudices against pomp" (p. 144). When describing aristocratic dress, Hawthorne comments favorably upon the "deep, rich, glowing splendor of our ancestors" (p. 151). His metaphor for the coming of the Revolution is decidedly repellent. Royal officials dreamed of American fiefdoms "until the prospective nobility were leveled with the mob, by the mere gathering of winds that preceded the storm of the Revolution" (p. 144).

"The Old Tory," the last of the three sketches in "Old News," is so dark a rendering of the Revolutionary era that it seems, like Cooper's *Wyandotté* (1843) and Melville's *Israel Potter* (1854), written with a desire to debunk all possibilities for Revolutionary heroics. Hawthorne begins with a transitional section in which he admits that his previous sketch has been "tinctured" with "antique prejudices" in favor of aristocracy and the province (p. 153). Curiously, however, the last sketch restates those prejudices all the more forcefully, releasing the feelings that have led Hawthorne to adopt the viewpoint – and his phrase is worth noting – of a "modern Tory":

> We shrink from the strangely-contrasted times, into which we emerge, like one of those immutable old Tories, who acknowledge no oppression in the Stamp-act. It may be the most effective method of going through the present file of papers, to follow out this idea, and transform ourself, perchance, from a modern Tory into such a sturdy king-man as once wore that pliable nickname. [P. 153]

Throughout his six-page monologue, Hawthorne's sturdy kingman proceeds to judge the tree of Revolution by its immediate fruits: confiscation of private property, worthless currency, Patriot deserters, privateers who in fact are pirates,[17] and agitators with mouths full of liberty. He even turns Hawthorne's chief justification for the Revolution against him.[18] Here it is the "Old Tory" who is the descendant of Puritans and the rebels who represent, not a resurgence of Puritan principles, but an abandonment of them. Looking at a "Patriot" newspaper, the old Tory exclaims, "In the next column, we have Scripture parodied in a squib against his Sacred Majesty. What would our Puritan great-grandsires have said to that? They never laughed at God's word, though they cut off a king's head" (p. 158).

"Old News" concludes with two paragraphs that leave one wondering why Hawthorne ever sought to justify the Revolution. The effects of all revolutions are held to be "pernicious to general morality" (p. 159); the American Revolution is not the exception to this rule, but the epitome of it:

> Almost all our impressions in regard to this period are unpleasant, whether referring to the state of civil society, or to the character of the contest, which, especially where native Americans were opposed to each other, was waged with the deadly hatred of fraternal enemies. It is the beauty of war, for men to commit mutual havoc with undisturbed good humor. [P. 160]

The chill of the last sentence bespeaks a mind aware of the price men have always paid for mere political ideas. This revolution is no popular uprising for a principle, but a civil war whose brutalities become bearable only if one rationalizes them. The three sketches of "Old News" constitute a view of the era, not as a progress from oppressive aristocracy to libertarian republic, but as a descent from civilization to fratricide. Out of old penny papers Hawthorne has wrought new news.

A NEW RACE OF MEN?

Hawthorne's historical doubts, kept under rhetorical control in *Grandfather's Chair*, could be portrayed more freely and more truthfully through the art of a mere storyteller. Whereas, in the character of Grandfather, Hawthorne evidently felt that he had to justify the Revolution, the romancer who created Robin Molineux's night in pre-Revolutionary Boston was free to revivify the feelings aroused by a Tory's expulsion. By deciding to write "Legends" about the Province House, Hawthorne could insist upon their inner historical truth, while tacitly scotching his declared purpose of maintaining a progressive viewpoint.

In "Old News" Hawthorne had described himself as a "modern Tory"; in "Legends of the Province-House," written three years later, he described himself as a "thorough-going democrat."[19] His selection and ordering of plot show the care he took to justify rebellion by uncovering the roots of colonial hostility. The first and fourth legends ("Howe's Masquerade" and "Old Esther Dudley") celebrate the loss and surrender of British power during the Revolutionary era. They enclose two tales ("Edward Randolph's Portrait" and "Lady Eleanor's Mantle") in which the prior oppressions that justify revolution are uncovered. Hawthorne may have chosen these four incidents to avoid the Loyalist sympathies and feelings of historical decline that had surfaced in "Old News." Or he may have sought to please the democratic and patriotic enthusiasms of his publisher, John Louis O'Sullivan. These possibilities should not lead us to conclude, however, that Hawthorne's claim to be a "thorough-going democrat" was hypocritical or untrue. The theoretical democrat in Hawthorne became a Tory when he contemplated the immediate events of the Revolution; the temperamental Tory in Hawthorne became a democrat when he contemplated high-handed acts of Parliament and the British military.

In fiction as in history, Hawthorne's primary justification for the Revolution is the rebirth of Puritanism, not the creation of the Republic. If the legends are rearranged in order of historical event, the steady re-emergence of the Puritan character over time becomes quite clear. The ur-American in "Lady Eleanor's Mantle," Dr. Clarke, is "a famous champion of the popular party" (p. 275) who has no sympathy for aristocratic splendor and who seems to relish Lady Eleanor's downfall. Never called a Puritan, Clarke nonetheless is stern, terse, and unyielding. In 1721, however, he can appear only briefly and in isolation.

By 1770, when Hutchinson signs Castle William over to Royal Troops in "Edward Randolph's Portrait," Puritan resistance has become difficult to suppress. Hutchinson is opposed not only by his niece and by the loyal captain of Castle William, but by the entire assemblage of Boston's selectmen, who are described as "plain, patriarchal fathers of the people, excellent representatives of the old puritanical fathers whose sombre strength had stamped so deep an impress upon the New England character" (p. 264). The selectmen embody the spirit of the Gray Champion in living beings, not in a supernatural symbol.

By the time of "Howe's Masquerade," the balance of personified historical forces shifts again, as the solitary figure of Governor Howe is juxtaposed against the Puritan patriots of two centuries. The procession of Massachusetts governors is an appropriate literary device for insisting both on historical continuity and on the primacy of the forefathers. The figures whom Howe first sees (Endicott, Winthrop, Vane, and Dudley) literally are the force that has undone him. Reclothed as Puritans, the Revolutionaries are revealing their true and ancient character before his eyes. Unable to perceive the masquerade as anything other than "tedious foolery" (p. 250), Howe can never understand the character of its organizer. Colonel Joliffe, a man of "known whig principles" and a "black puritanical scowl," is described as a "stern old figure . . . well representing the antique spirit of his native land" (p. 244).[20] In the person of Joliffe, the Puritan character, dormant in the early eighteenth century, has regained historical control.

Although Hawthorne carefully eliminates from the "Legends" all scenes of demagogic agitation (Liberty Tree rallies) or of popular violence (the Hutchinson mob), he does not withhold his responses to changes in the quality of life. Instead, the framing device for the series encourages an aesthetic response to history. The "faded magnificence" of the Province House – its graceful stairway, generous dimensions, and fine ornamentation – lead Hawthorne to a series of socially and aesthetically aristocratic discriminations (p. 240). He laments that the Province House, now a tavern, has been subdivided into small unconnected chambers, "its time-worn visage [hidden] behind an upstart modern building" (p. 242). His comment on the surrounding architecture implies that the ideal of individuality, associated by contemporaries with a democratic polity, should be associated with pre-Revolutionary times: "The buildings stood insulated and independent, not, as now, merging their separate existences into connected ranges, with a front of tiresome identity, – but each possessing features of its own" (p. 256).

In the midst of America's commercial democracy, with its "vulgar range of shoe-shops and dry-good stores," the reviving of the forgotten splendors of the Province House seems the only pathway to art (p. 271). Had Tocqueville been interested in the political implications of architectural change, he would surely have arrived at similar judgments. For Hawthorne, New England's hostility to art qualifies its political triumph. Although the Puritan ur-Revolutionaries in the "Legends" – Dr. Clarke, the selectmen, and Colonel Joliffe – may possess integrity, republican principle, and independent strength, they remain dark, joyless figures who look forward to ridding Massachusetts of graces they cannot appreciate.

Hawthorne's many-sided response is most evident in the last of the legends, "Old Esther Dudley." Like "Howe's Masquerade," the tale contrasts a representative of the old order (Esther) to a representative of the new (Hancock) in order to show beneficial changes in New England character. Somehow, however, the tidy, expected contrast between heroic Puritan Revolutionary and pathetically crazed aristocrat never emerges. When Hawthorne applies to Esther the same phrase ("a vision of faded magnificence" [p. 294]) he has applied to the Province House (p. 240), he shows admiring condescension toward those who cling to aristocratic dress, royal loyalties, and genteel manners. Because she loses all sense of time, Esther becomes as sadly displaced as Rip Van Winkle, but because she adheres to disgraced values, she remains as principled an individual as any Puritan. Unlike the dominant male Revolutionary of Puritan origin, Esther Dudley possesses both "a kindly and loving nature" (p. 297) and the romancer's power of imagination. In 1780, however, only children seem interested in her kindness or her stories.

Although the "Legends" build toward the liberating moment when elected Governor Hancock takes the keys of the Province House from old Esther Dudley, Hawthorne remains curiously reluctant to celebrate the triumph or to praise John Hancock. Hancock may be a Puritan in ancestry and a merchant in occupation, but he is "richly dressed" and speaks to Esther "with all the reverence that a courtier would have shown to a queen" (p. 301). His "reverence" must be in his manner, however, because his words are needlessly cruel in substance:

> "You have treasured up all that time has rendered worthless – the principles, feelings, manners, modes of being and acting, which another generation has flung aside – and you are a symbol of the past. And I, and these around me – we represent a new race of men – living no longer in the past, scarcely in the present – but projecting our lives forward into the future. Ceasing to model ourselves on ancestral superstitions, it is our faith and principle to press onward, onward! . . . We are no longer children of the Past." [Pp. 301–2]

Because this is a concluding and decisive speech, it has seemed persuasive. We should remember, however, that Hancock is Hawthorne's only Revolutionary to espouse a cult of novelty based on natural rights and a dismissal of the past. The Patriots in the three previous tales had been not "a new race of men," but ordinary citizens reborn because of old virtues. When Hancock urges his audience to forget the past, he dismisses the relevance and power of the historical imagination. Unlike Hancock, Hawthorne was never to forget the power the past exerts upon the mind, nor its value as a subject for fiction. Hancock's speech merely echoes Jacksonian clichés about the new race of Americans pressing on to some vague but assured destiny. Like Young Americans of a later era, Hancock speaks of "*projecting* our lives forward into the future," thereby making a country from the self. We may infer that Hawthorne's purpose, however, is to imbed such clichés in a fictional context that will deprive them of plausibility.

When Hancock picks up the key to the Province House from a dying woman who cries out, "God Save the King" (p. 302), Hawthorne reminds us that the triumph of republicans could have been achieved only by dispossession of Loyalists. The metaphor with which he describes Hancock's triumph, "his foot now trod upon humbled Royalty, as he ascended the steps of the Province-House" (p. 301), has acquired multiple associations. Lady Eleanor set her foot upon Jervayse Helwyse, Alice Vane said that Randolph "trampled on a people's rights" (p. 268), and Hutchinson contemptuously declared, "I set my foot upon the rabble, and defy them"

(p. 266).[21] The self-proclaimed new man, John Hancock, is unknowingly repeating the act of earlier royalists. The repetition of the metaphor implies that the injustice of trampling upon other people is of greater concern than any political cause that can rationalize it.

Elsewhere Hawthorne suggests that countinghouse Revolutionaries like Hancock were little better than demagogues. In "A Book of Autographs," Hancock is said to have been "more vulgar" than a princely merchant should be, and to have gained prominence "far more by an ornamental outside than by any intrinsic force or virtue." Hawthorne's sharpest judgment contrasts the first two governors of Massachusetts: "Adams acted from pure and rigid principle. Hancock, though he loved his country, yet thought quite as much of his own popularity, as he did of the people's rights."[22]

Why then did Hawthorne choose John Hancock, rather than Sam Adams, as the governor who would assume control of the Province House? Hawthorne may have decided that the new American should embody the Revolutionaries' skills at organizing violence, seeking publicity, and gaining profit. Having settled upon Hancock, Hawthorne may have refrained from outwardly expressing doubts about him in the pages of O'Sullivan's *Democratic Review*. Whatever the motives for his selection, the "thorough-going democrat" provided an ending that, however patriotic in plot, left his reader wondering whether the Revolution had not produced a generation of pretentious and aggressive worldlings rather than earnest Puritans.

Knowing the complexities of Hawthorne's response to the Revolution clarifies the historical significance of "My Kinsman, Major Molineux," the first and certainly the finest of Hawthorne's eighteenth-century tales. The most common historical interpretation remains that of Q. D. Leavis, who claimed that the tale could be subtitled "America Comes of Age." Robin Molineux, representative of Young America, having learned the necessity of casting off British political authority, rises to manhood by joining in the laughter at his uncle, a disgraced royalist father figure.[23] Because the tale seems to reaffirm the paradigm of America's Revolutionary season of youth,[24] the act of rebellion in the story has seemed justified. As in Bancroft's *History*, mob agitation can regretfully be condoned because it is the means by which an increasingly shrewd youth confronts his past, frees himself from it, and learns to rise in the world.[25]

This interpretation resembles John Hancock's view of the Revolution more than Hawthorne's. Hawthorne's later writings were to associate the achieving of Revolution with the strength of old Puritans, not the goodwill of country youth. The first paragraph of "My Kinsman, Major Molineux" conveys a sympathy for the plight of the provincial official similar to that of *Grandfather's Chair*. The word Hawthorne chooses to summarize the temper of the people on the evening of their rebellion is "inflammation."[26]

Through accumulation of consistent detail, "My Kinsman, Major Molineux" portrays the viciousness of Patriot mobs and the injustices done to Loyalists. Not one word in the story suggests that Major Molineux is anything but an "elderly man, of large and majestic person, and strong, square features, betokening a steady soul" (p. 228). The tarring and feathering of the major is precisely what Hawthorne says it is – "the foul disgrace of a head that had grown gray in honor" (p. 229). The phrases describing the procession form one coherent judgment: "counterfeited pomp," "senseless uproar," "fiends that throng in mockery round some dead potentate" (p. 230). A reader who recalls how John Hancock "trod upon humbled Royalty" might note Hawthorne's reference to the Patriot procession "trampling all on an old man's heart" (p. 230).

The memorable figure with the half-red, half-black face has been made the symbol of various kinds of psychic deviltries in man or repressed fears in Robin, none of which Hawthorne mentions. Surely it is of some importance that the figure is revealed to be the leader of the popular procession, and that Hawthorne likens him to "war personified" (p. 227). With his shaggy eyebrows, glaring eyes, and a face half-incendiary, half-deathlike, the leader just might embody all the animal violence and crazed belligerence that Hawthorne repeatedly associates with the Revolutionary War. Hawthorne's persistent suspicions of popular delusion during the witchcraft trials should prepare us for the suggestion that this diabolic figure may have been the true leader of a revolutionary people.

Unlike Robin, a perceptive reader soon senses that the people Robin meets, whom he persists in believing to be loyal, are conspiring to commit some unknown act. A pattern quickly develops in which the townspeople ridicule Robin, threaten him with various punishments, and take delight in keeping him confounded. Insidious traits that Hawthorne's contemporary readers would have ascribed to Tories are thus associated with makers of rebellion. Clichés about colonial grievances never appear, but a display of mob sadism does. In the entire tale, only the second sentence ("The people looked with most jealous scrutiny to the exercise of power, which did not emanate from themselves" [p. 208]) intimates that a political principle might have inspired the revolt.

Hawthorne's Revolutionaries are not young men needing to come of age. Robin may be young and dependent upon father figures, but he displays no will to rebel. The Revolutionaries in the tale are the figures Robin meets in the barber shop, tavern, streets, and procession. Like the Puritan Revolutionaries in "Howe's Masquerade," "Edward Randolph's Portrait," and Grandfather's Chair, they are elderly, decisive, and self-assured. They do not, however, exhibit the Puritan piety and integrity that Hawthorne was to claim for the Revolutionaries. In this tale, piety and integrity are qualities associated either with the major or, by Robin, with his father, a clergyman and "good man" in the seventeenth-century tradition, fond of "old thanksgivings" and of "old supplications," who lives in the country, and who is the cousin of Major Molineux (p. 223). The gentler virtues of the hypothetical Puritan are thus denied any part in Revolutionary gatherings.

The tarring and feathering of the major has been slighted or rationalized because it has seemed the necessary means to Robin's maturity. Yet Hawthorne never confirms that Robin has changed or grown. When the leader of the procession, already likened to "war personified," fixes his eye meaningfully upon Robin, Robin turns away sensing no hint of the future. The condemnations of the major's foul disgrace are written by Hawthorne, not spoken by Robin. Robin's joining into the common laughter may express no recognition of historical irony, and no repressed delight in disgracing father figures. Hawthorne, after all, wrote only, "The contagion was spreading among the multitude, when, all at once, it seized upon Robin" (p. 230). In context, the word "contagion" suggests that the widespread scorn for Loyalists is a disease, and the statement as a whole emphasizes Robin's passivity, not his awareness.

The ending of the tale, evidence of Robin's maturing to so many readers, can be regarded, equally plausibly, as evidence of his persistent naiveté. Robin says merely that he wishes to go to the ferry because he is "weary of a town life" (p. 231). Even if Robin is speaking with un-characteristic irony, he clearly prefers to avoid thinking about his experience. Because he seems not to acknowledge the political implications of what he has seen, his readiness to return to rural innocence may be ironically apt. It is only the old gentleman who suggests that Robin remain and gain success through independence: "Some few days hence, if you continue to wish it, I will speed you on your journey. Or, if you prefer to remain with us, perhaps, as you are a shrewd youth, you may rise in the world, without the help of your kinsman, Major Molineux" (p. 231). A regard for syntax shows Hawthorne's equivocation here. The statement presents two alternatives, each of which contains a conditional clause. Moreover, the second alternative, which is the one at issue, contains two further qualifications ("perhaps" and "you may rise"). Because the old gentleman knows Robin to be anything but shrewd, his words may show Hawthorne's desire to deflate Franklinian assurances about young men rising through self-help in pre-Revolutionary American cities.

The assumption that it is only Robin Molineux who represents Young America is equally arbitrary. Are we to assume that Robin represents America simply because he is young, innocent, and from the country, like other American Adams? Should not an alternative view of Young

America in the pre-Revolutionary era be sought, not in Robin Molineux, but in the crafty old tacticians who are creating the Revolution before our eyes? In haste to endow Robin with national dimensions, one may overlook the fact that Robin is not only a character but a narrative voice by which the reader's insight into aspects of human and historical experience is measured. Perhaps, then, Robin may resemble many of Hawthorne's contemporary, patriotic readers, who, even when confronted with violence and demagoguery, were unwilling or unable to recognize them.

At the end of his career, Hawthorne was implicitly to challenge the axiom, common to the entire commemorative tradition (including *Grandfather's Chair*), that the Revolutionary farmer had been inspired with the spirit of Puritan liberty. *Septimius Felton* contrasts two young men who have the opportunity to come of age through fighting the British during their retreat from Concord. Robert Hagburn, "a frank, cheerful, able, wholesome young man," eagerly shoots at invading redcoats, enlists in the Continental army, becomes a hero at the battle of Monmouth, marries, serves as a selectman, and in the process acquires "a simple perception of great thoughts, a free natural chivalry; so that the knight, the Homeric warrior, the hero, seemed to be here, or possible to be here, in this young New England rustic."[27] Throughout the tale, Robert's acquiring of maturity and authority is contrasted to the deepening failure of Septimius, who is repelled by the violence at Concord, withdraws from the Patriot cause, becomes obsessed with the elixir of life, and sacrifices both marriage and mental health to the quest for immortality. Hagburn's participation in the Revolutionary War "turned the ploughboy into the man" (p. 156), whereas Septimius, who "knew nothing, thought nothing, cared nothing about his country, or his country's battles" (p. 165), ends up "crushed and annihilated, as it were, by the failure of his magnificent and most absurd dreams" (p. 193).

Hawthorne, of course, is more sympathetic to Septimius's withdrawal than this contrast suggests, probably because Hawthorne's revulsion against the bloodshed of the Civil War permeates his account of Revolutionary Boston, a "new, uncomfortable world" (p. 131) where churches are converted to stables and young boys torment old Tories with mud balls. Moreover, Hagburn's achievements depend upon his insensitivity to the spiritual issues that trouble Septimius. And yet it is Hagburn who represents a healthy Young America and Septimius who ends defeated, crazed, and alone in England.

Robert Hagburn, however, is not a son who plucks his father's rifle from the mantel to fight for his forefathers' principles, nor is Septimius a wavering Anglophile like Cooper's Lionel Lincoln. The expected connections between origins and loyalties have been exactly reversed. Robert Hagburn, the ploughboy who becomes a man, has no known New

England past, no principles to inherit. Septimius Felton, who abandons the Revolution, is explicitly descended from Wyckliffites, Puritans, regicides, ministers, and a great-grandfather who "made the leaves wither on a tree with the fierceness of his blast against a sin" (p. 15). Having grown up in "an ordinary dwelling of a well-to-do New England farmer" (p. 5), Septimius graduates from Harvard and plans on entering the ministry. The local Congregational clergyman knows him thoroughly: "There is something of the Puritan character in you, Septimius, derived from holy men among your ancestors; as for instance a deep brooding turn, such as befits that heavy brow; a disposition to meditate upon things hidden; a turn for meditative inquiry" (p. 10). Although *Septimius Felton* is unfinished, Hawthorne seems finally to have suspected that the transmission of Puritan character during the Revolution pointed, not toward liberty-loving activism, but toward a deepening of the meditative self-absorption apparent in the third and fourth generations.

The Concord fight remained for Hawthorne, as it had for Everett, Webster, Cooper, Emerson, and countless others, a defining symbol of the Revolutionary temper. Years before writing *Septimius Felton*, Hawthorne indicated how deeply his response to the battle differed from theirs. Conducting the reader of "The Old Manse" to Concord Bridge, Hawthorne points out the granite obelisk memorializing "the very spots, on the western bank, where our countrymen fell down and died."[28] Shortly thereafter, however, he shows "a humbler token of the fight" (p. 9), the grave of a British soldier who, while wounded, was brained with an axe by a young New England patriot. The act, Hawthorne insists, was one of neither mercy nor villainy; it was simply "a nervous impulse, without purpose, without thought, and betokening a sensitive and impressible nature, rather than a hardened one" (p. 10). Hawthorne presumably did not recall Webster's insistence that "the axe was not among the instruments of its [the Revolution's] accomplishments."[29] But his dwelling upon the purposeless horror of this incident was surely intended as a rejoinder to the commemorative tradition: "This one circumstance has borne more fruit for me, than all that history tells us of the fight" (p. 10). Just as "Alice Doane's Appeal" offered the reader Gallows Hill as a counter-memorial to Bunker Hill, so "The Old Manse" offered the British soldier's grave as a counter-memorial to Concord's granite obelisk. One memorial does not cancel the other, but anyone who would see New England character whole should leave neither out of account.

As romancer and historian, Hawthorne was able to dramatize only a part of his contention that Revolutionary violence had been redeemed by its nobility of purpose. Because the brutalities of Revolutionary history seemed more real than any political abstraction, his revolutionaries could be nobly motivated only when they were said to possess Puritan traits idealized beyond the author's custom. When seen in action, however, Hawthorne's Revolutionary Puritan exhibits the single-minded self-righteousness and colorless sobriety of his seventeenth-century prototype. The truly worthy motives of the Revolution, which could not reside in superficial achievements such as the Constitution, westward expansion, or prosperity, remained perplexingly difficult to specify. If John Hancock was a representative new American, his ideas seemed as simplistic as Holgrave's, and he might act with as little discrimination as the reformers in "Earth's Holocaust."

Throughout the years in which Fourth of July rhetoric reached its shrillest depths, Hawthorne's acute historical imagination allowed him to preserve a disturbingly complex view of the Revolution. Accepting the premise that the Revolutionaries of 1776 must resemble the Puritans of 1630, he provided a continuity to colonial history that brought to the reader's attention the darker side of king-killing absolutism. We should recognize that his insistence on judging by deed rather than catchword, on revealing the character that creates law, rather than vice versa, was courageously atypical in an age and country that often sought external proof for its rising glory.

We must also recognize that, as Hawthorne's settings move toward the present, both intensity of tone and control of historical irony are proportionally weakened. Hawthorne's desire to praise the resurgence of Puritan principle in 1776 often seems merely dutiful. His fondness for eighteenth-century aristocratic culture seems to grow as he contemplates the turn into nineteenth-century democracy. Of all the tales and sketches concerned with the Revolutionary era, only "My Kinsman, Major Molineux" has the power of Hawthorne's seventeenth-century tales. And yet the achievement of "My Kinsman, Major Molineux" depends on total control of point of view, of metaphor, and of historical circumstance; in none of Hawthorne's writings concerned with the eighteenth century is there one character who in stature and significance can be placed beside John Endicott, Goodman Brown, or Hester Prynne. As New England character moves farther away from its seventeenth-century origins, material and political progress bring a cultural blandness that portends a relaxing of spiritual intensity. Only "our first Epoch," Grandfather warns – that bygone era when fallible men were truly imbued with "high religious and moral principle" – can still provide "a character of the truest and loftiest romance."[30]

4

A DIMINISHED THING

> Our forefathers walked in the world & went to their graves tormented
> with the fear of sin & the terror of the Day of Judgment. We are happily
> rid of these terrors, and our torment is the utter uncertainty & perplexity
> of what we ought to do.
>
> Emerson, *Journal* (1841)

The admirable American whose appearance Hawthorne anticipated was
to be neither a New Man, tilling a Western garden removed from time,
nor a limitless ego ordering an external chaos by imaginative possession.
His emergence could not be predicted by occupation, class, or any external
condition. In order to embody the promise of nineteenth-century New
England, he should combine the separate merits of John Hancock and
Esther Dudley, of Sam Adams and Governor Hutchinson. Without losing
all sense of aesthetics and social grace, the American had to preserve the
energy and will necessary to achieve practicable goals. Futuristic political
commitments to independence and equality of right should become sec-
ondary to moral living sustained by the power to love and to imagine.

Building upon the strengths of regional heritage thus entailed intricate
compromises. Because the new American was the old New Englander,
he had to acknowledge the shaping influence of the past, yet remain
sufficiently free from any obsession with it to be able to contribute toward
a healthy community. As an American of moral sensibility, he had to
guard the inviolate integrity of his individual soul without withdrawing
from the magnetic chain of humanity. Shaped by region and immersed
in time, an admirable contemporary above all had to embody the continuity
of Puritan character that Hawthorne hoped had been restrengthened in
Revolutionary New England. Such combinations of merit were not to

be attained by a simple resurrection of the spirit of the Gray Champion in times of crisis. Because the times that tried men's souls were gone, a progressive refinement of Puritan character was necessary. Somehow, the worst aspects of a John Endicott were to be discarded, and the best retained, to create a neo-Puritan American suited to a progressive Republic.

Vague though this figure might be, Hawthorne's model American was to have a tougher mind than Crèvecoeur's farmer, wider applicability than Franklin's builder of fortunes and towns (all Americans cannot finish first), and deeper cultural roots than the detached scholar-poet exalted by the Transcendentalist. And yet the convincing representation of his admired New Englander posed problems of no small difficulty. Hawthorne's standard of character was exacting in moral terms, yet curiously open in occupation, origin, and social attitudes. At a time of increasing self-assertion, Hawthorne foresaw a need to temper the age's individualism with a Puritan regard for communal concerns. To do so required a greater regard for others and for the true riches of regional heritage than many contemporaries were prepared to contemplate. Knowing the risk of impaling his fiction with morals, Hawthorne nonetheless sought to place his contemporaries within a tradition of regional character. His early New England sketches and his allegories of contemporary life measured his culture's present state by his own standards of expected improvement. Contemporaries who believed themselves freed from history discovered, upon reading either *The House of the Seven Gables* or *The Blithedale Romance*, that the present was inseparable from the past. By connecting contemporary Americans to their Puritan predecessors, both romances attempted to uncover the cleansing within the continuity.

Even in the early 1830s, when Hawthorne planned a collection of tales to be called "The Story Teller," the challenge of finding continuity of character in the present absorbed him.[1] The pseudonymous storyteller, sometimes called Oberon, is an orphaned free soul who has been strictly raised by one "Parson Thumpcushion" to be a devout Congregationalist, diligent in his calling in the true New England way.[2] Seeking goals prophetic of Thoreau's "Walking," the rebellious narrator discards the confining traditions of the old order by walking westward in search of unknown experiences that can give substance to a new self. Exhilarated by the open road, the narrator exclaims, "In truth, I had never felt such a delicious excitement, nor known what freedom was till that moment, when I gave up my home, and took the whole world in exchange." Like Thoreau striding from John Field's cabin toward newer worlds, the narrator hastens toward "a species of rainbow in the west, bestriding my intended road like a gigantic portal." Impelled by go-ahead notions, Oberon associates the rainbow with the "archway of futurity," the whole world into which he can project himself, rather than a covenant with specific conditions or prospects.[3]

Although we cannot now reconstruct the steps or causes of the narrator's disillusionment, his rainbow proves illusory, his open road leads to no new fulfillment, and the end of his westering freedom is indicated by the title of the sketch "My Home Return." The first of Hawthorne's rootless, shadowy Americans, Oberon recognizes that his pursuit of free self-creation has left him without community, hearth, wife, children, productive occupation, or feelings for his fellowman.

Oberon's melancholy end allows Hawthorne to state his book's intended "moral, which many a dreaming youth may profit by":[4]

> The world is a sad one for him who shrinks from its sober duties. My experience shall warn him to adopt some great and serious aim, such as manhood will cling to, that he may not feel himself, too late, a cumberer of this overladen earth, but a man among men. I will beseech him not to follow an eccentric path, nor, by stepping aside from the highway of human affairs, to relinquish his claim upon human sympathy. And often, as a text of deep and varied meaning, I will remind him that he is an American.[5]

After all the storyteller's new encounters are over, and all tales are told, he has had to recognize that the presumably archaic values of Parson Thumpcushion were largely correct. The parson had always been "a good and wise man" who had admonished him "in a style of paternal wisdom, and love, and reconciliation."[6] Oberon is even made to recognize, like Holgrave, the human worth of gold and houses: "The truly wise, after all their speculations, will be led into the common path, and, in homage to the human nature that pervades them, will gather gold, and till the earth, and set out trees, and build a house."[7] The climactic last sentence of Hawthorne's moral disassociates the highest Americanism from any westering spirit of free, solitary men in order to associate it with domestic and communal values embedded in the Congregational way. Rebellion against the forefathers, especially tempting to storytellers, leads to merely ephemeral creations. The highest Americanism lies in repudiating the free self-creation by which Americans were defining themselves.

Oberon may recognize that the Parson is correct, but he cannot change his character; by birth, choice, and temperament, he remains cut off from his heritage. At the end, the tubercular Oberon simply passes away, full of modern manners, vain regrets, and fruitless insight. As a new man, he may recognize the value of the old, but he is powerless to be what he recognizes. The heritage to be transmitted is little more than an idea of moral value, but the character who might embody it has neither place nor function. The narrator's home return thus poses a two-sided conundrum that Hawthorne himself was surely facing. Wholeheartedly to accept regional spheres of duty was to risk imaginative dullness; to step out of the New England way might better one's judgment, but only at the cost of those communal ties which preserve one's humanity.

The problem faced by the wandering storyteller, common to most of Hawthorne's fictive artists, is especially acute among those of New England origin because of long-standing regional hostility to art. Holgrave, Coverdale, and Kenyon, as well as less important figures like Drowne or the painter in "The Prophetic Pictures," show the marks of cultural prejudice. Their half-sought, troubling estrangement from their society resembles their creator's repeated insistence that he has remained at the wayside of contemporary life. Although Hawthorne may see more clearly in the clear brown twilight, his situation allows shadows to be cast across him, and foliage to grow up around him. Early sketches of Salem show how regretfully Hawthorne acknowledged that isolation was the necessary price of insight. His consistently melancholy narrator wanders out onto city streets in a midnight rain, clambers up a steeple to survey the town, observes Sunday service by staying at home, or transmutes himself into such still silent observers as the town pump or a tollgatherer.

The American Notebooks indicate that Hawthorne's removal to the wayside had causes other than gaining objectivity. To read the entries in sequence is to experience a willed search for the emblematic significance of ordinary New England lives. And yet the notebooks describe a world of stagnant rural communities and dreary factory towns, of peddlers, inns, stagecoach schedules, and humdrum prosperity, in which stimulation is afforded only by traveling caravans, dioramas, and lyceum lectures. This is the lamentably "thin" American posited by James's biography of Hawthorne, a world in which innumerable dull details almost never flower into fable. When a meaning is found, we are often offered sardonic reminders of life's ironies, as if contemporary New Englanders would no longer concede the grim ways by which time upsets the plans of man.

At times, these ironies even seem gratuitous. In his third notebook, for example, Hawthorne wrote down the source for a story dealing with his region's special holiday: "Thanksgiving at the Worcester Lunatic Asylum. A ball and dance of the inmates in the evening, – a furious lunatic dancing with the principal's wife. Thanksgiving in an alms-house might make a better sketch."[8] More commonly, however, the notations of a day's walk gutter into nothing or end in a concerted effort to drag some meaning from daily experience. Upon completing a long entry telling of an afternoon spent watching lawyers at Parker's bar, gazing at genteel houses along Temple Place, sitting for his portrait, and dining with fellow boarders, Hawthorne exclaims: "A thought to-day – Great men have to be lifted upon the shoulders of the whole world, in order to conceive their great ideas, or perform their great deeds. That is, there must be an atmosphere of greatness round them; – a hero cannot be a hero, unless in a heroic world" (p. 501).

The surmises of psychological or biographical criticism are not needed to explain why Hawthorne found New England to be no heroic world containing great men. Because the *Notebooks* struggle to make much of a diminished New England, an unwilling nostalgia underlies Hawthorne's meditations upon the just demise of great estates and imposing houses.[9] The merchants, mill managers, and military and civil officials whom we encounter are marked by a poverty of imagination, historical and cultural. Less prominent New Englanders fare no better. Throughout the *Notebooks*, the Hawthorne of presumed good feeling for the democratic commoner reveals sensitive distastes that recall those of his fallen aristocrats. A fellow passenger aboard the Worcester stage is declared to be "a genteel enough young man, but not a gentleman" (p. 83). Hawthorne is reluctant to shake hands with "an old, gray, bald-headed, wrinkled-visaged figure, decently dressed, . . . lest his hand should not be clean" (p. 89). Passengers to the Isle of Shoals are "rude, shrewd, and simple, and well behaved enough"; nonetheless, Hawthorne concludes, "People at just this stage of manners are more disagreeable than at any other stage. They are aware of some decencies, but not so deeply aware as to make them a matter of conscience" (p. 527). By implication, this last sentence forecloses the possibility that a common Yankee can possess the moral sense.

Hawthorne's wary distance from contemporary life bespeaks the clash between democratic politics and aristocratic taste that enriches Cooper's fiction. Hawthorne lingers over the Knox, Gardiner, and Browne estates both to approve the demise of privilege and to savor regret for vanished grandeur. Conversely, the energy and affability of contemporary New Englanders seem to have provided them with neither the manners nor the spiritual complexity that would make them worth deeper study. For the reader, the result is a curious dearth of signifying responses, as if a veil were dropped between the author and the beings he seeks to discover.

The degree of Hawthorne's estrangement from expansionist America can be shown by two unjustly neglected sketches titled "The Canal-Boat" (1835) and "The Old Apple Dealer" (1843). The narrator of "The Canal-Boat" is predisposed to accept his contemporaries' opinion that the Erie Canal is the wonder of American Internal Improvements, "a watery highway crowded with the commerce of two worlds."[10] Believing De Witt Clinton an "enchanter," and seeking "to be poetical about the Grand Canal," he intends to voyage its entire length "at least twice in the course of the summer" (p. 430). Although the narrator's account remains a credible description of immediate experience, Hawthorne also lends the westward canal trip an allegorical dimension of a journey through the new river of American time. Along the banks of the canal, the narrator sees the entire sequence of American civilization: unsettled forest, Indians, a log cabin, a thriving village, a commercial town, a city, and a group of immigrants. An Englishman is aboard who seeks to know America through the world of the canal boat, and who spends his time conceiving such representative character types as the Yankee yeoman, the American woman, the rural pedagogue and, most important, the avaricious American merchant.

The experience of passage offers only disillusionment. A dirty boat, surrounded by rusting commercial barges, creeps along "dismal swamps and unimpressive scenery . . . through a gloomy land and among a dull race of money-getting drudges" (pp. 430–2). Any current of progress is sluggish and without apparent destination; among all the sallow-faced settlers, only the Swiss immigrants are contented. The great wonder of Internal Improvements is in fact "an interminable mud-puddle . . . as dark and turbid as if every kennel in the land paid contribution to it" (p. 430). Hawthorne will not, however, allow his reader the easy consolation of revering American nature while denouncing American civilization. The remnants of the forest, now nearly erased by the rush of settlement, have never been more than the abode of barbarism. The conclusion Hawthorne offers his reader allows no consolation for either primitivists or progressives: "My fancy found another emblem. The wild Nature of America had been driven to this desert-place by the encroachments of civilized man. And even here, where the savage queen was throned on the ruins of her empire, did we penetrate, a vulgar and worldly throng, intruding on her latest solitude" (p. 437). Historically, these are the travelers and immigrants driven, in Tocqueville's phrase, by a "magnificent image of themselves . . . marching across these wilds, draining swamps, turning the course of rivers, peopling solitudes, and subduing nations."[11] Within Hawthorne's deeply estranged perspective, they emerge as "a vulgar and worldly throng" of invaders.

The narrator's responses to his increasing disillusionment form a revealing sequence. At first he is peevishly indignant, throwing apples at ducks in the filthy water while laughing at passengers too stupid to duck under the stream's inevitable low bridges. His growing boredom then leads to sexual fantasies in which he imagines that "the pure, modest, sensitive, and shrinking woman of America" (p. 435), posited by the Englishman, has in fact "disrobed herself without a blush" (p. 436) after an intervening curtain has fallen.[12] By midnight, the boat has reached a place known as "the long level," a seemingly interminable stretch with no rise or fall in the canal, surrounded by a forest whose majestic old trees have been felled. At this juncture, so evidently symbolic of the leveled present, the

narrator determines to get off the boat to examine one ruined old tree
that still casts a "phosphoric light" (p. 438). Discovering that this light
from the past is but a "delusive radiance, . . . a mass of diseased splendor,
which threw a ghastliness around" (p. 438), the narrator sadly resigns
himself to resuming his place upon the canal boat. In an ending subtly
prefiguring the place Hawthorne was to occupy in post-Jacksonian America,
the canal boat relentlessly maintains its snaillike pace, leaving the narrator
behind to walk alone, at midnight, his path lit only by a flambeau he
has taken from the old tree.

Attempting an eight-page sketch upon an old apple dealer, who sits
in one place, silent and unknown, carries to an extremity the literary
challenge of making something from nothing. Amid the hubbub of the
Salem train station, Hawthorne fastens the reader's attention upon the
one being who is the antithesis of everything the contemporary American
is supposed to represent. Unlike the train's bustling passengers, the old
apple dealer is utterly "devoid of hope," afflicted with a "frost-bitten
patient despondency" that renders him incapable of any acute or motivating
feeling.[13]

Hawthorne's characteristic literary strategy is to allow his narrative
voice to search in puzzled confusion for his subject's emblematic significance, and to provide it only at the very end: "I have him now. He and
the steam-fiend are each other's antipodes; the latter is the type of all
that go ahead – and the old man, the representative of that melancholy
class who, by some sad witchcraft, are doomed never to share in the
world's exulting progress."[14] To juxtapose one neglected apple dealer to
the powers of the railroad is an imaginative egalitarianism similar to
Whitman's linking of congressman and Cuff. Whereas Whitman's juxtapositions serve to bind, Hawthorne's serve to discriminate. Not one
trait of the old apple dealer is consonant with going ahead, but he is
nonetheless as deserving of concern, and perhaps as representative, as
the slogan by which Americans define themselves. Lest the import of
the old man pale beside the railroad, Hawthorne ends the sketch by
crediting the apple dealer with a soul. By sheer grace of writing Hawthorne
almost succeeds in obscuring an insoluble difficulty: Any merit the apple
dealer may possess can exist only through negative inference by the
author.

If the era's implacable energies wear down humane values, a palliative
can be sought through the burnishing of man's moral sense, traditionally
the office of New England's religious establishment. Precisely here, however, the breakup of older New England religious patterns gives cause
for redoubled doubt. In "Sunday at Home," the parishioners of the First
Church exhibit no sign of any motives save social ones for their two
weekly hours of religion; nor, one should add, does the narrator, whose

only expression of guilt for nonattendance ("Oh, I ought to have gone to church!") is caused by a dutiful habit, not spiritual conviction. Without suggesting any new source for faith, Hawthorne elsewhere observes: "I find that my respect for clerical people, as such, and my faith in the utility of their office, decreases daily. We certainly do need a new revelation – a new system – for there seems to be no life in the old one." Institutional religion has truly become bankrupt when dead Congregationalism is preferred to the vagaries of living Unitarianism: "The difference between the cold, lifeless, vaguely liberal clergyman of our own day, and the narrow but earnest cushion-thumper of puritanical times. On the whole, I prefer the last-mentioned variety of the black-coated tribe."[15]

It is only logical that Hawthorne should have sought a new faith for his new puritan, not in any ideological system, but in domestic love between man and woman. As Tocqueville had frequently noted, love and morality in America were to be found where protection from outside influence allowed them the freedom to grow – within the confines of home and hearth. Affirming the religion of love proved difficult, however, when the new spirit of economy and efficiency was infecting the home. A sketch appropriately titled "Fire-Worship" contrasts open-hearth fireplaces to closed stoves as signs of a change in domestic values. Whereas the open hearth drew the family together toward the heart's source of light and joy, the closed stove acts as a prison and a dispersant, locking up the reddening glow of life and encouraging people to separate into equally heated rooms.

"The Custom-House" judges contemporary Salem by alternating sardonic reminders of inner stagnation with reluctant recourse to the vitality of an older spiritual vision. Just as the railroad had been contrasted to one old man, so the ornamental pretension of the federal Custom House, replete with brightly colored flag and "an enormous specimen of the American eagle," presides over a dying commercial civilization characterized by "mud and dust, the dead level of site and sentiment, the chill east wind, and the chillest of social atmospheres."[16] Because of its declining economic prosperity (King Derby to dilapidated wharves), its failing governmental officials (Surveyor Pue to half-senile idlers), and its waning patriotic spirit (General Miller to the spoilsmen), Salem represents the still-unacknowledged decay of New England traditions. The nearest evidence of historical decline is the social, political, and religious demise of the author's own family, from William Hathorne, representative Puritan with Bible and sword, to "an idler like myself" (p. 9), whose real merit is merely literary. Only through a playful tone can Hawthorne minimize the lingering shame of publicly confessing that the Hathorne son has not proven worthy of his forefathers.

Because Hawthorne finds no sustaining value in contemporary Salem, he develops "a sort of home-feeling with the past, which I scarcely claim in reference to the present phase of the town" (p. 8). This seemingly personal statement then serves a literary end; the writing of *The Scarlet Letter* reminds the sons of their misunderstood if not forgotten origins. Because commercial Salem has discarded the scarlet letter as refuse in the governmental attic, Hawthorne's contemporaries have cut themselves off from that dark sense of Adam's Fall which gave stature and significance to New England civilization. By ferreting out the letter and placing it before dulled contemporaries, the mere storyteller can restore a gleam of redness to a graying civilization. Like a commemorative orator, Hawthorne is still, even in 1850, reminding sons of the forefathers' strength, but he now associates Puritan strength with a toughening sense of sin, rather than with a latent appreciation of freedom.

We should not doubt Hawthorne's sincerity in protesting that contemporary Salem would have provided a preferable subject for fiction. "A better book than I shall ever write was there," Hawthorne concedes. The higher artist would be determined "to seek, resolutely, the true and indestructible value that lay hidden in the petty and wearisome incidents, and ordinary characters, with whom I was now conversant" (p. 38). Although Hawthorne assumes the existence of some "true and indestructible value" in the present, New England life seems too wearisome and ordinary ever to yield it up. It is in the context of such present pettiness that his apologetic claim upon his Puritan heritage ("Let them scorn me as they will, strong traits of their nature have intertwined themselves with mine" [p. 9]) should be interpreted. Unless contemporaries will admit evil as a certainty, and sin as a possibility, their civilization and their art are doomed to a most limited significance.

A further cause of Hawthorne's returning to seventeenth-century New England as the setting for his first romance can be traced to his then most recent volume, *Mosses from an Old Manse*. To engage the present more directly than in many a twice-told tale, Hawthorne had written allegorical sketches of contemporary life so relentlessly distant in tone that the reader loses concern for the objects of satire. In these sketches, Hawthorne's reader is a passenger on a train, observer of a procession, tourist in a museum, guest at a banquet, onlooker at a bonfire, or clerk in an intelligence office. Society appears to be a collection of atomized types made to pass by author and reader for description, judgment, and dismissal. At first, the means of discrimination seem rightly democratic, because men are classified by their griefs rather than their titles, their desires rather than their class, their hatreds rather than their monies. When Hawthorne's classifications uncover no compensating sources of value, however, the disappearance of privilege seems to have resulted in faceless leveling.

An imperturbable coolness of tone creates ambivalence in fundamental responses. "The Intelligence Office," for example, portrays Bostonians as a line of unsatisfied applicants seeking infinite varieties of fulfillment. Among them are four figures Tocqueville would have recognized: an anxious man who knows only "I want my place," a white-haired man in search of tomorrow, a self-reliant philosopher who insists "I seek for Truth," and a man of deplorable success. At the end of the tale, however, there is no determination of their fate, no hint that happiness is unattainable, and no comment upon those who never sought the intelligence office. Hawthorne concludes by abruptly telling us, "What further secrets were then spoken, remains a mystery," and by hinting that his intelligence office may have been only his vaporous fancy anyway. Not infrequently, the author of these sketches seems so unsure of the contemporary world that he distrusts his own skepticism.[17]

The remarkable breadth of Hawthorne's satire is a sign that the lives of his contemporaries failed to engage his deepest imaginative responses. Plausible accusations of self-interest, monomania, myopia, or disregard for known experience are meted out to the following groups: State Street merchants, inventors, reformers, Millerites, bibliophiles, Transcendentalists, scientists, gentlemen of fashion, clergymen, lecturers, politicians, poets, feminists, Shakers, military officers, pacifists, manufacturers ("the manufactury where the demon of machinery annihilates the human soul"), Southern planters ("the cotton-field, where God's image becomes a beast of burthen"),[18] abolitionists, pastoral utopians, city dwellers, farmers, temperance men, topers, men of the world, recluses, knowing sinners, those who have never sinned, and those who hide sin in the heart. In some way, passionate pursuit of these occupations or ideals either breaks the magnetic chain of humanity or violates the sacred integrity of the individual soul.

In the best of these satires, the shapeless futurity of American life leads Hawthorne to expose the vagaries of the present by applying Puritan standards. Mr. Smooth-It-Away of "The Celestial Rail-road" is a fashionable modern "gentleman" wrongly convinced that the steps to salvation are dismissing the concept of sin and purchasing a seat on the railroad. A similar resurgence of outdated values occurs in "The Great Holocaust." The futility of creating an unbounded prairie utopia by burning all one's past is finally revealed by a "dark-visaged stranger" who, insisting on the "foul cavern" of the human heart, judges new Western reformers by an older Puritan spirit.[19]

Hawthorne sometimes cannot account for the behavior of contemporary New Englanders without recourse to a Puritan psychology they do not share. Prudence Inglefield, a New England country maiden turned Boston whore, returns for family Thanksgiving in tentative hopes of recovering her moral integrity. Suddenly and ungraciously, she departs to return to Boston, leaving before family worship but without guilt or sorrow. The terms by which Hawthorne accounts for her behavior would have been wholly acceptable to Arthur Dimmesdale: "Sin and evil passions glowed through [her face's] comeliness, and wrought a horrible deformity." "The fiend prevailed . . . Sin, alas! is careful of her bond slaves." His last words assert that Prudence has been led by infernal persuasion to some form of Hell: "The same dark power that drew Prudence Inglefield from her father's heart . . . would snatch a guilty soul from the gate of Heaven, and make its sin and its punishment alike eternal." Because the tale ends abruptly here, Hawthorne's intent must be to insist that only a Calvinistic sense of innate depravity can adequately account for so mysterious a power of blackness.[20]

In his sketches, notebooks, and allegories, Hawthorne habitually fashions from contemporary New England two symbols of opposing values, neither of which is wholly acceptable. The reader is confronted by an unpromising choice between the old apple dealer and the railroad, destructive reformers and a diabolic Puritan, frustrated Shakers and disappointed worldlings, sybaritic idealists and iron materialists. A characteristic passage of *The American Notebooks* contrasts Edmund Hosmer, "a yeoman . . . of homely and self acquired wisdom," with another man of Concord:

> A parallel between him and his admirer, Mr. Emerson – the mystic, stretching his hand out of cloud-land, in vain search for something real; and the man of sturdy sense, all whose ideas seem to be dug out of his mind, hard and substantial, as he digs potatoes, beets, carrots, and turnips, out of the earth. [P. 336]

In the many passages that reflect this habit of mind, it is impossible to determine the point at which accurately observed detail ceases and symbolic contrast begins. A description of one wasted branch of regional character calls forth its opposite, while a void remains where the trunk should be.

Aware of the warping effect of all callings, Hawthorne nonetheless strove to find a mediating way of life in which the Puritan character in its best form could survive. In fiction, autobiographical sketch, and political biography, he attempted a few literary realizations of his ideal New England American. The problems were at least threefold: to render him as a human reality, to trace his character inheritance from his New England past, and to immerse him at the center of contemporary New England life.

Because the genre of campaign biography demands the recreation of a living man as a national model of character, Hawthorne had a license, even an obligation, to present Franklin Pierce as an ideal New Englander, nationally electable. For many pages, the reader's attention is predictably directed to the candidate's father, General Benjamin Pierce, "one of the best specimens of sterling New England character."[21] Of an old yeoman family, Benjamin possessed all the external virtues appropriate to Revolutionary Americans: He was a "stripling at the plough" who immediately volunteered at Bunker Hill, a farmer who fathered eight children on a rural estate, and a governor whose selfless principles of public service made him "inflexibly democratic in his political faith" (p. 353). Befitting a newer age, son Franklin possesses "these same attributes, modified and softened by a finer texture of character, illuminated by higher intellectual culture" (p. 384). Unlike the sternly patriarchal governor, Franklin is endowed with a "liberal, generous, catholic sympathy" (p. 360), a "democracy of good feeling," which affects men like "a kind of sunshine" (p. 361). He thus represents, in theory, the progressive refinement of Puritan character.

Although Franklin Pierce gains the graces of a gentleman at Bowdoin, wisdom through his knowledge of law, political courage by association with Andrew Jackson, and pragmatic efficiency through military service, he is not merely a melding of all conceivably desirable qualities. Hawthorne is at pains to praise Pierce for not cultivating oratorical skills, for leaving Washington, for not seeking political office, and for not believing that government can solve any fundamental human problem. The prospective president's chief virtue is in fact not political: "He has learned, in his own behalf, the great lesson, that religious faith is the most valuable and most sacred of human possessions" (p. 425). In sum, Franklin Pierce is to be admired precisely because he has no peculiar vision, no distorting ideological crotchets, yet retains the greatness of an inherited regional character.

Fifteen years later, Hawthorne was to personify a similar definition of an exemplary life in "The Great Stone Face." The Old Man of the Mountains is Nature's eternal model of the ideal New England American, with his "original divinity intact," "a face benign and majestic," and, somehow, "the glory of a vast, warm heart."[22] While the stone face waits in silence, four characters embodying four generations of American values arrive in sequence to determine whether the likeness has been fulfilled. All four are loosely modeled on historical figures who are made to represent an age. Gathergold (Franklin and/or Hamilton), Old Blood and Thunder (Jackson), Old Stony Phiz (Webster), and the Poet (Bryant and/or Emerson) together constitute an historical continuum that ever more closely approximates the Great Stone Face.

The ideal American proves to be the common man whose only name is Ernest. Born in a cottage, self-educated, an industrious farmer, Ernest has stayed in the valley, never seeking money, power, oratorical skill, or poetic expression. Because he has not sought these qualities, not gone ahead, all four qualities have accrued to him, and he has become a natural aristocrat: "This simple husbandman has ideas unlike those of other men, not gained from books, but of a higher tone, – a tranquil and familiar majesty" (p. 42). The ultimate proof that Ernest has attained ideal stature is that he is too modest to credit the likeness.

Hawthorne's most convincing portrayal of the ideal New England American is achieved through architectural symbol rather than direct characterization. The Old Manse can sustain an admirable and fulfilling life because it represents the gradually purged house of New England history. Occupying the land where wigwams once stood, it has housed generations of Puritan divines, witnessed the brutal beginnings of the Revolution, and, more recently, yielded its hospitality to consciously moralistic artists. Remaining a Puritan's gray house, the Old Manse has nonetheless acquired, through the will of its new resident, a cheerful coat of interior paint enabling the "grim portraits of Puritan ministers" to recede.[23] Hawthorne can afford to condemn Puritan sermons as "dreary trash," because he has retained the essence of Puritan faith without Puritan theology: "So long as an unlettered soul can attain to saving grace, there would seem to be no deadly error in holding theological libraries to be accumulations of, for the most part, stupendous impertinence" (p. 19). The discarding of a theological vision, however, leads to no embracing of Emerson's newer light. The house and its inhabitants remain wary of immediate change in the name of any Idea: "How gently did its gray, homely aspect rebuke the speculative extravagances of the day!" Hawthorne exclaims, asserting a conservatism that ties history to psychology (p. 25).

Despite Hawthorne's will to affirm these three versions of the middle way, there remains in each of them something fundamentally unconvincing. Designed to embody the best aspects of common New England experience, they retain their virtues at a distance from the culture they represent. Franklin Pierce has shunned Washington for New Hampshire, Ernest has never left Mount Washington valley, and the inhabitant of the Old Manse has stepped back to choose his experiences. Secondly, the links between Puritan ancestors and their present representatives have become so attenuated that they threaten to disappear. Franklin Pierce is closely connected to a Revolutionary father, but not to Puritan forefathers. Although the great stone face shows resolute strength, it is created by Nature; no sadness mingles with its grandeur. Hawthorne may wish unlettered contemporaries to achieve saving grace, but the fact remains that he himself removed portraits of men who spoke of grace and sin from the manse. The problem here is not any denial of the ancestors, but a recognition that, in a democratic republic, any prolonged heritage is maintained with the greatest difficulty.

Despite the fair exterior of these admirable New Englanders, one wonders what their claims to mental and spiritual strength truly rest upon. The profound ideas Ernest utters from the rock are never specified; the price of happiness in the Old Manse is not completing a novel; the president even of a decentralized republic must have some ideas by which to assert leadership. Such a dearth of intellectual substance, combined with a retreat from vocation, breeds a shallowness, bordering upon vacuity, at the heart of those contemporaries Hawthorne would have us most admire.

Perhaps we can now more fully account for reasons why, despite its loose ends, "Ethan Brand" remains the most powerful and memorable of the tales of contemporary New England. Into the midst of a characteristically prosperous and dully livable country village, Hawthorne reinserts a grand figure whose mind, attitudes, and purposes belong to the Puritan past. Physically and spiritually, Ethan Brand is a pilgrim who has separated himself from the world of tavern and manufacturing in order to seek an absolute answer of God. The source of his search for the unpardonable sin dates from the era of Cotton Mather, not from his own. When Ethan returns to the kiln, Hawthorne reminds us that he is an anachronism: "The dead people, dead and buried for years, would have had more right to be at home, in any familiar spot, than he."[24] In the *North Adams Journal*, one can find contemporary sources for Bartram, lawyer Giles, little Joe, the stage agent, the dog, the tavern, and the kiln, but none for Ethan Brand, who had no contemporary existence, but was evoked to represent old Puritanism *in extremis*.[25]

To concentrate on Ethan Brand's corruption, without regard for the context in which he appears, oversimplifies Hawthorne's judgment of his stature. To search for an unpardonable sin is, admittedly, to delude oneself into believing that man can do something so heinous that God cannot forgive it. Nor can one deny that Ethan's search for an absolute "Idea" (p. 84) of sin has estranged him from mankind, destroyed an innocent woman, and literally calcified his heart.[26] Nonetheless, the alternative ways of conducting life are equally inhumane and of far lesser significance. Except for one child, the townspeople neither wish to understand Ethan Brand nor are able to; their two habitual responses to life are laughter and alcohol. It is the narrator, not Ethan Brand, who refers to Bartram as an "obtuse, middle-aged clown" (p. 83) and to the "low and vulgar modes of thought and feeling" (p. 93) common to the stage agent, lawyer, and doctor. The heartless act we experience in the tale is not Brand's ruin of Esther, which is passingly referred to, but Bartram's final desecration of Brand's heart with a pole.

Ethan Brand and the townspeople share only one quality – a self-absorption that confines them within the bounds of their differing obsessions. In a society valuing individual freedom, but lacking many social institutions that provide man a place, varying forms of self-enclosure are sure psychological consequences. Tocqueville conjectured that the individualism of a democracy not only must "make every man forget his ancestors, but it hides his descendants and separates his contemporaries from him; it throws him back forever upon himself alone and threatens in the end to confine him within the solitude of his own heart."[27] In Hawthorne's fiction, the thinness of contemporary New England, a growing tendency to live in the present moment, and reliance on one's own opinion combine to refashion his region as an almost insubstantial world of self-absorbed egoists. "Ethan Brand" shows us two differing consequences. The sole contemporary who retains a Puritan outlook has become so introspective that he commits suicide by throwing himself into a fire that mirrors back his own heart. Contemporaries who retain no trace of Puritanism have become indistinguishable in character because they see the world only as an extension of their petty desires.

To a writer like Hawthorne, who regarded his family and city as representative of his region, his sense of self should reflect his sense of culture. Tocqueville's comment that "in democratic countries, each citizen is habitually engaged in the contemplation of a very puny object; namely, himself"[28] is readily applicable to Hawthorne's "Monsieur du Miroir." The sketch is Hawthorne's willfully light-hearted admission that his mind and art inhabit a world of mirrors. Its narrator, who remains a nameless everyman but must be the writer, perceives his doubled image wherever he goes. Unable to discard his shadow, or to see the world beyond his own reflection, he is condemned to see his own "impenetrable mystery" mirrored in the void beyond.[29] "In old witch times, matters might have gone hard with him" (p. 165), Hawthorne wryly observes, but now such self-absorption is permitted and even encouraged. To see oneself in the outer world has become a common practice he must knowingly share.

The consequences of this narcissistic dilemma are appallingly real. Because it is so difficult to see beyond one's own "sunken eyes," the narrator's outward life seems sure to end in sluggish disappointment (p. 168). Instead of advancing with the times, Hawthorne is held back by his very perception of historical continuity: "I perceive that the tranquil gloom of a disappointed soul has darkened through his countenance, where the blackness of the future seems to mingle with the shadows of the past, giving him the aspect of a fated man" (p. 168). For Hawthorne as for Thoreau, the present moment thus stands on the brink of two eternities, but Hawthorne's present is fatally constricted by both the ambiguous past and the darkening future. In a phrase summarizing the difficulty of finding moral value in his contemporary world, the narrator then pictures his mind "chasing its own shadow through a chaos" (p. 107). Hawthorne's metaphor expresses the futile underside of the very mental process that Emerson was happily calling "projection." It is Hawthorne's darker image for the process, however, that proves pertinent to fictive Americans as diverse as Captain Ahab, Pierre Glendinning, Young Goodman Brown, and Miles Coverdale. Caught between a shadowy past and a black future, all four mirror artists' attempts to deal with chaos by imposing their imaginative visions upon it; they end by making themselves fated men.

5

BROKEN LINES

Our frank countrymen of the west and south have a taste for character
and like to know whether the New Englander is a substantial man, or
whether the hand can pass through him.

Emerson, "Character" (1844)

Hawthorne's early historical tales and *The Scarlet Letter* had implied that
contemporaries who contentedly persisted in building the sepulcher of
the forefathers were falsely idealizing them. His sketches and tales of the
New England present had implied that those who dismissed the past
were ignoring the cause of things and separating themselves from their
cultural roots. He needed to develop a fictional form that, by connecting
past to present directly, could remind contemporaries that they need not
worship patriarchal demigods and could not create themselves anew. The
ending of *The Scarlet Letter*, we know, had troubled Hawthorne because
it seemed to foreclose all hope. Perhaps a more supportive continuum
could be established by retrieving from the New England past a body
of family legend that, carefully selected, would acknowledge ancestral
failings while measuring the true changes within the inner self, then and
now.

One means by which Hawthorne could achieve a sunny close for his
second romance was to redeem the present from insignificance by uncovering within it a gradual reforming of Puritan character. From the
outset, the pattern of traits allotted to the Pyncheon and Maule lineages
lends a determinedly progressive shape to *The House of the Seven Gables*.
By retracing familial roots no farther back than the Salem witch trials,
Hawthorne posits an already corrupted Puritanism that reemerges in

cleansed forms within contemporary descendants who need not be compared to a Winthrop or an Endicott.

For these purposes, contrasting aspects of the Puritan temperament must evolve while they are recurring through hereditary descent. In the 1690s the dominant traits of Puritan character, embodied in Colonel Pyncheon, are religious hypocrisy, material greed, pride, and aristocratic social position. Because the Pyncheon mind is thoroughly empirical, it can control only the daylight world of money, public offices, and legal documents. The underside of the Puritan, first embodied in Matthew Maule, is characterized by dispossession, religious freethinking, democratic politics, and plebeian social position. Because handicrafts stimulate a conceptual imagination separate from the legal word, the Maules can control men only within the darker world of art, dreams, and spiritualism. The crux of familial conflict, the ever-blackening house of the seven gables, represents both the human heart and, as in "The Old Manse," the house of New England history.[1] When Matthew Maule swears providential revenge against the wrong done him by Colonel Pyncheon, descendants of both families become cursed with pride, cruelty, and an intense absorption in self. Complementary sides of a whole Puritan have evidently become bent on mutual destruction.

These clusters of qualities form character types that somehow descend, almost independent of external conditions, through generations of New England life. The Pyncheon family, for example, has its own underside – a line of sybaritic aesthetes beginning with Alice and extending through Clifford – whose weaknesses are explained not by their deference to European culture, but as a reaction to the dominant members of their own family. The wasting conflict between these two types of Puritan character can be resolved in the present by a symbolic marriage between them. Holgrave, embodying the best traits of the Maules, finally acquires control of the Pyncheons' monetary and social powers by becoming the husband of the youngest Pyncheon heir. Phoebe, embodying the best traits of the Pyncheons, first cleanses the house, then prompts Holgrave to forgo his intended vengeance, and finally submits to the virtues she has created in him.

To render the lifting of the curse convincing, Hawthorne faces formidable problems. First he must convince his reader that inherited character types determine the behavior of successive generations; then he must uncover, in descendants of the same families, traits that enable them to escape the curse. The Aeschylean resolution is regrettably inapplicable: Although the Eumenides exist in the hearts of both families, no Athena can suddenly appear to disperse them. Because the curse is not merely an avalanche of ill-gotten gold, but an inherited family character, only new traits can enable the families to transcend their seemingly unchangeable lineage.

Inherited character types must thus be shown to explain behavior, and then to be fundamentally changed from within, without the continuity of lineage being broken. When we consider that the curse has been inherited for some 150 years, but is then absolved by one generation in little more than a summer, it is small wonder that those contemporary characters who do not effect the change (Hepzibah, Clifford, the judge) have seemed more credible than those who do (Holgrave and Phoebe). The fault may lie neither in Hawthorne's inconsistency nor in his failure to prepare Holgrave's conversion, but in his requiring two slight contemporaries quickly and completely to lift an oppressive historical burden. The problem of Phoebe's and Holgrave's stature is compounded by a problem of origin. Inner strengths sufficient to redeem a blackened lineage cannot readily arise out of that lineage.

As the defining representatives of the dominant Puritan spirit, past and present, Judge Pyncheon and the colonel possess a physical solidity and imposing bearing that enable them to dominate family and community. In both men the Puritan devotion to the common weal serves to cloak an aggressive materialism that taints their region's character. Differences between their eras, however, force them to adopt different means toward the same ends. In the 1690s, the mask of hypocrisy was a Bible-carrying piety; in the nineteenth century, it is a form of demagoguery, Judge Pyncheon's "sultry, dog-day heat . . . of benevolence."[2] By making a show of egalitarian feeling, the judge displays the resentful superiority of the gentleman who must condescend to retain control. At bottom, however, it is an atavism of the old "hot fellness of purpose" (p. 129) who now walks down Pyncheon Street, tapping a gold-headed cane to replace the colonel's iron-hilted broadsword.

Although the colonel and the judge are convincingly sinister figures, Hawthorne denies them any trace of Puritan virtue – even the misguided zeal of a Cotton Mather. They have the stature and strength of the founding forefathers without any devotion to a community of virtue, be it theocratic or republican. They are as self-absorbed and monomaniacal as the generation of Goodman Brown, Father Hooper, and Leonard Doane, yet they retain no sense of the spiritual life. Judge Pyncheon devotes as much energy to public service as a neo-Puritan like Sam Adams, but the force of a political idea has no reality for him. During the long transmission of the Puritan character into contemporary Salem, its implacable exterior and underlying egoism have been retained, but all conviction of the reality of the spirit seems to have been lost.

The critical sign of this decline is Judge Pyncheon's inability to believe in sin, or to feel any guilt for his conduct toward his uncle, his wife, his son, Hepzibah, or Clifford. In a most unpuritanical fashion, the "Honorable Judge Pyncheon" has simply "shuffled it [his guilt] aside among the forgotten and forgiven frailties of his youth" (p. 312). The judge's amorality is then measured by standards that a conscientious Puritan judge would have applied. Note the unyielding severity with which Hawthorne condemns the sinful foundation of many a man's fair-seeming soul:

> Now and then, perchance, comes a seer, before whose sadly gifted eye the whole structure melts into thin air, leaving only the hidden nook, the bolted closet, with the cobwebs festooned over its forgotten door, or the deadly hole under the pavement, and the decaying corpse within. Here, then, we are to seek the true emblem of the man's character, and of the deed that gives whatever reality it possesses, to his life. [P. 230]

Although the present perceiver of sin is an imaginative seer rather than God the Father, the spiritual psychology of this passage is remarkably like that of Thomas Hooker's "A True Sight of Sin" (1659):

> Sin brings a Curse upon all our Comforts, blasts all our blessings, the best of all our endeavors, the use of all the choycest of all God's Ordinances; it's so evil and vile, that it makes the use of all good things, and all the most glorious, both Ordinances and Improvements, evil to us.[3]

Because sin brings all evil upon our good, both Hooker and Hawthorne contend that, for a true judgment, only our buried sins exist; absolutely no mitigating credit is granted for real services or for benevolences done for selfish motives.

The architectural imagery of Hawthorne's passage prefigures the climactic chapter in which the corpse of the judge is pictured in the parlor of the house through deepening night into dawn. Jaffrey's body has become the visual emblem of the sins that have brought about the decay of the house. Because pride of money and power has been the hidden cornerstone of both house and family, Hawthorne can complete his metaphor by saying of Jaffrey, "It is our belief, whatever show of honor he may have piled upon it, there was heavy sin at the base of this man's being" (p. 283).

Hawthorne stresses Jaffrey's sin because he, the townspeople, and perhaps the reader have all forgotten it. The specific charges in Hawthorne's address to the judge's corpse condemn him, not as a true Puritan, but as a contemporary man of affairs incapable of feeling guilt. Jaffrey is invoked as "Governor Pyncheon" – financier, Whig, country gentleman, supporter of charities, and pillar of society – a man who has always gone ahead. The only public connection between Jaffrey and his heritage is a thoroughly ironic campaign slogan. The judge is thought a suitable candidate for governor because he is "grounded by hereditary descent, in the faith and practice of the Puritans" (p. 274).

However closely Jaffrey may have been modeled upon C. W. Upham,[4] Hawthorne surely had more than a personal purpose for devoting an entire chapter to vengeance upon him. Hawthorne's mock address to the judge's dead body exposes the moral bankruptcy of a public Puritan tradition that commemorators had sought to keep alive. The toughness within the Puritan character has strengthened the material rather than spiritual concerns of its heritage, and has reduced the judge to the dead shell of an imposing tradition. In Hawthorne's view, a full chapter of ironic denunciation is needed to inform contemporaries how utterly phony such a respectable candidate's credentials – as either Puritan or gentleman – truly are.

Unlike Judge Pyncheon, Holgrave has inherited Puritan virtues that are publicly unrecognized but proved real under test. His encouraging Hepzibah to open the cent shop, his willingness to weed the garden, his skills at any handicraft, and his artistry as a daguerreotypist are all finally attributed to his having been, not simply a rootless commoner named Holgrave, but a Salemite named Holgrave Maule. A nineteenth-century democrat rather than a seventeenth-century plebeian, Holgrave has become a Yankee jack-of-all-trades able to act many parts as well as to brood over his wrongs. His return to his origins persuades him to qualify both his excessive attacks upon the past and his immediate embracing of reform measures. From Hepzibah he learns to value the generosity and courage of a lady; from the garden he learns that moonlight is the best of reformers; from Phoebe he understands the merits of a spirit that brings cheer because it embraces limits.

Hawthorne's endeavor to portray Holgrave as both the inheritor of the Maules' virtues and "the representative of many compeers in his native land" (p. 181) is inconsistent at one crucial point. Having inherited the Maule character, he has the ability and desire to pry into the recesses of another's soul. His mesmerism, Hawthorne claims, is to be understood as the nineteenth-century form of witchcraft. When Holgrave refuses to mesmerize Phoebe Pyncheon, he chooses not to reenact the spiritualistic vengeance of his ancestor Matthew Maule against Alice Pyncheon, and thereby contributes to the expiation of the curse. Although Hawthorne promptly credits Holgrave with "the rare and high quality of reverence for another's individuality" (p. 212), Hawthorne cannot account for that nineteenth-century virtue by transmission from the past or influence of the present.

Holgrave's merciful restraint is motivated by his disgust with a contemporary fad ("he had been a public lecturer on Mesmerism" [p. 176]) and by a need to renounce the chief weapon employed by his ancestors against their oppressors. Hawthorne's insistence that, despite years of shifting occupations and residence, Holgrave has "never lost his identity," and "never violated the innermost man, but . . . carried his conscience along with him" (p. 177), does not tell us whence his identity or conscience derived. A few pages later, we learn merely that "the true value of his character lay in that deep consciousness of inward strength" and in his "enthusiasm" (p. 180). These two qualities may belong to Hawthorne's most general notion of Puritan character, but they had surfaced in the judges at the witch trials as well as in the apostle Eliot. We are thus left with no satisfactory explanation for the source of Holgrave's principal virtue. Holgrave may be Hawthorne's Young American, but he proves to be a Puritan Maule in little else but name.

To carp at Hawthorne's admiring characterization of Phoebe Pyncheon as evidence of his sentimentality or naiveté can only be a profitless display of twentieth-century values, themselves possibly naive. Throughout the novel, she exemplifies virtues of home and hearth that become effective because she also has self-reliance and the gift of practical invention. Belonging to the "trim, orderly, and limit-loving class" (p. 131), Phoebe constitutes "a Religion in herself" (p. 168), able to cleanse the house and brighten the hearts of Clifford, Hepzibah, and Holgrave. While doing so, she has acquired, we should recall, qualities of maturity similar to Holgrave's: a deepened knowledge of life's sorrows, an awareness of the price of the past, and a consequent power to love. In all these ways, Phoebe seems Hawthorne's ideal New England American, appearing finally as a woman rather than a man.[5]

We must grant an author's conception of character, but not his manipulation of it. Like Holgrave, Phoebe cannot be made to fit plausibly within the determinants of lineage. Her name may be Pyncheon, but her common origin, frank sympathies, and cheery simplicity have no part in the Pyncheon traditions. When Hawthorne attempts to account for her virtues, he usually refers to her country upbringing rather than her branch of the family. His insistence that Phoebe Pyncheon represents "the stern old stuff of Puritanism, with a gold thread in the web," simply will not wash (p. 76). Free of ambition and self-absorption, but equally free of vengeance and a will to dominate, she possesses no traces of either form of Puritanism. Without the merits or benefits of an iron character, she is the New England girl of the 1850s whose cheery domesticity Hawthorne attempts to explain as a refurbished Puritanism.[6]

Hawthorne's difficulties in deriving his lovers' virtues from their lineages are aggravated by a problem of plotting. To preserve a sunny ending, Hawthorne must devise a means of transferring power over the house from Hepzibah's "old Gentility" to Phoebe's "new Plebeianism" without denying the judge his villainous control over the worlds of law and politics (p. 81). By conveniently arranging for Judge Pyncheon to fall dead in the ancestral chair, Hawthorne tacitly admits the weakness of the new generation. Instead of wresting control of the house from the judge, Holgrave and Phoebe can only be given control of it by external agency. Their love may flower into Eden over the dead body of the corrupted father, but neither the credit nor the inner strength belongs to them.

The text suggests three possible solutions to the recurrent question of who killed Judge Pyncheon: inherited pulmonary hemorrhage, a stroke upon seeing the "ghost" of Clifford, and the just Providence of God.[7] A fourth possibility is that the judge was killed by Nathaniel Hawthorne, who so detested the ascendent Protestant spirit of Mammon that he simply erased it, and then ended his triumphant flaying of the judge's corpse by proclaiming, "The Avenger is upon thee!" (p. 283). Whoever or whatever the Avenger may have been, the lovers' inability to contribute directly to the judge's defeat weakens the confidence we may repose in their future.

The romancer's narrative machinery may be rusty at the close, but his happy resolution in no way reverses the book's moral perspective. Holgrave's growth into humility and settled views is foretold when he is first introduced. His new commitments to the family, to permanent country houses, and to progress without organized reform are in exact accord with the values Hawthorne had praised in contemporary New Englanders since writing "The Story Teller." Like the narrator of "The Old Manse," Holgrave believes in continuing alteration of the interior of houses, while leaving the exterior to add "venerableness to its original beauty" (p. 314). By sending Phoebe and Holgrave to the judge's country seat and showering gold upon them, Hawthorne has not, as Matthiessen claimed, "overlooked the fact that he was sowing all over again the same seeds of evil."[8] The curse was caused by ambition and avarice, rather than large houses or the possession of money. Oberon's dying advice, we might remember, was to "gather gold, and till the earth, and set out trees, and build a house."[9] Because Holgrave and Phoebe have known the folly of privilege and the grasp of Mammon, the seeds of evil are not in them.

As Hawthorne's narrative develops, the growing presence of Phoebe and Holgrave causes the blackened house to brighten, while the reader's perspective widens to include the street and the railroad. These shifts render the house increasingly less repellent, because today's street life is a world of vendors and gossips whose only "patriarch" is Uncle Venner, a man of patches and clichés faced with the almshouse. While the townspeople gather to watch the organ-grinder, Hawthorne surmises that "more than one New-Englander" should find his moral state exemplified in the devilish black monkey, an "image of the Mammon of copper-coin, symbolizing the grossest form of the love of money" (p. 164). The effect of the hopefully liberating railroad is to sever passengers from surrounding life and to shatter all their stabilities until they see the world as through a kaleidoscope. Hawthorne, however, will not readily permit Pyncheon descendants simply to escape reborn into a world of futuristic flux. At the journey's end are a black church and black house that mirror back to Clifford and Hepzibah their unchanged inner lives.

Because neither the street nor the railroad offers any sustaining alternative to the house, Hawthorne must find a future for Holgrove and Phoebe separate from all three. The country estate allows them to realize the virtues of the middle way, and to develop their supposedly ancestral virtues for a new age. Because the house has enabled them to know the deeper aspects of the heart, Hawthorne chooses for them a large home similar to, but separate from, the house of seven gables. However appropriate this solution may be as an image of moral fulfillment, it nonetheless presents a problem of applicability to New England culture. Who other than Phoebe and Holgrave will benefit from or even observe their tempered virtues?

Hawthorne clearly does not intend Holgrave and Phoebe always to remain in rural retirement. Unable to imagine their place within contemporary Salem, he dispenses them in the dark green barouche to "take up their abode, *for the present,* at the elegant country-seat of the late Judge Pyncheon" (p. 314, italics mine). The problem of their residence, in turn, reflects Hawthorne's inability to resolve his contradictory attitudes toward historical progress. The narrative is shaped to demonstrate a benign evolution of New England character, yet Hawthorne also contends that there is "no reparation" for any major wrong, and that "no great mistake, whether acted or endured, in our mortal sphere, is ever really set right" (p. 313). The mechanical figures on the Italian boy's barrel organ allegorize life as a meaninglessly repetitive dance with a sudden end. Although this symbolic dance aptly describes the life of the street, the narrator explicitly rejects its moral as cynical falsity.

Quite understandably, critics have contended that Hawthorne approves Clifford's theory that human progress forms an "ascending spiral curve" (p. 259) by which we return to old ways but purify them.[10] A similar conception of history's movement was common to Bancroft, to Motley's *Merry Mount,* and to *Grandfather's Chair.* In a very general way, Clifford's theory is confirmed by the generational changes within the novel, yet we cannot forget that the theory is advanced by a crazed aesthete who knows little of history, and who gives vent to his "bubbling up-gush of ideas" in a "wild effervescence of mood" (p. 266).

With the issues of progress and residence unresolved, Holgrave and Phoebe are dispersed into a limbo of happiness. They have attained a substanceless life well described by Hawthorne's phrase "this visionary and impalable Now" (p. 149). Unconvincing though this solution may be, to blame its inadequacies upon Hawthorne is to assume that a more persuasive sunny ending was possible. After such knowledge of house, street, and railroad, we may well wonder where else Phoebe and Holgrave are to go.

When Hepzibah first descends into the cent shop, she is pictured "at the instant of time when the patrician lady is to be transformed into the plebeian woman" (p. 38). Pondering the meaning of such a change, Hawthorne confirms Chevalier's premonitions about the flux of American fortunes by applying the same metaphor:

> In this republican country, amid the fluctuating waves of our social life, somebody is always at the drowning-point. The tragedy is enacted with as continual a repetition as that of a popular drama on a holiday, and, nevertheless, is felt as deeply, perhaps, as when an hereditary noble sinks below his order. More deeply; since, with us, rank is the grosser substance of wealth and a splendid establishment, and has no spiritual existence after the death of these, but dies hopelessly along with them. [P. 38]

The novel's end suggests the depth of Hawthorne's feeling toward the "tragedy" of a patrician family's demise. Although the opening chapters treat Hepzibah's humiliation comically, Hawthorne will finally not permit the tragic demise to occur. Hepzibah is never transformed into a plebeian woman, the Pyncheon family never drowns, and a splendid establishment is restored to them. Although the moral announced by the preface may contend that "an avalanche of ill-gotten gold" will remain a curse "until the accumulated mass shall be scattered abroad in its original atoms," the novel's end regathers that accumulated mass in the family, and not among the people (p. 2). Hawthorne's will to pen such an ending should no longer surprise us. For a writer who wished to discover both a continuity and a cleansing of New England character through ancestral bloodlines, to have drowned the Pyncheons would have been tantamount to despair over his region. Despite all their faults the Pyncheons were the tenuous link back to the time of New England's sure significance.

SELF-CREATED MONSTERS

Perhaps the seams in the ending of Hawthorne's second romance were sufficiently visible to make him decide to reconsider from a new vantage point the prospects for a progressive Puritan spirit. However estranged the Pyncheons had been, they had remained within Salem, embedded in place, time, and family lineage. The members of Blithedale, by contrast, define themselves through removal from New England society. Except for Old Moodie, Hawthorne provides his characters no family legacy and no community of origin. By creating a separatist community in which time seems to begin anew, Hawthorne does not, as one might expect, ignore his characters' place in New England's regional heritage. Instead, he undermines the supposed novelty of Blithedale's futuristic claims by comparing its pastoral mission to the Pilgrims' attempt to create a theocracy two centuries earlier.

Miles Coverdale is quite conscious of "the puritanism, which, however diversified with later patchwork, still gives its prevailing tint to New England character."[11] And yet, despite his disillusionment with Blithedale, Coverdale discovers traces of Puritan qualities only among the new separatists. His comments on State Street, on the Irish, and on the world of Boston town houses suggest no Puritan heritage – sadistic or purposeful – in any of the three places. Whatever opportunity exists for re-forming New England character now lies outside the communities and families that have previously defined it.

As befits both his name and his intelligence, Miles Coverdale analyzes the Blithedale venture as a Protestant mission to plant a purer way of life.[12] After arriving during a snowstorm he notes, "A family of the old Pilgrims might have swung their kettle over precisely such a fire as this, only, no doubt, a bigger one" (p.13).[13] One of his companions anticipates that Blithedale will bring forth "regenerated men"; Coverdale says, "How difficult a task we had in hand, for the reformation of the world" (p. 12). To seek for moral law in such solitary sentinels as Emerson, Carlyle, and George Sand is eminently suitable "to pilgrims like ourselves, whose present bivouâc was considerably further into the waste of chaos than any mortal army of crusaders had ever marched before" (p. 52). Like their seventeenth-century prototypes, the Blithedalers ("our little army of saints and martyrs" [p. 62]) have withdrawn from a society corrupted by pride and materialism to form a regenerate community based upon cooperative economics, hard work, and love for fellowmen. To start anew may be a confession of decline, but it is also a sign of ineradicable utopian hopes. As late as chapter fourteen, the growth and prosperity of Blithedale have apparently convinced most members that they have succeeded where their predecessors fell short. Coverdale refers to his associates as "descendents of the Pilgrims, whose high enterprise . . . we sometimes flattered ourselves we had taken up, and were carrying it onward and aloft, to a point which they never dreamed of attaining" (p. 117).

Each of these comparisons, however, is touched by a satiric irony, always at the expense of contemporaries. The Blithedalers have made only a present bivouac, their army is weaker, they flatter themselves by comparison to forefathers, and even their fire is smaller. Because much of this badinage is gratuitous, Coverdale's irony often seems merely the self-protective device of a minor poet uncomfortably aware of the Puritans' greatness. When he and Hollingsworth contemplate their future status as founders of the reformation, Coverdale wishes to have Hollingsworth regarded as a father, but himself as a mere uncle. And yet Coverdale's self-mockery should gain our trust because he alone seems to have observed genuine, important distinctions between his brethren and their predecessors. Whereas the Puritans came to an untouched land to build a theocracy according to the Word, the Blithedalers scatter to pursue different avocations on Sundays. Their closest approximation of a binding religious purpose lies in their belief in "the spiritualization of labor," a belief that was to serve as "our form of prayer, and ceremonial of worship" (p. 65). This substitute for religion, far from being the progressive novelty the Blithedalers assume it to be, simply reclothes the transcendental self as the intellectual farmer so dear to the generation of Crèvecoeur and Jefferson. Having discovered that clods of dirt remain clods of dirt without being "etherialized into thought," Coverdale now knows that "the yeoman and the scholar . . . are two distinct individuals and can never be melted or welded into one substance" (p. 66).[14]

Although the Puritans had a model of Christian charity to follow, the Blithedalers have only their rejections to bind them. Blithedale, as Coverdale describes it, illustrates Tocqueville's and Grund's premonitions that the idea of personal liberty is America's only bonding value: "We were of all creeds and opinions, and generally tolerant of all, on every imaginable subject. Our bond, it seems to me, was not affirmative, but negative" (p. 63).[15] By remaining within a well-settled land, they have sacrificed the neutrality of removal: "As regarded society at large," Coverdale notes, "we stood in a position of new hostility, rather than new brotherhood" (p. 20). Although we should be wary of Coverdale's voyeuristic fantasies about individuals, we should not deny him societal perceptions caused by justifiable disillusionment.[16]

None of the major characters brings to the community the degree of commitment or Christian charity necessary to its errand. Coverdale's readiness to try work and trust in progress is accompanied by an equally strong desire to pry and then to write. Zenobia's feminist principles, essential to a community aiming at brotherhood and sisterhood, are increasingly wasted through her theatrical displays, her passion for Hollingsworth, and (if we believe Coverdale) the sheer sexuality of her presence. Although Hollingsworth may have come to Blithedale with a sincere commitment to its aims, he soon enlists support for his competing plan for reform. Less prominent characters offer little more to build upon. Yankees like Silas Foster may excel as yeomen, but they scorn to be scholars. Because Priscilla seeks to be dependent, her supposed virtues can have no effect until stronger wills are broken.

Among the four major characters, only Hollingsworth has the strength and the will to bring a better way of life into being. Able to instigate change by forcing crises, he has the solid stature of Hawthorne's Puritans, an "inflexible severity of purpose" (p. 43), and the most ironlike of callings. Hollingsworth speaks with the vocabulary of an Ethan Brand, referring to Fourier as a man who has committed "the Unpardonable Sin" by devising a "monstrous iniquity" for the sake of an "infernal regeneration" (p. 53). We should beware of readily accepting Coverdale's condemnation of Hollingsworth's "heartlessness" and "terrible egotism" (p. 55); Coverdale, after all, lacks all sense of purpose, and admits to "petty malice" toward Hollingsworth for "engrossing every thought of all the women" (p. 126). Among the few reliable facts of the novel are the following: Hollingsworth carries Priscilla to Blithedale, acts as a nurse to Coverdale, and saves Priscilla from Westervelt. Although Coverdale ascribes Hollingsworth's protective deeds to monetary or sexual designs, the only character actually pictured tilling a field is Hollingsworth. Coverdale complains about the weakness of contemporary agnosticism and then notes, almost in the same sentence, "Of all our apostolic society, whose mission was to bless mankind, Hollingsworth, I apprehend, was the only one who began the enterprise with prayer" (p. 39).[17]

In spite of old-time virtues, Hollingsworth decidedly fails to embody the purified Puritan character necessary for the reformation of contemporary New England. His plan for reconstituting Blithedale, even if it is not based upon a "terrible egotism," is subversively pursued and as inherently flawed as the spiritualization of labor. By proposing to reform criminals rather than men, Hollingsworth's plan would deal with society's outcasts rather than with sinners. As a contemporary Puritan, Hollingsworth's great failing is that, like Judge Pyncheon, he does not believe in human sin, least of all his own. Fourier's "Unpardonable Sin," Hollingsworth says, is to have chosen "the principle of all human wrong, the very blackness of man's heart, the portion of ourselves which we shudder at . . . as the master-workman of his system" (p. 53). Whether this is an accurate description of Fourierism or not, it exposes the discrepancy between Hollingsworth's mind and his manner: He would use Puritan vocabulary in pursuit of a reformation denying the central truth of the Puritan faith. In retrospect, Coverdale's first comment upon Hollingsworth's "impracticable plan" seems wholly undistorted by personal quarrels: "He ought to have commenced his investigation of the subject by perpetrating some huge sin, in his proper person, and examining the condition of his higher instincts, afterwards" (p. 36).

Hawthorne measures the failures of Hollingsworth and Blithedale by the same model of Puritan character he held forth in *Grandfather's Chair*. In chapter fourteen, Coverdale imagines John Eliot preaching beneath Pulpit Rock: "I used to see the holy Apostle of the Indians, with the sunlight flickering down upon him through the leaves, and glorifying his figure as with the half-perceptible glow of a transfiguration" (p. 119). Hollingsworth then ascends Eliot's pulpit and speaks the most affecting discourse Coverdale has ever heard. A close reading, however, reveals that Hollingsworth's Sunday discourses have an audience of three, and that the environs of Pulpit Rock have changed markedly since the seventeenth century. "The old pine-forest, through which the apostle's voice was wont to sound, had fallen, an immemorial time ago." Although the aftergrowth admits scattered sunlight, "the stately solemnity of the original forest" has been lost. The soil has "never been brought under tillage"; only "an entanglement of softer wildness" remains for contemporaries (p. 118).

Chapter twenty-five, "The Three Together," gathers the major characters beneath Pulpit Rock, where their mutual accusations will precipitate Zenobia's suicide and the shattering of Hollingsworth's will. Although Coverdale typically arrives too late to overhear the actual words of crisis, he plausibly surmises that Hollingsworth has rejected Zenobia either because of his preference for Priscilla or because, as Coverdale believes, Hollingsworth has learned that Zenobia has lost her inheritance. Whichever explanation is correct, Zenobia's bitter recriminations against Hollingsworth's treatment of women are confirmed. In all his speeches and acts toward Zenobia, Hollingsworth has steadily maintained a domineering condescension toward woman's presumed physical, intellectual, and moral inferiority.

Because Zenobia's outburst occurs under Pulpit Rock, Hollingsworth's male dominance is closely associated with his inherited, but unreformed, Puritan character. Observing the three together, Coverdale rightly perceives Hollingsworth's intransigent cruelty to women as a contemporary reversion to the nadir of 1692:

> I saw in Hollingsworth all that an artist could desire for the grim portrait of a Puritan magistrate, holding inquest of life and death in a case of witchcraft; in Zenobia, the sorceress herself, not aged, wrinkled, and decrepit, but fair enough to tempt Satan with a force reciprocal to his own; – and, in Priscilla, the pale victim, whose soul and body had been wasted by her spells. [P. 214]

Coverdale's fixing of his friends within this particular emblematic tableau resonates throughout the entire range of Hawthorne's fiction. The accusation of witchcraft is here linked with a judging male's higher purpose, punitive acts, and prurient desires. From Lady Arbella, through Goodman Brown's Faith, to Ethan Brand's Esther, a destructive aggression toward woman's moral purity has been an especially marked trait of many of Hawthorne's Puritans. In the later romances, however, the wrong done to woman by Westervelt, Hollingsworth, and Judge Pyncheon becomes a primary concern. During the nineteenth century, in contrast to the seventeenth, there was at least a possibility that woman's moral force might have measurable societal impact.

Miles Coverdale may perceive historical relationships in appropriately Puritan terminology, but he more closely resembles J. Alfred Prufrock than his namesake. In all known qualities, Coverdale is Hollingsworth's foil: a parasite deficient in emotion and will, a relativist so plagued with self-doubt that he can make no commitments, and an aesthete overly sensitive to rough manners and passing slights. The only important link between Coverdale's temperament and the Puritans' is his perpetual desire to delve into the recesses of others' souls. This quality, however, is common to many of Hawthorne's artists and scientists as well as his Puritans. Moreover, Coverdale's purposes in becoming a Paul Pry are quite different from, and possibly even less dignified than, those of Chillingworth or Ethan Brand. Whereas they search with cold determination after real sins, Coverdale is a voyeur seeking to know salacious personal details, preferably sexual. The modern Miles Coverdale could not be sure of sin even if he found it, because, as he himself admits, he has no religious sense.

Able to entertain all reasonable possibilities, but unable to decide or to do, Coverdale self-consciously adopts the role of chorus in a world that seems increasingly insubstantial. Lacking faith in a community agreeing only to be free, he is thrown back upon himself and becomes a Tocquevillean man of mirrors. Like the narrator of "Monsieur du Miroir," Coverdale is acutely aware of the dangers of a solipsism he cannot avoid. In chapter nine he speaks compellingly of the dangers to all men who see others as the "mirror of their purpose," thereby become enchanted with their own minds, and make of the mind a "false deity" or "priest" that can then only be "projected upon the surrounding darkness" (p. 70). Intended to describe Hollingsworth, the passage applies at least as accurately to Coverdale himself.

Acutely aware of the power of imagination, Coverdale is deeply troubled by the probability that his insights are self-projections. At one point, he warns the reader that the very book we are reading may contain little else:

> If we take the freedom to put a friend [Hollingsworth] under our microscope, we thereby insulate him from many of his true relations, magnify his peculiarities, inevitably tear him into parts, and, of course, patch him very clumsily together again. What wonder, then, should we be frightened by the aspect of a monster, which, after all – though we can point to every feature of his deformity in the real personage, – may be said to have been created mainly by ourselves! [P. 69]

Even the possibility of defining a man's character seems to have dissolved into the suspicion that fictional personages are only monstrous distortions created out of the self's needs.[18] Such a prospect undermines Coverdale's character as well as his words. Worried that his "colorless life" has rendered

him "but a poor and dim figure in my own narrative" (p. 245), Coverdale
will forever wish for some commitment that might endow his signifyings
with substance. His troubled recognition that the world he perceives may
be little more than a self-projection so saps him of energy that even the
equally egoistic Puritanism embodied in Hollingsworth seems finally
preferable. At least Hollingsworth retains the power to feel and the will
to act.

Although solipsism and protective flippancy are major causes of Coverdale's failure, so is his withdrawal – a withdrawal caused, in part, by
valid disillusionments that reach beyond Blithedale itself. To have seen
the failure of communal economics leads Coverdale to no approval of
State Street. The greatest merit he can find in the worlds of lawyers,
merchants, or the *North American Review* is that they provide a needed,
temporary corrective to Blithedale. Like the narrator of "Legends of the
Province-House," Coverdale sees Bostonians as dwelling in isolated cubicles
"cut out on one identical pattern like little wooden toy-people" (p. 149).

The tedium of Boston leads Coverdale to one of Massachusetts's "white
country-villages" (p. 196), where culture is dispensed through the lyceum,
partly by its standing exhibit of waxworks and partly by "that sober and
pallid, or rather, drab-colored, mode of winter evening entertainment,
the Lecture" (p. 196). When Coverdale discovers that the procession of
exhibitionist lecturers, including ventriloquists, thaumaturgists, itinerant
professors, and Ethiopian melodists, has descended to the dangerous
charlatanism of Westervelt's veiled lady, he bursts forth in an unusually
direct address:

> Alas, my countrymen, methinks we have fallen on an evil age! If these
> phenomena have not humbug at the bottom, so much the worse for
> us. What can they indicate, in a spiritual way, except that the soul of
> man is descending to a lower point than it has ever before reached,
> while incarnate? We are pursuing a downward course, in the eternal
> march, and thus bring ourselves into the same range with beings whom
> death, in requital of their gross and evil lives, has degraded below
> humanity. [P. 199]

Coverdale here challenges contemporary clichés about the progressive
march of civilization by showing that mesmerism is not merely a recurrence
of witchcraft, but a further decline.[19]

The downward march of which Coverdale speaks is most clearly embodied in Westervelt, who suddenly materializes as a presiding devil
among Blithedale's wood-paths, and whose name suggests the spirit of
the Western world. Westervelt combines professions of spiritual insight
with aggressively democratic manners, but directs them both toward
ends that, as his gold chain attests, are thoroughly materialistic. Forever
addressing others as "friend," Westervelt displays a "hard, coarse, forth-

putting freedom of expression" (p. 92) that is a more contemporary form of Judge Pyncheon's domineering demagoguery. A flashily handsome man of thirty, Westervelt knows the rhetoric of Young America. He speaks publicly of "a new era that was dawning upon the world; an era that would link soul to soul, and the present life to what we call futurity, with a closeness that should finally convert both worlds into one great, mutually conscious brotherhood" (p. 200). The hidden core of such futuristic idealism, Coverdale immediately detects, is its wholly materialistic premise: Westervelt's speech is "eloquent, ingenious, plausible, with a delusive show of spirituality, yet really imbued throughout with a cold and dead materialism" (p. 200). Another embodiment of the contemporary, grasping "gentleman," Westervelt may adopt mesmeric rather than statesmanlike behavior, but both he and Judge Pyncheon pervert older Puritan qualities to entirely selfish ends. In Westervelt's mannerisms, however, the sham has assumed proportions so theatrical that the man often seems a complete illusion.[20]

When the disillusioned Coverdale eagerly returns to Blithedale, he is greeted by a masquerade that unexpectedly destroys his hope for a "home" (p. 206). Because others have created this masquerade, it must be a symbolic rendering of the chaos that the perpetual playing of roles at Blithedale has caused. As in The Confidence-Man, Hawthorne's masquerade reveals the community's desire to act out life in ways that break down brotherhood by dissolving reality in word play. While Coverdale watches the masquerade unfold, he discovers that any meaningful order of historical character types has been lost. Kentucky woodsman, Jim Crow Negro, Shaker elder, Puritans, Silas Foster, Revolutionary officers, and Cavaliers all whirl around him like Alice's pack of cards. To reorder them would be an unappreciated exercise in imposing imagined patterns. When the entire "fantastic rabble" sets off in pursuit of author Coverdale, he wishes only to escape it (p. 211). Even though Coverdale writes The Blithedale Romance, he accepts the orderlessness of life's masquerade. Having finished his narrative, he acknowledges that he has no summary: "But what, after all, have I to tell? Nothing, nothing, nothing" (p. 245). The historical perspective through which the present can be known has collapsed, leaving Coverdale to know only a heap of broken images.

In one crucial respect Hawthorne cannot resist reaffirming continuity of character. Like Holgrave and Phoebe, Hollingsworth and Priscilla embody a chastened form of New England Puritanism upon which any viable future must rest. Unlike The House of the Seven Gables, however, The Blithedale Romance does not encourage any culturally redemptive prospects through the marriage. Absorbed in his past sin, Hollingsworth remains locked within an earlier form of Puritan guilt. When Coverdale observes that "the powerfully built man showed a self-distrustful weakness, and a childlike, or childish, tendency to press close, and closer still," to Priscilla, we can only conclude that Hollingsworth remains at the very beginning of self-renewal (p. 242). Nor does Priscilla possess more than a faint trace of the cheering energies of Phoebe Pyncheon. One of Westervelt's few credible statements is his explanation for Priscilla's weak purity: "She is one of these delicate, nervous young creatures, not uncommon in New England, and whom I suppose to have become what we find them by the gradual refining away of the physical system, among your women" (p. 95). Whereas Phoebe's merits are active yet unconvincingly Puritan, Priscilla's thin pallor may be traced back among Hawthorne's New England women to the victimized Anna Gower Endicott. To entrust Hollingsworth's future to Priscilla's "protective and watchful quality," to her "deep, submissive, unquestioning reverence," is to lean upon the slenderest of reeds (p. 242).

A HOME ELSEWHERE

Hawthorne's famous complaint about the vexations of writing American romance reflects the altered perspective of his European years:

> No author, without a trial, can conceive of the difficulty of writing a Romance about a country where there is no shadow, no antiquity, no mystery, no picturesque and gloomy wrong, nor anything but a commonplace prosperity, in broad and simple daylight, as is happily the case with my dear native land.

The verb tenses of the passage show that Hawthorne would deny antiquities, shadows, and wrongs only to the American present. Because sources for romance are declared to be lacking "in the annals of our stalwart Republic," we may presume their continuing existence in a pre-republican era. And yet this sentence also serves abruptly to sever continuities between the American past and the American present. If in 1851 Hawthorne had believed America to be devoid of antiquity, mystery, and wrong, *The House of the Seven Gables* would not have been conceived. The consoling tone of the phrase "my dear native land" (Scott had written only "my native land") presumes a nation in which the possible presence of Judge Pyncheon has been forgotten.[21]

Hawthorne's statement may be a tacit admission of difficulties he confronted in showing that a Puritan past has led to a neo-Puritan present. Phoebe's status as a Pyncheon, Holgrave's status as a Maule, Hollingsworth's or Coverdale's ties to Puritan forefathers – all posed problems of rendering credible the development of a heritage. Now, however, Hawthorne seems to embrace the separation of past from present. Readers of Hawthorne's earlier sketches of contemporary life found the daylight world of common prosperity treated with ironic ridicule because contemporaries lacked a sufficient vision of evil to see many of the signifying realities of life. The experience of Europe, however, has apparently led Hawthorne to contend that to be free of shadows is "happily" the American norm. Ignorance of evil and the past, once a diminishment of the citizen as well as the artist, is now a loss only for the romancer.

The two Americans in *The Marble Faun* are creations of a mind resolutely determined to associate American virtue with moral innocence and a commonplace prosperity. The energy, blackness, and intelligence that once constituted the American Puritan character are now associated with Rome, Catholicism, and Europeans. As Rome embodies the decay and historical guilt once prominent in Salem, so Hilda and Kenyon represent the health of an Adamic America. In previous fictions, Hawthorne created a New England at least as ghost-ridden as old England; from within the perspective of Rome, however, Hawthorne accepts his countrymen's treasured assumption that the blessed American Republic is the sole exception to a fallen world.

Hawthorne attempts to embody in Hilda and Kenyon a new compromise between the zeal of ignorance and oppression by shadows. As redemptive Americans, they are to be made aware of the Old World's evil, but are not personally to experience it; they must see sins without committing them. For them, Rome is to be a theoretical education by which innocence of character can somehow be preserved while knowledge of experience is acquired. Through the characterization of Hilda, Hawthorne would now persuade us that a New England woman can become Able and Angel without being a sinner. Kenyon would illustrate how a young New Englander, like Robin Molineux, can come to a fallen city and mature without joining in compulsive laughter at the stained traditions he must supersede.

Kenyon is introduced as "a young American sculptor, of high promise, and rapidly increasing celebrity" (p. 21). Physically he possesses "features finely cut, as if already marble; an ideal forehead, deeply set eyes, and a mouth . . . sensitive and delicate" (p. 116); his spirit is one "of refined taste, and . . . of delicate sensibility" (p. 286). Possessing such virtues, Kenyon can do nothing to confirm them save to comment on art objects and offer moral advice to his friends. He can have no shadowy past that might sully his cheery decency, no strong ideas that might upset his objectivity, no firm purpose that might endanger another. His notion of happiness is to remove Hilda from Rome to a retreat like Monte Beni: He describes his role as mentor by saying, "I shall tell Hilda nothing that would give her pain" (p. 287). The blandest of heroes, Kenyon shows us the almost total vacuity of Hawthorne's new compromise. To deprive the contemporary American of his past and of the experience of sin, while leaving him the character virtues of the middle way, is to reduce him to a prig.

The same problem recurs in the characterization of Hilda. This "brown-haired, fair-cheeked, Anglo-Saxon girl" (p. 389) is said to be "a daughter of the Puritans" who believes in "the faith of her forefathers" (p. 54). However, Hilda has never considered the fact of evil; her status as heroine depends upon keeping her free of any complicity in sin. Her tower, like Kenyon's studio, is a hermitage from which Rome may be contemplated. Hilda's one crisis is a wholly egoistic need to rid herself of sins observed in others. When she avails herself of confession for the sake of psychological release, and then repulses the priest, purportedly because "I am a daughter of the Puritans" (p. 362), she is clearly justifying a complacent affront by a false reason.

Hawthorne nonetheless seeks to praise Hilda's self-enclosed innocence. While gazing at the portrait of Beatrice Cenci, Hilda wonders, "Am I, too, stained with guilt?" whereupon the narrator interjects, "Not so, thank heaven!" (p. 205). Hawthorne clearly intends to compliment Hilda by observing that, "with respect to whatever was evil, foul, and ugly, in this populous and corrupt city, she had trodden as if invisible, and not only so, but blind" (p. 387). Whereas Phoebe Pyncheon went into the house of the seven gables, dealt with its shadows, and brought about visible change, Hilda's visit to the Palazzo Cenci, seemingly so important to the novel's plot, remains both unexplained and finally inconsequential. The virtues of New England purity seem to have acquired a self-protective shield.

Surrounded by the wreckage of two civilizations, one pagan and the other Catholic, Hilda and Kenyon project an image of New England that will limit their environment to clear, clean places and a knowable present. Kenyon tells Donatello: "You should go with me to my native country. . . . In that fortunate land, each generation has only its own sins and sorrows to bear. Here, it seems as if all the weary and dreary Past were piled upon the back of the Present" (p. 302). Hilda summons up "vivid scenes of her native village, with its great, old elm-trees; and the neat, comfortable houses, scattered along the wide, grassy margin of its street, and the white meeting-house, and her mother's very door" (p. 342). The happiness of such a life depends upon the absence of all untoward occurrence; Hilda longs for "that native homeliness, those familiar sights, those faces which she had known always, those days that never brought any strange event" (p. 342). To be freed from the experience of evil, once a sign of weakening innocence, is now accepted for the sake of contentment.

All these qualities contribute to a "home" that more closely resembles the New England villages known to Currier and Ives than those known to Ethan Brand or Hepzibah Pyncheon. There is, however, no suggestion of authorial irony when Hilda and Kenyon imagine their New England future. Instead, we find Hawthorne confirming their anticipations. "The Italians," the narrator declares, "appear to possess none of that emulative pride which we see in our New England villages, where every householder, according to his taste and means, endeavours to make his homestead an ornament to the grassy and elm-shadowed wayside" (p. 295). When Kenyon turns to Hilda and says, "Oh, Hilda, guide me home!" (p. 461), he is sincerely appealing, like Holgrave and Hollingsworth before him, to a New England maiden as a source of redemption. Unlike them, however, he has no known failings. Moreover, he and Hilda have conceived a changeless village future where all art will be domesticated and Hilda "enshrined and worshipped as a household Saint, in the light of her husband's fireside" (p. 461). It is fitting that the novel's final line, "But Hilda had a hopeful soul, and saw sunlight on the mountain-tops" (p. 462), has no intended ironic context. A sentence so riddled with clichés of thought and diction shows us the shrinking of Hawthorne's regional hopes. When no true continuity can be established between seventeenth-century Puritans and their nineteenth-century descendants, the empty banalities of Kenyon and Hilda constitute a last resort.

Despite the declaration of the preface, Hawthorne could not quite reconcile himself to simple affirmation of the virtues of being happy, shadowless, prosperous, and American. His relentlessly cheery ending cannot erase his troubled response to the Fortunate Fall either from his memory or from ours. When Miriam first advances the Miltonic and hardly heretical notion of education through sin, Kenyon admonishes her. When Kenyon tentatively mentions the idea to Hilda, she in turn admonishes him. Although the idea is thereby relegated to mistaken Europeans, it nonetheless keeps recurring. More important, it is confirmed by Miriam's passionate intelligence and by Donatello's undeniable growth.

Hawthorne's submerged distrust of his patriotic pieties remains in his responses to setting. Any thinking reader must infer that the trim decencies of the American village can have been attained only at the expense of all the art and human history that are Rome. In the remarkable paragraph that opens chapter thirty-six, Hawthorne heaps up every imaginable just charge that an American democrat could hurl against the Old World: its decay, brutality, filth, poverty, crime, lethargy, and disregard for individual rights (pp. 325–6). As this single 380-word sentence unfolds its catalogue of atrocities, the reader anticipates a conclusion similar to Kenyon's outcry, "Oh, Hilda, guide me home!" Without offering one reason to account for the change, Hawthorne suddenly reverses the thrust of his sentence: "When we have left Rome in such mood as this, we are astonished by the discovery, by-and-by, that our heartstrings have mysteriously attached themselves to the Eternal City, and are drawing us thitherward again, as if it were more familiar, more intimately our home, than even the spot where we were born" (p. 326). Evidently, an even more resolute control of characterization and of the ending would have been necessary for Hawthorne to persuade his reader, and perhaps himself as well, where home truly was.[22]

The title of Hawthorne's last completed book implies the existence of a new home to replace our old one. Its nostalgic tone, however, suggests a doubt whether American daylight prosperity has proved to be permanently livable. Throughout *Our Old Home*, Hawthorne shifts back and forth in his responses toward England and America, sometimes condemning the opposed customs of both cultures, sometimes complimenting one nation only to contradict himself elsewhere. As an eminent writer contributing to the long tradition of Anglo-American travel volumes, he pursues the graceful double game of being a patriotic American who nonetheless loves his old home. Almost as frequently, however, he speaks as a deracinated observer who has little patience with either the American's spirit of novelty or the Englishman's acceptance of tradition. Rarely embittered, often amused, but predominantly melancholy, the author of *Our Old Home* seems reconciled to a homelessness he cannot publicly acknowledge.

Final judgments upon long-standing concerns show no consistent resolution, no arrival at sustaining values. Hawthorne's well-known observations upon English women complain comically of their elephantine mass and domineering conventionality. American women, however, exhibit the opposite defects: "a certain meagreness, (Heaven forbid that I should call it scrawniness!), a deficiency of physical development, . . . a paleness of complexion, a thinness of voice."[23] The lack of any known alternative to these febrile qualities (so appropriate to Hilda, Priscilla, and their predecessors) only makes Hawthorne "resolve so much the more sturdily to uphold these fair creatures as angels" (p. 334).

Many passages from *Our Old Home* could support a claim that Hawthorne found consummate value in the peaceful beauty of the English country estate. Nuneham Courtenay, Hawthorne declares, is "as perfect as anything earthly can be"; because it illustrates "the splendid results of long hereditary possession," it deserves the envy of "we Republicans, whose households melt away like new-fallen snow in a spring morning" (p. 191). And yet Hawthorne's similarly reverential picture of another ancestral estate ends in a self-conscious reversion to American values: "A lodging in a wigwam or under a tent has really as many advantages, when we come to know them, as a home beneath the roof-tree of Charlecote Hall" (p. 119). The Englishman's respect for his moss-grown past leads Hawthorne to exclaim: "Old associations are sure to be fragrant herbs in English nostrils; we pull them up as weeds" (p. 51). A very few pages later, he assumes the opposite attitude, embracing American progressivism as a feeling as well as a principle:

> An American visitor . . . becomes sensible of the heavy air of a spot where the forefathers and fore-mothers have grown up together, intermarried, and died, through a long succession of lives, without any intermixture of new elements, till family features and character are all run in the same inevitable mould . . . Better than this is the lot of our restless countrymen, whose modern instinct bids them tend always towards "fresh woods and pastures new." [Pp. 59–60]

In neither nation, apparently, can our needs for roots and for change both be satisfied.

An inevitable result of such contrary impulses is the creation of two opposed national types, neither of which is consistent with itself. In some passages John Bull is beefy, bumbling, and obtuse; in others he is affectionate, quick-witted, and energetic. Hawthorne credits his own countrymen with "American acuteness of intellect, quick-wittedness, and diversity of talent" (p. 35); elsewhere, these same qualities are associated with "our national paleness and lean habit of flesh" (p. 319). Faced once more with trying to find an ideal compromise between equally flawed extremes, Hawthorne proposes that Englishmen be transferred to the virgin West and Americans be repatriated to their old home:

> I used to wish that we could annex it [England], transferring their thirty millions of inhabitants to some convenient wilderness in the great West, and putting half or a quarter as many of ourselves into their places. The change would be beneficial to both parties. We, in our dry atmosphere, are getting too nervous, haggard, dyspeptic, extenuated, unsubstantial, theoretic, and need to be made grosser. John Bull, on the other hand, has grown bulbous, long-bodied, short-legged, heavy-witted, material, and, in a word, too intensely English. [P. 64]

Superficially, the passage contends for mutual benefits. If sustained by graceful tradition, the restless, anxious American, so familiar to readers of Tocqueville, could be humanized. If freed by the unformed West, the Englishman could quicken his body and open his mind. But the significance of the passage lies in its obviously calculated absurdity. Because the enriching compromise of character types now takes place only in imagined kingdoms, both alternatives are facetiously offered only to be thrown away.

At the end, Hawthorne suspected that he might have found no home. An entry in the *English Notebooks* recalls a dispiriting evening spent contemplating a long list that recalled "how many times we have changed our home since we were married." It ends by including his remaining European years within a period of two decades, "during all of which we shall have no real home."[24] The only house Hawthorne was ever to own, however, still lay in his future. Its name, the Wayside, suggests a persistent hope of living the mediating ideal he had created in "The Old Manse." As his volume on England attests, however, he was to find no new home in Concord. And so the significance of his house was to be subtly shifted: "I call it the wayside . . . because I never feel as if I were more permanently located than the traveller who sits down to rest by the road which he is plodding along."[25] Like Oberon in "The Story-Teller," Hawthorne seems to have returned home only to discover, at the last, his own rootlessness.

Hawthorne's unceasing search for a home mirrors his inability as a writer to embody the exemplary New England American in a secure present. His attempts to trace a progressive continuity of regional character back to Puritan strengths repeatedly foundered against his contemporaries' disregard for the bonds of community and the fact of evil. Contemporary New England, as Hawthorne saw it, was shifting steadily toward a commercial and egalitarian society; its declining faith and rising prosperity brought a sham spiritualism that was itself a sign of restlessness. When Hawthorne attempted to represent worthy neo-Puritan contemporaries, he could do so only by removing them to rural retirement, thereby depriving their integrity of power.

There are historical as well as fictional reasons why, among the four romances, only *The Scarlet Letter* has a satisfying ending. Hester Prynne returns to a community that has a defining purpose and spiritual values. Because Hester can never be more than half-penitent, her dwelling has to remain between town and forest. Unlike Holgrave and Phoebe, Hollingsworth and Priscilla, Kenyon and Hilda, Hester occupies an enriching marginal place that is realized for us. We can envision it because Hester's grim and shadowy perception of life, subversive though it is, is linked to a society of demonstrable value. Without the context provided by a contemporary community bonded in spirit, Hawthorne's supposedly neo-Puritan couples can only be dispersed into a visionary and impalpable Now.

PART II

MELVILLE

While freely acknowledging all excellence everywhere, we should refrain from unduly lauding foreign writers, and, at the same time, duly recognize the meritorious writers that are our own; – those writers who breathe that unshackled, democratic spirit of Christianity in all things.

Melville, "Hawthorne and His Mosses" (1850)

From this morbid self-esteem, coupled with a most unbounded love of notoriety, spring all Mr. Melville's efforts, all his rhetorical contortions, all his declamatory abuse of society, all his inflated sentiment, and all his insinuating licentiousness.

Review of *Moby-Dick, United States Magazine and Democratic Review* (1852)

6

DISTRUST IN
CONFIDENCE

And now the future is all before us, and Providence our guide. When
the children of Israel, after forty years of wanderings in the wilderness,
were about to enter upon the promised land, their leader, Moses, . . .
commanded that when the Lord their God should have brought them
into the land, they should put the curse upon Mount Ebal, and the
blessing upon Mount Gerizim . . . Fellow citizens, the ark of your
covenant is the Declaration of Independence. Your Mount Ebal, is the
confederacy of separate state sovereignties, and your Mount Gerizim is
the Constitution of the United States . . . Lay up these principles, then,
in your hearts, and in your souls – bind them for signs upon your hands,
and teach them to your children . . . So may your children's children,
at the next return of this day of jubilee, after a full century of experience
under your national Constitution, celebrate it again.

John Quincy Adams, "The Jubilee of the Constitution" (1838)

LUSTY DEFENSES AND GLORIOUS AREOPAGITICAS

By his thirtieth year (1849), Herman Melville had experienced
more family tragedies and personal reversals, in America and on American
ships, than most men experience in a lifetime. Nonetheless, during the
years from 1849 to 1851, he became convinced that America was shortly
to realize the seventeenth-century Puritan's dream of a New Israel. Like
John Quincy Adams, Melville assumed that the New Israel could only
be created, not in a Calvinistic theocracy, but in a libertarian republic
where democratic principles had received heaven's sanction through the
gift of a paradisiacal land. At the very moment when Melville felt his
literary powers unfolding within him, he was projecting a future of
limitless glory for his country. If Tocqueville's model of the workings

of the American mind is valid, Melville was surely ascribing to his country the energizing creativity he felt within himself.

Even more explicitly than O'Sullivan or Adams, Melville pursued a theology of democratic politics. Through one lengthy exhortation by White-Jacket, Melville defined, as authoritatively as anyone of the era, the covenant of his nation's promise:

> And we Americans are the peculiar, chosen people – the Israel of our time; we bear the ark of the liberties of the world. Seventy years ago we escaped from thrall; and, besides our first birth-right – embracing one continent of earth – God has given to us, for a future inheritance, the broad domains of the political pagans, that shall yet come and lie down under the shade of our ark, without bloody hands being lifted. God has predestinated, mankind expects, great things from our race; and great things we feel in our souls. The rest of the nations must soon be in our rear. We are the pioneers of the world; the advance-guard, sent on through the wilderness of untried things, to break a new path in the New World that is ours. In our youth is our strength; in our inexperience, our wisdom. At a period when other nations have but lisped, our deep voice is heard afar. Long enough have we been skeptics with regard to ourselves, and doubted whether, indeed, the political Messiah had come. But he has come in *us*, if we would but give utterance to his promptings. And let us always remember that with ourselves, almost for the first time in the history of earth, national selfishness is unbounded philanthropy, for we can not do a good to America but we give alms to the world.[1]

Such assurance of tone discourages the reader from attending closely to troublesome assumptions. By comparing the untried future to a readily conquerable wilderness, Melville can include all Americans within the elect because all are pioneers, pathfinders whose rebelliousness in the name of liberty and equality merits divine protection. The forward-looking energy of the adolescent nation quickly turns into deep-voiced strength because innocence (or "inexperience") is synonymous with wisdom. Although all who inhabit lands outside the American polity are political pagans, they will be bloodlessly assimilated within the conquering culture, presumably because they recognize its superiority. Only if the individuals who constitute the people are innately virtuous can "selfishness" feasibly be said to serve public good.

Visions of paradise are often beheld most clearly by men in infernal conditions. Experiencing the brutalities of the American navy leads White-Jacket both to denounce the miseries of a man-of-war world and to anticipate the coming of the political messiah in America. While the credibility of the passage depends on logic of statement, its power depends upon the literary rendering of a will to believe.

To a writer baptized in the Dutch Reformed Church, the coming of a messiah posed a threat of judgment as well as the promise of a kingdom. But if America's political messiah was to be its democratic ideas, the kingdom could spread over the open continent without any need of destructive wrath. When Redburn prophesies the Millennium in America, he contends that the land permits a wholly peaceful reversal of the decree of Genesis:

> We are the heirs of all time, and with all nations we divide our inheritance. On this Western Hemisphere all tribes and people are forming into one federated whole; and there is a future which shall see the estranged children of Adam restored as to the old hearth-stone in Eden.
> The other world beyond this, which was longed for by the devout before Columbus' time, was found in the New; and the deep-sea-lead, that first struck these soundings, brought up the soil of Earth's paradise. Not a Paradise then, or now; but to be made so, at God's good pleasure, and in the fullness and mellowness of time. The seed is sown, and the harvest must come; and our children's children, on the world's jubilee morning, shall all go with their sickles to the reaping.[2]

The coming of this Millennium is a totally beneficent and restorative act, a remaking of the "soil of Earth's paradise" that will somehow re-create Eden rather than supersede it. The sign of paradise will be a harvest of unspecified produce assumed to be good because its seeds were sown in 1776 and 1787.

Although Redburn amasses alliterative phrases and metaphors of the jubilee into a form of written oratory, his unexpected use of the words "federated" and "estranged" reveals a longing distinct from the pre-millennial rhetoric of the day. His vision of the disparate strengths of many peoples fused into a mighty nation of free men who remain equal despite their differences is something more than the cliché of the melting pot. It implies that, in fact, the ordinary American is an unusually solitary individual who longs for paternity or community. The biblical explanation for the jubilee, we might recall, specifies that "it shall be a jubilee for you, when each of you shall return to his property and each of you shall return to his family" (Lev. 25:10). Elsewhere in his book, Redburn acknowledges that, by anticipating a national mingling of bloodstreams, he quiets his fear that he, like all Americans, is a cultural orphan: "Our blood is as the flood of the Amazon, made up of a thousand noble currents all pouring into one. We are not a nation, so much as a world; for unless we may claim all the world for our sire, like Melchisedec, we are without father or mother."[3] Like Holgrave, he wishes to believe it both possible and good to inhabit a world without fathers. To be an American is to make a collective claim upon the entire world, yet Redburn knows that collective claims deny the intimacy of blood.

Redburn's use of the word "federated" ("On this Western Hemisphere all tribes and people are forming into one federated whole") creates a revealing political analogy. In America the fusion of bloodstreams is to be furthered by the federal system of united, independent states; the national polity is to unite men by honoring their natural rights as individuals. These expectations help to account for Melville's fascination with Anacharsis Clootz, who, in 1790, had gathered peoples from all nations before the French National Assembly to represent collected humanity.[4] In *Moby-Dick*, *The Confidence-Man*, and *Billy Budd* Melville was to compare his ship's journey to Clootz's pilgrimage, thereby creating a parallel between his national and his universal hopes. The sailors aboard the *Pequod*, for example, form "an Anacharsis Clootz deputation from all isles of the sea," a deputation made up of "*Isolatoes*" who have become, Ishmael trusts, "federated along one keel."[5] To expansionists like O'Sullivan, the principle of federation was merely a means of maximizing liberty within an endlessly enlarging polity. To Melville, federation had an added psychological dimension. Like the federal union, Melville's ships hold forth the possibility of escaping from the isolation of self-reliance, from that frightening tendency of democracies to make men free, equal, indistinguishable, and consequently, as Tocqueville knew, insignificant.

As the logic of justifying the republican faith demands, Melville's prophecies of the New Israel and hymns to liberty and equality are based upon his faith in the dignity of the democratic individual. Consider Ishmael's crucial invocation of the "great democratic God," the "just spirit of Equality," as the muse that allows him to ascribe "high qualities, though dark" to "meanest mariners and renegades and castaways":

> But this august dignity I treat of, is not the dignity of kings and robes, but that abounding dignity which has no robed investiture. Thou shalt see it shining in the arm that wields a pick or drives a spike; that democratic dignity which, on all hands, radiates without end from God; Himself! The Great God absolute! The centre and circumference of all democracy! His omnipresence, our divine equality!

The spirit of divine equality in each workman, so foreign to Hawthorne's view of the contemporary common man, becomes a force for an unknowably grand future. Ishmael's invocation echoes the third sentence of the essay "Circles," in which Emerson noted, "St. Augustine described the nature of God as a circle whose center was everywhere and its circumference nowhere." In both passages, the divine power of the self is free to expand in ever-widening circles toward a circumference without fixed limit. Not surprisingly, chapter fourteen of *Moby-Dick* is a hymn to Nantucket whalemen, who, starting from their island center, will soon master the globe. The last sentence of *Moby-Dick* may submerge Ishmael in a chaotic vortex, but he finds survival by recovering its center.[6]

The individual who feels his own immaculate manliness, who possesses an insular Tahiti at the center of his democratic soul, thus becomes an ideal that Melville associates with the American character. Even aboard autocratic American ships like the *Neversink* and the *Pequod*, insistence upon the natural dignity of common men allows us to entertain the promise of equality of value. For Ishmael, the political term "equality" becomes synonymous with the democratic God dwelling within every man. As a narrative voice, Ishmael illustrates Grund's claim that, for citizens of the United States, America is a state of psychological becoming without geographical boundary. The specific terms of Ishmael's invocation confirm Tocqueville's surmise that the democratic mind, seeking union because of its own lonely insignificance, would transcend solitude through pantheism.

Melville's intense national optimism was also founded upon feelings less aggressively transcendental: a dismissal of the past, pride in the American Revolutionary era, love of the Western spirit, and the promise of democratic good fellowship. Like so many of his American contemporaries, Melville sought to arouse the individual's energies by denying the constricting power of the past. Though the future must remain a blank page, White-Jacket insists that it will provide a new scripture:

> The past is dead, and has no resurrection; but the Future is endowed with such a life, that it lives to us even in anticipation. The past is, in many things, the foe of mankind; the Future is, in all things, our friend. In the past is no hope; the Future is both hope and fruition. The Past is the text-book of tyrants; the Future the Bible of the Free.[7]

When Holgrave or John Hancock expressed such sentiments, Hawthorne placed them within an ironic context. Throughout *White-Jacket*, however, Melville is prepared to celebrate the fact that democratic ideology, the absence of a codified legal tradition, and the waiting expanses of the West are creating a national mentality fixed upon future expectations. Because the Articles of War embody a dying *ancien régime*, doubts about the American future may be contemplated but not credited.

Melville suspected that only Calvinism could account for the compellingly dark side of human behavior, yet he had no pre-Revolutionary heritage through which to measure the generational continuities of American development. He therefore assessed contemporary American realities against a standard of Revolutionary heroism without having to work out, as Hawthorne did, the problems of its origin. The American navy of 1849 is judged by the Bill of Rights; Pierre attempts to live up to the image of his grandfather; both Ungar and Jack Gentian compare the 1870s to the 1780s. Although the pattern of historical comparison thus was simpler for Melville than for Hawthorne, the burden of heroic legacy was no less intense; it was merely shifted to another era. Whereas Hawthorne's family had been most prominent in the seventeenth century, Melville's ancestors had performed acclaimed heroic service during the Revolution. Because Melville's maternal grandfather had commanded the successful defense of Fort Stanwix, and his paternal grandfather was the last surviving participant of the Boston Tea Party, Melville had good reason to inform Secretary of State Buchanan of "the services which so many of my family in many ways have rendered the country."[8] By visiting the Melvill estate, Broadhall, as a boy, and purchasing contiguous property when a man, Melville sought to link himself to the remnants of his family's Revolutionary heritage.[9]

Unlike Whig orators who argued that the Revolution had ended all need for political change, Melville admired the fathers' heroism while seeking a continuing revolution. However, the continuing revolution would have to proceed through admittedly lesser men. Although White-Jacket protests that the founding fathers merely provided the constitutional framework for a more glorious future, he also recognizes that Jefferson's heroic intellectual courage will be difficult to equal, impossible to surpass. Throughout Melville's works, Revolutionary Americans are repeatedly described as principled, self-reliant liberators who created institutions that release human potential. George Washington, Ethan Allen, and – to a much lesser extent – Grandfather Pierre become enlarged figures of a national mythology, men who possess the godlike combination of moral courage, physical stature, and Christian gentleness.

Melville shares his contemporaries' fondness for sculpting the founding fathers into *figurae* of Freedom. Ishmael informs us that "George Washington, too, stands high aloft on his towering main-mast in Baltimore, and like one of Hercules' pillars, his column marks that point of human grandeur beyond which few mortals will go." Even in a novel as disillusioning as *Israel Potter*, Melville praises "that fearless self-reliance and independence which conducted our forefathers to national freedom." As a class, the seemingly crude settlers of the Berkshires are elevated to the outsized stature of their leaders: "That they should have accomplished such herculean undertakings with so slight prospect of reward . . . gives us a significant hint of the temper of the men of the revolutionary era." Only the recurring Herculean note suggests Melville's preference for crude, creative labor rather than the statesmanly self-control of an Augustus Caesar.[10]

Whereas Hawthorne's storyteller walked away from the canal boat and returned home, Melville's regard for the future induced him to seek the true American spirit in the West. A six-month trip to Illinois in 1840 filled his mind with images of boundless prairies, leafy forests, and mighty rivers that were to recur throughout his writings and make him especially sympathetic to the scenic descriptions called for by literary nationalists of the Young America movement. No matter how violent or crude frontier life might still be, the land seemed to permit expansive self-fulfillment, and to offer the environs necessary for redemption to Adamic stature. Though Galena's lead mines provided no living, the deprivation was surely temporary. The national exhilaration of open expanses was so great that it led even the tempered Emerson of "Experience" (1844) to proclaim, "I am ready to die out of nature and be born again into this new yet unapproachable America I have found in the West."[11]

Although Melville imagined the American as a geographical and spiritual pioneer, the journey forward in space should be a journey backward in time. The restoration of paradise, the regeneration of man, the reaping of jubilee were the nation's aims. The White Steed of the Prairies, for instance, embodied "a most imperial and arch-angelical apparition of that unfallen, western world, which to the eyes of the old trappers and hunters *revived* the glories of those primeval times when Adam walked majestic as a god, bluff-bowed and fearless as this mighty steed."[12] While legend released Melville's latent nostalgia, he also accepted progressive economic reasons for the West's future greatness. Both in *Mardi* and in *Clarel*, he anticipated Frederick Jackson Turner's belief that the democratizing influence of the frontier would serve as America's safety valve for pressures of inequality building up in Eastern society.

To Melville, the republican polity and the Western land were necessary preconditions, but not determinants, of heroic traits in American man. If Eden were to be re-created, the expanse of virgin soil had to be settled by citizens who exemplified a democratic variant of Milton's "Paradise Within." When Ishmael asserts, "Columbus sailed over numberless unknown worlds to discover his one superficial western one," he reminds us that the deeper quest of an exemplary explorer was spiritual.[13] The "Paradise Within" that contemporary pioneers had to bring to the West was to consist of the heroic traits of Revolutionary fathers: magnanimity, physical courage, democratic politics, and Christian behavior, if not Christian belief. Born of Revolutionary rather than Calvinistic virtues, Melville's emerging American was to be a physically prepossessing libertarian, sprung from the kingly commons, utterly frank yet with a touch of the poet – a man, above all, who valued political freedom as a means toward community, toward establishing a fellowship of shared interests.

Wherever Melville found traces of this American spirit in contemporary life, he praised them. Reviewing *The California and Oregon Trail*, he singled out Henry Chatillon as an especially powerful characterization of the free, gallant, good-natured, and utterly competent Western trapper, and then concluded: "For this Henry Chatillon we feel a fresh and unbounded love." A few months later, Melville shaped Hawthorne into a Titan-like imaginative genius, imbued with the Western character, one of a future American fellowship of heroic artistic hearts. He saw Bulkington as an admirable and grand figure, not primarily because he was a sizable mountain man but because he aroused manly sociability in others. The courage of Northern soldiers attacking Fort Donelson was traced to their "vim from Western prairies won." Rolfe's friendly aplomb and honest skepticism were partially explained by the years he had spent as a trapper. Whereas Hawthorne sought to bind men and women in a magnetic chain of humanity from which chastened love could grow, Melville sought to liberate men to engage in a fellowship nearly independent of social context.[14]

Among praiseworthy American qualities, none was more important to Melville than frankness. Plain dealing between man and man, so rare in aristocratic Europe, was to develop in an unsettled land where the national polity encouraged it. The waning of feudal forms and the guaranteeing of individual rights had made manly directness possible upon a national scale: "For I hold it a verity, that even Shakespeare, was not a frank man to the uttermost. And, indeed, who in this intolerant Universe is, or can be? But the Declaration of Independence makes a difference." In tone as well as content, Melville's letters to Hawthorne display the ebullient, democratic frankness that Melville cherished. When Melville visited Hiram Powers's studio in Florence in 1858, he described Powers, a Cincinnati artisan turned sculptor, as an "open, plain man. Fine specimen of an American." Just as Melville's vision of male comradeship anticipated Whitman's "Calamus" poems, so Melville was to assert, like Whitman, that the horrors of Civil War had brought forth the best qualities of the American character. Observing "manly greatness" in fellow soldiers, Northern infantrymen and observing poets were able to "feel the bonds that draw" and realize that "Nothing can lift the heart of man / Like manhood in a fellow-man."[15]

Each facet of this heroic image – Revolutionary Patriot, Western pioneer, frank democrat – is touched with the innocence of the primitive. Grandfather Pierre is described as a childlike Titan; Ishmael's half-serious comparison of Queequeg to George Washington (unthinkable to a commemorative orator) characterizes both parties. Bulkington, Steelkilt, Pitch, and Rolfe, all of them Westerners, retain an ability to think deeply and independently, an ability that is explicitly disassociated from the bookish productions of the civilized intellect, and associated with the influence of their environs. Melville's democrats, from Jack Chase through Israel Potter to Billy Budd, seem to have obtained their democratic impulses from the most direct experience of life. Jack Chase can often be gaily literary, but it is questionable whether Israel or Billy is capable of intellectual abstraction, let alone of reading. Melville never devalues human simplicity, even the simplicity of a *naïf*, by branding it as mere credulity. Like the French woodchopper in *Walden*, Israel and Billy arouse both their creator's respect for instinctive virtue and his pity for their unknowing trust.

The primitivistic strain in Melville's image of American heroic character is partly attributable to his experience in the South Seas, as well as in Illinois. Having known the virtues of both the savage and the civilized states, Melville hoped that Americans, with their vast expanse of wilderness, might combine them. Among civilized Western peoples, Americans alone might still redevelop the bodily health, candor, and feelings of tribal brotherhood that Melville had known in the Marquesas. The metaphor that Ishmael finds appropriate for the core of a whole man is "one insular Tahiti, full of peace and joy." Although Melville fled from the barbaric cannibalism and religious practices of the Typees, he was deeply offended by Parkman's contempt for the American Indian as an inferior savage. The red man might be a political pagan, but he was still a man, and his culture was of considerable value. By insisting that "we are all of us – Anglo-Saxons, Dyaks, and Indians – sprung from one head, and made in one image. And if we regret this brotherhood now, we shall be forced to join hands hereafter," Melville reminded readers that traits considered primitive by Parkman were considered divine in Genesis. If the divinity common to Indian and Anglo-Saxon was to be utterly erased with the spread of civilization, the bonds of deepest "brotherhood" would be lost.[16]

Melville's resentment of Parkman's racism indicates a hope that the happier life of man's origin, now lost to European aristocracies, might in desirable measure be recovered in the unspoiled American Republic. In the valley of the Typees, Tommo shows us an Edenic agrarian community, a civilization without great wealth or poverty, without industrial machinery, without cities, courts of law, or police. Preservation of social order depends upon the individual's obeying the dictates of a universal moral law – a hope crucial to the libertarian premises of many contemporaries. Tommo notes: "There were no legal provisions whatever for the well-being and conservation of society, the enlightened end of civilized legislation." He then accounts for this utopian state of individual freedom by explaining that all members of the community voluntarily obey "that sort of tacit common-sense law which, say what they will of the inborn lawlessness of the human race, has its precepts graven on every breast." Tommo ultimately discovers that such freedom is an illusion, but he is deprived of his liberty because of the community's religious barbarism, not its social or economic mores. In all save religious customs, the Typees have extended equality, individual freedom, and limited government to their ultimate by staying behind rather than going ahead. When the garden proves to have no machine, Melville leads us to wonder whether Americans must not progress backward to achieve their political dreams.[17]

Among the many American readers of *Typee*, few could have shared Tommo's forthright approval of certain nonpolitical aspects of Polynesian life. The shared moral sense of the Typees depends upon cooperative communal labor, which in turn serves to break down the isolated competitiveness of family units, and shifts love of kindred into a "general love . . . where all were treated as brothers and sisters."[18] Only readers who felt themselves displaced from midcentury American domesticity could have welcomed such inferences, yet Melville was to develop them further. None of his solitary seekers, from Tommo through Rolfe, wishes finally to join a family; they yearn to know their paternity and then to create a community of free heroic hearts. His grandest characters – Taji, Ahab, Pierre – show that self-realization and spiritual growth depend upon breaking away from the domestic, familial pieties dear to contemporary American culture, even if death be the price. Sharing Oberon's rebellious desires, all three men prefer heroic suicide to a chastened return home.

In the valley of the Typees, communal fellowship and the moral sense depend upon retaining private property in goods, but abolishing private property in land. This combination prevents the human wrangling caused by boundary stones or locks:

> Whether the land of the valley was the joint property of its inhabitants, or whether it was parcelled out among a certain number of landed proprietors who allowed everyone to "squat" and "poach" as much as he or she pleased, I never could ascertain. At any rate, musty parchments and title deeds there were none on the island; and I am half inclined to believe that its inhabitants hold their broad valleys in fee simple from Nature herself; to have and to hold, so long as grass grows and water runs.[19]

Phrases such as "landed proprietors," "musty parchments and title deeds," and "fee simple," written in the autumn of 1845 by a young man from Lansingburgh, New York, were surely provoked by the Anti-Rent Wars, which were reaching their peak of violence in 1845 in counties around Albany.[20] Melville's evident distaste for manorial estates, apparent here and in *Pierre*, indicates his willingness to entertain the abolition of private property in land as a necessary element of the western New Israel. Such passages would have seemed dangerous to Webster and foolish to Hawthorne. If readers of *Typee* or *Pierre* ever perceived the implications of such remarks (the reviewers did not), Melville's suggestions would have been ill-received – by those who defended the landowners, by the many who argued for abolishment of leasehold contracts, and even by most of the tenants, who wished to own their own farms. Cooper's uncompromising defense of private property in his Anti-Rent trilogy (1845–6), despite his unwelcome praise for landlords, more closely reflected popular opinion on the issue.

Only in 1854, after Melville's expectation of a New Israel had largely faded, did he embody all of these ideal qualities of the American character in one grand culture hero. Ethan Allen, captor of Fort Ticonderoga, appears as a godlike figure, a Revolutionary Patriot who by sheer daring won liberty and individual equality under law for his fellows. Allen is as physically imposing as Samson, "a martial man of Patagonian stature." Huge, unkempt, costumed like an Indian and a backwoodsman, Allen represents natural man governed by inner moral law and utterly scornful of parchments. His instinctual abilities to lead men in a libertarian cause elicit awe from his English tormentors and love from all sympathizers. By insisting that the leader of the Green Mountain Boys embodies the truly American, Western spirit, Melville combines the Revolutionary father from New England with the contemporary Western pioneer:

> Allen seems to have been a curious combination of a Hercules, a Joe Miller, a Bayard, and a Tom Hyer; had a person like the Belgian giants; mountain music in him like a Swiss; a heart plump as Coeur de Lion's. Though born in New England, he exhibited no trace of her character. He was frank; bluff; companionable as a Pagan; convivial; a Roman; hearty as a harvest. His spirit was essentially Western; and herein is his peculiar Americanism; for the Western spirit is, or will yet be (for no other is, or can be), the true American one.

Traits of folk heroes from Europe and America here melt into one Western hero. The gigantic laborer, jokester, chivalrous knight, and wrestler fuse into an ingenuous, wholly competent good fellow whose skills as a Yankee actor are momentarily forgotten. The gallantry of Bayard is redirected toward democratic ends; sheer physical strength somehow blends into Western conviviality. Though pagan in manner, the essential American spirit remains Christian at heart. Partly a Revolutionary gentleman, partly a medieval knight, and partly a sociable pioneer, Allen devotes all of his heroic qualities to national service. As a type of the national character, he resembles Hawthorne's neo-Puritans in only one crucial detail: He promises more virtues than any culture could deliver.[21]

For Melville's purposes, the New England deist he encountered in the *Narrative of Colonel Ethan Allen's Captivity* had to be refashioned to represent "the unshackled, democratic spirit of Christianity in all things." Although the historical man declared, "I was a full blooded Yankee,"[22] while speaking in proper latinate abstractions, Melville portrays Allen as a backwoods roarer. One comparative detail will illustrate the Allen that Melville seeks to vivify. In his *Narrative*, Allen referred to "the doleful scene of inhumanity exercised by Gen. Sir Wm. Howe, and the army under his command, towards the prisoners taken on Long Island, on the 27th day of August, 1776, sundry of whom were in an inhuman and barbarous manner, murdered after they had surrendered their arms."[23] Melville's Ethan Allen calls Howe "that toad-hearted king's lick-spittle of a scarlet poltroon; the vilest wriggler in God's worm-hole below!"[24]

Ethan Allen is very like the heroic national figure that Whitman was to create, one year later, in the first edition of *Leaves of Grass*. "Walt Whitman, an American, one of the roughs," singer of liberty and equality, is a huge protean self who incorporates all European and American blood strains. Scornful of books, often speaking in metaphoric slang, Whitman's persona celebrates the vitality of nature, the union of soul and body. He reverences "The friendly and flowing savage" in himself, yet insists that his truest identity is Christ. Phrases such as "Behavior lawless as snowflakes . . . words simple as grass . . . uncombed head and laughter and naivete" could all, except for the last word, apply equally well to Ethan Allen. Combining savagery, Christianity, democratic values and immense physical energy, Whitman's imagined self and Melville's Ethan Allen are embodiments of a Western spirit claimed as a national spirit. Of the differences between them, their placement in time is the most telling. By an unrelenting process of projection, Whitman portrays an ideal self that is latent in all of us, yet sure to emerge. Ethan Allen may be invoked as a future Western spirit, but he actually appears as a historical personality bound in chains; the other Americans in *Israel Potter* embody his virtues only in perverted forms.[25]

In the fictions written just before midcentury, Melville did not envision the spirit of Ethan Allen bound in chains. For whatever reasons – association with the Young America movement, a touch of Manifest Destiny, or a projection of his own creative energies – the years in which *Redburn* and *White-Jacket* were written, and *Moby-Dick* begun, were a time of an almost unqualified national faith. Melville delighted in portraying shrewd American sailors aboard the *Neversink* and the *Pequod* outsailing and outthinking the British, French, and Germans. We are invited to share White-Jacket's ridicule of the Brazilian emperor's foppish pretensions. Wellingborough Redburn may be a gentleman's son gulled of his wages, but his seamanship earns him the grudging acceptance of the *Highlander*'s crew. Jack Chase is an Englishman, but his political allegiances and hearty sociality are republican qualities; he clearly belongs to the Columbia of the Spirit that Melville, like Emerson, was ready to anticipate.

Evidence outside Melville's fiction shows that, during these years, he was quite capable of cheeky, self-conscious Americanism. Like Cooper before him and Twain after him, but unlike Hawthorne, Melville was ready to play the American traveler's role of practical, democratic Jonathan laughing at the Old World. He described Albert as "the prince of whales" and Victoria as "an amiable domesticated woman" who needs "Q. Rowland's Calydore for clarifying the complexion." He assured himself that the American side of a silly, half-century cultural quarrel was correct: "The old ruins & arch were glorious – but the river Rhine is not the Hudson." And he knew how to react to Scott's son-in-law, J. G. Lockhart, who, even before Cooper's attack upon him, had seemed to literary Americans a perfect example of the ridiculous, autocratic Tory. Melville found Lockhart to be a "half galvanized ghost," "a customer who was full of himself and expected great homage," "a thorough-going Tory & fish-blooded Churchman & conservative, & withal, editor of the Quarterly." And yet Melville, like Cooper, Twain, and Hawthorne, also felt the classless American's fascination for, if not envy of, European aristocracy. Melville refused a visit to the Duke of Rutland's castle with great difficulty, and noted in his journal, "I should much like to know what the highest English aristocracy really & practically is."[26]

Just as early nineteenth-century American writers commonly project personal hopes upon their nation, so they associate literary and national promise. Adopting the role of poet-priest leads Emerson and Whitman to reflect on the nation's spiritual prospects. Once Hawthorne has provided Melville a model of the American writer, Melville can express his most ebullient Americanism. When he calls for "those writers who breathe that unshackled, democratic spirit of Christianity in all things, which now takes the practical lead in this world, though at the same time led by ourselves – us Americans," he claims his cultural vision for his entire people by positing a literary spirit that propels them both.[27]

Such literary energies are assumed to be good, not only because Nathaniel Hawthorne has proved them so, but because they are conveyed through such metaphors as the "broad prairies" and "roaring Niagara" of the author's soul. Recognizing that good spirits need no shackling, Melville is freed to delight in metaphors of virtually unlimited size. The indigenous American genius is to be a large man with a large heart, one who scorns graceful elegance in favor of imperfect grandeur, and who delivers an original literature, "though at first it be crabbed and ugly as our own pine knots."[28] Like Ethan Allen, the American writer can possess both a democratic spirit that exhorts to practical action and a Christian spirit that demands creedless charity for all. Melville's decision to pose as a Virginian living in the Green Mountain State is a stratagem for inclusion rather than secrecy; his essay can thereby illustrate America's federated literary spirit, just as Ethan Allen incorporates all bloodstreams within one expansive self.

In certain passages of Melville's review, he very nearly accepts the Emersonian faith that America will become what its literary genius imagines. When he claims, "The world is as young to-day as when it was created; and this Vermont morning dew is as wet to my feet, as Eden's dew to Adam's," he denies the past any influence upon the present, thereby implying that, in America, citizens and writers can at any time create themselves anew. The far-away truths of a Shakespeare will henceforth be uttered only by "an American, a man who is bound to carry republican progressiveness into Literature as well as into Life." The final incorporation of all Americans into the one spirit of a master genius permits Melville to extend the prospect for the national character to its extremity: "Call him an American and have done, for you cannot say a nobler thing of him."[29]

Melville's heroic national ideal raised, as he well knew, numerous problems. A figure like Ethan Allen would have seemed tempestuous and uncompromising in any Victorian parlor, including Melville's parlors at Arrowhead and 103 Fourth Avenue. Allen represents a precarious combination of possibly incompatible virtues: frank but not naive, natural but not savage, democratic but not egalitarian. By reverencing men like Ethan Allen, Melville calls for perpetual self-re-creation through a heroic national spirit – a continuum difficult to maintain. Allen's Christian conduct may be combined with democratic principles, but Christianity is not easily practiced on the frontier, where democracy as an institutional polity is quite absent.

The narrator of "The Apple-Tree Table" whimsically describes himself as a waverer between the opinions of Cotton Mather and of Burton's Christianius Democritus. Whenever man's condition seems to confirm the assumptions of Cotton Mather, confidence in the liberating West, in a New Israel, and in American innocence becomes suspect, if not foolish. Although the prairies might be an "unfallen western world," man's entrance into earth's paradise will be likely to corrupt it. The Puritan conception of New Israel was selective. To democratize it, to declare that all may enter, all bloodstreams contribute, requires that one view the immigrant European as a potential Adam; this is an imaginative feat that Redburn, observing the plight of stolid immigrants aboard the *Highlander*, finds difficult to perform. Both in *Redburn* and in *White-Jacket*, Melville eulogizes America as an Eden of confident, Western Adams. The known experiences of Redburn and White-Jacket suggest, however, that a loss of confidence and innocence is both necessary and desirable.

"Hawthorne and His Mosses" contains inconsistencies that derive from the same divided vision. When Melville thinks of Hawthorne as the representative American genius, he praises him for possessing a Western, democratic heart. When Melville looks directly at Hawthorne's short stories, literary genius is suddenly associated with the power of blackness. Whether the great national writer should look backward toward the power of Calvinism or forward to republican progressivism is never clarified. According to the terms Melville establishes, however, it is not possible to do both. The Revolutionary spirit is too Promethean to allow for the kind of compromise between Puritan origins and republican gentlemanliness that Hawthorne tried to work out in the figures of Sam Adams or Franklin Pierce, Ernest or Holgrave.

THE CHRONIC MALADY

An alternative American future had been imagined before *Redburn*, *White-Jacket*, and "Hawthorne and His Mosses" were written. When Taji set off into the Mardian archipelago in search of Yillah, Melville's writing entered upon an uncharted expanse of autonomous self-creation aptly called "the world of mind."[30] Freed from literary strictures, Melville was equally freed to express skeptical attitudes toward accepted cultural prophecy. In the chapters describing the Northern, Southern, and capital regions of Vivenza (the United States), Melville's satire is pointedly directed against the presumption, shared by himself among many others, that America is the world's political messiah.

In the nation's capital, the Western spirit proves to be the truly American spirit, but the expressions of Western temperament are neither free, frank, democratic, nor manly. Most members of Congress appear to be primitives of the tobacco-chewing, teeth-picking kind, half of them asleep and the others striking poses. Governmental business is transacted in the congressional basement during squalid feasts in which conviviality reigns only because legislators are snatching manly portions of the public trust. Nationalistic rhetoric has become a parody of itself. Neither Melville's appreciation for assertive speech nor his belonging to a "Democratic family . . . which has done much for its party"[31] precludes his ridiculing Democratic Senator William Allen of Ohio (Alanno of Hio-Hio) as a crazy imperialist and word-drunk orator who works up jingoistic feelings by appealing to false fears of an aristocratic conspiracy.[32] Everywhere in Washington, the travelers find that manly patriotism expresses itself in bragging about the size of American beards, thighs, trees, mountains, and rivers. In a scene that recalls Cooper's *Home As Found*, Melville introduces a figure named Znobbi, an immigrant European turned democratic hustler, who uses such Jack Cade–like phrases as "all Kings here – all equal. Every thing's in common" (p. 521) as a means of picking his listener's pocket. Like Steadfast Dodge or Aristabulus Bragg, Znobbi shows how vulnerable a democratic polity is to egalitarian demagoguery.

In *Mardi*, in the last paragraph of *White-Jacket*, in "The House-top," and in *Billy Budd*, Melville expresses scorn and fear for the destructive upheaval that accompanies political revolution. More enthusiastic in support of libertarian revolutionary principles than Hawthorne, he is no less wary of the illiberal violence necessary to promote them. When the Mardian travelers visit northeastern Vivenza, they discover that the heritage of 1776 has made it difficult for some Americans to distinguish between needed reforms and unneeded violence. The revolutions of 1848, described in images of volcanic fire,[33] are gleefully welcomed by Northerners, simply because they have been undertaken in the name of liberty and equality. Such a situation prompts Melville to protest that American greatness should be defined not by political freedom, but by the human qualities that freedom might create:

> It is not the prime end, and chief blessing, to be politically free. And freedom is only good as a means; is no end in itself. Nor, did man fight it out against his masters to the haft, not then, would he uncollar his neck from the yoke. A born thrall to the last, yelping out his liberty, he still remains a slave unto Oro [God]. [Pp. 527–8]

Northerners have forgotten what Ishmael was always to know ("Who aint a slave?") and Ahab was gradually to recognize ("I would be free as air; and I'm down in the whole world's books").[34] Their fundamental delusion is that liberty was somehow born within the nineteenth-century American's character. Lest futuristic Vivenzans forget the ancient origins of American independence, New Yorker Melville cites New England's argument that the Revolution was fought primarily to maintain Pilgrim tradition: "Your nation enjoyed no little independence before your Declaration declared it. Your ancient pilgrims fathered your liberty; and your wild woods harbored the nursling" (p. 528).

Melville's yearning to envision an America peopled by Northern democratic spirits, made congenial in a Western paradise, repeatedly left sectional and regional problems out of account. His readiness to imagine the worst of Southern slavery in *Mardi* and then, in the following year, to write unqualified hymns to the democratic New Israel illustrates the antebellum American's need to repress grave issues by imagining one's own region's merits as the nation's norm. To Melville, slavery may be the South's sin, but it originates in the human exercise of patriarchal power. Because the brutality of Southern overseers is maintained through the hypocrisies of planters and politicians, he bluntly confronts the inconsistency between Jeffersonian creed and Southern fact: "In this re-publi-can-land-all-men-are-born-free-and-equal . . . Except-the-tribe-of-Hamo" (pp. 512–13). In the mind of a Calhounite named Nulli, owning slaves is a constitutional freedom, and imprisoning any traveler who protests slavery will merely protect one's free state. The hypocrisies of slavery are similarly apparent to Redburn, who, observing free blacks in Liverpool, comments, "In some things, we Americans leave to other countries the carrying out of the principle that stands at the head of our Declaration of Independence."[35]

Only when projecting the nation's future in the North's image is Melville able to disregard the potential danger of such ironies.

Searching for a humane and practicable policy toward slavery, the travelers debate extensively but arrive at no solution. When Yoomy enthusiastically calls for abolitionists to support a slave rebellion, Nulli prophetically declares, "The first blow struck for them, dissolves the union of Vivenza's vales" (p. 533). Among the travelers, Babbalanja best understands the historical causes of chattel slavery, and it is he who, sharply disagreeing with Yoomy, says, "Better present woes for some, than future woes for all" (p. 534). All of the travelers, including King Media, deplore slavery on religious and political grounds, yet none of them, after hearing Babbalanja's comments, can suggest any workable remedy for the South other than the Hunker Democrat's remedy of time. In the 1870s Melville was to create two troubled Civil War veterans of Southern birth, Ungar and Jack Gentian, who even with the advantage of hindsight could find no political solution for their region's peculiar institution. Nothing in Melville's later writings contradicts Babbalanja's unwilling admission: "It can not be, that misery is perpetually entailed; though, in a land proscribing primogeniture, the first-born and last of Hamo's tribe must still succeed to all their sires' wrongs" (p. 535).

Melville's most worrisome doubts about America are expressed in the sardonic commentary of an anonymous scroll read to a throng of excitable Northern democrats.[36] At first, the author of the scroll reaffirms the familiar tribute to Young America as "a fine, florid youth, full of fiery impulse, and hard to restrain; his strong hand nobly championing his heart" (p. 526). Because rebellious youths often settle into compromised adulthood, however, the course of an American's life will probably prove to be a cyclical rather than linear development: "He who hated oppressors, is become an oppressor himself" (p. 526). The sheer will to go ahead provides no defense against the inevitability of aging.

The author of the scroll anticipates that political abstractions sacrosanct to the crowd may work toward unexpected ends. Subverting the hackneyed metaphor of the melting pot, he predicts Tocquevillean leveling and hints of a flood: "Republics are as vast reservoirs, draining down all streams to one level; and so, breeding a fullness which can not remain full, without overflowing" (p. 525). Because he mistrusts America's unthinking faith in the merits of the franchise, he reminds the crowd that true freedom is a quality of the mind, not a political right created by paper constitutions. (To him, the Declaration of Independence does not in fact "make a difference.") Criticizing the expansionist tendency to project the self into all of space and time, he distinguishes between individual freedom and the "freedom to filch" neighboring territories (p. 529). His most effective weapon is repeatedly calling his listeners "Sovereign-Kings." Through this two-word taunt, he probes at a problem of national self-definition: However much a democratic man may delight in imagining his own aggrandizement, equal individuals cannot all be sovereign.

The author of the scroll may accept the well-worn analogy of the American and Roman republics, but he insists upon its unwelcome end – the cataclysm that Webster had heatedly denied. America, like Rome, is likely to fall to its own imperialistic ventures and collapse through overreaching. The national totem of the eagle, once Roman and now American, should perhaps have been a bloody, rapacious hawk. This rather odd prophecy is subtly reaffirmed in *Moby-Dick*. Melville recalls Livy's story of an eagle that foretold Tarquin's kingship by snatching away, and then replacing, Tarquin's cap; in the following sentences, a hawk suddenly swoops down, carries off Ahab's hat, but then disappears.[37] The true sign of this transformation can appropriately appear only in the last chapter, when Tashtego nails a hawk's wing to the flag and mainmast of the sinking *Pequod*.

The author of the scroll is not concerned with laws, institutions, or political measures. He argues by metaphors, and all of his metaphors (American as a boy, beehive, reservoir, or hawk) reveal that his skepticism is based upon his sense of national character. Convinced that American innocence is potentially dangerous, he justifies his hardheaded political opinions by reminding listeners that they neglect the Puritan view of man at their peril: "And though all evils may be assuaged; all evils can not be done away. For evil is the chronic malady of the universe; and checked in one place, breaks forth in another" (p. 529). This particular malady then serves to justify the author's sardonic conclusion that republicanism may in fact destroy itself: "And the grand error of your nation, sovereign-kings! seems this: – the conceit that Mardi is now in the last scene of the last act of her drama; and that all preceding events were ordained, to bring about the catastrophe you believe to be at hand – a universal and permanent Republic" (p. 525). The startling appearance of the word "catastrophe" in this context is an ironic variant of a familiar rhetorical mode. To release civic energies by suspending the nation on the brink of "a universal and permanent republic" had been John Louis O'Sullivan's way of justifying predictions of a secular millennium.

When Melville exclaimed, "How profound, nay appalling, is the moral evoked by 'Earth's Holocaust,' " he may have felt gratified by similarities between Hawthorne's story and the scroll he had inserted into *Mardi*.[38] Like the diabolic figure who appears at the end of Hawthorne's tale, the author of the scroll is a skeptical Calvinist who has the courage to confront a crowd of ultra-democratic reformers. Sweeping the best of the past away with the worst, both crowds assume that the good of the inner man is sufficient for all things. For a dramatic moment, the solitary skeptics gain great authority while reminding the mob that they are depriving themselves of everything save the chronic blackness of the human heart. Both speakers try to force their audience to consider that, if evil is inherent in human nature rather than political systems, republicans will merely give evil its freest reign. In Hawthorne's tale, the stunned crowd remains silent while the ashes accumulate; in *Mardi*, however, the scroll is torn to bits by enraged Northern democrats.

Despite the courage and force of their solitary figures' words, neither Hawthorne nor Melville is prepared unequivocally to sanction them. Hawthorne's gloomy prophet is repellent in person and in manner, and the author of the destroyed scroll remains unknown. Melville does not know or will not divulge whether he places any faith in the scroll's content. If the author is Babbalanja, the reader must recognize that the scroll's opinions are those of a decidedly Melvillean thinker, but if Media is its author, one could reasonably dismiss the scroll as royalist propaganda.

Although Melville postpones settlement of the question of authorship for five hundred years, Media seems the more likely possibility. Melville tells us that the scroll is "too dogmatic and conservative" (p. 530) for Babbalanja, but provides for Media only the lame, debatable excuse that the scroll is too boldly written to suit a tactful demigod. We should also remember that, throughout the entire political section of *Mardi* (chapters 145–68), Melville's satire is lighthearted, and that the ridicule of Dominora (England) and Verdanna (Ireland) is sharper than the ridicule of America. The contrasting connotations of the names Vivenza and Porpheero (Europe) are favorable to New World politics. Before Melville mocked the idea of the political messiah, he described Vivenza through the following similes: "a young tropic tree . . . laden down with greenness," "St. John . . . with prophetic voice crying to the nations from the wilderness," and "a young Messiah, to whose discourse the bearded rabbis bowed" (p. 472). Even the author of the scroll expresses the national confidence he criticizes: "But, as in stars you have written it on the welkin, sovereign-kings! you are a great and glorious people. And verily, yours is the best and happiest land under the sun" (p. 528). Yillah is not to be found in Vivenza, but Yoomy is right to say that, among political kingdoms, she will exist "there or nowhere" (p. 501).

Doubts expressed openly in Melville's portrait of Vivenza emerge only as self-contradictions in *Redburn* and *White-Jacket*. In both works, Melville's assurances about the New Jerusalem appear in an exactly similar context. A young American sailor, experiencing the autocratic tyranny of the Old World, associates paradise with the New World and longs to return to America. Melville approves his characters' nationalism by expressing their assurances about the New Israel through the auctorial voice. On the one hand, Melville hymns Americans as godly innocents; on the other, he associates maturity with journeying away from America and discarding a white jacket. More than any other works in the Melville canon, *Redburn* and *White-Jacket* associate evil with exterior oppression (militarism, imperialism, capitalism) and virtue with exterior conditions of freedom (the Declaration of Independence, the American land).[39] And yet, in the very midst of these microcosmic ships Melville places Bland and Jackson, two Cains afloat whose evil natures cannot be explained by merely external conditions.

Melville's Dickensian description of Liverpool as an inferno of urban poverty and human neglect leads him to exalt the promise of the New World. At the very moment Melville invokes divine judgment upon the Old World, however, his Calvinistic heritage prevents his exempting America from the conditions of Liverpool:

> Adam and Eve! If indeed ye are yet alive and in heaven, may it be no part of your immortality to look down upon the world ye have left. For as all these sufferers and cripples are as much your family as young Abel, so, to you, the sight of the world's woes would be a parental torment indeed.[40]

Twice in these sentences, Melville writes "the world" rather than "the Old World," yet the passage occurs only a few pages after he has told us of earth's certain paradise in the West. At the end of the tale, the issue remains unresolved. Redburn rightly extols the beauties of harbor and city, of the Purple Palisades and the shoreline's "glorious green" (p. 300), but he also soon learns of severe unemployment problems. The call to joy in such a sentence as "Hurra! hurra! and ten thousand times hurra! down goes our old anchor, fathoms down into the free and independent Yankee mud, one handful of which was now worth a broad manor in England" (p. 301) becomes suspect as soon as one considers the ironies of fastening an anchor into free mud.

White-Jacket only compounds the question whether America can be a separable paradise. Melville is anxious to distinguish the despotism, oppression, and depravity aboard an American man-of-war from the advance guard of youthful pioneers on the American land. The American navy, he assures us, is only a feudal blot upon a democratic America:

> Our institutions claim to be based upon broad principles of political liberty and equality. Whereas, it would hardly affect one iota the condition on shipboard of an American man-of-war's man, were he transformed to the Russian Navy and made a subject of the Czar.
>
> As a sailor, he shares none of our civil immunities; the law of our soil in no respect accompanies the national floating timbers grown thereon, and to which he clings as his home. For him our Revolution was in vain; to him our Declaration of Independence is a lie. [P. 144]

Melville also insists that the detested Articles of War derive, not from Americans or any American tradition, but from tyrannical British codes of an obsolete past; flogging, for example, is to be regarded as "a lingering trace of the worst times of a barbarous feudal aristocracy" (p. 146). At the same time, however, Melville's tendency to seek a static emblem for the order of the world causes him to see his frigate as "The World in a Man-of-War." The last chapter assures us that the inscrutability, militarism, and autocracy of our battleship world are unending; earlier, however, he has declared, "Who knows that, when men-of-war shall be no more, 'White-Jacket' may not be quoted to show to the people in the Millennium what a man-of-war was?" (p. 282). If Melville changed his ship's actual name (the *United States*) to the *Neversink* in order to separate Jeffersonian America from the Articles of War, his allegorizing ultimately defeats his purpose.

Naiveté was perhaps implicit in Melville's early ideas of the American character, but greed of the kind embodied in Judge Pyncheon was not. The gold rush raised the possibility that many Americans would journey west only if the New Jerusalem held forth the promise of lucre. Sailing along Kolumbo's western shore, the Mardian travelers hear a goldrusher's song that proclaims, "But joyful now, with eager eye, / Fast to the Promised Land we fly" (p. 546). Through metaphors Thoreau was to use in "Life without Principle," Melville pictures the prospector as a hunter who, mistaking material gold for spiritual, digs his way into a golden hell without recognizing that "gold is the only poverty."[41] This image of the Western gold hunter evidently lingered in Melville's mind. Among his undated "Miscellaneous Poems" is a terse, direct lyric, "Gold in the Mountain":

> Gold in the mountain
> And gold in the glen,
> And greed in the heart,
> Heaven having no part,
> And unsatisfied men.[42]

After completing *White-Jacket*, Melville was to explore the implications of this poem in far greater depth. Captain Ahab, himself the most unmaterial of Americans, knows that the souls of most New Bedford sailors may be bound by transfixing a gold doubloon to the mainmast.

Until Melville recast *Moby-Dick*, his ideas of national destiny were expressed as oratorical insertions that proved to be as improvisational and open-ended as the America they create. The shadowy writer of the Vivenza scroll is no less liable to the charge of masking fantasy as prophecy than is Redburn or White-Jacket. The two visions, however, have almost nothing in common. Unlike Hawthorne's steady attempt to imbed notions of national character in historical contexts, Melville's early speculations about America display the self-contradictory energies Tocqueville anticipated in democratic literature:

> Style will frequently be fantastic, incorrect, overburdened and loose, almost always vehement and bold . . . Literary performances will bear marks of an untutored and rude vigour of thought, frequently of great variety and singular fecundity . . . American readers require strong and rapid emotions, startling passages, truths or errors brilliant enough to raise them up and plunge them at once, as if by violence, into the midst of the subject.[43]

Although all prophetic utterance has these qualities, prophecy for a nation with few traditions save its own great expectations, written by an author who would dare to write *Mardi*, must display them to the fullest.

Considered together, these passages define tensions and problems of Melville's cultural thought, but they are not integrated into a fictive action that gives them resonance. While writing *White-Jacket*, Melville discovered literary means of making a ship serve as an emblem of the world. One year later, he discovered means of making a whaler an emblem of national culture. Because of its thirsty federated seamen, multinational crew, and racial hierarchies, the *Pequod* resembles the American ship of state on its pioneering voyage through time.[44] The *Bachelor's Delight* and the *Fidèle* would also possess a symbolic national dimension, though one of very different import. Pierre and Israel Potter were explicitly to represent the Young American. Whereas Melville's first five novels offer abstract, untested ideas about American culture, his later fictions immerse representative Americans in microcosmic worlds that have a decided national reference. Beginning with *Moby-Dick*, we must seek Melville's sense of national destiny, not in extractable passages, but in the experience of his characters.

7

MIRROR MEN

For every seeing soul there are two absorbing facts, I and the Abyss.

Emerson, *Journal* (1866)

When Melville wrote Hawthorne his expansive letter of praise for *The House of the Seven Gables*, he began with graceful compliments on Hawthorne's romance, moved on to consider the "tragicalness of human thought" embodied in Hawthorne's literary spirit, and then ended with a long tribute to the human courage of which "we mortals" are capable. This process of turning ever inward, a kind of mental ingression common to many of Melville's letters, did not escape his own notice. Toward the end of his next letter to Hawthorne, he acknowledged: "I talk all about myself, and this is selfishness and egotism. Granted. But how help it? I am writing to you; I know little about you, but something about myself. So I write about myself, – at least to you." To proceed imaginatively from the world without to the world within is the complement, not the opposite, of imaginative projection. Projection extends a self upon the universe without; ingression claims that the outer universe lies within; but both processes fuse inner and outer worlds rather than distinguishing them.[1]

Melville sought literary fraternity of feeling so intensely that he once asserted a union of souls through sacramental metaphors: "Whence come you, Hawthorne? By what right do you drink from my flagon of life? And when I put it to my lips – lo, they are yours and not mine. I feel that the Godhead is broken up like the bread at the Supper, and that we are the pieces." We should recall, however, that this extraordinary statement was written after Melville had received Hawthorne's letter praising *Moby-Dick*. This fact suggests that Nathaniel Hawthorne, the American master spirit, and fictional portrayals of it had all become parts of one continuum in Melville's mind. When Melville formulated ways in which his spirit was at one with Hawthorne's, he described traits we find in Ahab, Ishmael, and Pierre. Through all three characters, as well as Nathaniel Hawthorne, Melville exalted the metaphysical seeker who would assault Heaven in order to find truth and to treat with "all Powers upon an equal basis."[2]

The place Melville hoped his admired seekers might occupy is as important as their aims. The man who insists upon "sovereignty in myself" and the man who says "No! in Thunder" – all such men will find themselves "in the happy condition of judicious, unincumbered travellers in Europe; they cross the frontiers into Eternity with nothing but a carpet-bag, – that is to say, the Ego."[3] Recognizing that Americans are accumulating so much baggage that many can no longer get through the customhouse, Melville associates the happy man with the American traveler in Europe. The true advantages of travel, however, have nothing to do with the customary acquiring of cultural knowledge and artifacts. To be happy is to be an utterly unencumbered spiritual pioneer. Melville's traveler is in no particular place and is surrounded by nothing, because he carries in himself the only essential piece of baggage – his ego. To be great is to move through this formless world toward eternity while crossing undefinable frontiers. In describing America's master literary spirit, Melville is in effect idealizing a disembodied mind that, belonging nowhere, moves throughout vacant space and infinite time.

The man who crosses placeless frontiers into eternity with only an ego is not likely to discover worlds separate from himself. The novels Melville was then writing show that he was acutely aware of this problem. Ahab and Pierre try to free themselves from the past, cross every spiritual and physical frontier, and perceive ultimate truth in the void they then face. Here, too, however, Melville is fortunate in recognizing that Hawthorne has already confronted the consequences of such a search. Among the many pieces in *Mosses from an Old Manse*, Melville selects a short, seemingly innocuous sketch for special commendation: "What, to all readers, can be more charming than the piece entitled 'Monsieur du Miroir,' and to a reader at all capable of fully fathoming it, what, at the same time, can possess more mystical depth of meaning? – yes, there he sits and looks at me, – this 'shape of mystery,' this 'identical Monsieur du Miroir.' " Evidently, Melville recognizes that he, like Hawthorne, is engaged in "chasing [his] own shadow through a chaos." As thinkers or writers, Ahab, Ishmael, and Pierre are to do the same.[4]

THAT APOSTOLIC LANCER, BROTHER JONATHAN

One of the wondrous achievements of *Moby-Dick* is Melville's ability to entertain many conflicting views of his subjects without allowing contradiction to result in a suffocating sense of ambiguity or skepticism.

His treatment of national character and national myth is no exception. Melville's Yankees have the traits of cunning peddlers (Peter Coffin, Bildad) and of green Jonathans (Ishmael himself); the physical power of the Westerner takes the forms of inspirational goodwill (Bulkington), of stubbornness provoked to murderous rage (Steelkilt), and of a careless profligacy (the Canallers). Melville celebrates the size, technological expertise, and heroic courage of American whalemen, but also provides his reader a convincing critique of the exploitation and waste of American industry. At different moments of the narrative, Melville persuades us that these whalemen are heroes, victims, competent workmen, sharks who are capable of great humanity, and divine democrats who act like beasts. The cumulative effect is to make us recognize that the whaling man is all of these and more.

As the novel progresses, Melville focuses our attention upon the relationship between Ishmael as narrator and Ahab as actor. Although these two figures embody Melville's deepest feelings about the American character, he never allows us to forget that Starbuck, Stubb, and Flask represent other alternatives. The gams remind us that the *Pequod* represents only one view of the ship of state; the crazy religiosity of the *Jeroboam*, the mindlessly happy prosperity of the *Bachelor*, and the humanitarian piety of the *Rachel* all have their sources in contemporary American culture, just as the *Pequod* does. Melville's book is so comprehensive in its scope, so balanced in its attitudes, that any interpretation of it, including this one, must oversimplify. Poised between the hypothetical millennialism of *White-Jacket* and the pervasive skepticism of *The Confidence-Man, Moby-Dick* holds contradictions in suspension without reaching impulsively after ultimate certainties, or denying that they might be obtained.

The persistency with which Melville applies images of the American prairies to the whale and the sea reflects the important cultural fact that the American of 1850 saw his nation taking possession of two frontiers simultaneously.[5] Ishmael describes sailors as pioneers, the whale's forehead as "The Prairie," and rolling billows as grassy Western glades. In the "Extracts," Melville quotes Obed Macey's belief that the sea is "a green pasture where our children's grand-children will go for bread."[6] The green pasture has a way of masking the white devil, however. Because the white whale serves, on one level, as a symbol of untamed natural force, Nantucketers turn him into a legend they seek to destroy.[7] By their very indefiniteness, the sea prairie and the white whale shadow forth heartless voids and immensities that man cannot abide. They represent Melville's equivalent for the open and limitless vacancy, "the Abyss," which surrounds an Emersonian psyche. *Moby-Dick* thus conveys a fear of wilderness that Melville, in previous works, had been able only to assert: When Babbalanja had contemplated the Vivenzans' continent, he could merely say, "Here your foes are forests, struck down with bloodless maces."[8]

Twentieth-century readers are likely to slight Melville's exultation over the American's bloody conquest of his frontiers. Ishmael relishes statistics proving the superiority of American whalemen, and devotes a chapter to hymning the enterprising spirit of Nantucketers – those Alexanders who, conquering the world in ever-widening circles, know that the sea is their "plantation" (p. 98). Ishmael describes Nantucketers in accord with his cherished national image; the whale ship is "the pioneer" who "at last eventuated the liberation of Peru, Chile, and Bolivia from the yoke of Old Spain, and the establishment of the eternal democracy in those parts" (p. 153). The whalemen in the Spouter Inn have the natural energies of Melvillean Westerners: "a brown and brawny company, with bosky beards; an unshorn, shaggy set, all wearing monkey jackets for morning gowns" (p. 57). Throughout his book, Ishmael serves as the advocate for whalemen, elevating them into medieval knights or epic heroes, describing in fond detail the immense practical skill evident in whaling operations, and dwelling on the sheer size of the whale itself.[9]

As an emblem for the American ship of state, however, the *Pequod* more often resembles an industrial sweatshop than the free ways of pioneering. Although the term "capitalism" was not current in 1850, Ishmael provides a thorough analysis of the procuring, manufacturing, and marketing of a natural and presumably national resource. Aboard the *Pequod*, butchery, waste, and indifference to worker but not to product are as apparent as technological efficiency. Ahab is not so absorbed in metaphysics as to be unaware that "the permanent constitutional condition of the manufactured man . . . is sordidness" (p. 285). Characters such as Flask, who measures Moby-Dick by monetary value, and the carpenter, an unreflecting factotum who mutters, "I do as I do" (p. 665), lend substance to Ahab's opinion. As one unit in an economic system, the *Pequod* is a manufactory owned by absentee Yankee capitalists, commanded by a despotic manager, and operated by Yankee knights who transmit orders to multinational workers through black, Indian, and Polynesian squires. Observing tiny Flask sitting atop the gigantic shoulders of Daggoo, Ishmael comments that, in the American military, merchant marine, and engineering corps, "the native American liberally provides the brains, the rest of the world as generously supplying the muscles" (p. 166). By appealing to hierarchies of command, and by sheer force of will, Ahab turns all his seamen save Ishmael and Starbuck into mechanical cogs turned by larger cogs. Ishmael may be whaling's "advocate," but he is equally right to complain that the Fates assigned him "this shabby part of a whaling voyage" (p. 29).

Despite his ponderings of fate and predestination, Ishmael gradually perceives that both the *Pequod* as a manufactory and Ahab as its manager can only prove self-destructive. It is he who notes the irony that the whaleman feeds upon the creature that feeds his lamp, and he who finds the sight of sharks devouring their own disembowelments to be morbidly fascinating. Only after extended consideration does Ishmael wrongly predict that the sperm whale, unlike the plains buffalo, cannot be slaughtered to the verge of extinction. Nor is it accidental that Ishmael finally and firmly resolves to condemn Ahab's quest while observing the climactic moment of the manufacturing process. Toward the end of "The Try-Works," Ishmael has a vision of the *Pequod* as a red hell, a civilization rushing from all havens astern, consuming itself while burning blubber down to oil. This vision, which comes to him as a revelation, is later confirmed by the narrative. Ahab is killed not by Moby-Dick, but by the coiled ropes with which the whale is to be captured. Whatever metaphysical meaning one may ascribe to the whale, the *Pequod* remains a microcosm of a pioneering industrial world sailing willfully to its annihilation.

The primitive qualities Melville seeks in Western man recall Chateaubriand's Indians rather than Parkman's, Uncas rather than Magua, the gentle rather than the brutal aspects of the Typees. On the sea frontier of *Moby-Dick*, however, the cannibalistic aspects of natural man are clearly emerging. Peleg's calculating compliment "No harpooner is worth a straw who aint pretty sharkish" (p. 131) shades readily into Ishmael's admission that "your true whale-hunter is as much a savage as an Iroquois" (p. 358). Fleece senses that, in many respects, sharks, whales, and men are not distinguishable, that a jolly Cape Codder like Stubb, probing with his lance for the whale's inmost life, has in him "more of a shark dan Massa Shark hisself" (p. 391). When Ishmael later applies Fleece's observation about Stubb to the entire nation ("What to that apostolic lancer, Brother Jonathan, is Texas but a Fast-Fish?" [p. 510]), he recognizes that the hunting of Texas and whales is impelled by one ostensibly religious mission. The metaphors of loose and fast fish, in turn, lead Ishmael to question whether the most treasured republican doctrines do not provide sanctions for unrestrained force. The unpursued implications of his rhetorical question "What are the Rights of Man and the Liberties of the World but Loose-Fish?" (p. 510) obviate any chance for a just, permanent civil polity.[10] How the savage sharkishness of the *Pequod* can be squared with Ishmael's praise of everyman's inner divinity is a problem Melville does not choose to address. He clearly intends his reader to recognize, however, that the spirit of the warring Pequods has not quite become extinct in the American character.

Melville's growing estrangement from American values is clearly apparent in his characterization of Starbuck, who embodies conventional virtues in their highest form. Honest, decent, rational, and preeminently competent, Starbuck has committed himself to hard work, reasonable profits, and Christian family, and serves them all with a courage "always at hand upon all mortally practical occasions" (p. 159). In Melville's view, however, such virtues are not in command of the American ship of state, but have become first mate to a grander madness. Starbuck's failing is not ultimately one of courage but one of understanding and loyalty. Too empirical to perceive the "little lower layer" (p. 220) and too dutiful to wrest control from his captain, Starbuck cannot withstand Ahab's "more spiritual terrors" (p. 159). Ahab knows that Starbuck's conventional virtues are in fact his undoing: "Thou art but too good a fellow, Starbuck" (p. 605), he murmurs, after quelling Starbuck's rebelliousness by sheer force of will. In the context of the entire novel, Melville allows revealingly little space to Starbuck's humane protest; Starbuck's virtues so circumscribe his power that he becomes of limited interest and significance.

In a letter to Hawthorne, written as *Moby-Dick* was nearing completion, Melville confronted a fundamental problem vexing to Americans of discriminating mind and democratic faith:

> It is true that there have been those who, while earnest in behalf of political equality, still accept the intellectual estates. And I can well perceive, I think, how a man of superior mind can, by its intense cultivation, bring himself, as it were, into a certain spontaneous aristocracy of feeling, – exceedingly nice and fastidious, – similar to that which, in an English Howard, conveys a torpedo-fish thrill at the slightest contact with a social plebeian. So, when you see or hear of my ruthless democracy on all sides, you may possibly feel a touch of a shrink, or something of the sort. It is but nature to be shy of a mortal who boldly declares that a thief in jail is as honorable a person as Gen. George Washington. This is ludicrous . . .
>
> It seems an inconsistency to assert unconditional democracy in all things, and yet confess a dislike to all mankind – in the mass. But not so.[11]

It is revealing that Melville's letter does not attempt to resolve this supposedly resolvable inconsistency, but turns to other matters. Evidently, Melville's distinguished family heritage, personal intellectual development, and recognition of inequality of worth (not inequality of station) were troublingly at odds with his egalitarian political faith. Many antebellum writers, Cooper and Hawthorne among them, had known similar causes for their "aristocracy of feeling," but few if any could claim that their democratic faith was as "ruthless" in its breadth.

Melville's sharply divided responses to this issue furnish the major source of ethical conflict between and within the characters of *Moby-Dick*. Ishmael invokes "the just Spirit of Equality," the "democratic dignity" of the "great God absolute" (p. 160) as his Muse, but then proceeds to create, as the hero-villain of his noble tragedy, a Byronic sultan of a commander whose willed isolation and intellectual superiority are everywhere evident, and who scorns his crew as "unrecking and unworshipping things" or "pagan leopards" with "cheeks of spotted tawn" (p. 222). As a tragic hero Ahab may have sprung from the kingly commons, but his grand condescension hardly suits an author who has recently committed himself to "that unshackled democratic spirit of Christianity in all things."[12] To exalt Ahab is to forsake the Christian, democratic spirit, but to accept Starbuck's values is to blind oneself to Ahab's greatness.

It is far too simple to conclude that Ahab is an expression of Melville's "spontaneous aristocracy of feeling" whereas Ishmael represents Melville's "ruthless democracy." Both characters are self-divided. Ishmael is often awed by Ahab's innate superiority; "royal," "exalted," "kingly," and especially "noble" are commendatory adjectives in Ishmael's vocabulary. It is Ishmael, not Ahab, who says, "Take mankind in mass, and for the most part, they seem a mob of unnecessary duplicates" (p. 593). However strongly Ahab may believe in the intellectual estates, and use the authority of his position in overbearing ways, he nonetheless seeks autocratic power only as a means to a theoretically noble end. Ishmael can never be wholly certain whether Ahab is motivated by revenge, by self-assertion, or by a noble desire to rid the world of evil. But he does know that Ahab has quelled his humanities only at the cost of a considerable inner strength. Whereas Stubb coolly calculates that "a whale would sell for thirty times what you would, Pip, in Alabama" (p. 529), Ahab practices the Indian belief that one must love a crazed fool because he is holy.

Although Melville's aristocratic and democratic impulses are shared by both major characters, the increasingly ominous direction of Ahab's quest forces them finally to separate. By applying animal and machine metaphors to the mob, Ahab can harden his heart against natural sorrow. As the *Pequod*'s end approaches, Ishmael is brought to condemn Ahab by the democratic, if not Christian, standard that Ahab has become a tyrant sacrificing the welfare of his community to his monomania. Behind these graspings for single judgment, we sense Melville's complex responses to aristocratic discriminations and democratic feeling. In a fluid society where all are presumed equal in merit and in right, Melville expresses his admiration for superior thinkers of high purpose through the figure and speech of Ahab. Because the same society allows men of dangerous will to gain power, however, Melville must convey his longings for democratic brotherhood and human community through the voice of the solitary Ishmael.

Although ethical differences between Ahab and Ishmael may originate from tensions within Melville himself, the two characters also share the solitary, futuristic traits that Tocqueville had found to be characteristically American. Tocqueville had observed that the American spirit of individuality ultimately broke down family structure and that the search for freedom, especially on the frontier, created loneliness if not fear. Questioning widespread assumptions about the happiness of the Republic, Tocqueville had contended that the eternally hopeful spirit of Americans made them restless and dissatisfied because their souls were gripped by unrealizable future expectations, not necessarily material in kind. Both Ahab and Ishmael are rootless solitaries, men without surname and virtually without parents; they pride themselves on their self-reliance while quietly regretting their lack of human ties. Because Ahab lives only to destroy the whale, all satisfaction must be postponed to the future; a man with so fixed and forward-looking a glance must, in the midst of paradise, find himself damned (p. 226). Ishmael seems to derive greater pleasure from re-creating the voyage than he did in living it. When first setting pen to paper, he withholds his worldly name in order to insist upon his deeper identity as a lonely outcast. After hearing Bildad's psalm, Ishmael acknowledges that his mind repeatedly wanders to "meads and glades . . . eternally vernal," "sweet fields beyond the swelling flood," which he knows he will never reach (pp. 145–6). Unlike the non-Arian squires, Ishmael and Ahab cannot fully taste whatever joys the present moment affords because, in differing ways, they must both search for an ungraspable ultimate in the whale.

Sailors aboard the *Pequod* often share Tocqueville's response to untouched frontiers. In "Quinze Jours au Desert," Tocqueville had noted that vast Michigan forests arouse an uneasiness that borders upon fear: "Again in the solitudes of the New World we felt, perhaps more strongly and poignantly, that sense of isolation and of abandonment that had weighed on us so heavily in the middle of the Atlantic."[13] On different occasions, Queequeg, Pip, and Ishmael are all described floating forlornly on an endless sea; all share Pip's fear of "the intense concentration of self in the middle of such a heartless immensity" (p. 529). Tocqueville had been surprised that America's "cold, tenacious and relentless" pioneers showed so little appreciation for natural beauty; because of fear, indifference, or greed, they seemed grimly determined to assert their mastery over the wilderness.[14] Among the white sailors aboard the *Pequod*, only Ishmael appears to have a sense of wonder for the beauty and sublimity of the sea. All the mates, including Starbuck, pride themselves on being men of affairs; until "The Symphony," Ahab's pursuit of the whale is so relentless that he will not recognize that Nature has benign as well as malevolent moments.

Because Tocqueville's precise terms are so pertinent, his summary of the distinctive qualities of the American imagination deserves recall:

> To evade the bondage of system and habit, of family maxims, class opinions, and, in some degree, of national prejudices; to accept tradition only as a means of information, and existing facts only as a lesson to be used in doing otherwise and doing better; to seek the reason of things for oneself, and in oneself alone; to tend to results without being bound to means, and to strike through the form to the substance – such are the principal characteristics of what I shall call the philosophical method of the Americans.[15]

Like Emerson's poet and Tocqueville's American, Ahab has been led to "think untraditionally and independently; receiving all nature's sweet or savage impressions fresh from her own virgin voluntary and confiding breast" (p. 111). He shares the characteristically American beliefs that all can be known, that the agent or principal of evil can be destroyed, and that life is a linear progress toward an ultimate goal. His special hatred for the inscrutable leads him to believe that he can "strike through the mask" (p. 220) – a phrase tellingly similar to Tocqueville's "strike through the form to the substance [*viser au fond à travers la forme*]." Obsessed with the end of his quest, Ahab has little regard for the inhumanity of his means. By identifying all of the world's evil with one natural beast, he exhibits what Tocqueville felt to be the characteristically American "craving to discover general laws in everything," the American need "to explain a mass of facts by a single cause."[16] Accepting only his own intuitions about Moby-Dick, Ahab proceeds to explain the world by the whale, rather than the whale by the world.[17]

The nihilistic end of Ahab's journey warns us that Americans who solipsistically "seek the reason of things for oneself, and in oneself alone," transform themselves into suicidal mirror men. Like a Transcendentalist and like Tocqueville's American, Ahab cries out, "O Nature, and O Soul of Man! How far beyond all utterance are your linked analogies" (p. 406). Seeing his own pride, courage, and presumed victory in the doubloon, Ahab momentarily recognizes that the coin "is but the image of the rounder globe, which, like a magician's glass, to each and every man in turn but mirrors back his own mysterious self" (p. 551). Instead of observing the whale in order to find a linked analogy with his own soul, Ahab creates Moby-Dick solely in accord with his own mirror image.[18] By ascribing his own rage, his own inscrutability, and his own craving for vengeance to the beast who mutilated him, Ahab aggrandizes his personal character into a divine power, and then seeks to destroy it.

Ethan Brand eventually understood that the unpardonable sin was not a preexistent abstraction, but the heartless self he was creating in the very process of his search. Ahab never attains such self-awareness. Although Ahab momentarily acknowledges that his view of the coin is a self-projection, he will not admit that his view of the whale is equally narcissistic. Only Ishmael is aware that white is the colorless all-color of "dumb blankness" (p. 264), a void that causes us "to throw the same snowy mantle round our phantoms" (p. 258). Consequently, only Ishamael can perceive that Ahab has become a Prometheus who is creating the spiritual vulture that consumes him (p. 272). In hopes of striking through form to substance, Ahab worships a fire that, rather than bringing knowledge to men, ends in destruction of self and community. Attempting fully to live out ideals of freedom and self-reliance, he exemplifies the disastrous possibilities of a culture that, by defying tradition, seeks ultimate truth *in* a very imperfect self.

Marvin Meyers has argued persuasively that commitment to both equality of human worth and individual freedom creates a contradiction within Tocqueville's hypothetical American. In some passages, Tocqueville pictures the American as self-reliant man in his fullest pride – radically independent and triumphantly individualistic. In other passages, however, his American is a lost, lonely figure, one among a gray mass of equals, longing for "submergence in the brotherhood."[19] Although *Moby-Dick* holds both possibilities before us, only Ishmael survives the voyage. Ahab's intransigent pride, limitless self-assertion, and contempt for inferiors develop through time into a sublime but suicidal insanity. By comparison, Ishmael can seem little more than a surviving voice. His virtual namelessness and his long absences as actor and narrator show his recognition that he is lost, lonely, and all too equal.

In a spiritual as well as physical sense, Ishmael's self-recognition may contribute to his survival. Gazing into the mirror of the sea, he is transfixed by the God in the soul, but he knows that such reveries are treacherously self-enclosed. Preferring to seek Christian, democratic fellowship by be-friending a savage, he discovers that moments of brotherhood are no less fleeting than pantheistic ecstasies at mastheads. After the *Pequod* disappears beneath the sea, Ishmael remains as he began – a Yankee Jonathan stuffing shirts into a carpetbag, seeking relief from a "splintered heart and maddened hand" (p. 83). By knowing that he must always be "another orphan" (p. 724), Ishmael has gained effective psychic defenses against the treacheries of the watery wilderness. He can entertain all possibilities, because no one of them is truth; when ironies accumulate unbearably, he can control them by adopting the laughing indifference he has observed in the hyena.[20]

The sailor who calls himself Ishmael is only the most interesting of a series of similar figures in Melville's novels. Tommo, Redburn, White-Jacket, Pierre, Bartleby, Israel Potter, Pitch, Clarel, Rolfe, and Ungar all share Ishmael's qualities: In all but four of these instances, the association is explicit. Every one of them is an American. Melville's fascination with the figure of Ishmael may be biographically revealing,[21] but the characters themselves, who are not Herman Melville, also constitute a tacit comment upon American culture. For these men, equality proves a lie, and freedom, when obtainable, is difficult to distinguish from loneliness. Melville's Ishmaels remain Young Americans in embryo, men with no sure sense of values, no tradition, nothing to belong to. Each is a detached self, a blank integer, what Ishmael calls an "*Isolato*, living on a separate continent of his own" (p. 166). These characters are often prone to pantheistic reveries because, exactly in accord with Tocqueville's model, they seek some consoling way of connecting their solitary selves with the immense uniform world around them. When moments of ecstatic union fade, however, Melville's Ishmaels are left in precisely the situation Tocqueville predicted: "Thus not only does democracy make every man forget his ancestors, but it hides his descendants and separates his contemporaries from him; it throws him back forever upon himself alone and threatens in the end to confine him entirely within the solitude of his own heart."[22]

The biblical Ishmael was an outcast who was destined to inherit a nation. Redburn, White-Jacket, and Melville's Ishmael all conclude their voyages by returning to America with evident relief and, in the two former cases, with hopes for the New Israel. During their journeys away from America, the Ishmael figures in Melville's early fiction find all communities and ways of life to be deficient. Typee, beachcombing, all isles of the Mardian archipelago, Liverpool, London, the American navy – none of these provides Ishmael the community he seeks. Speaking for Redburn and White-Jacket, Melville utters his strongest assurances about America's millennial destiny from distant ship decks in mid-ocean. After *Moby-Dick*, however, Ishmael comes home; the fiction Melville was to write between 1852 and 1857 portrays the disillusionment of the nearer view.

In a sense, the epitaph of the American character had already been implied. Neither Ishmael nor Ahab was a whole man; neither represented the ideal American figure Melville was seeking. When Melville discarded Bulkington as the hero of his whaling voyage, he in effect excluded his heroic American. "The Lee Shore" is an elegy to a Western mountaineer of awesome physical presence, a man who had become a metaphysical seeker without sacrificing human decency. Ahab stifles his humanities; Ishmael retains them, but lacks Ahab's force of character. We cannot determine whether Melville dropped Bulkington because he felt that such a hero would be a cultural lie; we know, however, that Bulkington's disappearance left the *Pequod* to dangerously fractional men.

A DEMOCRATIC KNIGHT

Although Pierre becomes defiantly immersed in the self-enclosed world of his mind, the chapter title "Young America in Literature" suggests that Melville intended his supposedly "regular romance" to have national implications.[23] In context the words "Young America" can refer to a concept, to Duyckinck's literary movement, and to Pierre himself. The family history of the Glendinnings, like the family history of the Pyncheons and the Maules, mirrors the inner development of American society from the Revolution to the near present. The physical journey of Pierre thus becomes a visual metaphor for his spiritual journey: In him, Young America seems to have evolved from rural innocence, an aristocratic society, and aristocratic ideals toward urban corruption and egalitarian values. On the superficial level of physical setting, the change from Saddle Meadows to New York suggests cultural degeneration; the concomitant awakening of Pierre's mind, however, suggests a growth into cultural maturity, which is then made perplexingly ambiguous.

When Melville wrote Richard Bentley that *Pierre* would describe "a new & elevated aspect of American life,"[24] he was probably sincere about his desire to convey social history through a family of station, but ironic about the degree of moral elevation that the Glendinning legacy had retained. Melville's characterization of Pierre's parents acknowledges, and then attacks, the persistence of aristocratic economic forces within a democratic republic; his portrayal of Pierre himself, however, implies that democratic idealism might prove equally destructive. Beginning as a naive soul toddler for whom Nature intended a rare and original development, Pierre is gradually transformed into a self-willed democratic knight whose idealism brings death and degradation upon his family as well as himself. Although the old order perpetuates deceit and injustice, the uncompromising innocence of Young America, whether admirable or absurd, seems only to kill.

No novel of the era better conveys the self-defeating burden assumed by sons trained to believe in the founding fathers' heroism. The comparisons among generations of Glendinnings, all made from the perspective of the present, argue that heroic qualities of the American character are fading as the Revolutionary era recedes. Grandfather Pierre – huge in stature, mild in manner, courageous in Revolutionary action – provides Pierre a model he despairingly strives to emulate. Because his forefather's possessions are the only remaining proof of his character, Pierre must trust in his grandfather's heroic image. Although there was a deadly naiveté in the family patriarch (Grandfather Pierre bludgeoned Indians' heads), he also displayed a benign grandeur that made him seem the "fit image of his God."[25] A slave-owning aristocrat who is compared to Abraham, Grandfather Pierre represents Revolutionary America. Although Melville suggests that Grandfather's heroic image is suspect, Pierre believes that Grandfather's virtues passed away from the national character "in A.D. 1812" (p. 31).[26] Young Pierre's absurdly inadequate attempts to fit the symbols of his grandfather's authority imply that Young America, despite all its claims of giantism, is becoming increasingly less prepossessing.

Antidemocratic impulses in the post-Revolutionary generation are responsible for the family's fall from heroic innocence. Setting themselves against new practices of political equality, Pierre's parents aspire to retain his grandfather's social status. To maintain the estate at Saddle Meadows they must perpetuate feudal land laws permitting leasehold, the quarter sale, and days' works. Such policies may have provided a needed spirit of community during colonial times, but Melville criticizes them as a debilitating anachronism once a republican polity has been formed. His imagery may associate Saddle Meadows with an American paradise, but he never lets his reader forget that the paradise is insular, achieved by economic oppression of citizens whom the family would prefer to ignore.

Unlike Cooper, whose Anti-Rent trilogy pictured admirable landlords declaring political truth, Melville recognizes that the legalizing of permanently unequal land rights harms the gentry as well as the tenants. Whereas Grandfather Pierre was proud of his deeds, Mary Glendinning can be proud only of her station. Young Pierre, who is to inherit the title of lord of the manor, is still a soul toddler at nineteen, largely because his privileged position has protected him from life. Although the narrator frequently mocks Pierre's naiveté, he never mocks Pierre's growing recognition of aristocratic injustice; Melville's denunciation of a patroon as a "worm that but crawls through the soil he so imperially claims" (p. 11) is more explicit than any similar criticism by Pierre himself. Imagery arising from the setting suggests that the underside of Melville's filiopietism is appearing. The irony of the book's dedication to "The Most Excellent Purple Majesty of Greylock" becomes clear only when Pierre dreams that he is an American Enceladus warring against the "cunning purpleness" of the Mount of Titans near his ancestral manor (pp. 344–6). Not only do author and character evidently share a subversive desire to defy the burden of Titan-like forefathers; they recognize that their particular republican families have developed a tradition of decidedly monarchical coloring.

Pierre's father bequeaths his son an Eden, but deprives him of the respect for ancestral integrity necessary to enjoy it. The family sin most tormenting to Pierre, his father's probable refusal to acknowledge his illegitimate daughter, has often-overlooked cultural implications. In a land professing to welcome the immigrant poor, Pierre's father apparently seduced and then abandoned a French immigrant, in a smiling, secretive manner that is utterly unlike Melville's ideal of democratic candor. The aristocratic prejudices underlying the abandoning of Isabel's mother are laid bare when Mary Glendinning describes her son's presumed marriage to Isabel as "mixing the choicest wine with filthy water from the plebeian pool, and so turning all to undistinguishable rankness" (p. 194).[27]

The decline of family character is not confined to aristocrats with legal privilege. Melville's assessment of Charlie Millthorpe's father seems an almost parodic tribute to the merits of Jefferson's natural aristocracy:

> Millthorpe was the son of a very respectable farmer – now dead – of more than common intelligence, and whose bowed shoulders and homely garb had still been surmounted by a head fit for a Greek philosopher, and features so fine and regular that they would have well graced an opulent gentleman. The political and social levellings and confoundings of all manner of human elements in America, produce many striking individual anomalies unknown in other lands. Pierre well remembered old farmer Millthorpe: – the handsome, melancholy, calm-tempered, mute, old man; in whose countenance – refinedly ennobled by nature, and yet coarsely tanned and attenuated by many a prolonged day's work in the harvest – rusticity and classicalness were strangely united. The delicate profile of his face bespoke the loftiest aristocracy; his knobbed and bony hands resembled a beggar's. [P. 275]

Even though Melville is slyly jeering at "old farmer Millthorpe" as a shopworn cultural cliché, the passage compliments the Revolutionary era at the expense of the thriving social aristocracy represented by Mary Glendinning. Gentleman, philosopher, and farmer, Millthorpe has now become "mute" and "melancholy" because he can no longer meet the rent due the Glendinnings and must sell his farm. Millthorpe's son Charlie proves to be a charming nonentity for whom Idealism is merely a jolly game without intellectual exhilaration or spiritual risk.

Within the context of familial degeneration from prominent ancestry, Melville considers the consequences of fully believing and practicing the democratic faith. In the first chapter, he challenges presumably complacent readers by bluntly stating, "You will pronounce Pierre a thorough-going Democrat in time; perhaps a little too Radical altogether to your fancy" (p. 13).[28] Renouncing the injustices of his heritage, reverencing "Truth, and Earnestness, and Independence" (p. 165), Melville's young American becomes a moral absolutist determined to remake himself in the heroic image of his grandfather. Knowing that he cannot measure up to old Pierre's bedstead, phaeton, or sword, Pierre nonetheless conceives of himself as a revolutionary knight who will purge the Glendinning line of its stained inheritance. When Melville asserts, about Pierre, that "in the Enthusiast to Duty, the heaven-begotten Christ is born" (p. 106), all components of the ideal national character theoretically coalesce. Pierre becomes the first Melvillean protagonist to set out to practice, in America, the creed of "the unshackled democratic spirit of Christianity in all things."

In earlier years Melville assumed that the Christian democratic spirit could be realized only in American culture. Casting off America's aristocratic past, Pierre experiences none of that spirit in contemporary American life. Conventional society, represented by the social circles of Mrs. Glendinning, Glen Stanly, and Mrs. Tartan, is preoccupied with matchmaking and snobbish mannerisms. When Pierre turns to Reverend Falsgrave for ethical advice, he discovers that the church is serving the injustices of the upper class with imperturbable grace. Pierre's first evening in New York is quite like Robin Molineux's evening in Boston; to both up-country adolescents, the city seems a nightmarish world of prostitutes, sharpsters, madmen, and gilded aristocrats – the old city re-created in the New World. Pierre is soon disillusioned with the state of American letters. Having apparently abandoned "republican progressiveness," Young America in Literature is content to exploit sentimentality and to purvey uplifting orthodoxies in gift books and annuals. More honest, ambitious literary efforts seem to have dwindled to the circle of indigent bohemian crazies in the Church of the Apostles, artists who are estranged from society and naively committed to "the hasty and premature advance of some unknown great political and religious Millennium" (p. 269).

Melville's conventional attack on urban vice does not lead him to idealize rural life. Millthorpe's father, we are reminded, represents a standard of physiocratic virtue that is long departed; the constant laboring for dollars has caused the American farmer to fail his trust and decline into "that strangely wilful race, who, in the sordid traffickings of clay and mud, are ever seeking to *denationalize* the natural heavenliness of their souls" (p. 139, italics mine). Man may have made the town, but God will not acknowledge whether He made the country. In the heart of the "infinite inhumanities of those profoundest forests" (p. 110) is the Memnon Stone, with its cryptic nonmessage from Solomon the Wise. Gazing into an unspoiled lake, Pierre perceives none of the energizing inner purity Thoreau discovered at Walden; he sees only the Emersonian abyss – "one sheet of blankness and of dumbness," "the imaged muteness of the unfeatured heavens" (p. 109).

Pierre is forced to recognize that he lives in "a bantering, barren, and prosaic, heartless age" (p. 191), but he is never ultimately concerned with his social disillusionments. By crossing his Rubicon, he commits himself to Young America's total confidence in the self's sufficiency: "Henceforth, cast-out Pierre hath no paternity, and no past; and since the Future is one blank to all; therefore, twice-disinherited Pierre stands untrammeledly his ever-present self! – free to do his own self-will and present fancy to whatever end!" (p. 199). Pierre's creed, so reminiscent of Emerson's "Self-Reliance," is one that Tocqueville had defined as representative of democratic man. Libertarian impulses drive Pierre to cut himself off from everything past, to treasure freedom above all, to live in the present moment, to assume that the self is an all-sustaining world. When Pierre declares, "I will no more have a father" (p. 87) and burns all written evidence of his past, he resembles, not only Young America casting off English aristocracy, but Holgrave and Clifford attempting to discard their ancestral heritage and live solely within their present selves.

The American Ishmaels in Melville's earlier fiction were parentless: Pierre, however, is a self-exile ("twice-disinherited") who drives himself "an infant Ishmael into the desert, with no maternal Hagar to accompany and comfort him" (p. 89). The relentlessly negative terms through which he affirms his freedom to create himself ("no paternity," "no past," "cast-out," a "blank" future) imply a defiant recognition of his possible failure. Only subconsciously does he understand that selves are not created through negation. By indulging in self-pity over his voluntary defection from an evil society, Pierre sometimes speaks like a grotesquely latinate parody of Leatherstocking: "This day I will forsake the censuses of men, and seek the suffrages of the god-like population of the trees, which now seem to me a nobler race than man" (p. 106).

The end of Pierre's quest provides perhaps the most chilling portrayal of the consequences of total self-reliance in our literature. Pierre sits alone in a tawdry, barren room, writing himself into blindness, impervious to the merrymakings and seasonal changes around him. Hoping to provide the gospel for a new age, he angrily pours forth fragments of tortuous, overly internalized philosophy. Because his projections make no contact with the world beyond, they return upon him in deathly forms of ingression. Having assumed that the self is the source of truth, Pierre discovers that the self is a dark cave, or a staircase endlessly descending into blackness. The passages Melville cites from Pierre's book are evidence only of his egoism, self-hate, and despair. No human being, and surely no institution, can touch him: "One in a city of hundreds of thousands of human beings, Pierre was solitary as at the Pole" (p. 338). By tunneling into the self, Pierre abandons all ethical standards and finally descends to murder and suicide because of despair over spiritual ambiguities. Even for Young America, no further degree of solipsism seems possible.

Pierre's absolutist gestures, his compulsive desire to be totally free, have cut him off from the possibility of practicing within society the democratic, Christian principles he professes. He liberates himself only to be lost in himself:

> Now look around in that most miserable room, and at that most miserable of all the pursuits of a man, and say if here be the place, and this be the trade, that God intended him for. A rickety chair, two hollow barrels, a plank, paper, pens, and infernally black ink, four leprously dingy white walls, no carpet, a cup of water, and a dry biscuit or two. Oh, I hear the leap of the Texan Camanche, as at this moment he goes crashing like a wild deer through the green underbrush; I hear his glorious whoop of savage and untamable health; and then I look in at Pierre. If physical, practical unreason make the savage, which is he? Civilization, Philosophy, Ideal Virtue! behold your victim! [P. 302]

This passage suggests that Melville's ideal American character is made of self-destructive and incompatible parts. Pierre is declared to be the victim of his own "Ideal Virtue" (the democratic spirit of Christianity) and of his "Philosophy" (extreme individualism), as well as of a mediocre civilization's indifference. By pursuing ideal virtue, Pierre has deprived himself of the "savage and untamable health" necessary to any Western man who responds to the possibilities of his environment.

Pierre's world becomes so wholly self-enclosed, so narcissistic, that it becomes difficult for him – and sometimes for the reader – to separate the Me from the Not Me. Just as Emerson began to doubt whether natural laws were not simply an extension of self,[29] the reader of *Pierre* suspects that Saddle Meadows is a projection of his disillusionment. Lucy and Isabel begin to seem, not separate personalities, but Pierre's projections of the Good and Bad Angels within himself. When Pierre looks at nature, he ascribes to it his own despair and irresolution. Melville explicitly tells us that "Nature is not so much her own ever-sweet interpreter, as the mere supplier of that cunning alphabet, whereby selecting and combining as he pleases, each man reads his own peculiar lesson according to his peculiar mind and mood" (p. 342). Because Pierre does not recognize his own narcissism, he has no means for distinguishing between object and fantasy, between other people and his need to reshape them spiritually. His insistence upon freeing the self thereby renders him increasingly unable to make necessary human distinctions: His mother becomes his fiancée, his fiancée his sister, and his sister his lover.[30]

After casting aside his flawed heritage, Pierre faces the challenge of having to create a new self in a world that, like a void, has no discernible order or limit. His ordeal is a familiar one in American literature. Emerson's poet, the narrator of *Walden*, Isaac McCaslin, Jay Gatsby (who "sprang from his platonic conception of himself"),[31] and Stephen Rojack in Mailer's *An American Dream* all face the same task. Perhaps Pierre most resembles

Whitman's "noiseless patient spider" who stands isolated on a promontory, spinning "filament, filament, filament" out of himself in hope that his soul will catch "somewhere."[32] These other Americans, with the possible exception of Isaac McCaslin, find something to fill their inner void, be it the Oversoul, a spiritual Camerado, or a green light. Pierre, however, finds only death. As Pierre leaves Saddle Meadows, Melville speaks of things "foetally forming in him" (p. 106). When Pierre writes his gospel, however, Melville comments, "Better might one be pushed off into the material spaces beyond the uttermost orbit of our sun, than once feel himself fairly *afloat in himself!*" (p. 284, italics mine). As the book concludes, Melville emphasizes that Pierre's new self can be little more than the despairing will to die. Confined within a cell that symbolizes his self-imprisonment, Pierre ironically trusts that death will enable his soul finally to be born: "Now, to my soul, were a sword my midwife!" (p. 360). Pierre's democratic feelings have proven so ruthless that they can be satisfied only in death. "I joy that Death is this Democrat and [remain] hopeless of all other real and permanent democracies" (p. 278).

At the beginning of the novel, Melville encourages the illusion that the aristocratic life of the Hudson River gentry is desirable and permanent. Families like the Glendinnings are offered to the reader as a welcome refutation of a familiar European charge against the New World: "In demagoguical [sic] America the sacred Past hath no fixed statues erected to it, but all things irreverently seethe and boil in the vulgar cauldron of an everlasting uncrystalizing present" (p. 8). By the end of the novel this charge has proved oddly prophetic. The last of the Glendinnings has, indeed, torn down all statues of a past he had thought sacred. The metaphor of a cauldron, seething with irreverent and uncrystallizing fragments, is strikingly appropriate to the final condition of Pierre's mind and Pierre's art. To the extent that he is a representative figure, his end suggests the directionless confusion of contemporary American culture.

Pierre's grossest delusion is his belief that he is free to create a new self in accord with "Truth, and Earnestness, and Independence." Having first deified and then rejected his father's memory, Pierre later sacrifices himself to uphold his father's reputation for virtue. Pierre's Christ-like gestures are devoted to maintaining the false appearances of Saddle Meadows and to shielding his mother from truth. He burns his heritage before leaving Saddle Meadows, but remains obsessed with that heritage in New York. Having dedicated his life to absolute virtue, he spends his last days tormented by the suspicion that he has committed the unpardonable sin of forsaking his inheritance, his mother, his fiancée. Try though he may to live by the democratic spirit, his "one only prospect [is] a black, bottomless gulf of guilt" (p. 337).

By insisting upon the bottomlessness of Pierre's guilt, Melville has brought the cultural conflict of *The House of the Seven Gables* to a discouraging resolution. In both novels, the pride, greed, and dominance of an aristocratic order fasten the past's dead hand upon the republican present. Like Holgrave, Pierre is an American radical who professes to dismiss ancestral sins for the sake of a limitless future, yet remains secretly ashamed of the ancestral heritage that lives on inside him. Yet, Pierre can never be dissuaded from his revenge upon the past, because his solipsism prevents him from sharing Holgrave's reverence for another's individuality. In Melville's novel, there is neither a contemporary symbol of familial sins who conveniently passes away (the judge) nor a contemporary symbol of the family's energizing love who appears as a redeemer (Phoebe). The decline of the Glendinnings proves to be total because Melville's hero harbors desires for incest and parricide that he justifies as parts of his Christian, democratic purpose. In such a situation, Lucy Tartan can be only a parodic rendition of Phoebe Pyncheon, a *naïf* fair heroine who utterly fails to save Pierre from himself, because she can neither comprehend Pierre's failings nor withstand his will to despair.

In mind and attitude, Pierre more closely resembles Young Goodman Brown than Holgrave. Trusting in the goodness of ancestors, yet prone to believe all kinds of spectral evidence, Goodman Brown and Pierre experience a shattering vision of the blackness in the human soul. Neither will acknowledge his desire to deface the saintliness of his father. Both subsequently try to exempt themselves from their own complicity in evil, but thereby end as virtual misanthropes who can never quite be sure that their blackest visions are true. Any truths hidden in forest, meadows, or city can never be known, because neither young man can perceive his environs as tangible realities separate from his own mind. Faith has as little influence on Goodman Brown as Lucy does on Pierre. To despair of all things, after hoping in all things, is to remain forever innocent, forever young. It is little wonder that Melville found Hawthorne's tale "deep as Dante."[33]

By the end of the novel, Melville has led his reader to question even the purity of Pierre's Christian and democratic intentions. Like Melville, Pierre approves of Christian conduct while declaring his contempt for un-Christian, tormenting Gods. Pierre thinks of himself as a "heaven-begotten Christ" (p. 106) who will act on chronometrical principles, yet his only action that can remotely be called Christian, the protection he affords Isabel and Delly Ulver, is partly undertaken to reify his unproved virtue. Once Pierre moves his entourage to New York, he strives to shut both women out of his consciousness. Similarly, Pierre's "Radical Democracy" never develops any social expression; it seems to emerge only as an immense pride in his own powers and a contempt for the mediocrity of American civilization. Qualities of Melville's ideal American character are again proved contradictory; Pierre's self-reliance and struggle for inner purity lead to an egoism that precludes Christian, democratic actions.

To be sure, Pierre is as much the victim of American society as he is the victim of his own solipsism and innocence. When one's aristocratic heritage and one's contemporary society both fail to provide moral value, when God is silent if not malicious, where is Pierre to turn save to the resources of his own soul? His self is insufficient to sustain him because it is neither fully democratic (he seeks to maintain the aristocratic facade of Saddle Meadows) nor fully Christian (he confuses Samaritan behavior with incestuous desire). Melville, however, does not criticize democratic feeling or Christian action; he upholds them in principle, while mistrusting their application. The "unshackled" spirit of democracy is criticized only when it leads to the assumption that one's past can be discarded. The "unshackled" spirit of Christianity is criticized only when it leads the self-proclaimed Christ to un-Christian pride. Nothing in the novel suggests that Melville sanctions Plinlimmon's conclusion that the Christian act of returning good for evil must be morally "false" simply because it has proved "entirely impracticable" (p. 215). Plinlimmon, a Tennessee Welshman who has "no family or blood ties of any sort" (p. 290), cannot begin to understand the needs that drive a son to perverse imitation of his forefathers' presumably exemplary spirit of democratic Christianity.

8

CONFIDENCE IN
DISTRUST

This country has not fulfilled what seemed the reasonable expectation of mankind. Men looked, when all feudal straps and bandages were snapped asunder, that nature, too long the mother of dwarfs, should reimburse itself by a brood of Titans, who should laugh and leap in the continent, and run up the mountains of the West with the errand of genius and of love.

Emerson, "Literary Ethics" (1838)

The Americans portrayed in Melville's later fiction fail to substantiate Jacksonian expectations of progress, let alone the millennial predictions of Redburn and White-Jacket. Places as diverse as New England factories, Berkshire farms, Grace Church, and Wall Street shape human lives that are imprisoned and sterile, atomized and leveled, poor and lonely.[1] Long-established institutions exert such constricting force that the roads of the future never open. Americans who combine the vitality, Christian feeling, and democratic politics of Ethan Allen or Bulkington cannot appear in such settings. The Ishmael figure, be he Pierre, Bartleby, Israel Potter, or Pitch, becomes disillusioned both with American society, and with his place within it, yet finds no association of heroic hearts to ease his solitude. As prospects for democratic community fade, demagogic confidence men gradually emerge as the true leaders of American culture.

Heroism is still applicable to the American character, though it is redefined as compassionate endurance rather than libertarian action. The admirable American perceives realities rather than prophesying them. He acknowledges that expected national virtues have surfaced in less desirable forms, that youthful frankness has shaded into credulity and Western energy into savage barbarity. Rather than growing embittered over these changes, Melville becomes increasingly resigned to them.

175

Shocked by recognizing that American society is undemocratic, Pierre unburdened himself in fruitless denunciation and self-destructive posturing. The narrators of Melville's short stories accept their disillusionment and then search for responses that will salvage the most for life. The author of *The Confidence-Man*, who has no national hopes, surveys a ship of fools and knaves with saving humor and admirable artistic control.

THE FAILINGS OF CHARITY

Melville's magazine stories focus upon national concerns that are of little importance in the major romances. The American looking-glass business, pursued to its ultimate end in *Pierre*, gives way to social problems visible in ordinary life. We see less of Young America's search for ultimate truth, but more of middle-aged Americans struggling to live with one another. Even the standard by which men are judged shifts in emphasis. As the attaining of the self's grand goals seems less feasible, it becomes less important; men now prove their Christian democratic spirit by showing charity to one another, rather than by pursuing the future.

Long sketches that immerse the reader in poverty and failure subvert any belief that America is a land of plenty and opportunity. "Cock-A-Doodle-Doo!" and "Poor Man's Pudding" portray depleted soil, inadequate diet, and grasping "squires" as permanent conditions of a rural life that has no Western safety valve. The penury of these Americans is persistently aggravated by democratic beliefs that they themselves accept. Self-reliance renders it as difficult for needy Americans to accept charity as it is for wealthy Americans to bestow it:

> The native American poor never lose their delicacy or pride; hence, though unreduced to the physical degradation of the European pauper, they yet suffer more in mind than the poor of any other people in the world. Those peculiar social sensibilities nourished by our own peculiar political principles, while they enhance the true dignity of a prosperous American, do but minister to the added wretchedness of the unfortunate; first, by prohibiting their acceptance of what little random relief charity may offer; and, second, by furnishing them with the keenest appreciation of the smarting distinction between their ideal of universal equality and their grindstone experience of the practical misery and infamy of poverty – a misery and infamy which is, ever has been, and ever will be, precisely the same in India, England, and America.[2]

Such an essayistic declaration emphasizes an intricate, unacknowledged irony: The poor man's assumption that he is the equal of the rich impedes equality of condition.

In none of his sketches of poverty and failure does Melville imply that the kinds of legal reform demanded in *White-Jacket* could alleviate the problems. Instead he concentrates upon the insidious effect of confidence men like the poet Blandmour or the cock Beneventano, who voice soothing platitudes of hope and self-reliance while the Coulters' want deepens and the Merrymusks sink to their death. The miseries of poverty are no longer glossed over by such political assurances as Redburn's belief that "to be a born American citizen seems a guarantee against pauperism; and this, perhaps, springs from the virtue of a vote."[3]

Two sketches in "The Encantadas" suggest the bases for Melville's recognition that libertarian government is no guarantee against inequality. The third sketch, "Rock Rodondo," is an allegory describing man's condition in the State of Nature. Left to themselves, the birds arrange themselves into a social hierarchy upon a vertical rock tower. "Disposed in order of their magnitude," with misshapen ugly penguins at the base and brilliant butterflies at the top, the birds form "thrones, princedoms, powers, dominating one above another in senatorial array." In Melville's conception of the State of Nature, any Lockean equality of right can exist only until two beings attempt to live in one space.[4]

The seventh sketch, tracing the history of Charles Isle, should be interpreted as a hidden allegory of American history. A freebooting soldier gathers eighty colonists and sails westward from Peru to populate "the promised land." The settlers, whom Melville calls an "inferior rabble," "a citizen mob," and "pilgrims," grow restive under the autocratic rule of "His Majesty" and his majesty's police dogs. After a number of years, the citizenry successfully revolt, drive the king into exile back over the ocean, and proclaim a republic. Welcoming every downtrodden immigrant as "a ragged citizen of this universal nation," Charles Isle proclaims itself "the asylum of the oppressed." The promised land, however, is never realized. The vicious individualism of the pilgrims subverts their republican confederation and turns the island into an "Anathema – a sea Alsatia – the unassailed lurking-place of all sorts of desperadoes, who in the name of liberty did just what they pleased." Without offering any solution, Melville arrives at an appropriately Federalist scorn for revolutionary license: "Nay, it was no democracy at all, but a permanent *Riotocracy*, which gloried in having no law but lawlessness."[5]

As long as the Old World was kept imaginatively separate from the New, antebellum Americans could maintain a belief that, however disappointing conditions in America might be, conditions in Europe were surely worse. In 1854 and 1855, Melville wrote six sketches, organized as three diptychs, which force the reader to make direct comparisons between America and England. The subtlety of the tales depends upon showing the reader expectedly different social customs while revealing an unsolved universal problem that lies beneath them. The narrator of "The Two Temples" discovers that, in democratic America, the common citizen is barred from worshiping in a socially exclusive church, and can be fined for trespassing on its premises. In England, the narrator is given a free ticket to a theater only to discover that the drama has become the Englishman's substitute for religion. By a similar kind of contrast, "Poor Man's Pudding" reveals how ideals of liberty and equality conveniently allow Americans not to be charitable; "Rich Man's Crumbs" portrays British aristocrats displaying charity through public spectacles, thereby reinforcing class distinctions and arousing popular resentment at "the intrinsic contempt of the alms."[6] The logical conclusion to be drawn from juxtaposing these two stories is that men of every nation will use their ingenuity to avoid giving alms until charity is in their self-interest.

The title "The Paradise of Bachelors and the Tartarus of Maids" promises a contrast that extends only to the tales' settings. The hearty conviviality that Melville had sought in American life seems to be found among the London bachelors of Temple Bar. Maids in New England factories, by contrast, have been reduced to cogs by the machines they serve. The self-consciously masculine seedsman who narrates "The Tartarus of Maids" observes that factory employment has leveled workers to desexualized solitaries who doggedly produce foolscap rather than royal sheets. His memorable sentence "At rows of blank-looking counters sat rows of blank-looking girls, with blank, white folders in their blank hands, all blankly folding blank paper," combines Ahab's recognition of the effect of machinery with Ishmael's fear of becoming a blank integer.[7] The sexual puns that the seedsman scatters throughout his sketch might be amusing, were they not so obviously inappropriate.

The utter blankness of the maids implies that the worst effects of the industrial revolution may be transpiring in New England rather than old. Taken together, however, the tales constitute no simple inversion. Although the bachelors inhabit the house of the Knights Templar, they have exchanged the helmet for a wig, sacrificed thought to comfort, dismissed pain and trouble as "preposterous to their bachelor imaginations" (p. 237), and thus reduced the field of their energies to "the heavy artillary of the feast" (p. 234). The bachelors, like the maids, have lost the ability to feel and the will to think along with the power of sexuality. By parodying the Anglophile geniality of *The Sketch Book*, Melville suggests that the Englishman's love of tradition yields the same psychological paralysis as the American's will to produce. At the next level of abstraction, Melville's allegory may imply that Paradise and Tartarus, Heaven and Hell, are essentially the same.[8]

The attitudes that Melville's narrators adopt toward poverty and failure are revealingly consistent. William and Martha Coulter, Jimmy Rose, the Merrymusks, Hautboy, and the inventor uncle of "The Happy Failure" – all earn pitying respect for their abilities to recognize misery, bear it uncomplainingly, and gather whatever joys may be salvaged by remaining in their place. Their gentle acquiescence, so foolish by worldly standards, derives from a deeper source than philosophic fatalism, and gains a dignity surpassing flight or anger. A similar equanimity prevails in the stories that are closest to known biographical circumstances. The narrator of "I and My Chimney" and "The Apple-Tree Table" is a thoroughly congenial man, fond of the dark artifacts of New England forefathers, but unsure of any answers. Although his wife reveals herself as an aggressive democrat whose "infatuate juvenility" expresses itself in a thirst for novelty, her opinions do not make him bitter or reactionary, even when she schemes to tear down the symbols of his ego.[9]

Melville's two major achievements in short fiction deal with the obligations of charity that the privileged assume toward the less privileged. The lawyer in "Bartleby" and Amasa Delano in "Benito Cereno" are both conceived as successful, middle-aged Americans who pride themselves on their Christian benevolence and practical good will. Melville confronts both men with disturbingly complex situations that their Christian benevolence and practical goodwill cannot solve.[10] The lawyer and Delano, each of them in nominal command of a commercial enterprise, grope toward an understanding of dark ironies that their cheery American optimism has denied. The characterization of both men thus implies that the very success of the nation's commercial endeavors can protect Americans against the loss of their innocence, and of their generosity, well into their middle years.

In both stories, the fictional point of view is skillfully controlled to emphasize these issues. Melville describes the mental qualities of the lawyer and Delano at the outset, but thereafter requires the reader to view their experiences solely through their eyes. By treating his narrators in the manner of a Jamesian reflector, Melville invites his readers to measure their own acuity against the acuity of the lawyer and of Delano. Because readers know only as much of Bartleby or the *San Dominick* as the lawyer or Delano knows, they must judge their own perceptivity in light of the traits attributed to the narrator. Perhaps Melville intends the more honest of his American readers to recognize that their own innocence shades into credulity, and that their own Christian benevolence, if sincere, can be blinding.

The lawyer of "Bartleby the Scrivener" is an engagingly frank man who is perfectly willing to tell his reader that he is proud of his prudence, his association with John Jacob Astor, his financial success, and his conviction that "the easiest way of life is the best."[11] He struggles honestly to understand and to aid Bartleby, but never fully realizes that Bartleby's perplexing reveries in front of blank walls are due partly to Bartleby's recognition that Wall Street is a psychological prison for its employees. After Bartleby is dead, the lawyer surmises that Bartleby's suicidal aimlessness may be attributable to years of handling and then copying dead letters in Washington. He never seems to recognize, however, that Bartleby has been asked to copy equally dead letters in New York. Most important, the lawyer cannot begin to understand that Bartleby's colorless blank wall represents a mind so self-imprisoned that it can see nothing beyond itself.[12] Committed to a world of safe routine and financial reward, the lawyer can never perceive how the conditions of Bartleby's life have brought him to near silence and to a seemingly purposeless form of passive resistance.

Although the lawyer believes he is writing a tale about "Bartleby the Scrivener," he can tell us precious little about Bartleby, yet he unwittingly reveals things about himself that he little suspects. Throughout the story, the lawyer tries to maintain an attitude toward Bartleby that is both Christian and businesslike. He may speak of Bartleby as a "valuable acquisition" (p. 37), but he is also anxious to convince himself that, as a devout churchgoer, he treats the scrivener in a wholly Christian manner.

The major conflict within the tale is not between Bartleby and the lawyer, but between the lawyer and himself. The lawyer's human pity is forever at odds with his business ethics, but his business ethics usually predominate. Melville deftly exposes the rationalization by which the lawyer makes Christian principles square with unchristian impulses. After resisting a temptation to throttle Bartleby, the lawyer takes a rather smug pride in his self-restraint:

> But when this old Adam of resentment rose in me and tempted me concerning Bartleby, I grappled him and threw him. How? Why, simply by recalling the divine injunction: "A new commandment give I unto you, that ye love one another." Yes, this it was that saved me. Aside from higher considerations, charity often operates as a vastly wise and prudent principle – a great safeguard to its possessor. Men have committed murder for jealousy's sake, and anger's sake, and hatred's sake, and selfishness' sake, and spiritual pride's sake; but no man, that ever I heard of, ever committed a diabolical murder for sweet charity's sake. Mere self-interest, then, if no better motive can be enlisted, should, especially with high-tempered men, prompt all beings to charity and philanthropy. [P. 52]

By the end of this passage, the lawyer has unwittingly confused Pauline *caritas* (love of man for love of God in man) with "charity" in the sense of succoring the less fortunate. This confusion has then led him to justify Christian restraint by appealing to prudence and self-interest.

Although the lawyer makes charity subservient to worldliness, he is not a hypocrite; he is bedeviled by an honest confusion of values. The Christian and the businessman have become so intermingled in his psyche that he can discuss morality only in business metaphors. When he congratulates himself on his generosity in allowing Bartleby to remain in his offices, he thinks: "Here I can cheaply purchase a delicious self-approval. To befriend Bartleby; to humour him in his strange wilfulness, will cost me little or nothing, while I lay up in my soul what will eventually prove a sweet morsel for my conscience" (p. 34). Because he contemplates moral decisions through a vocabulary of cost and gain, his reasoning follows in the tradition of Franklin's *Autobiography*. Tocqueville had remarked of the lawyer's contemporaries: "Not only do the Americans follow their religion from interest, but they often place in this world the interest that makes them follow it . . . and it is often difficult to ascertain from their discourses whether the principal object of religion is to procure eternal felicity in the other world or prosperity in this."[13]

Although the lawyer eventually removes his offices from Bartleby's presence, Melville surely does not share Bartleby's condemnation of the lawyer: "I know you . . . and I want nothing to say to you" (p. 61). Few men of affairs in any profession would be equally patient and good-humored in dealing with an employee of such nonnegotiable preferences.[14] Wall Street and the Tombs, two enclosures made of high walls and blank conformity, define the lawyer's world, and unless he would forsake his world entirely, he has no choice but to rid himself of Bartleby, and salve his Christian conscience as he may. Ironically, however, it is not only Bartleby but the lawyer who is "pallidly neat, pitiably respectable, incurably forlorn" (p. 27): The lawyer's mind and business habits are pallidly neat, his reaching out for approval is pitiably respectable, and he seems, at the tale's end, more than a little forlorn. Perhaps Bartleby has made him aware that, in the world of Wall Street, effective charity entails more than extending material comforts. At least, however, the lawyer has experienced the difficulties of assuming that businessman and Christian are readily compatible identities.

Amasa Delano of Duxbury, Massachusetts, is introduced as "a person of singularly undistrustful good-nature, not liable, except on extraordinary and repeated incentives, and hardly then, to indulge in personal alarms, any way involving the imputation of malign evil in man."[15] Captain of an American merchantman, suggestively named the *Bachelor's Delight*, Delano leaves his prosperous, orderly ship to confront the real, fallen, and explicitly European world of the *San Dominick*. Mentally prepared only for a simple world of black-or-white absolutes, Delano sets off on an errand of mercy into a gray morning and a shadowy gray sky. Whereas the *Bachelor's Delight* recalls the thoughtless wealth of that Nantucket whaler the *Bachelor* in *Moby-Dick*, the *San Dominick* resembles the American antebellum world inverted. It is a microcosm in which slave is master and master is slave, where a stutter is eloquent but smooth speech is a lie, and where Christopher Columbus, figurehead pointing to a new world, has been replaced by the rotting skeleton of a slave owner. Setting off on a commendable errand of mercy, Delano hopes to ease the *San*

Dominick's distress by providing physical relief. The situation does not seem to demand a more complex form of mission, nor can he conceive of one.

Delano's mind is filled with the cultural prejudices of ordinary antebellum Americans. According to him, the American is a charitable, practical man, but the European is something else, and the Spaniard is almost beyond humanity. Because Don Benito looks like the stereotype of a haughty, tattered, aristocratic Spaniard, Delano assumes that he is a cutthroat and deceiver. Sure that Benito Cereno must be a "paper captain" (p. 85), an impractical aristocrat who has gained command in a European system of birth rather than merit, Delano muses that "the very word Spaniard has a curious, conspirator, Guy-Fawkish twang to it" (p. 113). Delano also believes in the nineteenth-century stereotype of the black man as a happy darky, a "Newfoundland Dog" who makes a fine valet or hairdresser. Delano describes the black man by such phrases as "the great gift of good-humour," "the unaspiring contentment of a limited mind," and "the bland attachment sometimes inhering in indisputable inferiors" (pp. 120–1). He has none of Ishmael's awareness that "the sinews and souls of . . . Republican slaves [are] but Fast-Fish, whereof possession is the whole of the law."[16]

Because these racial attitudes are commonly accepted as fact, Delano makes merely passing mention of them. An attentive reader, however, will be immediately aware that these stereotypes are preventing Delano from perceiving truth. Again and again, appearances lead him momentarily to distrust the blacks, yet he can never assume that they would have been capable of armed rebellion. He can only turn his eyes upon Don Benito and assume that the "horrible Spaniard" (p. 111) must be nursing a plot against him.

Despite Delano's racial misconceptions, he might have been undeceived had it not been for his instinctual and consoling piety. Delano's trust that divine Providence rules a just world allows him to conquer his suspicions. Fearing that Cereno might murder him, he dismisses his supposedly childlike fears with a few childlike phrases: "Who would murder Amasa Delano? His conscience is clean. There is someone above" (p. 111). Melville's contradictory attitudes toward Pierre indicated that he reverenced the spirit of Christian knighthood but mistrusted Pierre's self-centered application of it. Delano's motives and actions are truly generous, but his underlying religious attitudes remain unexamined and naive. Surely "Hawthorne and His Mosses" called for a spirit of American Christianity that would be of tougher mind than the sentimental Deism of Amasa Delano.

"Benito Cereno" disquiets readers of all parties because it implies that the institution of chattel slavery, the viciousness of slave revolts, and the whites' retaliation (Babo's head fixed on a pike in the square in Lima) are all atrocities for which no palliative can be offered. The tale's point of view suggests that Melville is concerned not to make any statement about slavery, but to study the failure of a representative American's perception and to suggest its consequences. The most discouraging outcome of the tale is Delano's inability to learn anything from his experiences. During the final conversation between Delano and Benito, Benito tries to make Delano understand that his psyche has been shattered by experiencing the shadow of racial and universal blackness contained in the simple words "the negro." Delano's reply reveals that he is incapable of abandoning the thoughtless optimism, dismissal of evil, and dismissal of the past that seems ingrained in the national character: "You generalise, Don Benito; and mournfully enough. But the past is past; why moralize upon it? Forget it. See, yon bright sun has forgotten it all, and the blue sea, and the blue sky; these have turned over new leaves" (p. 168).

Like "Bartleby the Scrivener," "Benito Cereno" offers no prospect for effective humanitarian action based upon a disillusioned view of man. Although Melville implies that Delano and his New World need the Old World's knowledge of human complexities, he suggests that the price of such knowledge is psychic debility. Because Benito Cereno has no physical malady, his death must be attributed to the effect of his experiences upon his mind. Delano, however, can cheerfully prepare himself for other voyages because he remains unwilling to impute malign evil to all mankind. The figurehead of Christopher Colon should in retrospect have suggested something of America's origins to Delano, yet he never makes the connection. Unlike Redburn, White-Jacket, or Ishmael, Captain Delano retains his moral naiveté along with his goodwill; he can be horrified by atrocities without speculating upon their cause. Like the townsfolk in "The Apple-Tree Table," Delano has relegated Cotton Mather's knowledge of inner deviltry to "a very old garret of a very old house in an old-fashioned quarter of one of the oldest towns in America."[17] The persistence of such innocence allows him to continue on errands of physical salvation that can have no lasting ethical benefit.

A GLORIFIED SHROUD

When Melville offered *Israel Potter* to Putnam's, he assured his publisher that the serialized story would "contain nothing of any sort to shock the fastidious. There will be very little reflective writing in it; nothing weighty. It is adventure."[18] As promised, the completed tale proved to be an adventure serial about the familiar matter of the American Revolution, but it was hardly a historical novel in the customary filiopietistic mode. Nor was Melville concerned, as Hawthorne had been, with tracing the Puritan origins of American Revolutionaries. Knowing that national readers expected to hear of Christian gentlemen and Yankee farmers,

Melville offered them a sardonic view of the American character by questioning the status of popular heroes. Three figures in the national pantheon – Benjamin Franklin, John Paul Jones, and Ethan Allen – are juxtaposed to the title protagonist, an unknown farmer from the Berkshires. Whereas Hawthorne was greatly concerned with the historical accuracy of his re-created pasts, Melville alters Israel Potter's autobiography for purposes more personal than historical. Melville adds, deletes, and changes with a freedom that shows a will to confirm his suspicions about the present American character by uncovering their origins in the Revolutionary era. To have selected so forgotten a tale of woe indicates that Melville sought to subvert contemporary assumptions of heroic grandeur by placing an unknown historical victim at the center of a narrative that would picture culture heroes as tainted, ineffective, or peripheral. By subtitling Israel's revised life "A Fourth of July Story," Melville surely intended to shock patriotic readers, if not fastidious ones.[19]

Melville's first chapter, which has no equivalent in his source, prepares the reader for a customary tale of historical heroism. Because the Berkshires have become a cultural backwater of neglected farms and exhausted soil, the abandoned houses of Revolutionary settlers now seem of "extraordinary size, compared with modern farmhouses."[20] The remains of their huge stone fences indicate "herculean undertakings" where "the very Titans seemed to have been at work." So that the reader may expect great things of his title character, Melville declares, "Nor could a fitter country be found for the birth place of the devoted patriot, Israel Potter" (p. 5). Throughout the book, Israel acts and thinks in ways that every American reader, however unsophisticated, could emulate. Farm laborer, landowner, surveyor, trapper, peddler, sailor, gardener, soldier, marksman at Bunker Hill – Israel is, like Franklin, "Jack of all trades, master of each and mastered by none – the type and genius of his land" (p. 48). Wholly unselfish and of common origin, Israel has an unreflecting faith in God, in country, and in a future where honest decency receives its due. In accord with commemorative tradition, he is a libertarian without being a professional revolutionary; when he tells George III that all men are born equal, his manner is polite, friendly, and firm. Melville's young rebel, however, is much more of a new man than Hawthorne's. Instead of following the known political ideals of the forefathers, Israel develops his democratic faith only after revolting against "the tyranny of his father" (p. 8). To sever Israel from any Puritan ancestry, yet keep him a representative American, Melville even renders him momentarily fatherless by referring to "the country which gave birth to our hero" (p. 6).

Thus Melville's hero is Israel, the new nation; gradually, however, Melville reveals to us that Israel is also made of potter's clay. He proves to be too innocent and trusting to make his way successfully in the callous, indifferent worlds of Revolutionary America, the British navy, Paris, and England. Melville explicitly states that "the peculiar disinterested fidelity of our adventurer's patriotism" (p. 32) is one cause of his undoing. Because Israel remains unwilling to advance himself at the expense of his democratic principles, he is ignored by his country and finally reduced to sullen submission.

Unlike the shifty Yankee peddler, who retains his individuality beneath his mask, Israel is gradually deprived of whatever personal identity he might have had. Forced to adopt disguise after disguise, he literally becomes, at one moment of the narrative, the ghost of himself. In reply to the repeated, troubling question "Who are you?" Israel can answer only, "A poor persecuted fellow at your service, sir" (p. 138). Somber beyond his years, Israel never acquires either the expansive joy or the vigorous self expected of Young America. Near the end of his pilgrimage, he finally recognizes that his last name is more appropriate than his first: "Brick is no bad name for any son of Adam; Eden was but a brick-yard; what is a mortal but a few luckless shovelfuls of clay, moulded in a mould, laid out on a sheet to dry, and ere long quickened into his queer caprices by the sun?" (p. 156).

Israel is most effectively conned, not by the English nor by the Tories, but by Revolutionary heroes and American sympathizers. Sir John Millet and George III offer him sympathy and employment, but Horne Tooke, John Woodcock, and Benjamin Franklin lock him up in closets, deprive him of food, use him as an errand boy for the Revolutionary cause, and casually discard him. John Paul Jones befriends him only until he is no longer useful as a marine. The jeering tone of Melville's dedication, "To his Highness, the Bunker-Hill Monument," is finally confirmed. Instead of setting Israel free, the battle of Bunker Hill introduces him to a series of Revolutionary patriots who confine him and cast him aside, leaving him to a new life without order, cohesion, or progress.

The ending of *Israel Potter* contains Melville's first explicit declaration that the very idea of the New Canaan is a preposterous and self-destroying illusion. Despite all mistreatment, Israel has maintained his patriotism through forty years of London exile. His longings to return to America are expressed through metaphors dear to Americans of both Puritan and Revolutionary generations. America, Israel is certain, has remained "the Fortunate Isles of the Free," "Canaan beyond the sea," and "the Promised Land" (p. 166). Melville changes his source to enable Israel to disembark near Faneuil Hall on the Fourth of July, 1825, less than a month after Webster has delivered "The Bunker Hill Monument" before the multitudes. Israel, yeoman Patriot of Bunker Hill, is nearly run over by noisy democrats who, intoxicated with Independence Day rhetoric, carry a banner commemorating "the heroes that fought" (p. 167). Instead of joining the procession to Charlestown to commemorate the battle yet again, Israel retreats to Copp's Hill to spend the entire day sitting "mute, gazing blankly about him," his cross-shaped wound on his chest (p. 167). His dazed silence is Melville's counterpart to the dazed silence with which Esther Dudley suffers Hancock's callousness. Although both scenes expose the falsities of commemorative tradition, Hawthorne arouses sympathy for Loyalists, whereas Melville arouses contempt for the hypocrisies of both the American present and the American past.

Hoping to retreat to his pre-Revolutionary past, Israel returns to his beloved Berkshires, but discovers only burned homesteads, buried hearthstones, and untended fields. All generational continuities have been erased; new Israel, already old, has no place in the present; he can no longer conceive of a future. In such circumstances, the brutal miseries of the revolution ironically seem the lesser evil. Melville concludes with a natural analogy implying that, no matter how ill-used and unfulfilled Israel may have been, his honesty and patriotism made him grander than the present generation. Melville's last words, "He died the same day that the oldest oak on his native hills was blown down" (p. 169), imply that the New Israel reached the height of its natural and historical cycle (no matter how low it was) before many a reader was born.

Israel Potter's pamphlet provided Melville his source, but the completed novel belongs to the tradition of historical romances about the American Revolution begun by Fenimore Cooper's *The Spy* (1821). Israel Potter, like Harvey Birch, is a lowborn Yankee whose democratic principles induce him to act as an undercover agent in the Revolutionary cause. Skilled for any physical task and adept at necessary deceptions, Israel and Harvey perform real services, but can have no recognized status in the new world they are helping to create. Both men spend their post-Revolutionary years in grudging self-exile. Lest the virtue of the Revolution be finally discredited by scavenger "Patriots" like the Skinners, Cooper arranges for Harvey Birch to receive the spoken blessing and written gratitude of his impossibly noble commander, George Washington. Israel Potter can receive no recognition whatever, because gentlemen Patriots like Cooper's Mr. Harper (Washington) do not exist in his world. Whereas Harvey Birch dies gloriously in the War of 1812, clutching Washington's written tribute to his breast, Israel Potter is compelled to recognize that Americans will continue to care more for commemorative rhetoric than for the Revolutionaries who inspired it.

The two Revolutionary heroes who directly influence Israel's life are declared to be typical of the national character, yet they are wholly destructive of American traits that Melville formerly had praised. Benjamin Franklin may be "the type and genius of his land" (p. 48), but the first description of him suggests a comic mountebank and necromancer, not a principled sage, and certainly not a companionable democrat. By posing as the simple, practical, plain-dealing American, Franklin works his will on his own countrymen as well as the Parisian court. The juxtaposition of Franklin and Israel shows that the American jack-of-all-trades appears in two equally unsatisfactory guises. Franklin is a Yankee as a protean actor, successful through deception; Israel Potter is a Yankee as a protean servant, victimized by his own innocence.

Melville's characterization of John Paul Jones reveals his growing fear that freedom from the constraints of Old World civilization might render Western man barbarous rather than natural, violent rather than sociable. Jones is portrayed as a self-advertiser, a freebooter, and a militarist whose thirst for glory makes him remarkably casual about human life. As a fictional character Jones has a cocky charm, but as a type for the national future, his traits become wholly sinister: "Intrepid, unprincipled, reckless, predatory, with boundless ambition, civilised in externals, but a savage at heart, America is, or may yet be, the Paul Jones of nations" (p. 120). Even if this passage is read as a tentative prophecy, rather than a description, it contends that the unlimited energies and intransigent will of Americans are losing control and direction. Repeatedly compared to American Indians, Jones exemplifies a savage spirit without any of the accompanying restraints of the Christian or the democrat.

Despite the obvious differences between Franklin and Jones, Melville suggests that there is a prophetic link between them. The savage spirit in the American character, which seems to have superseded the Christian, democratic spirit, rationalizes its violence by citing Franklin's creed. Jones names the *Bon Homme Richard* in honor of the maxim "God helps them that help themselves" (p. 61). Throughout a two-chapter description of the fight between the *Bon Homme Richard* and the *Serapis*, Melville explores the consequences of self-help when practiced by an egotist like Jones. Although Melville's readers doubtless expected to read a glorious account of the most celebrated of American Revolutionary naval victories, Melville impartially pictures the methodical decimation of the ships and the piling up of bodies. By summarizing such an event with a question ("Is civilization a thing distinct, or is it an advanced stage of barbarism?" [p. 130]), he leads an attentive reader to wonder whether Franklin's self-reliance may not lead the march of American civilization backward into savagery.

Melville conceived of the battle of the *Bon Homme Richard* and the *Serapis*, not only as a revision of Revolutionary history, but as a prophecy of civil war.[21] The battle is offered to the reader as a triple emblem: "a type, a parallel and a prophecy" (p. 120). The *Richard* and the *Serapis*, unlike England and America, but like the North and the South, are "Siamese Twins" joined together over a "disputed frontier" (p. 125). The death struggle between the two ships thus suggests that civil war is likely to occur because libertarian doctrines of self-help, coupled with the savage individualism in the American character, will prove both uncontainable and self-destructive. This vision of civil war contains no mention of slavery as its cause. As in "Benito Cereno," the reader can only conjecture that slavery is an institutional symptom of underlying human failures.

Melville's portraits of Franklin and Jones imply that the rites of the Fourth of July do not celebrate an uprising of the folk against oppressive redcoats; they dignify a rebellion manipulated by self-seeking leaders who use the common citizen's libertarian feelings.[22] Only after Melville has undercut the character of two celebrated heroes does he introduce true Americanism in a less well known Revolutionary father, Ethan Allen. Allen possesses Israel's honesty without Israel's weakness, Franklin's acuity without Franklin's duplicity, and Jones's physical power without Jones's cruelty. Allen's "essentially Western," "true American" spirit holds forth a promise of the convivial fellowship that Franklin and Jones, in differing ways, effectively stifle (p. 149).

Melville offers Ethan Allen to the reader much as Franklin offers brandy to Israel: He arouses hope, then snatches it away. Not only is Ethan Allen seen solely in chains or in prison; he looms up suddenly from the past, dominates the stage for one chapter, and recedes back into the past. Although Israel Potter is abused by Jones and Franklin for many days and several chapters, Israel is never able to meet Ethan Allen or to experience the virtues that Allen embodies. The chaining of the truly heroic American seems to have left the controlling American spirit to confidence men like Franklin, violent individualists like Jones, and lonely victims like Israel. By Melville's admission, Ethan Allen cannot be representative of the nation; to keep him fully admirable, Melville specifies, "Though born in New England, he exhibited no trace of her character" (p. 148).

Melville's "Fourth of July Story" challenges commemorative affirmation at every turn. America's heroic past seems a lie, its present tawdry and barren, and its future clouded by prophecies of civil war. Comparison of Melville's adventure story to its source, the *Life and Remarkable Adventures of Israel Potter*, reveals how thoroughly Melville abandoned the national flattery of Israel's autobiography. Israel Potter never mentioned Ethan Allen, never claimed to have met John Paul Jones, and hurried over his interview with Benjamin Franklin in two pages. He described Franklin as "that great and good man (whose humanity and generosity have been the theme of infinitely abler pens than mine)."[23] Jones was passingly mentioned as a patriotic hero: "There was no one engaged in the cause of America, that did more to establish her fame in England, and to satisfy the high boasting Britains of the bravery and unconquerable resolutions of the Yankees, than that bold adventurer Capt. Paul Jones" (pp. 58–60). Upon returning to America, the original Israel Potter was welcomed in New York, was tenderly reunited to his son, and made a tranquil, reverent pilgrimage to Bunker Hill. By making his Israel Potter more innocent and more disinterested than the historical man, Melville increased both the injustice and the pathos of his victimization.

Melville's deletions from his source are as revealing as his additions. Half of the original autobiography was concerned with Israel's description of his years in London. Potter repeatedly contrasted London crime to American rural security, and inserted lengthy protests against English poverty, English disease, and English pickpockets. After his return from exile, the historical man was confident that America remained the Promised land. Potter solemnly assured his reader that "our own country . . . like a phoenix from her ashes, having emerged from a long, an expensive and bloody war, and established a constitution upon the broad and immovable basis of natural equality, now promises to become the permanent residence of peace, liberty, science, and national felicity" (p. 77). With tiresome frequency the autobiography reiterated that Americans were "blessed with the sweets of liberty, and the undisturbed enjoyment of their natural rights" (p. 77), or that "the poorest class of inhabitants of America . . . ought not to murmur, but have reason to thank the Almighty that they were born Americans" (p. 75). Not a trace of these sentiments remains in Melville's novel.

In 1824 Israel Potter wrote a self-denying tribute to his country in hopes of obtaining a war pension. Thirty years later, Melville reshaped Potter's meager story into an entertaining portrayal of the ways in which qualities of the American character have betrayed republican dreams. Whatever self the New Israel might have developed had gradually been effaced. One cannot imagine Melville's Israel Potter remaining forever undeceived about America; nor can one imagine the historical Israel Potter referring to the American flag as a "glorified shroud" (p. 112). In a fiction designed for popular audiences, Melville thus offered an alternative meaning for the gaining of independence. So brutal a revolution provides no basis for national progress, no continuity of truly democratic character, and no hope for pressing onward into a new future.

SHIFTY IN A NEW COUNTRY

The last work of fiction Melville was to publish during his lifetime, *The Confidence-Man* (1857), reveals the total dissolution of his hopes for a Young America to be realized in the West. The citizens aboard the *Fidèle* know how to use the articles of national faith to their own advantage, but their creator has no faith in them. Abandoning the national promise expressed in his recent characterization of Ethan Allen, Melville portrays American society as a ship of many knaves and more fools, of limited folk betrayed by their own innocence and their own greed. As the second chapter specifies, all passengers are to be regarded as merchants, strangers, and hunters simultaneously – but not as convivial, hearty democrats. Carrying the hopes of humanity, the *Fidèle* remains "an Anacharsis Clootz congress of all kinds of that multiform pilgrim species, man," but the ship's pilgrimage is a journey southward that has no ethical destination and arrives nowhere.[24] The *Fidèle* embarks at sunrise (chapter 1), emerges into daylight (chapter 16), slips into "dark twilight" (chapter 23), and concludes in the blackness of midnight with hints of apocalypse, but no promises of a new kingdom to follow.

However disillusioned with America Melville may have been when writing *Pierre* or *Israel Potter*, both novels dealt with actions and decisions that had significant consequences for nation, family, and individual human beings. *The Confidence-Man* pictures American life as an inconclusive succession of discrete, unconnected conversations. Aboard the *Fidèle*, to do is to act, but to act is only to talk, and the end of all talking is the exchange of a few dollars in petty games of confidence. Language is no longer merely the vehicle for describing reality; it becomes, by the end of many conversations, the only reality that exists.

The creeds of freedom and equality seem to have resulted in a nation of faceless people; with few exceptions, Melville's passengers have no heritage, no origin, no name, and no character. They are not individuals but types (senile miser, student, good merchant, charitable lady) who exist only in their words and clothes, who emerge from the murky crowd of passengers for a moment and are promptly forgotten. Emotional relationships between them are not possible. The significance of the conversational exchanges, even their effect upon the participants, is deliberately withheld from the reader. The Confidence-Man can practice his wiles with impunity because there is no social order by which he might be identified, no system of knights and squires that creates identity by allocating responsibility. Because all ride as equals for a price, the *Fidèle* can never be more than an amalgam of continually shifting *Isolatoes* ("strangers still more strange" [p. 51]), a nation of actors whose only bond is the masquerade of the confidence game itself. It is significant that the eight avatars of the Confidence-Man become the only means of perceiving any continuity in the nonevents that occur. Although the Confidence-Man lends some continuity to the voyage, he also seeks to create ethical confusion, to subvert frankness through language. One of the few reliable judgments of the voyage suggests that the American journey has become an unreal dream accelerating toward nowhere: "Speeds the daedal boat as a dream" (p. 65).

In *Moby-Dick* and *Pierre*, Melville expressed fears that his hopes for a convivial, Christian, Western democracy might be betrayed by the violence, solipsism, or blackness in the American character. The deceptive banality of life aboard the *Fidèle* has causes neither so complex nor so profound. Evil motives and solipsistic perception are not common among the passengers; violence, though it exists, is offstage. The victims of the Confidence-Man are, for the most part, drearily ordinary people who are betrayed by either their own selfishness or their own credulity. Melville tends to divide his nation into deceivers and gulls. Of those who commend charity, most are duped fools and the others only mouth the word; of those who condemn charity, most are misers and the others misanthropes.

Although Melville placed the "essentially Western" spirit of Ethan Allen in chains, his lingering hope for the survival of Allen's qualities was implied by the end of the sentence, "Herein is his peculiar Americanism; for the Western spirit is, or will yet be (for no other is, or can be), the true American one."[25] From the perspective of 1778, the open reaches of the West allowed this expectation to flourish. Melville's comment upon Ethan Allen is therefore quite consonant with his assurance about the American literary genius being imbued with roaring Niagaras and virgin forests. When Melville finally wrote a novel with a Western setting, however, he confined his characters within a maze of indistinguishable rooms and omitted tributes to the natural sublime. The few characters in *The Confidence-Man* who have known the open West are not deluded by its theoretical sublimity. After listening to the Yarb Doctor's palaver about confidence in "Dame Nature," the Missouri bachelor asks, "Who froze to death my teamster on the prairie?" (p. 91); "Whose hailstones smashed my windows?" (p. 94).

At first Melville invites the reader to share his former confidence in the heroic Western character. The second chapter concludes with the following summary description of the hunters aboard the *Fidèle*:

> As pine, beech, birch, ash, hackmatack, hemlock, spruce, basswood, maple, interweave their foliage in the natural wood, so these varieties of mortals blended their varieties of visage and garb. A Tartar-like picturesqueness;[26] a sort of pagan abandonment and assurance. Here reigned the dashing and all-fusing spirit of the West, whose type is the Mississippi itself, which, uniting the streams of the most distant and opposite zones, pours them along, helter-skelter, in one cosmopolitan and confident tide. [P. 6]

Upon a first reading, this passage seems to reaffirm the cliché of the American melting pot by invoking the unifying power of the Mississippi – itself a literary cliché. When grouped at a distance, the passengers thus appear to possess at least some of the qualities of Ethan Allen: his paganism, abandonment, and assurance. Only upon rereading the novel can one detect the ironic intent of the passage. Few of the passengers show any trace of paganism; those who are abandoned or assured are the quickest to be gulled. Rather than elevating Americans to heroic stature, the

Western environment appears to deprive them of any individuating inner character. By the time the man in cream colors adopts his last disguise as the Cosmopolitan, he has leveled nearly all the passengers to one confident tide. Even Melville's method of composition resembles the action of the Mississippi. Myriads of disparate characters are whirled along in a series of parables concerning the bestowal of confidence. When characters first appear their clothing or occupations sharply delineate them, but they are soon forgotten in the confusion of the crowd and the triteness of their words. Like the voyage itself, few of the characters have a goal that might make them memorable.

"The River," a prose fragment almost surely deleted from *The Confidence-Man*, provides an even clearer illustration of Melville's inversion of clichés. The passage begins by invoking the Mississippi as "the father of a great multitude of waters," uniting all streams into "the Golden Age of the billow" and flowing through grand, pure Northern forests. At St. Louis, however (where the *Fidèle*'s voyage begins), the "sacred river" is invaded by the "yellow-jacked Missouri," its clear waters are muddied, and its islands disappear. "The Father of Waters" thus serves as Melville's metaphor for the leveling, muddying, and erosion that have entered national history. Its corruption is apparent to none of the passengers, who prefer to regard the river as the conventional symbol of American unity and strength.[27]

Traces of the ideal Western spirit remain in Pitch and the Invalid Titan in Homespun. Like Ethan Allen, both are prepossessing, manly figures – wholly honest, blunt of speech, and skilled in practical affairs. Significantly, however, they retain neither Ethan Allen's devotion to liberty nor his hearty spirit. The Invalid Titan is one of the very few passengers to sense that the Confidence-Man may be a "profane fiddler on heart-strings" and a "snake" (p. 75), but the Titan's voice is "lonesome enough to come from the bottom of an abandoned coal-shaft" (p. 73), he is seeking "insensibility," and his face is "lividly epileptic with hypochondriac mania" (pp. 74–5). If his perceptions are true, none will believe him; moreover, the reader is prompted to wonder whether the Titan's understanding is worth so costly a spiritual price.

A preferable model for living with disillusionment can perhaps be found in Pitch, who is surely the most sympathetic character aboard the *Fidèle* precisely because he has "confidence in distrust" (p. 93) without having totally lost his humanities. And yet Melville tells us that Pitch, who puts his faith in machinery, not men, is a fool for having trust in even one more boy; "his too indulgent, too artless and companionable nature betrayed him" (p. 113). Although Pitch is a Westerner, he has no faith in democracy. He is compared to Ishmael because he wisely preserves his own solitude, not because solitude is thrust upon him. Taken together, the Invalid Titan and Pitch suggest that perception creates misanthropy and that the manly, Western manner, if it is to endure, must admit that liberty and good fellowship are dangerous illusions. The very name "Pitch" suggests that Melville's Western man can retain heroic qualities only by adopting a Calvinistic view of man.

As *The Confidence-Man* draws near its inconclusive conclusion, debased but even more representative Westerners appear. Charlie Noble, who approaches the Cosmopolitan "with the bluff *abord* of the West" (p. 121), proves to be another confidence man trading upon presumed nobility. Noble is the last Westerner we see, and his middle name, Arnold, suggests that his calculated dishonesty is the betrayal of a fundamental Western virtue. Even Charlie Noble's deception seems trivial, however, when compared to the controlled violence of John Moredock. A legislator and a Christian gentleman amid white society, Moredock indulges deeper desires in periodic monomaniacal urges to slaughter all Indians. Like the American character anticipated in John Paul Jones, Moredock is civilized in externals, but a savage at heart. His schizophrenia implies that Western settlers, if they are to justify continental conquest, must generalize wrongs done by individual Indians into a murderous hatred for the entire red race. To avenge a personal injury upon a whole people is a projection akin to Ahab's, but Moredock's red enemies are supposed contributors to America's interracial character, a component of our universal humanity.

Paraphrasing Judge James Hall, Charlie Noble delivers a conventional but apparently sincere oratorical tribute to the American backwoodsman:

> Though held in a sort a barbarian, the backwoodsman would seem to America what Alexander was to Asia – captain in the vanguard of conquering civilization. Whatever the nation's growing opulence or power, does it not lackey his heels? Pathfinder, provider of security to those who come after him, for himself he asks nothing but hardship. Worthy to be compared with Moses in the Exodus, or the emperor Julian in Gaul. [P. 126]

Because this eulogy serves to introduce the character of John Moredock, however, Melville is subtly parodying contemporary rhetoric in praise of the conquering pioneer. Such a passage not only reminds us that Cooper's Pathfinder had been an idealization (Moredock is later called "a Leather-stocking Nemesis" [p. 130]); it ironically recalls the numerous passages in *Moby-Dick* that glorified American pioneering.

Melville's portrait of John Moredock should not lead a careful reader to assume that Melville is sentimentalizing the Indian as the noble victim of white injustice. It is the Confidence-Man who calls Indians "one of the finest of the primitive races, possessed of many heroic virtues," and who says, "When I think of Pocahontas, I am ready to love Indians" (p.

122). By specifying that Moredock's mother was thrice widowed by a
tomahawk, Melville does not exonerate Moredock, but he does emphasize
red savagery, and thereby suggest why his comparison of John Paul
Jones to American Indians was complimentary to neither party. In a
little-discussed sketch titled "The 'Gees,' " written one year before *The
Confidence-Man* was published, Melville gently ridiculed Dartmouth College, "that venerable institution," for "having been originally founded
partly with the object of finishing off wild Indians in the classics and
higher mathematics."[28] The days when Melville dwelt upon the gentler
qualities of primitive tribes, whether in Polynesia or in America, were
decidely gone.

The conversations aboard the *Fidèle* contain many speeches that recall
Melville's joyous faith in the American spirit. Because they are all spoken
by confidence men, however, the alert reader should regard them as the
songs of democratic sirens. The Confidence-Man eulogizes the free press,
declares that "the voice of the people is the voice of truth" (p. 142), and
predicts that a new era, free of evil, will arise from the advance of the
humanitarian spirit. The Soldier of Fortune is subjected to a verbal assault
in praise of the divine nature of republican government and the duty of
patriotism. By calling a fraudulent real estate venture in Minnesota the
"New Jerusalem," the Confidence-Man turns America's fondest hope
into a commercial trick (p. 43).

Neither the Confidence-Man nor the reader nor the writer can believe
the articles of national faith advanced in these speeches. In the context of
the devious motives and tawdry character of the passengers, such samples
of contemporary patriotic rhetoric collapse into parodies of themselves or,
even worse, word games. The Confidence-Man perverts the democratic
credo to such demagogic, trivial purposes that the reader eventually grows
weary and suspicious of the creed, as well as of its misapplication. Faith in
a free new world becomes only a series of phrases mouthed in a hypocritical
ritual to elicit confidence, and deceive the unwary.

Pitch, as usual, seems to be one of the few who grasp the harsher
political realities: "Aye, for come from Maine or Georgia, you come
from a slave-state, and a slave-pen, where the best breeds are to be bought
up at any price from a livelihood to the Presidency. Abolitionism, ye
Gods, but expresses the fellow-feeling of slave for slave" (p. 97). In 1857
this angry denial of freedom would have been unacceptable to hopeful
unionists, and offensive to a Southerner as well as an abolitionist. No
words are truer, however, to the world Melville has created. Aboard the
Fidèle, true liberty, which is a matter of the mind rather than political
franchise, is the rarest of qualities. A psychological as well as an economic
determinist, Pitch insists that every man has his price and that every man
is a slave to his own inner weakness. Although the Confidence-Man

would never outwardly assent to either of these propositions, he knows them to be true and "acts" upon them with continued success.

As soon as the Confidence-Man writes on his slate, "Charity thinketh no evil," charity becomes the standard by which the nation's Christian spirit is to be judged. All the characters except Pitch, Mark Winsome, and Egbert promptly restrict the meaning of charity either to confidence or to the giving of alms. Like the lawyer of "Bartleby," they thus trivialize the meaning of *caritas* that 1 Corinthians refers to. The Confidence-Man encourages this trivialization, because the reduction of *caritas* to confidence or alms creates a field for the winning of petty financial and confidential victories. Pitch, with his Augustinian sense of original sin, knows that true *caritas* "suffereth long" and "endureth" all things. When he at last succumbs (by having faith in a boy, not by giving anyone money), the Confidence-Man earns a victory that ends in Pitch's disillusionment, but is not to Pitch's discredit. To the degree that the passengers prove unreceptive to *caritas*, or even to almsgiving, the Confidence-Man deserves his Christ-like, sorrowful appearance during moments of solitude. Far more frequently, however, the lamblike stranger is a false Christ who bilks Americans by appealing to their tendency to confuse giving money with aiding the soul.

Accounts of Melville's meetings with Duyckinck, Adler, Hawthorne, and other friends convey the joy Melville found in sharing drink and frank conversation about deep, far-away things. Melville's conception of Western democracy as a free association of heroic hearts subsumed these same values. On the lips of the Confidence-Man, however, wine and words are weapons used to confuse his listener, to arouse his confidence, and then to fool him. The controlling spirit aboard the *Fidèle* may talk confidence, but confidence ultimately destroys fellowship by creating eventual mistrust. The last name that the Confidence-Man assumes, Frank Goodman, suggests that widespread pretending to Young America's virtues has destroyed frankness and perverted goodness.

Melville's deepening interest in the popular mind enables him to express his disillusionment through folk types rather than symbolic historical figures. Constance Rourke's analysis of the three recurrent folk heroes in antebellum America applies precisely to Melville's novel. The Yankee peddler, the backwoodsman, and Jim Crow – all three, Rourke showed, are lonely wanderers, hostile to any settled society, men who treat life as a game and present a mask to the world in order to conquer or to survive. The Yankee peddler and the backwoodsman become protean shape-shifters who alternate between rhapsodic tall tales and laconic understatement as means of confirming the mental superiority of the democratic commoner to the Whig, the merchant, or the town sophisticate. Whatever the underlying sociological reasons may be, Americans have created latently rebellious folk heroes who slide through established society by hoodwinking it.[29] Character, Rourke's work implies, is not something an American has, but something he can don and use.

The Confidence-Man portrays dark variants of all three folk types. Black Guinea is a Jim Crow who plays the cripple; his function is to reveal American stinginess and American racism, as well as to act the clown. Pitch may be a backwoodsman, but he is no ring-tailed roarer; he speaks in simple declarative sentences and tells no tall tales either about prodigious Western fecundity or about his own achievements. He has too much Melvillean disillusionment and too little faith in nature ever to talk like a Crockett almanac.

Because the Confidence-Man first appears as the "mysterious imposter, supposed to have recently arrived from the East" (p. 1), his origins as a character type should surely be traced to the Yankee peddler. Delighting in small deceptions, shifting masks in a moment, relishing tall tales, the Confidence-Man is, like the peddler, an unknowable figure who seems to have no family and no home. It is revealing that the Yankee peddler is the most successful confidence man aboard a Western steamboat; Ethan Allen notwithstanding, New England seems to have had the last laugh in shaping Western character. Melville's Confidence-Man, however, speaks in ways unlike such literary New England peddlers as Jack Downing and Sam Slick. When he wishes to deceive, he uses a ponderously proper style full of abstract latinate nouns, qualifying phrases, and philosophical double-talk. Whereas Jack Downing had been a libertarian whose ridicule of Jackson had been quite good-natured, Melville makes the Confidence-Man a mouthpiece for American clichés in order to expose them.

The Confidence-Man confirms many of Tocqueville's least complimentary observations about American life. Tocqueville believed that "in the ages of equality all men are independent of each other, isolated, and weak" and that Western Americans are in an especially unpromising situation: "They are unknown to one another; they have neither traditions, family feeling, nor the force of example to check their excesses." Americans are frequently described as job shifters without "rooted habits," men whose commitment to "perpetual change" turns their existence into a "perpetual feverish agitation" so great that "the whole life of an American is passed like a game of chance." Americans may claim to value liberty of opinion, but they submit to the majority's progressivist prejudices. The future orientation of the American mind, Tocqueville believed, is leading to an "ill-defined excitement and a kind of feverish impatience that creates a multitude of innovations." Because improvement is defined as the acquisition of things by a large number of people, each individual must anxiously pursue his own material betterment. Tocqueville devoted a chapter to the American passion for physical comfort, and emphasized the American's taste for "easy success and present enjoyment."[30]

Serving as a Melvillean "original character," the Confidence-Man illuminates these weaknesses like a revolving Drummond light (p. 205). The ever-changing, disconnected staging of life aboard the *Fidèle* is a necessary precondition of his success. By shifting masks of employment, he reduces life to a game of coins and words. He repeatedly hoaxes his victims by appealing to sacrosanct notions of perfectibility and social progress. Three of his most successful gimmicks, the Samaritan Pain Dissuader, the Omni-Balsamic Reinvigorator, and the Protean Easy Chair are products catering to the passengers' unattainable desire for total physical comfort. The Confidence-Man even speaks like Tocqueville's hypothetical American. Tocqueville noted that Americans were fond of fuzzy abstractions because their mobility of fortune made all ideas unsettled and potentially profitable. The Confidence-Man uses abstract language for the same reason, and with the same effect, as Tocqueville's American: "An abstract term is like a box with a false bottom; you may put in it what ideas you please, and take them out again without being observed."[31] The only American who can create himself anew in this formless world is the Confidence-Man himself.

Considered as a whole, *The Confidence-Man* is a mordant critique of Melville's declared literary creed, "republican progressiveness in Literature as in Life."[32] American society is certainly not "unshackled," its democratic spirit results in lonely leveling, and its occasionally Christian spirit ends in sentimental gestures of charity. It is misleading to conclude, however, that *The Confidence-Man* is a satire without a controlling system of authorial values. Melville recognizes that the "unshackled democratic spirit of Christianity" has been thoroughly betrayed in contemporary life, and he suggests no means for restoring it; nonetheless, that standard remains the one by which the *Fidèle* is judged and found wanting. Nowhere in any of Melville's writings between *Pierre* and *The Confidence-Man* does he indicate that the values he should like to see realized in American society have been altered.[33]

When one considers the deep cultural disillusionment that *The Confidence-Man* discloses, its tone seems all the more surprising. The bitterness and wrath that surface often in *Pierre* and occasionally in *Israel Potter* have virtually disappeared. The narrator of *The Confidence-Man* seems coldly ironic, bemused, and detached. Melville's sense of national mediocrity seems to have grown to the point where outright anger has become pointless. Consequently, indignation is washed away in puns, preposterously inventive tales, and seemingly offhand improvisation. Melville's refusal to believe in ultimate truth (human nature is "past finding out" [p. 59]) yields artistic fruit. *The Confidence-Man* is surely the most subtly crafted of his works, but the more we know of its art, the more we acknowledge that the book's spiritual and philosophic issues are past resolution.[34] Melville's masquerade has been assembled with such ingenuity, such regard for detail, that one suspects him of reveling in the contrivance of art as a way of controlling chaos.

LOYAL OUTSIDER

One cause for the frequently hostile reception of Melville's fiction during the 1850s was the reviewers' insistence that his portrayal of the national character was a lie. One reads complaints that no such madman as Ahab ever commanded an American whaler, that the *Pequod*'s seamen are profane, that no American family was ever so degenerate as the Glendinnings, that no American novelist should deal with incest, and that both Franklin and John Paul Jones are unfair caricatures.[35] The short notice of *The Confidence-Man* that appeared in the *Berkshire County Eagle* conveys the curt response that became customary after *Pierre*:

> THE CONFIDENCE MAN – By Herman Melville – is much praised in the English papers. – One [journal] says of its picture of American society, – "The money-getting spirit which appears to pervade every class of men in the States, almost like a monomania, is vividly portrayed in this satire, together with the want of trust or honor, and the innumerable 'operations' or 'dodges' which it is certain to engender. We gladly hail the assistance of so powerful a satirist as Mr. Melville in attacking the most dangerous and debasing tendency of the age." We need not say to those who have read the book that as a picture of American society, it is *slightly* distorted.[36]

For most reviewers, however, it was not Melville's specific criticisms of America that proved offensive, but his attitude toward democratic, Christian civilization in general. A popular American novelist simply should not indulge in attacks on missionaries, satire of demagogues, agnostic speculations, irreverent views of family life, or queries about the present meaning and extent of charity.

Uncomplimentary reviewers seem not to have perceived that Melville was questioning the present condition of Western civilization, rather than its underlying ethical or political ideals. The puzzled displeasure of many reviewers reveals their fundamental confusion between facts and principles. Melville's criticisms of the failure of Western civilization to create a free, democratic, and humanitarian society were treated as if they were attacks on the unshackled democratic spirit of Christianity itself. Melville knew that similar distortions and comparable critical neglect had befallen Cooper in the late 1830s when he had turned from popular romances to social criticism.[37] No matter how principled or patriotic an author might be, vigorous criticism of Western man and his national future continued to be unacceptable. When the literary ambitions of Cooper and Melville moved beyond their proved skills as popular entertainers, both writers violated the pietistic, progressive, and chauvinistic canons of popular taste, and of the many reviewers who depended upon it.

Although "Hawthorne and His Mosses" was published only seven years before *The Confidence-Man*, Melville's views of American society and American art seem altered beyond recognition. Redburn's expectation of paradise regained is literally a world apart from the *Fidèle*. Millennial prophecy has ended in apocalyptic darkness; the democratic embrace of Western pioneering has changed to Whiggish premonitions about leveling and the loss of communal spirit. To trace the change is easier than to account for it. Surely the nation itself had not undergone such a sorry decline in so short a period. One cannot point to the various imperialistic ventures of the 1840s, to the drift of national government during the 1850s, or to impending civil war to account for Melville's disillusionment, for these matters were never his primary national concern. The argument that Melville became critical of his countrymen because they rejected him puts the cart before the horse, implies that he was supersensitive to literary reviews, and ignores the underlying toughness and good humor in his character – qualities that Newton Arvin and Edward Rosenberry have emphasized and that are everywhere evident, especially in *The Confidence-Man*. In 1856 Melville's relations with Duyckinck and Hawthorne were quite amicable, and one should remember that many of the comments about Melville's excitability and nervous disorders between 1852 and 1855 were part of a family campaign to gain him a political appointment. An author able to write and to publish books of the quality of *Israel Potter* or *The Confidence-Man* was by no means a victim of crippling melancholy or critical rejection.

To be sure, Melville had learned much since the writing of *Typee* about the simplicity of literary nationalism, the labor of earning a living as an American writer, the cultural demand for conventional reassurance, and the difficulty of remaining popular while fulfilling one's artistic aims. And yet these biographical facts cannot begin to account for the immense change separating these two summary statements: "Call him an American and have done, for you cannot say a nobler thing of him"; "Intrepid, unprincipled, reckless, predatory, with boundless ambition, civilized in externals, but a savage at heart, America is, or may yet be, the Paul Jones of nations."[38] One may conclude that Melville's excessively high cultural expectations were bound to end in an equally excessive disillusionment. Or one might select characters like Amasa Delano, the lawyer in "Bartleby," and the innocent gulls and acquisitive hunters aboard the *Fidèle*, and then cite them as Melville's accurate representation of the common midcentury

American mind. Unfortunately, either argument would reveal more about the critic than about Melville or his culture. Perhaps the truer explanation is that Melville's conception of America was a projection of his own changing state of mind, a barometer of his creative energies, his self writ large. This assertion, however, is probably as inadequate as the others; it ignores Melville's negative capability and slights his awareness that narcissism is the key to it all. Although the changes in Melville's national attitudes may be understood, he nowhere accounts for them, and they probably must remain unexplained.

9

TRUE BRIDGE
OF SIGHS

By a kind of instinct, for the poor purposes of gleaning relief to fear,
I obey the propensity of my nation and rake praises out of futurity.

Emerson to John Boynton Hill (1822)

Best swallow this pill of America which Fate brings you & sing a land
unsung.

Emerson, *Journal* (1843)

For a quarter of a century after the Civil War, Melville remained a distant, skeptical, but remarkably even-minded observer of the American scene. For him, as for writers of a newer generation, changing social forces were rendering the ideals of Young America, New Israel, and the redemptive West touchingly obsolete. The poet of *Battle-Pieces* clearly recognized that by 1865 America was emerging into an era of industrialization, religious doubt, growing federal power, and interest in scientific rather than moral law. These social changes left men of Melville's national persuasion in a most uneasy position. Inevitably, there were moments of nostalgia for the heroic American who, although he never had appeared, could no longer even be anticipated. Simultaneously, however, Melville was too much a realist not to be uneasy while indulging in simplistic reminiscence. The pursuits of the newly reunited people had the virtues of experience and energy, if nothing else. Whenever Melville re-created hearty, manly, antebellum figures like Jack Gentian, the sailors in *John Marr*, or even Billy Budd, his portraits of them were both sentimental and wryly ironic, as if he were defensive about resurrecting a possibly childlike, heroic age that contemporaries would neither credit nor respect.

Throughout *Battle-Pieces*, Melville contends that the disillusionment of civil war has marked the end of naive American credulity and trusts that a more mature national character will evolve. Self-consciously Christian innocents, whether they be like Amasa Delano or like Pierre, do not figure in Melville's conception of postwar America. The problem faced by Americans in *Clarel* is neither their moral innocence nor the illusions of their national faith, but the Arnoldian problem of wandering between worlds in search of something worthy of commitment. The fact that neither Rolfe, Clarel, Vine, nor Ungar finds any satisfying or practicable aim for living may suggest why, after completing *Clarel*, Melville turns back to characters from a past that seems to be grand, naive, and heroic, but recoverable only through an act of imagining.

THE MANFUL SOLDIER-VIEW

In 1860, when the United States of America ceased to exist, many Northerners who believed in the democratic spirit of Christianity justified their army's cause as a holy war to preserve the Union or a holy war to abolish slavery. "The Battle Hymn of the Republic," fervently sung by soldiers, citizens, and GAR veterans for decades, appealed to Old Testament assurances of a vengeful God, the Last Judgment, and the ultimate victory of right. Without a trace of doubt, Mrs. Howe's hymn equates Northern trampling of Southern vineyards with the coming of the Lord, pictures God in the "watchfires of a hundred circling camps," and urges Christ's soldiers to rout Satan's legions.[1] The exalted demands that singers of the hymn thus placed upon themselves ("Let the Hero, born of woman, crush the Serpent with his heel"; "As he died to make men holy, let us die to make men free") did not allow for mercy or reconciliation. Until God and Truth had marched on and rooted out Evil, other considerations were simply unthinkable.

When Melville applied Miltonic imagery to historical personages of the Civil War, he showed how deeply he shared this understandable need for cosmic justification. Hawthorne, however, who had closely studied the Puritan spirit among the Revolutionaries of 1776, could no longer seriously consider the possible righteousness of God's charge to any army. Passing comments in scattered letters reveal how impartial and iconoclastic his opinions of the war were: Abolitionists "look at matters with an awful squint"; old men create wars but young men die in them; slave owners, abolitionists, and unionists all know that God is somehow on their side; the war's true outcome will be new political power for some "bullet headed general." On one occasion Hawthorne facetiously suggested that New England secede and join Canada; on another, he urged that the Union army fight for the Northern slave states and "let the rest go."[2] In 1863 he wrote to Henry Bright acknowledging both the isolation of his political stance and the limits of his loyalty: "I have been publicly accused of treasonable sympathies; whereas – I sympathize with nobody and approve of nothing; and if I have any wishes on the subject, it is that New England might be a nation by itself."[3] At the moment when Mrs. Howe's hymn was binding New England to the war effort by appealing to biblical analogues of long-standing tradition, Hawthorne was concerned to preserve his ideal New England, which had never been realized.

All of Hawthorne's expectations were not as parochial and bitter as these comments suggest. Assuming the role of "a peacable man" in "Chiefly about War Matters," he satirized the stupidities of the military, but his criticisms were of procedures, not men. His private embracing of New England separatism may have been wry bluster; in public print, he still hoped that the war might somehow allow the best New England characteristics to become national. Before the legendizing of Father Abraham began, Hawthorne had described Lincoln as a cross between Uncle Sam and Ichabod Crane, a homely, serious, and kindly man with "a great deal of native sense" and "a sort of tact and wisdom that are akin to craft." Despite Lincoln's "sallow queer sagacious visage," Hawthorne "would as lief have Uncle Abe for a ruler as any man whom it would have been practical to put in his place." Seeking a regional identity for Lincoln, Hawthorne inverted the customary practice of claiming admirable Easterners like Ethan Allen for the West. Lincoln might be a Kentuckian by birth and Western in residence, but he should be regarded as "the essential representative of all Yankees." Lincoln's wit, craft, schoolmasterish appearance, and "exaggerated Yankee port and demeanor" provided Hawthorne a New England character that could then be enlarged into a model for the nation: "And yet it seemed as if I had been in the habit of seeing him daily, and had shaken hands with him a thousand times in some village street; so true he was to the aspect of the pattern American."[4]

Three years after "Chiefly about War Matters" was published, James Russell Lowell delivered his "Ode Recited at the Harvard Commemoration." Long revered for its nobility of statement, Lowell's poem offered a high-minded, benign view of the war that appealed both to popular feeling about Lincoln's martyrdom and to the genteel tradition that Lowell was then beginning to embody. The intense spiritual and political mission pervading Mrs. Howe's hymn is as foreign to Lowell's ode as the disillusioned acuity of Hawthorne's essay. Lowell's Abraham Lincoln does not emerge from the folk roots Hawthorne specified; instead, he is Christ, the Western pioneer, and American self-reliance combined. By detaching Lincoln from all origins and then concluding that he is the "New birth of our new soil, the first American," Lowell incurs the problem of defining the American in a void that Crèvecoeur, Emerson, and Tocqueville had faced before him. Lowell's slain collegians, unlike Melville's, have died for some Harvardian *veritas* that Lowell never defines, but that will "certify to earth a new imperial race." Because the war was fought to preserve the Union, America has been wholly saved; she remains "The open soul and open door / With room about her hearth for all mankind." Writing while the South is in ruins and Northern Radical Republicans prepare for Reconstruction, Lowell nonetheless reasserts an old hope: "We sit here in the Promised Land / That flows with Freedom's honey and milk."[5]

Melville shares Lowell's understandable desire to believe in national redemption, but questions whether such self-assurances are justified. Throughout *Battle-Pieces*, he never forgets that the nation that was to fuse individuals into an egalitarian republic has divided in two because republicans legalized slavery. The outbreak of battle acts as "The tempest bursting from the waste of Time / On the world's fairest hope linked with man's foulest crime."[6] Unlike Lowell, Melville perceives that the centralization of federal power necessary for reunification has made minimal government a future impossibility. He also believes, as Lowell does not, that the mythology of man's restoration to Adamic innocence in the Promised Land has resulted only in an historical reenactment of the Fall.

Whether the national fall has proved to be fortunate is a vexing problem Melville seeks to resolve through poems that are to confront historical fact while reassuring readers that Providence decreed the carnage for national good. Many of Melville's poems portray battles as a struggle of moral forces in which the militantly Christian North emerges victorious over the satanic South, Freedom conquers Slavery, and Right conquers Wrong. Many other poems, however, sympathetically describe human individuals who can find no redemptive value whatever. Still others suggest that the Southerner is in fact the victim of his region's economic and legal past. This multiple perspective gives Melville's poems a cultural complexity quite unique among the battle verse of his contemporaries. His willingness to weigh historical fact against religious justification enables him to avoid the sectional self-righteousness of Whittier or Timrod, the blandness of Lowell, or the confining personalism of Whitman, who yearns to serve as the entire nation's spiritual and physical wound dresser.

The sequence of poems describing historical battles justifies the North by citing biblical analogues or adopting Milton's divine machinery. In "The Conflict of Convictions," "Donelson," "The Battle for the Mississippi," "Gettysburg," "Look-out Mountain," and "The Fall of Richmond," Melville pictures Satan, Raphael, Michael, and Moloch acting on cosmic battlefields that are transferred to the American South. Victory at Gettysburg, for example, ends in the defeat of Dagon; the fall of Richmond is conceived as the fall of "helmeted dilated Lucifer" (p. 125). Six poems are eulogies of Northern battle heroes. In nearly all the battle poems, Melville portrays

God acting in history through heavenly or earthly emissaries to punish
a rebellious, aristocratic oligarchy.

Despite the absolute standards applied to historical battles, there are
many poems in which Melville puts aside the paradigms of the war in
Heaven, the Fall of Man, the hierarchical order, and the analogies of
Exodus. Even the title indicates that more than one voice is addressing
us. Among the battle pieces, poems that elevate slaughter into a holy
war, are other poems, "Aspects of the War," in which, without a priori
ideas, Melville looks at battle as an experience rather than as a fulfillment
of the moral imperatives of Providence. His poems thus form an early
bridge between providential and empirical conceptions of American history.

Under such scrutiny any glory that warfare might have had quickly
fades. When Fort Donelson finally surrenders, the haggard victors are
too sickened by battle to rejoice ("Donelson"). During the Wilderness
Campaign, indistinguishable armies haphazardly slaughter each other on
a bleak field littered with the rotting corpses and rusting battle gear of
past years ("The Armies of the Wilderness"). By contrasting the melancholy
demise of the wooden *Temeraire* with the "Pivot, and screw" (p. 70)
workings of contemporary ironclads, Melville implies that the conduct
of naval warfare has become even less glorious, even more distant and
mechanical, than it was in the days of Jones or Nelson. One of the last
poems of the volume, "The Apparition," compares the Civil War to a
volcano that capriciously devastates a green land and its uncomprehending
people. No deity decrees that the cataclysm will end in historical progress.

Whenever Melville puts aside his concern for historical justification,
his cast of biblical or Miltonic figures disappears, and he looks sympathetically and directly at the human individual, Northerner or Southerner,
trapped in a historical disaster over which he has no control. A listless,
crazed prisoner suddenly drops dead under the barren glare of the sun
("In the Prison Pen"). A suffering liberated slave knows that hope is
reasonable only for future black generations ("Formerly a Slave"). Deprived
of all illusions about regional merit, a freed Confederate prisoner is shown
wandering, stricken and confused, through the alien North ("The Released
Rebel Prisoner"). One suspects that Melville may have ascribed some of
his own wary bewilderment to the "College Colonel," W. F. Bartlett,
who led his troops back to Pittsfield in 1863. Returning amid unwanted
popular huzzahs, crippled in his moment of triumph, the colonel realizes
– much like Hunilla or Bartleby – that the truth that has come to him
is past utterance ("The College Colonel").

At such moments, justification of Northern righteousness dissolves
into pity for the suffering individual. Poems that seem to proclaim a holy
war of abstract principles are sometimes resolved in surprising ways. In
"The Swamp Angel," for example, Michael and the Negro, destroying

Charleston with self-righteous calm, are finally made to seem unduly complacent about the virtue of their cause:

> Who weeps for the woeful City
> Let him weep for our guilty kind;
> Who joys at her wild despairing –
> Christ, the Forgiver, convert his mind.
> [P. 106]

After readers have been led to assume that vengeance on Charleston is just, they suddenly discover that it is they who may be in need of forgiveness. When Fort Donelson finally falls after a protracted and wearying assault, the triumph is celebrated by the lines "Ah, God! may Time with happy haste / Bring wail and triumph to a waste, / And war be done" (p. 63).

Melville is acutely aware of his divided attitude toward the war. In the "Supplement," he concludes: "Noble was the gesture into which patriotic passion surprised the people in a utilitarian time and country; yet the glory of the war falls short of its pathos – a pathos which now at last ought to disarm all animosity" (p. 198). When these two attitudes bear upon the question of national reconciliation, Melville's divided feelings make any unqualified prophecies, including his own, seem simplistic. The cosmic analogy of the war in Heaven leads him to predict and to celebrate national reunion after national fall. Yet his urge to see the conflict in terms of right and wrong has made reconciliation seem not only less possible, but less desirable. The poet who has observed the sufferings of Northern or Southern individuals, and therefore yearned for national reconciliation, runs afoul of the poet who has cast the South in the role of Satan.

In some poems, the distancing abstractions of the biblical or Miltonic paradigm allow Melville to assert that reconciliation is not only feasible but certain. "A Canticle" prophesies national union by endowing the hackneyed comparison of America to Niagara with complex meaning. The opposing waters of the nation converge in a mighty fall dictated by God. Moving in ordered power, the merging waters fall only to rise anew from the depths into an overarching rainbow, symbol of a new national covenant. The Fall has become the Fortunate Fall, enabling Melville to end his poem with prophecies of a steadfast state and a more humane citizenry.

If the years of bloodshed have reconfirmed the Fortunate Fall, the Civil War can readily be seen as a purgative national tragedy. The "Supplement" thus suggests that Aristotelian terms are applicable to the entire American people: "Let us pray that the terrible historic tragedy of our time may not have been enacted without instructing our whole beloved country through terror and pity; and may fulfillment verify in the end those

expectations which kindle the bards of Progress and Humanity" (p. 202).
The poem that ends the first section of *Battle-Pieces*, "America," affirms
that national catharsis is an accomplished fact. America awakens from
the nightmare of civil war:

> And in her aspect turned to heaven
> No trace of passion or of strife –
> A clear calm look. It spake of pain,
> But such as purifies from stain –
> Sharp pangs that never come again –
> And triumph repressed by knowledge meet,
> Power dedicate, and hope grown wise.
>
> [P. 146]

The qualities Melville here associates with national redemption – pain,
knowledge, power, and wisdom – are those of a people who, somewhat
to the poet's regret, have grown beyond innocence or liberty. As in "A
Canticle," however, the abstract quality of the poem's central metaphor,
through which America is conventionally personified as nourishing mother
and awesome goddess, makes it difficult to describe specific details of
the supposedly purified future.

When Melville considers the historical aftermath of the war, he fears
that the Fortunate Fall and national catharsis are unrealizable hopes. Satan
and God, Moloch and Michael, rebellious enslaver and liberating hero –
the struggle between such opponents has been so long and mighty that
Melville sees little prospect of reconciliation. The poem "Magnanimity
Baffled" concerns a Northern conquerer who, proud of his magnanimity,
grasps a Southern hand, only to find it dead. By the end of the volume,
reconciliation has become a matter of poetic tone as well as national
politics. Because he associates the South with hellish evil, it becomes
difficult for the poet fully to accept the humane spirit of reconciliation.
Having dedicated his *Battle-Pieces* to slain Union soldiers, Melville follows
"America" with thirteen epitaph poems titled "Verses Inscriptive and
Memorial." Although these poems are elegiac, they also eulogize the just
cause for which the righteous died.

Melville's commitment to "man's later fall" has thus forced him to
affirm a national reconciliation whose historical probability he cannot
fully accept. And, conversely, the author's yearning for an end to regional
bitterness, so eloquently voiced in the "Supplement" and the personal
poems, has been impeded by the judgments of providential history.
Melville himself becomes uncomfortably aware that, by glorifying a war
for right and then adding hymns of victory and poetic epitaphs, he has
blocked the reconciliation that many of his poems embraced and predicted:

> In looking over the battle-pieces in the foregoing collection, I have been
> tempted to withdraw or modify some of them, fearful lest in presenting,

though but dramatically and by way of a poetic record, the passions and epithets of civil war, I might be contributing to a bitterness which every sensible American must wish at an end. So, too, with the emotion of victory as reproduced on some pages, and particularly toward the close. It should not be construed into an exultation misapplied – an exultation as ungenerous as unwise. [P. 198]

Aware also that the conflict within the poem is but a reflection of a conflict within himself, Melville ends his last poem with a plea that is personal as well as national:

> O, now that brave men yield the sword,
> Mine be the manful soldier-view;
> By how much more they boldly warred,
> By so much more is mercy due.
>
> [P. 195]

At the conclusion of *Battle-Pieces*, the dead hand and the rainbow remain; the certainties of "A Canticle" end in prayerful pleading.

Battle-Pieces is written by an author of growing conservative convictions. Many poems describe the Northern armies as an inchoate mass of naive boys who need the discipline and leadership that Farragut or Grant can provide. Many of Melville's most effective ironies concern young American innocents who "Perish, enlightened by the vollied glare" (p. 44), or who "Went from the North and came from the South, / With golden mottoes in the mouth / To lie down midway on a bloody bed" (p. 143). The ideal of the equality of man has only an ironic place in a world made up of great heroes and slain collegians. Melville has wholly reversed the expectations of *White-Jacket*, in which the narrator said of Americans, "In our youth is our strength; in our inexperience our wisdom."[7]

Looking backward to determine the causes of the war, Melville suggests that liberty was as much to blame as slavery. The "Supplement" makes a perceptive distinction between the motive of Southern secession and the reasoning that supported it:

> It was in subserviency to the slave-interest that Secession was plotted; but it was under the plea, plausibly urged, that certain inestimable rights guaranteed by the Constitution was [*sic*] directly menaced, that the people of the South were cajoled into revolution. Through the arts of conspirators and the perversity of fortune, the most sensitive love of liberty was entrapped into the support of a war whose implied end was the erecting in our advanced century of an Anglo-American empire based upon the systematic degradation of man. [Pp. 196–7]

How "plausible" the argument of the Calhounites, who, with unrelenting constitutional logic, had cited constitutional liberties as a justification for slavery! Melville also acknowledges that abolitionists had contributed to secession through the self-righteousness with which they vilified slave owners in the name of divine laws of human liberty. With quiet tact he states that "those unfraternal denunciations, continued through the years, and which at last inflamed to deeds that ended in bloodshed, were reciprocal" (p. 199). Thus a prophecy advanced without certainty in *Mardi* had proved true: The author of the scroll had feared that Northern Vivenzans might precipitate a revolution by their crusading zeal for total personal liberty. Now, however, Melville recognizes that the war was hastened because the American pursuit of liberty was misapplied in both regions simultaneously.

In *White-Jacket*, Melville was quick to protest against the feudalism of the laws governing the man-of-war world. The conditions of national life in 1865, however, have altered his feelings. When liberty has proved a rationale for slavery and equality a lie, the firm rule of law seems more desirable. Describing Dupont's victory over the Confederate fleet at Port Royal, Melville praises the "victory of LAW" (p. 49). Grant taking Richmond is proof that "Right through might is Law" (p. 125). Speaking to Congress in 1865, Melville's Robert E. Lee says, "What sounder fruit than re-established Law?" (p. 191). In all of these instances the rule of law, be it divine or man-made, is associated with the authority of a powerful figure, not with the will of the people.

Despite the frequency of tributes to law, Melville laments the necessity of repression at the very moment he praises its benefits. "The House-top," Melville's fine poem concerning the draft riots of 1863, seems to praise the maintaining of civil order through force when civil statutes fail. In the revolt against conscription, Melville sees a civil war on a reduced scale, in which an "Atheist roar of riot" is let loose by uncontrolled "rats" deprived of "All civil charms / And priestly spells which late held hearts in awe / Fear-bound, subjected to a better sway / Than sway of self" (p. 89). And yet Melville deeply regrets that the sway of self must be relinquished, even to a "better" power. The prompt quelling of the riot by federal troops is a sad desecration of the national ideal of liberty and individual dignity:

> Wise Draco comes, deep in the midnight roll
> Of black artillery; he comes, though late;
> In code corroborating Calvin's creed
> And cynic tyrannies of honest kings;
> He comes, nor parlies; and the Town, redeemed,
> Gives thanks devout; nor, being thankful, heeds
> The grimy slur on the Republic's faith implied,
> Which holds that Man is naturally good,
> And – more – is Nature's Roman, never to be scourged.
>
> [P. 90]

The passage reflects the complex attitudes of a republican who acknowledges the darker facts of human nature. Melville insists upon our recognizing that the rioters, whom he describes as "tawny tigers," are not "naturally good." And yet the insidious black imagery applied to Draco and the harsh alliteration of the third line cause readers to fear and to protest the "wise" Calvinism they know is necessary. Kings who establish "cynic tyrannies" are nonetheless "honest." The Conscription Act is a legalized scourging of free man that the war renders inevitable. No matter how condemnatory Melville's view of the rabble may be, he regrets that society's need for order has caused Americans to forget their right to liberty.

Throughout *Battle-Pieces*, Melville treats the new iron dome of the Capitol building as a symbol for the needed reestablishment of federal law. Yet he also recognizes that the new order will mark the end of the libertarian dream dear to Revolutionary America:

> Power unanointed may come –
> Dominion (unsought by the free)
>   And the Iron Dome,
> Stronger for stress and strain,
>   Fling her huge shadow athwart the main;
> But the Founders' dream shall flee.
>   [P. 40]

Although the war has made a stronger federal government both likely and necessary, the new powers remain shadowy, "unanointed," and "unsought." Individual freedoms, once considered the basis for a glorious future, are now associated with the past. Although Liberty was never more than the "Founder's dream," it ennobled a national youth that Melville half wishes could be retained.

The older values of innocence, democracy, and Western heartiness are being replaced by the rule of law, the spread of empire, and a tempered wisdom gained through suffering national disaster. At the end of the volume, however, these new virtues remain abstractions; they are never embodied in human characters. Nor can Melville convince the reader, or himself, that reconciliation and magnanimity have been achieved. Nonetheless, his attempts to portray the Civil War as tragedy, and to apply Miltonic imagery to battle descriptions, reveal his belief that the Civil War has given the nation new dignity and grandeur. Whereas Aristotle and Milton would have been ludicrously inappropriate to the world of *The Confidence-Man*, Melville's battle poems presume that the Civil War has raised Americans above either materialism or utilitarian practicality. Divine Providence, utterly absent from the *Fidèle*, operates in Civil War history. Imagery of Eden and the Fall can once more be seriously applied to national life, thereby showing that "Battle can heroes and bards restore" (p. 156).

The author of *The Confidence-Man* was as elusive, deceptive, and protean as its title character. The poet of *Battle-Pieces* is a moderate, rational Christian who addresses his reader seriously and directly. He declares that "with certain evils men must be more or less patient" and urges his readers to "be Christians toward our fellow-whites, as well as philanthropists toward the blacks, our fellow-men" (p. 200). His faith in Christian philanthropy and his hope for progress are feelings that the Confidence-Man used as tools of deception. The chastened sadness and quiet hopes that surface in *Battle-Pieces*, so unlike the ebullience or the irony of Melville's earlier writings, are a striking confirmation of Henry James's statement about the psychological effect of the Civil War: "The collective sense of what had occurred was of a sadness too noble not somehow to inspire, and it was truly in the air that, whatever we had as a nation produced or failed to produce, we could at least gather round this perfection of a classic woe."[8]

AT DOUBT'S FREEZING POLE

Although the most important pilgrims in *Clarel* – Rolfe, Ungar, Vine, and Clarel himself – are American wanderers who have no families, no surnames, and the sketchiest of pasts, they are not shallow type characters. Concerned with America's complex fate, they have gained from the Old World a critical detachment that the passengers aboard the *Fidèle*, immersed in the national masquerade, could never attain. Rolfe, Clarel, and Ungar may be strangers and pilgrims, but they search for life's sustaining values rather than personal gain, and they submit to no confidence games. Their earnestness, honesty, and intellectual acuity lend them a dignity that largely precludes satire. And yet these personal virtues never lead them beyond their awareness of the world's contraries. Their attempts to form lasting human attachments (Clarel with Ruth, Clarel with Vine, Rolfe with Vine) are thwarted by fate or by the human will to independence. Although each of the three has a searching intelligence, they all find much to bewilder, more to criticize, little to believe in. At the end of the pilgrimage, all four are simply left in Jerusalem – men without a country, without a social creed, and except for Ungar, without religious faith.

The national purgation foretold in *Battle-Pieces* seems not to have taken place. No character claims that any demonstrable good has resulted from the Civil War, which the poet refers to as "That evil day, / Black in the New World's calendar," a day that formed a "True Bridge of Sighs," a "Sad arch between contrasted eras."[9] When Melville declares that the killing of America's "pick and flower of sons" was endured to maintain "A paper pact, with points abstruse / As theologic ones" (p. 422), one crucial justification for the war is explicitly abandoned. All four American characters are struck by the contrast between the dry, stony rubble of the Old World and their memories of the green fertility of the New. By the end of their journey, however, they recognize that distinctions based upon environment alone are superficial. Rolfe declares that "Our New World bold / Had fain improved upon the Old; / But the hemispheres are counterparts" (p. 422). Ungar sees no fortunate prospects in the fact that America represents "New confirmation of the fall / Of Adam" (p. 483). To be sure, the very disillusionment of these characters implies that the war has brought the nation to flawed maturity. Innocent, benign progressivism, formerly associated with an American like Delano, is now associated with the Anglican priest Derwent. Nonetheless, the criticisms of Melville's Americans are directed against a people who, in the main, have remained thoughtlessly optimistic and committed to material gain.

All three of the Americans who grasp after religious certainty, Nathan, Nehemiah, and Ungar, return to Old World faiths. Part I, canto 17, the longest canto in the poem, shapes the life history of Nathan, Ruth's Zionist father, into a very Melvillean summary of national experience. Nathan has sprung from the "worthy stock" of seventeenth-century Puritans, a people whom Melville describes as "Austere, ascetical, but free" (p. 57). As Nathan's ancestors emigrate westward, their inner and outer lives prosper: "At each remove a goodlier wain, / A heart more large, an ampler shore, / With legacies of farms behind" (p. 57). After Nathan's father dies and the family moves to Illinois, Nathan begins to doubt that God and Nature are just to man, and he finally abandons his Puritan faith when he reads a Deist (probably Thomas Paine).[10] During this period of his life, Nathan is likened to an American Adam who has spiritually fallen even though he lives in Paradise. Illinois may be "a turf divine / Of promise" (p. 58), but when Melville describes Nathan tilling Illinois soil, he refers to "Adam's frame / When thrust from Eden out to dearth / And blest no more, and wise in shame" (p. 61). Obsessed with his lost faith, Nathan attempts, like Ishmael, to ease his loneliness through Pantheism, a philosophy that "tenants our maiden hemisphere" (p. 61). Pantheism, however, provides no permanent faith, bountiful harvests no longer please, and Nathan eventually finds himself, like Pierre, "at Doubt's freezing pole" (p. 62). Before Nathan leaves America, he thus stands as the embodiment of Western pioneering, and of the evolution of the American mind from Puritanism through Deism and Pantheism to honest confusion.

Like Clarel, and somewhat like Pierre, Nathan tries to resolve his doubt by making a religion of romantic love. His love for the Jewish maiden Agar, however, ultimately causes him to embrace Zionism, to emigrate to Israel, and to try to refound the New Jerusalem. Melville distinguishes between Nathan's doubts, which are perceptive and inevitable, and Nathan's

Zionist solution, which is illusory. He leads his reader to feel that Nathan is right to recognize that the New Jerusalem cannot be found in the New World, but wrong to believe that a New England Puritan can rebuild Zion in fallen Palestine.

A similar pattern develops in Melville's characterization of Nehemiah. Because of some unspecified woe that befell him in America, Nehemiah has concluded that the Millennium can be sought only in Palestine. After years of unsuccessful proselytizing, he sees a vision of the New Jerusalem hovering above the Dead Sea's horizon, and then kills himself while attempting to reach it. His vision of the New Jerusalem, however, is based upon memories he thinks he has discarded:

> Scythes hang in orchard, hay-cocks loom
> After eve-showers, the mossed roofs gloom
> Greenly beneath the homestead trees.
>
> [P. 245]

Although American millennialists must seek fulfillment of their visions beyond America, the visions can be expressed only through images of the New Israel that has betrayed them.

Because Nathan and Nehemiah are deranged and ineffectual, they recede in the second half of the poem and make no lasting impression upon the other travelers. In the fourth part of *Clarel*, commentary on the national character is virtually confined to the pronouncements of Ungar, an ex-Confederate soldier who has recently joined the pilgrimage. Ungar speaks with such intensity and clarity that he awes his listeners and nearly dominates the poem. In speech after speech, he declares dark prophecies of Melville's earlier writings to be present American fact. The American is developing a savage spirit that will make him the "new Hun"; Anglo-Saxons are "Grave, canting, Mammonite freebooters, / Who in the name of Christ and Trade / . . . Deflower the world's last sylvan glade!" (p. 434); extension of the suffrage is extension of demagoguery; the American people are a mass of unchristian solitaries whose commitment to accelerating change will end (once more) in civil strife.

Ungar's vision of the American future is one that both the Confidence-Man and the author of the Vivenza scroll would have recognized:

> Myriads playing pygmy parts –
> Debased into equality:
> In glut of all material arts
> A civic barbarism may be:
> Man disennobled – brutalized
> By popular science – Atheized
> Into a smatterer –
> . . . .
> Yet knowing all self need to know

In self's base little fallacy;
Dead level of rank common-place:
An Anglo-Saxon China, see,
May on your vast plains shame the race
In the Dark Ages of Democracy.
    America!

[P. 438]

Ungar's prophecy that Americans will prove to be barbaric role players, leveled to mediocrity and dulled with material success, assumes the dominance of the worst qualities of John Paul Jones as well as of the passengers aboard the *Fidèle*. Following long-standing traditions of cultural prophecy, Ungar discovers the national future in the West; to him, however, the "vast plains" show the "shame" of "the Dark Ages of Democracy." Nearly all the specific charges of Ungar's diatribe were less abrasively phrased by Tocqueville, who would surely have understood how the American belief in the self's sufficiency for all things is here condemned as "self's base little fallacy." Only the forthrightness of the attack on science and atheism indicates that Ungar is condemning the America of the 1870s rather than the 1840s.

Melville's characterization of Ungar raises a perplexing question of rhetorical credibility. After Ungar's tirade is concluded, Rolfe, Vine, and Clarel look at him with silent amazement. They are unwilling to agree with him, but have no rebuttal to offer. Rolfe, perhaps the most consistently sensible of the pilgrims, later defends Ungar's ideas against Derwent and flatly declares, "He's wise" (p. 487). Previously, Rolfe has called Ungar a "brave soldier and stout thinker" and has compared him to "Mars in funeral of reminiscence" (p. 466). And yet Ungar's ideas must be weighed against his obsessive concern with the defeated South and his fondness for absolute statement. Rolfe may not disagree with Ungar's ideas, but he rightly tells him, "you do but generalize / In void abstractions" (p. 481).

Ungar is a Southerner, part Indian, essentially Catholic, and a humorless political reactionary who reveres the *ancien régime*. In none of these respects does he resemble either Herman Melville or the hypothetical representative American. Ungar has a gift for exaggerated metaphors, such as his descriptions of democracy as "Harlot on Horseback" and "Arch strumpet of an impious age" (p. 481). Although Melville expresses his darkest national feelings through Ungar, he clearly disassociates himself from Ungar's character and language. The pleasure Ungar derives from verbal shock reveals only that the jeremiad depends on overstated denunciation. Referring to James Thomson's supposed pessimism, Melville was to imply that, in the 1880s, cultural criticism needed to be audibly shrill:

"I relish it in the verse if for nothing else than as a counterpoise to the exorbitant hopefulness, juvenile and shallow, that makes such a bluster in these days."[11]

Throughout *Clarel* Melville never lets his reader forget that a man's ideas are an outgrowth of his personality. It therefore follows that Ungar is of greater importance as a national character type than as a mouthpiece for ideas that Melville may or may not share. Ungar is described both as "A wandering Ishmael from the West" (p. 441) and as "An Ethan Allen, by my troth" (p. 466). He combines the rootless, solitary wandering of Melville's Ishmaels with the honesty, blunt words, and military bearing of Ethan Allen. Like Melville's ideal American, Ungar has the Indian, the colonial, and the Westerner in him. All of these qualities that Melville admired, however, now appear in a less attractive, contemporary form. Wishing to be heard rather than to listen, Ungar cares little for human fellowship or natural beauty. His Catholic leanings have nothing to do with humanitarian actions; his blunt honesty and military virtues are in the service of wholly reactionary political principles, rather than the Rights of Man. Neither Rolfe nor Vine nor Clarel can conceive that Ungar, given his high national expectations and recent disillusionment, could be other than he is. Surely, Melville's concern is not to commend or castigate Ungar's opinions, but to reveal that new, darker expressions of older American traits have become inevitable.

The characterization of Rolfe confirms the chastening of Melville's ideal American. He is introduced as a jack-of-all-trades – trapper, pioneer, seaman, scholar – a man who possesses "a genial heart, a brain austere" (p. 99). Rolfe's good nature and honest skepticism make him a sympathetic figure both to other pilgrims and to the reader. His Western qualities are not, however, accompanied by a strong democratic faith. Much like the author of *Battle-Pieces*, he trusts that the outcome of the class war will be "The first firm founding of the state" (p. 482). And he even sounds very like Ungar when referring to "King Common-place – whose rule abhorred / Yearly extends in vulgar sway, / Absorbs Atlantis and Cathay" (p. 112).

Pitch was a Westerner whose knowing Calvinism and personal reserve cut him off from fools and made him difficult to cheat. Because Rolfe is equally skeptical, yet full of hearty goodwill, he engages the reader's sympathy more readily than any of Melville's Americans since Ethan Allen. And yet, among the self-protective pilgrims who surround him, Rolfe's bluff decency gains him no lasting attachments. "Too frank, too unreserved, may be, / And indiscreet in honesty" (p. 100), Rolfe finds that none of the pilgrims is receptive to the comradeship he offers. Moreover, his readiness to entertain all ideas makes him unable to commit

himself to anything except personable equanimity and a life of wandering.
A reliable critic without creative values, Rolfe is aware that his personal
dilemma has cultural origins:

> Tis the New World that mannered me
> Yes, gave me this vile liberty
> To reverence naught, not even herself.
>
> [P. 234]

He has arrived at the Hawthornian perception that the pursuit of liberty
dissuades men from making any fulfilling commitment, and thereby leads
thinking people ultimately to mistrust liberty itself. Rolfe's mistrust,
however, gains him little benefit. Because vile liberty is the New World's
irrefusable "gift" to her citizens, Rolfe cannot seem to abandon either
his broad-minded irreverence or his wandering ways.

Ungar's diatribe against American democracy is surely excessive, but
there is not one American in *Clarel* who eulogizes the New Israel, the
democratic Western spirit, or Revolutionary heroism. As far as we know,
none of the characters decides to return to America, because there is no
new world to return to. Rolfe, Vine, and Clarel, no matter how much
they object to Ungar's particular crotchets, agree with him in substance:

> They felt how far beyond the scope
> Of elder Europe's saddest thought
> Might be the New World's sudden brought
> In youth to share old age's pains –
> To feel the arrest of hope's advance,
> And squandered last inheritance;
> And cry – "To Terminus build fanes!
> Columbus ended earth's romance:
> No New World to mankind remains!"
>
> [P. 484]

By agreeing that the New World has evolved from youthful innocence
to premature age without enjoying its heroic manhood, all three characters
reject an expectation once cherished by Melville as well as the commemorative historians. None of the characters, however, fixes the blame for
missed cultural manhood upon the war or industrialization. Republican
citizens have squandered their own inheritance; as soon as Columbus
entered the New World garden, it was corrupted.

Although Melville forecloses any hope for distinctions of cultural merit
between the Old and the New World, his American characters are clearly
more attractive, complex, and rounded than his Europeans. To represent
the Old World, Melville introduces a narrow Scottish Covenanter, a
materialistic Levantine banker, an utterly positivistic Jewish geologist, a
misanthropic Swedish revolutionary, and a worldly Anglican churchman
of calculated good cheer. Except for Derwent, all of these figures are

one-dimensional caricatures who serve a momentary purpose, but do not have the intellectual command or sophistication to carry forward the poem's far-ranging debates.

Because the poem as a whole offers no particular creed, polity, culture, or place as a source of value, its affirmative epilogue is effectively surprising. In spite of all contemporary doubt and disillusionment, Melville quietly declares that faith and despair have always hovered around the sphinx, that stoics may yet be astounded into heaven, and that man may "like the crocus budding through the snow . . . prove that death but routs life into victory" (p. 523). Such a consolation is mainly religious, but partly cultural, and all the more moving because it holds forth possibilities whose empirical bases the poet has been at pains to deny.

LEAVINGS

Melville's travels in Greece and Italy during the spring of 1857 were the source of numerous passages in later writings that unfavorably measure the nineteenth century by standards of classical civilization. Both *Clarel* (1876) and *Timoleon* (1891) develop Arnoldian contrasts between the beauty and wholeness of Greek culture and the fragmentation of the contemporary age. In 1870 Melville acquired *The Conduct of Life*, read Emerson's rhetorical question, "You do not think you will find anything there [in Europe] which you have not seen at home?" and rebuffed Emerson with the following marginal comment: "Yet possibly, Rome or Athens has something to show or suggest that Chicago has not." "Statues in Rome," a lecture Melville delivered to lyceum audiences in 1857 and 1858, holds up Roman architecture and sculpture as standards of beauty in art and of grandeur in human nature. In all probability, Melville delighted in piquing his audiences by implying that undue Christian humility might have been responsible for the diminution of man: "There was about all the Romans a heroic tone peculiar to ancient life. Their virtues were great and noble, and these virtues made them great and noble . . . It is to be hoped that this [natural majesty] is not wholly lost from the world, although the sense of earthly vanity inculcated by Christianity may have swallowed it up in humility."[12]

These are the responses of a man who, for the sake of an ultimate standard, accepts the idealization of classical sculpture as a portrayal of cultural reality. Because magnificent classical artifacts have proved to be lasting and tangible, while the era of Revolutionary hope has grown more remote, Melville's measure of cultural worth is often, in later years, moved backward by two thousand years. "The Age of the Antonines," first written before 1877 and then revised for publication in Melville's last year, is his final attempt to assess the general condition of American life. By summoning up the classical virtues praised in the opening three chapters of Gibbon's *The Decline and Fall of the Roman Empire*, Melville posits a standard for defining the deficiencies of postwar America.

Because of the poem's unfamiliarity, Melville's final version is here quoted in full:

The Age of the Antonines

While faith forecasts millennial years
  Spite Europe's embattled lines,
Back to the Past one glance be cast –
  The Age of the Antonines!
O summit of fate, O zenith of time
When a pagan gentleman reigned,
And the olive was nailed to the inn of the world
Nor the peace of the just was feigned.
  A halcyon Age, afar it shines,
Solstice of Man and the Antonines.

Hymns to the nation's friendly gods
Went up from the fellowly shrines,
No demagogue beat the pulpit-drum
  In the age of the Antonines!
The sting was not dreamed to be taken from death,
No Paradise pledged or sought,
But they reasoned of fate at the flowing feast,
Nor stifled the fluent thought.
  We sham, we shuffle while faith declines –
They were frank in the Age of the Antonines.

Orders and ranks they kept degree,
Few felt how the parvenu pines,
No law-maker took the lawless one's fee
  In the age of the Antonines!
Under law made will the world reposed
And the ruler's right confessed,
For the heavens elected the Emperor then,
The foremost of men the best.
  Ah, might we read in America's signs
The Age restored of the Antonines.[13]

While contemporaries project a future millennium, Melville recalls all the lost virtues of his ideal American Republic, but attributes them to second-century Rome. Religious fellowship, the inquiring mind, appreciation of the senses, self-assurance, and manly frankness – all these familiar ideals are now associated with an irrecoverable world. Melville imagines a society ruled by a figure who is both a "pagan" and a "gentleman" (Marcus Aurelius), a society that respects free thought yet allows for heroism because it admits that death is final. Characteristically, Melville suggests that the Romans achieved their ideal state because, unlike Americans, they acted for peace rather than talking of paradise.

Although the Antonines embody Melville's unchanging cultural and personal values, these values are now associated with a form of republicanism that would have been repellent to Jack Chase or Ethan Allen. The "halcyon Age," Melville insists, is one in which law makes will, not vice versa. Gibbon had explained with great care that the government of the Antonines was only a nominal republic. The citizens of Rome, a small minority of the people, elected emperors who then ruled with firm dedication to the welfare of the state and minimal regard for popularity. By the time of Marcus Aurelius, Gibbon argued, the emperor was encouraging the people to believe that he ruled by divine right.[14] Melville's poem does not incorporate Gibbon's analysis of specific political institutions, but it clearly accepts the premises of Gibbon's argument. Second-century Rome has evolved a polity that, unlike America's, puts the best men in power ("the foremost of men the best") and eliminates demagoguery by inducing the people to wish to maintain degree. Hearty frankness and communal fellowship are thereby linked, not to a democratic republic, but to a disguised monarchy. Melville is not so undiscerning as to believe that the *ancien régime* can be recreated, nor so reactionary that he explicitly advocates its reinstatement. He simply confronts his reader with the possibility that democratic social virtues are compatible only with a predemocratic polity.

Because George Bancroft was confident that a new Roman empire was arising to supersede the old, he made a strikingly different use of Gibbon's passage. In a speech at Williams College in 1835, Bancroft claimed that the Age of the Antonines showed how any culture, no matter how refined in mind or noble in intent, will degenerate if it does not develop democratic political institutions supported by a moral people:

> It is only by infusing great principles into the common mind, that revolutions in human society are brought about. They never have been, they never can be, effected by superior individual excellence. The Age of the Antonines is the age of the greatest glory of the Roman empire. Men distinguished by every accomplishment of culture and science, for a century in succession, possessed undisputed sway over more than a hundred millions of men; till at last, in the person of Marcus Aurelius, philosophy herself seemed to mount the throne. And did she stay the downward tendencies of the Roman empire? Did she infuse new elements of life into the decaying constitution? Did she commence one great, beneficent reform? Not one permanent amelioration was effected; philosophy was clothed with absolute power; and yet absolute power accomplished nothing for Humanity. It could accomplish nothing. Had it been possible, Aurelius would have wrought a change. Society can be regenerated, the human race can be advanced, only by moral principles diffused through the multitude.[15]

To Bancroft, the combined promise of art, philosophy, science, and power is as nothing without an egalitarian polity and popular virtue. To

Melville, a nation must be judged by its quality of life; its citizenry cannot possibly attain a higher culture unless the most enlightened men have the courage to lead. By 1891 Melville had evidently forsaken the most fundamental antebellum assumption about the ways in which men can collectively better their condition.

At an unknown time after the centennial celebration, Melville wrote four posthumous sketches concerning Major Jack Gentian.[16] The last American character Melville was to develop in any detail, Gentian is a complex figure woven from Melville's heritage, his sense of his own position in postwar America, his observations on war veterans, and, no doubt, his fondness for charming eccentrics in the pages of Irving, Lamb, and Dickens. A lover of wine and frank talk, liberally enlivened with oaths, Gentian is "captain of the good fellows" in the Burgundian Club of New York (p. 353). A Southern gentleman and Harvard graduate, Gentian fought under Grant during the war, but he refuses to vilify the South or to participate in the mindless GAR parades of the 1870s. He believes that "fate, working through force" (p. 357), made the South succumb; the narrator remarks that Gentian could never have been a righteous partisan because "for all the free thought that beats in thy brain, at heart thou art the captive of Christ, yea, even something of a Christian" (p. 359). Both of Gentian's grandfathers were heroes of the Revolutionary War; he loves nothing more than to regale his audience with stories of the Revolution, and he remains far more proud of his family's membership in the Order of the Cincinnati than of his own services during the War of Secession.

Melville carefully distinguishes between Gentian's dress, manners, and social attitudes, which are aristocratic relics, and his political feelings, which remain libertarian. Despite Gentian's likings for classical culture and European travel, he is "not too dignified to be humane; a democrat, though less of the stump than the heart" (p. 372). From the 1850s through the 1870s, he has retained democratic feelings despite his disillusioned view of man; he gaily reminds his fellows that "all mankind, not excluding Americans, are sinners – miserable sinners, as even no few Bostonians themselves nowadays contritely respond in the liturgy" (p. 359). Rather than attempting to explain how Gentian can logically combine democratic feelings with Calvinistic principles, Melville persuades his reader to appreciate Gentian's engaging, national traits; the narrator twice exclaims, "Ah, Dean of the Burgundians, but I love thee!" (p. 358).

The narrator knows, however, that his love for Jack Gentian is not widely shared. Except for the narrator and one other aging gentleman, there appear to be no club members available to listen to Gentian's tales, partly because he dispenses "considerable old-school hospitalities of the board, hardly practicable for the 'business-man' of our day" (pp. 353–

4), and partly because Melville seems so fond of Gentian that he does not wish him to be contradicted. When Gentian travels to Newport, he prefers to talk with genial house servants rather than the respectable worthies who sit on the hotel veranda talking stocks and bonds. Gentian discovers that almsgiving is as socially unacceptable in the 1870s as it was in Tocqueville's time. After he gives money to an old vagabond, his act of kindness is criticized by a "middle-aged merchant and vestryman, the comfortable president of a charity" (p. 369), on the grounds that, in a democracy, charity demeans the receiver.

Gentian is tolerated because he has a comfortable income, but his cosmopolitan tastes and old-school manners are resented as aristocratic, when they are not dismissed for their eccentricity. An anonymous news-paper slur mistakes Gentian's aristocratic social standards for aristocratic politics, and his pride in the Cincinnati for a love of the Bourbons. Because Gentian must obviously be "undemocratic," the writer urges that he never be considered for an office of public trust: "And is such a man – I put it to your conscience – the sort of man to take place with the law-makers of a people, the chosen people, the advance-guard of progress, a friendly people, the Levite of the nations, to whose custody Jehovah has entrusted the sacred ark of freedom?" (p. 375). The same millennial phrases that White-Jacket uttered seriously are here made into a parody of stump oratory. Although these clichés are cynically used for the purpose of personal defamation, Jack Gentian senses that he can do nothing to refute his accuser, even after he learns that the article was written by a man named Colonel J. Bunkum.

Gentian may be an objective study of the remnants of heroic American character or a self-indulgent autobiographical projection. Depending upon the reader's prejudice, Gentian may seem ridiculous or noble, sentimental or heroic, an idealist or a man of principle. We can reach no conclusion because Gentian, like the sailors in John Marr, exists in a cultural void and does not engage in any social action by which the true value of his character might be determined.

Even Billy Budd, despite its perplexing ironies and British setting, reveals Melville's nostalgia for lost American ideals. Although Billy at-tributes no symbolic import to his waving goodbye to the Rights of Man, Melville clearly does. The author, who recognizes that the rights of man are being discarded, sadly disassociates himself from the innocence of his titular hero, who is only making a gay physical gesture. The question that the scene raises, but does not answer, is whether the rights of man may be considered an adequate standard by which to judge the execution that will occur aboard Billy's new ship.

Billy has many of the qualities that Melville, forty years earlier, had considered admirably American: frankness, decency, compassion, and hearty goodwill. His physical magnificence and practical skills make him the Handsome Sailor, capable of unconsciously drawing others into convivial fellowship. Like Melville's Ishmaels, Billy has no family, no heritage, not even a birthplace; he exemplifies Redburn's statement about all Americans: "Unless we may claim all the world for our sire, like Melchisedec, we are without father or mother."[17] Aboard the *Bellipotent*, however, none of these virtues proves to be as important as the credulity and naive innocence that accompany them. Billy's faith in his superiors prevents him from perceiving or challenging the harshness of the *Bellipotent*'s naval codes. His inability to articulate any protest enables Claggart to take advantage of him, and his need for a father, common to many of Melville's orphans, leads him to an unquestioning reverence for Captain Vere. Because Billy proves unable to discard his Adamic qualities, he cannot survive. Whether Billy's execution, described as a transfiguration, is sentimental or ironic in tone, it remains a farewell to that most vulnerable of foundlings – the America of the Spirit.

"Benito Cereno" provides a suggestive analogue by which to measure Billy's innocence. The *Bellipotent*, like the *San Dominick*, is a world of dark reality in which neither divine nor natural justice operates. Although life aboard both ships abounds with deceit, violence, and autocracy, Melville persistently implies that these ships symbolize the actual conditions of contemporary life. When, therefore, in the first few pages of both novellas, Amasa Delano and Billy Budd disembark on an unknown ship, their arrival suggests the possible birth of a new soul. Conversely, the *Rights of Man* and the *Bachelor's Delight* seem to represent a state of prior innocence that adequately symbolizes the hero's character, but that must be discarded. Because Delano and Billy are never capable of satire or irony, never able to understand the "mystery of iniquity" in their new world,[18] the psychological states symbolized by their former ships seem increasingly childish. The price of innocence, however, has grown. Whereas Delano blundered through to nominal success, while recognizing that acuity would have cost him his life, Billy is hanged with probably unnecessary dispatch, and his character is deliberately misconstrued in the official report of his execution.

Readers of *Billy Budd* who believe that Melville condemns Captain Vere for violating moral justice in the name of expediency overlook the growing conservative leanings of Melville's later years. Melville's insistence in *Battle-Pieces* on the need for law, Rolfe's anticipation of "the first firm founding of the state," and the reactionary implications of "The Age of the Antonines" are quite consonant with Vere's speech to his drumhead court. Between 1860 and 1890 Melville was clearly inclining toward Starry Vere's belief that "with mankind . . . forms, measured forms, are everything" (p. 128). The narrator of *Billy Budd* shares Vere's distrust for the consequences of the French Revolution; he refers to the "irrational combustion" (p. 54) and "revolutionary chaos" (p. 166) caused by libertarian thought.

Melville's sympathy with Vere's conservative principles does not extend to approval of the code of naval regulations under which Billy is sentenced. There seems to be no mediating polity between the vanished rights of man and the *Bellipotent*, no hope that better laws could make better men, and not even a hint that better men will make better laws. Vere chooses to remain loyal to a code that he declares to be radically unjust by standards of divine or natural justice. Although the author of *White-Jacket* would surely have condemned Vere as a hypocrite and an autocrat, the narrator of *Billy Budd* is wary of any absolute, and painfully conscious of the necessity of civil restraint. In neither *Battle-Pieces* nor *Clarel* nor "The Age of the Antonines" had Melville justified the firm rule of man-made law on the grounds that man-made law corresponds to divine law. He had simply recognized that if men would live in this world they must become aware of the necessity of unjust compromise. To such a mind, the innocent energies of Young America, even if they still existed, could pose only dangerous prospects.

Considered as a sequential whole, Melville's writings show that the millennial expectations of Redburn or White-Jacket were an unrealizable national myth, a cultural hope so deeply rooted that it was expressed in overly assured terms. For a few years at midcentury, an author with a Calvinistic and socially elite heritage treasured the expectation that men of the New World would combine the best qualities of the pioneer, the Christian, the democrat, and the primitive. When Melville attempted to embody this impossibly ideal conception of American man in fictional characters, he produced the fragmentary sketches of Bulkington, Grandfather Pierre, and Ethan Allen, figures who hold forth a promise or re-create a memory, but who have no permanence in the present world. The representative American whose literary presence Melville could realize and sustain proved to be a far different figure, a wandering outcast destined to inherit a nation that somehow never appears. Although Melville's concern for Ishmaelic qualities drew upon personal experience, it had special resonance for American culture, in which freedom so readily creates loneliness. In national spirit, as in geography and politics, Melville's fictions show us why nineteenth-century America could have been both the vanguard of the future and the Ishmael of nations.

Beginning with *Moby-Dick*, Melville's writings suggest that the different facets of heroic American virtue are in fact incompatible. Pierre's innocence

and supposedly Christian radicalism end in destructive pride and a withdrawal from the natural rhythms of life. The primitive Western energies
of Paul Jones and Moredock are perverted into outbreaks of savagery
that preclude democratic feeling and Christian conduct. The changing
facets of innocence we see in Redburn, Pierre, Israel Potter, Delano, and
Billy Budd suggest that Adamic ingenuousness shades into an increasingly
vulnerable naiveté. As the behavior of the deceived aboard the *Fidèle*
shows, the outward expression of American innocence has been shifting
from genial fellowship and physical courage to sentimental philanthropy
and an unthinking pursuit of physical comfort. Even the fictional form
Melville chooses for *The Confidence-Man* forces the reader to conclude
that egalitarian strains in democratic thought are leveling and atomizing
American society, not energizing it for heroic deeds.

Unfortunately, the contemporary expressions of national political faith
were providing no answers to these dilemmas. By using the consoling
clichés of a democratic progressive civilization for selfish or trivial ends,
Franklin and the Confidence-Man create confusion and mistrust. No
character in *The Confidence-Man* or *Clarel* adheres to the hardheaded,
Revolutionary vision of Western society that Ethan Allen both proclaims
and embodies. Those who still reverence heroic behavior (Ungar, Gentian,
John Marr) have become either reactionaries or genteel sentimentalists,
men who feel isolated and outmoded in a world they never made. Melville's
most dispiriting recognition is voiced, as one might expect, by Rolfe:
The national commitment to self-reliance has created a spirit of "vile
liberty" that has obviated all possibility for a frank community of heroic
hearts.

In Melville's view, the ultimate source of betrayal resides not in the
Constitution, or in the structure of American society, or in the land, but
in the heart of the American himself. Consequently, his final warnings
about the need for law can have no substantive content, and are offered
without hope. Melville never specifies precisely what kinds of laws should
be enacted, or what form of civilization should replace the ideal America
whose promise has never been fulfilled. The unshackled democratic spirit
of Christianity has proved utterly impracticable, but Melville cannot
envision any other society worth an American's commitment.

Having inherited the contradictions of an American mythology that
he could not discard, Melville had to abandon national hymns and content
himself with exploring insoluble ironies. At periodic times in our history,
Americans of many persuasions have sought for Melvillean ideals of
community, social honesty, and a life more open and natural than the
structure of American society has seemed to allow. As long as man can
be assumed to be naturally good, Young America cannot discard the
possibility that the failings of the Republic are soluble. For Melville as

for all people, disillusionment is the measure, and sometimes the price, of unabandoned hopes. Creative energy is not expended upon ideals to which we have become indifferent. The substance of Melville's heroic national vision can never now be attained, but the vision itself is not likely to be abandoned. It is the ineradicable, ever-receding future that our cultural heritage inflicts upon us.

CONCLUSION:
FLOATING AT WILL

If, as Tocqueville predicted, Americans had to imagine the national character by generalizing from self to nation, Hawthorne and Melville were all too aware that they too were engaged in the looking-glass business. Warning his reader against the distortions of fiction, Miles Coverdale speaks of creating monsters out of the self, and of forming grand ideals "projected upon the surrounding darkness." At the time Pierre tries to create Young America through literature, Melville declares, "All the great books in the world are but the mutilated shadowings-forth of invisible and eternally unembodied images in the soul; so that they are but the mirrors, distortedly reflecting to us our own things." After Hawthorne had whimsically acknowledged that Monsieur du Miroir went everywhere with him, Melville appropriated the same figure for himself: "Yes, there he sits and looks at me, – this 'shape of mystery,' this 'identical Monsieur du Miroir.' "[1]

Convinced that the free assertion of the dark self must have destructive consequences, Hawthorne and Melville nonetheless shared in their contemporaries' need to discover a Young American worthy of a presumably progressive republic. In spite of their attempts to invoke or characterize such a person, Hawthorne's humane neo-Puritan and Melville's congenial Western democrat remained, like other variants of Young America, less a present reality than an implausible possibility. In part, both writers shared the assumption that Young America was only in the process of becoming. In part, they were keenly aware of the unrecognized dangers of aggressive innocence. But their inability to embody the promised American must also be traced to their own insistent evasions. Convincing projections of a national self must be based on a firmly realized literary self. Whereas Emerson, Thoreau, Whitman, and Dickinson wrote within a comparatively direct autobiographical mode, Hawthorne and Melville were forever in hiding. Tommo, Redburn, White-Jacket, Ishmael, and

226

Pierre undergo Melville's experiences, but the author's self is always concealed behind a fictive persona. Hawthorne's and Coverdale's constant reminders that they keep the inmost Me behind a veil serve not to create an authorial self, but to mask that self, if not to obviate its individuality entirely.

The use of such self-concealing personae was not due to the simple fact that Hawthorne and Melville wrote fiction; they wrote romances because they were convinced that the self was undefinable. Monsieur du Miroir, Melville and Hawthorne agreed, must forever remain a "shape of mystery." Whatever self these writers might claim for Young America was therefore, from the outset, an assumed identity. Their acknowledgment that they were assuming a self became in turn their greatest insight into the fantasizing imbedded in all evocations of the American character. Whereas Whitman used every conceivable device to make readers believe they could touch the singer of "Song of Myself," the very names Ishmael and White-Jacket force us to acknowledge that, whatever Young America they may represent, only a fiction gives them their identity.

Later historians have shown that neither the importance nor the impossibility of defining the American character was to lessen merely because the Civil War had ended the nation's youth. Henry Adams devoted the last chapter of the last volume of the *History of the United States of America during the Administrations of Jefferson and Madison* to defining "American Character." Accepting the Tocquevillean premise that "the nation could only be understood by studying the individual," Adams concluded that by 1817, "The traits of American character *were fixed.*" Logically proceeding to enumerate those American traits, Adams could merely make vague mention of "intelligence, rapidity, and mildness." He therefore ended the *History* with eight consecutive questions to be answered before anyone could truly know "what kind of people these millions *were to be.*"[2]

If forever asserting its newness has been America's only tradition, then the continual anxiety to define the American has been caused by the fact that there can be no single, representative national identity. Until quite recently, each individual has claimed imminent reality for a future American projected in the individual's own image. Noting that Americans have a "somewhat compulsive preoccupation with the question of their Americanism," David M. Potter has asserted that the two dominant models of American character have always been Jefferson's independent farmer and Tocqueville's anxious, conforming materialist. Whether both of these American types have retained their centrality may be questioned, but no one should dispute Potter's metaphor that searching for the American is an unending quest into the looking glass: "Through many decades of self-scrutiny, Americans have been seeing one or the other of these images whenever they looked into the mirror of self-analysis."[3]

Two passages by Emerson show why the raking of praises from futurity and the berating of contemporary inadequacies have been perpetually self-reinforcing processes. No one has more clearly voiced the limitless expectations of the American self:

> I dreamed that I floated at will in the great Ether, and I saw this world floating also not far off, but diminished to the size of an apple. Then an angel took it in his hand & brought it to me and said "This thou must eat!" And I ate the world.[4]

As Tocqueville predicted, there is in this American's dream no intermediary between the self and the world. Because Emerson's universe has no form, he may engage it wherever and whenever he chooses, expanding himself until the entire world becomes his hand-held possession. In the old dispensation, the Lord God forbade man to eat of the apple. In the new, the angel commands man to partake of forbidden fruit as if consumption were a sacramental duty.

Emerson's dream concerns only the act of eating the apple, only the process by which the self satisfies its new and unbounded privileges. Aware that America was a process of becoming, Emerson also knew that the tree must ultimately be known by its fruits:

> Irresistibility of the American; no conscience; his motto like nature's is, "our country right or wrong." He builds shingle palaces and shingle cities; yes, but in any altered mood perhaps this afternoon he will build stone ones with equal celerity. Tall restless Kentucky strength; great race, but tho' an admirable fruit, you shall not find one good sound well-developed apple on the bough. Nature herself was in a hurry with these hasters & never finished one.[5]

Like the Emersonian dreamer, this go-ahead American possesses the will, strength, and size necessary to transform his universe. His energies, however, are devoted to the process of transformation, not to any particular goal, and certainly not to any moral idea. Committed to undirected growth, the American can have no lasting identity save the exertion of force, the sheer power of self-creation. Although Kentucky strength can do anything, there is not yet one well-developed apple on the bough. For Emerson, fortunately, there were always the possibilities of tomorrow; for Hawthorne, there could be peace in the heart that acknowledges limits; but for Melville, there was only the wry pain of understanding his forever-disillusioning commitment to vile liberty.

NOTES

PREFACE

1 Larzer Ziff, *Literary Democracy: The Declaration of Cultural Independence in America* (New York: Viking, 1981), pp. 262, 11.

2 Henry James, *Hawthorne* (Ithaca, N.Y.: Cornell University Press, 1966), p. 22.

3 John P. McWilliams, " 'Drum Taps' and *Battle-Pieces*: The Blossom of War," *American Quarterly*, 23 (1971), pp. 181–201, and "Fictions of Merry Mount," *American Quarterly*, 29 (1977), pp. 3–30, published by the University of Pennsylvania, copyright 1971/1977, Trustees of the University of Pennsylvania; John P. McWilliams, Jr., " 'Thorough-Going Democrat' and 'Modern Tory': Hawthorne and the Puritan Revolution of 1776," *Studies in Romanticism*, 15 (1976), pp. 549–71.

INTRODUCTION

1 This summary is based upon the following sources: Joseph Blau, ed., *Social Theories of Jacksonian Democracy* (Indianapolis: Bobbs-Merrill, 1954); Marcus Cunliffe, *The Nation Takes Shape: 1789–1837* (Chicago: University of Chicago Press, 1959); Arthur Ekirch, *The Idea of Progress in America: 1815–1860* (New York: Columbia University Press, 1951); Paul Nagel, *This Sacred Trust: American Nationality, 1798–1898* (New York: Oxford University Press, 1971); Russell Nye, *Society and Culture in America: 1830–1860* (New York: Harper & Row, 1974); Russell Nye, *This Almost Chosen People* (Lansing: Michigan State University Press, 1966); George Probst, ed., *The Happy Republic* (New York: Harper & Bros., 1962); Ernest Tuveson, *Redeemer Nation* (Chicago: University of Chicago Press, 1974); Rush Welter, *The Mind of America, 1820–1860* (New York: Columbia University Press, 1975). Recent summaries of the consensus may be found in Welter, *The Mind of America*, p. 331, and in the first chapter of Nye's *Society and Culture*.

2 Andrew Jackson, "Farewell Address," in *The Statesmanship of Andrew Jackson*, ed. F. N. Thorpe (New York: Tandy-Thomas, 1909), pp. 514–15.

3 Melville, *Moby-Dick; or, The Whale*, ed. Charles Feidelson (New York: Bobbs-Merrill, 1964), pp. 160–1.

4 Michael Rogin has summarized the meaning of Jackson's appeal as follows: "Jackson forged American national identity in westward expansion and Indian Removal. The struggle with the Indians produced a powerful nationalism, a militant liberal egalitarianism, and a charismatic national political figure . . . He developed the mixture of primitive rage, agrarian nostalgia and acquisitive capitalism which formed the core of Jacksonian Democracy" (*Fathers and Children: Andrew Jackson and the Subjugation of the American Indian* [New York: Random House, 1975], p. 167).

5 George Bancroft, "Introduction" to *The History of the United States of America*, 2nd ed. (Boston: Little, Brown, 1837), I, pp. 4, 1.

6 Jackson, "Farewell Address," p. 501; letter of Noah Webster quoted in Cunliffe, *The Nation Takes Shape*, p. 128; Richard D. Rust, "Washington Irving's 'American Essays,' " *Resources for American Literary Study*, 10 (1980), pp. 3–27; Ralph Waldo Emerson, "Permanent Traits of the English National Genius" (1835), in *The Early Lectures of Ralph Waldo Emerson*, ed. S. E. Whicher and R. E. Spiller (Cambridge, Mass.: Harvard University Press, 1959), I, p. 234.

7 J. Hector St. John de Crèvecoeur, *Letters from an American Farmer* (New York: Dutton, 1957), p. 39.

8 Alexis de Tocqueville, *Democracy in America*, trans. Henry Reeve, ed. Phillips Bradley (New York: Random House, 1945), I, p. 422; Harriet Martineau, *Society in America* (New York: Saunders & Oatley, 1837), II, p. 152; Adam G. de Gurowski, *America and Europe* (New York: Appleton, 1857), p. 334; Philip Schaff, *America: A Sketch of Its Political, Social and Religious Character* (1855), reprinted with an introduction by Perry Miller (Cambridge, Mass.: Harvard University Press, 1961), pp. 46, 49.

9 William Evans Arthur, *Oration* (Covington, Ky., 1850), p. 38, quoted in Sacvan Bercovitch, *The American Jeremiad* (Madison: University of Wisconsin Press, 1978), p. 151.

10 Emerson, "Politics," from *Essays, Second Series*, in *Complete Works of Ralph Waldo Emerson*, ed. E. W. Emerson (Boston: Houghton Mifflin, 1903–4), III, p. 216 (hereafter cited as *Works*); Emerson, entry of 1840 in *Journals and Miscellaneous Notebooks of Ralph Waldo Emerson*, ed. A. W. Plumstead and Harrison Hayford (Cambridge, Mass.: Harvard University Press, 1969), VII, p. 334 (hereafter abbreviated *JMN*).

11 Joel Porte notes that, after Webster supported the Fugitive Slave Bill and *Representative Men* was published, Emerson hung a portrait of Washington in his dining room and reflected upon the greater grandeur of Washington's character. See Joel Porte, *Representative Man* (New York: Oxford University Press, 1979), p. 318.

12 See Bercovitch, *The American Jeremiad*, especially chaps. 5 and 6.

13 William Gilpin, letter of 1846, quoted in Henry Nash Smith, *Virgin Land* (Cambridge, Mass.: Harvard University Press, 1970), p. 37; Walt Whitman, November 1846 editorial in the *Daily Eagle*, reprinted in *The Gathering of Forces* (New York: Putnam, 1920), I, p. 28.

14 Emerson, *JMN*, II, p. 3; Gulian C. Verplanck, "The Advantages and Disadvantages of the American Scholar" (1836), in *American Philosophic Addresses*,

ed. J. L. Blau (New York: Columbia University Press, 1946), p. 122; Martineau, *Society in America*, I, p. 120.

15 Tocqueville, *Democracy in America*, II, p. 35; George Bancroft to Evert Duyck-inck, May 26, 1855, Duyckinck papers, New York Public Library.

16 Emerson, entry of 1846, *JMN*, IX, p. 385; Tocqueville, "Author's Introduction" to *Democracy in America*, I, p. 15; Horace Bushnell, *The Fathers of New England* (New York: Putnam, 1850), p. 37; Francis Grund, *The Americans in Their Moral, Social and Political Relations* (Boston: Marsh, Capen & Lyon, 1837), p. 149.

17 Grund, *The Americans*, p. 151.

18 Tocqueville, *Democracy in America*, II, p. 3.

19 Henry Reeve has here translated Tocqueville's phrase quite precisely: "chercher par soi-même et en soi seul la raison des choses" (*De la Democratie en Amerique*, ed. André Gain [Paris: Librairie de Medicis, 1951], II, p. 12).

20 Tocqueville, *Democracy in America*, II, pp. 77, 16, 32, 4.

21 See Leo Marx, ed., *The Americanness of Walt Whitman* (Boston: Heath, 1960), pp. 44–9.

22 Tocqueville, *Democracy in America*, II, p. 78; Tocqueville, "Quinze Jours au Desert," in *Tocqueville in America*, ed. G. W. Pierson (New York: Oxford University Press, 1938), p. 235; Whitman, *Daily Eagle*, June 1846, reprinted in *The Gathering of Forces*, p. 17; Grund, *The Americans*, pp. 240–1; Verplanck, "Advantages and Disadvantages of the American Scholar," p. 124.

23 Merk is summarizing a speech by Senator William Breese of Illinois. Merk notes that Breese's view was accepted by Secretary of State Buchanan in the *Pennsylvanian*, and then spread by war correspondents through major newspapers in all sections of the country. See Frederick Merk, *Manifest Destiny and Mission in American History: A Reinterpretation* (New York: Random House, 1966), pp. 160–1.

24 Emerson, entries of 1836, *JMN*, V, pp. 221, 259; Tocqueville, *Democracy in America*, II, pp. 16, 77–8.

25 This single sentence constitutes the entire entry, *JMN*, VII, p. 84. These were the years in which Emerson was most intensely preoccupied with "Essaying to Be" (Porte, *Representative Man*, pp. 134–60). The concept of projection then came readily to his mind; in 1837 he claimed, "A divine life I create, scenes & persons around & for me, and unfold my thought by a perpetual successive projection" (*JMN*, V, p. 337).

26 Emerson, *JMN*, VII, p. 24, V, p. 448, IV, p. 104; Emerson, "The Over-Soul," from *Essays, First Series*, in *Works*, II, p. 274. Emerson once extended his vale of soul making to the following extreme: "The state of me makes Massachusetts & the United States out there" (*JMN*, IX, p. 85).

27 Cunliffe, *The Nation Takes Shape*, p. 164.

28 Emerson, *JMN*, IX, p. 206; Charles Sumner, "Francis J. Grund's *The Americans*," *North American Review*, 46 (1838), pp. 106–7.

29 Tocqueville, *Democracy in America*, II, p. 80; Emerson, *Nature*, in *Works*, I, p. 10; Emerson, "The Poet," from *Essays, Second Series*, in *Works*, III, p. 14.

30 "A solitary quest for perfection of individual character was at the very heart of democratic hope. Yet all Cooper's loyalty to republicanism and all his

fictional inventiveness could not show him how to expand Natty's figure within society" (Kay Seymour House, *Cooper's Americans* [Columbus: Ohio State University Press, 1965], p. 327).

31 See John Stafford, *The Literary Criticism of "Young America"* (Berkeley: University of California Press, 1952); and Perry Miller, *The Raven and the Whale* (New York: Harcourt, Brace & World, 1956).

32 Arlin Turner, *Nathaniel Hawthorne: A Biography* (New York: Oxford University Press, 1980), pp. 167, 168, 275.

33 F. L. Mott, *A History of American Magazines* (New York: Appleton, 1930), I, p. 683. For information on O'Sullivan's life see Julius W. Pratt, "John O'Sullivan and Manifest Destiny," *New York History*, 14 (1933), pp. 213–34. Julian Hawthorne called O'Sullivan one of his father's "very dear friends" (*Hawthorne and His Wife* [Boston: Osgood, 1885; reprint, Saint Clair Shores, Mich.: Scholarly Press, 1968], p. 160).

34 O'Sullivan, "Introduction" to the *United States Magazine and Democratic Review*, 1 (1837), pp. 1–15.

35 O'Sullivan, "The Great Nation of Futurity," *United States Magazine and Democratic Review*, 6 (1839), pp. 426–30. Although O'Sullivan did not edit the *Democratic Review* during late 1839 and early 1840, Julius Pratt believes that he wrote this particular essay ("John O'Sullivan and Manifest Destiny," p. 222).

36 Grund, *The Americans*, p. 107; Michel Chevalier, *Society, Manners and Politics in the United States* (Boston: Weeks & Jordan, 1839), p. 369; Tocqueville, *Democracy in America*, II, p. 99.

37 O'Sullivan, "Democracy," *United States Magazine and Democratic Review*, 7 (1840), pp. 215–29. Although this essay is unsigned, O'Sullivan is again its likely author. Many of his favorite phrases – "freedom of act and thought," "less and less government," "divine origin of human rights" – are repeated. "Democracy" expresses ideas that recur in two later essays published after O'Sullivan had resumed the editorship: "The Progress of Society" in vol. 8 (1840), pp. 67–87; and "Democracy and Literature" in vol. 11 (1842), pp. 196–200.

38 O'Sullivan, "Annexation," *United States Magazine and Democratic Review*, 17 (1846), pp. 5–10.

39 O'Sullivan's writings thus provide a politically influential illustration of Quentin Anderson's insight that "our dreams of empire have had to do with imperial selves" (*The Imperial Self: An Essay in American Literary and Cultural History* [New York: Knopf, 1971], p. 18).

40 Emerson, "The Young American," in *Works*, I, pp. 363–95. Evert Duyckinck became literary editor of the *Democratic Review* in 1845 (Stafford, *Literary Criticism of "Young America,"* p. 6). Perry Miller noted that in 1844 Duyckinck had become literary editor of O'Sullivan's newspaper, the *Morning News* (*The Raven and the Whale*, p. 110). Miller did not suggest that Emerson's lecture influenced the New York based movement at all. Robert E. May claimed in passing that "John L. O'Sullivan adopted Emerson's phrase of 'Young America' in the *Democratic Review* and connected the idea with the concept of 'Manifest Destiny'" (*The Southern Dream of a Caribbean Empire, 1854–1861* [Baton Rouge:

Louisiana State University Press, 1973], p. 21 n). I suspect that the phrase "Young America" originated precisely in this manner and not in the Tetractys Club or in the fuddled enthusiasms of Cornelius Matthews. In a long, laudatory review of *Essays, Second Series* in the *Democratic Review*, the reviewer proclaimed, "No man is better adapted than Emerson to comprehend the spirit of the age and to interpret its mission. His insight is marvelously clear" (*United States Magazine and Democratic Review*, 15 [1845], p. 591).

41 Chevalier, *Society, Manners and Politics*, p. 309.

42 Martineau, *Society in America*, II, p. 185. Whereas Southern writers tended to ignore "worldly anxiety" by escaping into cavalier plantation fantasies, Northern writers had to make the best of it. In William R. Taylor's words, "If swift change and social mobility of an unprecedented kind produced glowing optimism and expectations of a secular millennium, they also produced nostalgia and disquietude" (*Cavalier and Yankee: The Old South and American National Character* [New York: Harper & Row, 1961], p. 18).

43 Hubert J. Hoeltje, *Inward Sky: The Mind and Heart of Nathaniel Hawthorne* (Durham, N.C.: Duke University Press, 1962), pp. 226, 270–2; Turner, *Nathaniel Hawthorne*, pp. 162, 169.

44 Melville, *White-Jacket; or, The World in a Man-of-War*, ed. Harrison Hayford, Hershel Parker, and Thomas Tanselle (Chicago: Northwestern-Newberry, 1970), p. 395; *Letters of Hawthorne to William D. Ticknor, 1851–1864* (Newark, N.J.: Carteret Book Club, 1910; reprint, Bloomfield Hills, Mich.: Bruccoli-Clark, 1972), I, pp. 42–3; Melville, "The House-top," in *The Battle-Pieces of Herman Melville*, ed. Hennig Cohen (New York: Thomas Yoseloff, 1963), p. 90. Emerson scorned "the flippant mistaking for freedom of some paper preamble like a Declaration of Independence" ("Fate," from *The Conduct of Life*, in *Works*, VI, p. 23). Melville described the U.S. Constitution as "A paper pact, with points abstruse / As theologic ones" (*Clarel: A Poem and Pilgrimage in the Holy Land*, ed. W. E. Bezanson [New York: Hendricks House, 1960], p. 242).

45 Melville, "Hawthorne and His Mosses," in *Herman Melville: Representative Selections*, ed. Willard Thorp (New York: American Book Co., 1938), pp. 335–6, 333, 339. Miller, *The Raven and the Whale*, pp. 284–6; Hawthorne, *The American Notebooks*, ed. Claude M. Simpson, vol. VIII of the Centenary Edition (Columbus: Ohio State University Press, 1972), p. 237.

46 Richard Wilbur, "The House of Poe," in *Anniversary Lectures: 1959*, reprinted in *Poe: A Collection of Critical Essays*, ed. Robert Regan (Englewood Cliffs, N.J.: Prentice-Hall, 1967), pp. 98–120. Also see Michael Bell, *The Development of American Romance* (Chicago: University of Chicago Press, 1980), p. 112.

47 Simms, "Preface" to *The Wigwam and the Cabin* (New York: Redfield, 1856), p. 4; Hawthorne, letter of 1857, in Horatio Bridge, *Personal Recollections of Nathaniel Hawthorne* (New York: Harper & Bros., 1893), p. 155.

1. JOHN ENDICOTT AND THE FICTIONS OF ORATORY

1 Hawthorne, *The Scarlet Letter*, intro. by Larzer Ziff, reprint of the Centenary Edition (Indianapolis: Bobbs-Merrill, 1963), p. 34.

2 Nina Baym, *The Shape of Hawthorne's Career* (Ithaca, N.Y.: Cornell University Press, 1976), pp. 17–19, 54–5, 74, 99–102.

3 Melville, *Pierre; or, The Ambiguities* (Chicago: Northwestern-Newberry, 1971), p. 278.

4 See David Levin, *History as Romantic Art* (Stanford, Calif.: Stanford University Press, 1959).

5 J. Q. Adams, *An Oration Delivered at Plymouth* (Boston: Russel & Cutter, 1802), p. 11.

6 Rufus Choate, *The Colonial Age of New England* (delivered at the Ipswich Bicentennial; Boston: Carter & Hendee, 1834), reprinted in *Works of Rufus Choate* (Boston: Little, Brown, 1862), I, p. 356 (all quotations are from the reprint); Edward Everett, *An Oration Delivered at Plymouth, December 22, 1824* (Boston: Cummings, Hilliard, 1824), p. 11; Josiah Quincy, *An Address to the Citizens of Boston* (Boston: J. H. Eastburn, 1830), p. 16.

7 Daniel Webster, *A Discourse Delivered at Plymouth* (Boston: Wells & Lilly, 1821), reprinted in *Writings and Speeches of Daniel Webster* (Boston: Little, Brown, 1903), I, p. 183 (all quotations are from the reprint); Joseph Story, *A Discourse in Commemoration of the First Settlement of Salem* (Boston: Hilliard, Gray, 1828), p. 54.

8 Joseph Story, *Discourse in Commemoration of the First Settlement of Salem*, p. 62.

9 Rufus Choate, "The Age of the Pilgrims the Heroic Period of Our History" (delivered in New York, 1843), in *Works*, I, p. 385.

10 J. V. Matthews observes that, for New England Whigs, "the Revolution was natural, legitimate – and over" ("Whig History: The New England Whigs and a Usable Past," *New England Quarterly*, 51 [1978], p. 202). In the Massachusetts commemorative addresses, however, such utterances seem to have no particular party focus. Not all the orators were Whigs, and the speeches contain scarcely one party innuendo.

11 J. Q. Adams, *An Address for Celebrating the Anniversary of Independence* (Cambridge, Mass.: Hilliard & Metcalf, 1821), p. 8.

12 Rufus Choate, "The Importance of Illustrating New England History by a Series of Romances Like the Waverley Novels: An Address Delivered at Salem, 1833," in *Works*, I, p. 330; Quincy, *Address to the Citizens of Boston*, p. 41.

13 Webster, *Discourse Delivered at Plymouth*, p. 204.

14 Choate, "Importance of Illustrating New England History," p. 333; Choate, *Colonial Age*, p. 361; Choate, "Age of the Pilgrims," p. 373; Everett, *Oration Delivered at Plymouth*, p. 21; Story, *Discourse in Commemoration of the First Settlement of Salem*, pp. 67, 88; Quincy, *Address to the Citizens of Boston*, p. 50.

15 Choate, "Age of the Pilgrims," p. 337; J. Q. Adams, *Oration Delivered at Plymouth*, p. 9; Quincy, *Address to the Citizens of Boston*, p. 53; Choate, *Colonial Age*, p. 353; Edward Everett, *An Address on the Anniversary of the Arrival of Governor Winthrop at Charlestown* (Boston: Carter & Hendee, 1830), p. 52.

16 Quincy, *Address to the Citizens of Boston*, p. 18; Joseph Story, *An Oration Pronounced at Salem on the Fourth Day of July, 1804* (Salem: William Carlton, 1804), p. 18 (John Hathorne, Jr., served on the committee of arrangements for this occasion); Webster, *Discourse Delivered at Plymouth*, p. 207.

17 Choate, "Importance of Illustrating New England History," pp. 339–40. After hearing a Forefathers Day speech at Plymouth, Harriet Martineau commented, "No man of common sense could be made to believe that any community of mortal men has ever been what the orator described the inhabitants of New England to have attained." According to Martineau, the large but restive audience was tired of rehearsed praisings of "the intensity of the New England character." After the speech, one young woman exclaimed, "I am heart-sick of this boasting. When I think of our forefathers, I want to cry, 'God be merciful to us sinners' " (*Society in America* [New York: Saunders & Oatley, 1837], I, pp. 104–5).

18 Everett, "*Address on the Anniversary of the Arrival of Governor Winthrop*," p. 52.

19 Story, *Discourse in Commemoration of the First Settlement of Salem*, p. 56.

20 Everett, *Address on the Anniversary of the Arrival of Governor Winthrop*, p. 32; J. Q. Adams, *Oration Delivered at Plymouth*, p. 8; Webster, *Discourse Delivered at Plymouth*, p. 183.

21 Choate, *Colonial Age*, p. 393; Everett, *Address on the Anniversary of the Arrival of Governor Winthrop*, pp. 50, 51.

22 Story, *Discourse in Commemoration of the First Settlement of Salem*, pp. 12–13, 89.

23 Choate, *Colonial Age*, p. 350.

24 Everett, *Address on the Anniversary of the Arrival of Governor Winthrop*, p. 37.

25 Webster, *Discourse Delivered at Plymouth*, p. 226.

26 George Bancroft, *The History of the United States of America*, 2nd ed. (Boston: Little, Brown, 1837), I, pp. 267, 467, 310, 323. The second edition is probably the one Hawthorne read.

27 Ibid., 4th ed. (1838), II, p. 451.

28 Ibid., 4th ed. (1840), III, p. 98.

29 Ibid., 2nd ed., I, pp. 343, 313, 348, 359, 460–4.

30 Ibid., pp. 394, 396, 354.

31 Ibid., p. 355.

32 Ibid., 6th ed. (1869), VII, p. 398. Bancroft's Jefferson has similar traits: "Always temperate in his mode of life and decorous in his manners, he [Jefferson] was a perfect master of his passions"; "the nursling of his country, the offspring of his time, he set about the work of a practical statesman"; even in religion, "he believed more than he himself was aware of" (ibid., 5th ed. [1866], VIII, pp. 463, 465, 464).

33 Ibid., III, p. 2.

34 Ibid., 2nd ed., I, pp. 341, 388.

35 Hawthorne, "Preface" to *The Whole History of Grandfather's Chair*, in *True Stories from History and Biography*, ed. R. H. Pearce, vol. VI of the Centenary Edition (Columbus: Ohio State University Press, 1972), pp. 5–6.

36 See especially the two addresses delivered in Salem by Joseph Story (*Discourse in Commemoration of the First Settlement of Salem*, pp. 70–8) and by Rufus Choate (*Colonial Age*, pp. 330–40).

37 Unlike Bancroft, the first generation of post-Revolutionary New England historians overlooked Puritan failings and seventeenth-century political realities

almost entirely. Hannah Adams praised the Boston Puritans, not Roger Williams, for adhering to "the sacred rights of conscience." She forthrightly reclothed Puritans as Revolutionary Whigs: "An ardent love of liberty, an unshaken attachment to the rights of man, with a desire to transmit them to their latest posterity, were the principles which governed their conduct" (*A Summary History of New England* [Dedham, Mass.: Mann & Adams, 1799], pp. 36, 22.

38 Washington Irving, *A History of New York from the Beginning of the World to the Dutch Dynasty* (New York: Inskeep & Bradford, 1809), II, p. 179, I, pp. 170, 175, 220, 172.

39 James Fenimore Cooper, *The Wept of Wish-ton-Wish* (New York: W. A. Townsend, 1859), pp. 151, 23.

40 Michael D. Bell, *Hawthorne and the Historical Romance of New England* (Princeton, N.J.: Princeton University Press, 1971), chap. 2; David S. Reynolds, *Faith in Fiction* (Cambridge, Mass.: Harvard University Press, 1981), pp. 106 ff. Lawrence Buehl has recently compared the ways in which Hawthorne and Stowe turned these simplistic contrasts into persuasive historical fiction ("Rival Romantic Interpretations of New England Puritanism: Hawthorne versus Stowe," *Texas Studies in Literature and Language*, 25 [1983], pp. 77–99).

41 Lydia Maria Child, *Hobomok: A Tale of Early Times* (Boston: Cummings, Hilliard, 1824), pp. 7, 6; Catharine Maria Sedgwick, *Hope Leslie; or, Early Times in Massachusetts* (London: John Miller, 1828), I, p. 172.

42 Hawthorne, "Alice Doane's Appeal," in *The Snow-Image and Uncollected Tales*, ed. J. D. Crowley, vol. XI of the Centenary Edition (Columbus: Ohio State University Press, 1974), p. 278.

43 Hawthorne, "Sir William Phips," in *Tales, Sketches and Other Papers*, vol. XII of the Riverside Edition (Cambridge, Mass.: Houghton Mifflin, 1883), p. 227.

44 Quoted in Randall Stewart, "Hawthorne's Contributions to *The Salem Advertiser*," *American Literature*, 5 (1934), pp. 331, 332.

45 Hawthorne, "The May-pole of Merry Mount," in *Twice-Told Tales*, ed. J. D. Crowley, vol. IX of the Centenary Edition (Columbus: Ohio State University Press, 1974). For discussions of the contribution of Hawthorne's tale to the literature of Merry Mount see Richard Sterne, "Puritans at Merry Mount: Variations on a Theme," *American Quarterly*, 22 (1970), pp. 846–58; and John McWilliams, Jr., "Fictions of Merry Mount," *American Quarterly*, 29 (1977), pp. 3–30.

46 John Lothrop Motley, *Merry Mount: A Romance of the Massachusetts Colony* (Boston: James Munroe, 1849), II, p. 249.

47 Hawthorne, "Mrs. Hutchinson," in *Tales, Sketches and Other Papers*, p. 223, italics mine.

48 Hawthorne, "Main-Street," in *The Snow-Image*, p. 55; Hawthorne, "The Gentle Boy," in *Twice-Told Tales*, p. 69.

49 Hawthorne, "The Custom-House," in *The Scarlet Letter*, p. 8.

50 Hawthorne, "Endicott and the Red Cross," in *Twice-Told Tales*, p. 433.

51 Neal Doubleday has discussed Hawthorne's use of Felt's *Annals* for the details concerning the wolf's blood, the cleft stick, and the scarlet letter (*Hawthorne's Early Tales* [Durham, N.C.: Duke University Press, 1972], pp. 104–8). Sacvan

Bercovitch has identified the Wanton Gospeller as John Clarke ("Endicott's Breastplate: Symbolism and Typology in 'Endicott and the Red Cross,'" *Studies in Short Fiction*, 8 [1972], p. 297). The Anglican in the pillory is probably Samuel Brown, banished by Endicott in 1629 (Joseph Felt, *The Annals of Salem* [Salem, Mass.: W. & S. B. Ives, 1827], p. 39). Felt excused Brown's banishment for the astounding reasons that "the policy was common to successors in the colonial administration, was frequently complained of by the sovereigns of England, and ultimately became the cause of our independence" (ibid.). The mention of cropped ears surely refers to Philip Radcliff, who had been whipped and banished by Endicott's order (ibid., p. 54).

52 I am here indebted to Michael Bell, *Hawthorne and the Historical Romance of New England*, pp. 56–60.

53 E. J. Gallagher, "History in 'Endicott and the Red Cross,'" *Emerson Society Quarterly*, 50 (1968), pp. 62–5; Doubleday, *Hawthorne's Early Tales*, pp. 101–2.

54 John Winthrop, *The History of New England*, ed. James Savage (Boston: Phelps & Farnham, 1825), I, p. 147. See also Cotton Mather, *Magnalia Christi Americana* (Hartford, Conn.: S. Andrus, 1853), II, p. 449; Daniel Neal, *The History of New England* (London: J. Clark, 1720), p. 142; Thomas Hutchinson, *The History of the Colony and Province of Massachusetts Bay*, ed. L. S. Mayo (1764; reprint, Cambridge, Mass.: Harvard University Press, 1936), I, p. 35; and Felt, *Annals of Salem*, pp. 72–6.

2. NARROWER SOULS

1 Perry Miller, *The New England Mind: From Colony to Province* (Boston: Beacon Press, 1961), bk. 1, pp. 19–104; Sacvan Bercovitch, *The American Jeremiad* (Madison: University of Wisconsin Press, 1978), pp. 31–61.

2 Bancroft, *The History of the United States of America*, 6th ed. (Boston: Little, Brown, 1869), II, p. 92.

3 Cooper, *The Wept of Wish-ton-Wish* (New York: W. A. Townsend, 1859), p. 471.

4 Hawthorne, "Main-Street," in *The Snow-Image and Uncollected Tales*, ed. J. D. Crowley, vol. XI of the Centenary Edition (Columbus: Ohio State University Press, 1974), p. 68.

5 Hawthorne, *The Scarlet Letter*, intro. by Larzer Ziff, reprint of the Centenary Edition (Indianapolis: Bobbs-Merrill, 1963), p. 223.

6 See chap. 7, "Puritan Tribalism," in Edmund S. Morgan, *The Puritan Family* (New York: Harper & Row, 1966), pp. 161–86.

7 Perry Miller, "Declension in a Bible Commonwealth," in *Nature's Nation* (Cambridge, Mass.: Harvard University Press, 1967), p. 26.

8 See, for example, Larzer Ziff's *Puritanism in America* (New York: Viking, 1973), pp. 147–8.

9 Hawthorne, "Mrs. Hutchinson," in *Tales, Sketches and Other Papers*, vol. XII of the Riverside Edition (Cambridge, Mass.: Houghton Mifflin, 1883), p. 224; Hawthorne, "Dr. Bullivant," in *Tales, Sketches and Other Papers*, p. 82; Hawthorne, *The Whole History of Grandfather's Chair*, in *True Stories from History and Biography*, ed. R. H. Pearce, vol. VI of the Centenary Edition (Columbus: Ohio State University Press, 1972), p. 96.

10 Hawthorne, "The Gentle Boy," *Twice-Told Tales*, ed. J. D. Crowley, vol. IX of the Centenary Edition (Columbus: Ohio State University Press, 1974), p. 92.

11 The relationship between Catharine and the Puritan authorities illustrates Kai Erikson's conclusion that deviant Quakers and backsliding Puritans had been eager to reaffirm their separate identities by engaging in patterned hostilities (*Wayward Puritans* [New York: Wiley, 1966], pp. 107–36).

12 Cotton Mather, *Magnalia Christi Americana* (Hartford, Conn.: S. Andrus, 1835), II, pp. 522–8; Daniel Neal, *The History of New England* (London: J. Clark, 1720), I, pp. 291–330; Thomas Hutchinson, *The History of the Colony and Province of Massachusetts Bay*, ed. L. S. Mayo (1764; reprint, Cambridge, Mass.: Harvard University Press, 1936), I, pp. 166–74; Bancroft, *History*, 2nd ed., I, pp. 450–3.

13 Hawthorne's descriptions of Endicott, of the minister's diatribe against Quakers, and of Puritan harassment of Quaker sympathizers were drawn from this source. See William Sewel, *The History of the Rise, Increase and Progress of the People Called Quakers* (Philadelphia: B. & T. Kite, 1823), I, pp. 291–3, 403–9, 584–8, 592–600.

14 Mather, *Magnalia*, I, pp. 178–81; Neal, *History of New England*, 428–33; Hutchinson, *History of . . . Massachusetts Bay*, I, pp. 316–22; Bancroft, *History*, 2nd ed., II, pp. 427–30, 446–51; Daniel Webster, *A Discourse Delivered at Plymouth* (Boston: Wells & Lilly, 1821), reprinted in *Writings and Speeches of Daniel Webster* (Boston: Little, Brown, 1903), I, p. 204; and Rufus Choate, *The Colonial Age of New England* (Boston: Carter & Hendee, 1834), reprinted in *Works of Rufus Choate* (Boston: Little, Brown, 1862), I, pp. 356–61.

15 Hawthorne, "The Gray Champion," in *Twice-Told Tales*, pp. 10, 9.

16 Mather, *Magnalia*, I, pp. 179–80. The two factions were called the "Country party" or "Popular party" and the "Moderate party." On the day of the revolt, sporadic violence and seizure of British officials continued until such principal gentlemen as Waitstill Winthrop and Simon Bradstreet met in the Town House, assumed control of the revolt, and confronted Andros. The Popular party was largely composed of landowners whose loss of title had threatened their livelihood. The merchants and ministers of the Moderate party, who stood to lose more through an unsuccessful rebellion, counseled restraint. The presence of both groups, together with some good fortune, enabled the overthrow of Andros to be bloodless. (See Michael Hall, *Edward Randolph and the American Colonies* [Chapel Hill: University of North Carolina Press, 1960], pp. 121–3; David Levin, *Cotton Mather: The Young Life of the Lord's Remembrancer, 1663–1703* [Cambridge, Mass.: Harvard University Press, 1978], pp. 162–73; and Ziff, *Puritanism in America*, pp. 222–32).

17 Josiah Quincy, *An Address to the Citizens of Boston* (Boston: J. H. Eastburn, 1830), p. 38; Hawthorne, "The Gray Champion," p. 12.

18 G. Harrison Orians, "The Angel of Hadley in Fiction," *American Literature*, 4 (1932), pp. 257–69.

19 Hawthorne, *Grandfather's Chair*, p. 79.

20 Neal, *History of New England*, II, pp. 490–630; Hutchinson, *History of . . . Massachusetts Bay*, II, pp. 16–47; Joseph Felt, *The Annals of Salem* (Salem,

Mass.: W. & S. B. Ives, 1827), pp. 304–14; Abiel Abbot, *History of Andover* (Andover, Mass.: Flagg & Gould, 1829), pp. 153–73; C. W. Upham, *Lectures on Witchcraft* (Boston: Carter & Hendee, 1831); Bancroft, *History*, 4th ed. (1840), III, pp. 72–100. Among Hawthorne's known source readings, only Cotton Mather's *Magnalia* and *The Wonders of the Invisible World* (London: J. R. Smith, 1862) attempt to defend the power of witchcraft or the conduct of civil and ecclesiastical authorities during the trials. On spectral evidence and "Young Goodman Brown" see David Levin, "Shadows of Doubt: Specter Evidence in Hawthorne's 'Young Goodman Brown,'" *American Literature*, 34 (1962), pp. 344–52; and Michael J. Colacurcio, "Visible Sanctity and Specter Evidence: The Moral Vision of Hawthorne's 'Young Goodman Brown,'" *Essex Institute Historical Collections*, 110 (1974), pp. 259–99.

21 Upham, *Lectures on Witchcraft*, p. 33. See also Abbot's *History of Andover*, p. 173; and Felt's *Annals of Salem*, p. 314.

22 Hyatt H. Waggoner, *Hawthorne: A Critical Study* (Cambridge, Mass.: Harvard University Press, 1955), pp. 37–45; Frederick Crews, *The Sins of the Fathers: Hawthorne's Psychological Themes* (London: Oxford University Press, 1976), pp. 44–60; Nina Baym, *The Shape of Hawthorne's Career* (Ithaca, N.Y.: Cornell University Press, 1976), pp. 24–6, 37–8. My interpretation of the tale develops the argument of Helen L. Elias in "Alice Doane's Innocence: The Wizard Absolved," *Emerson Society Quarterly*, 62 (1971), pp. 28–31.

23 Hawthorne, "Alice Doane's Appeal," in *The Snow-Image*, p. 271.

24 In "Main-Street," Hawthorne was to imply that any devil present must have deceived the judge: "May not the Arch-Fiend have been too subtle for the court and jury, and betrayed them – laughing in his sleeve the while – into the awful error of pouring out sanctified blood as an acceptable sacrifice upon God's altar" (p. 77). Hawthorne does not seem to recall that Cotton Mather had expressed similar fears in *Wonders of the Invisible World*.

25 Hawthorne, "Young Goodman Brown," in *Mosses from an Old Manse*, ed. William Charvat, R. H. Pearce, and Claude Simpson, vol. X of the Centenary Edition (Columbus: Ohio State University Press, 1974), p. 77.

26 Mather's presence as the presiding spirit of the trials appears to have influenced even Young Goodman Brown, who is made to repeat Mather's infamous judgment of Martha Carrier as a "rampant hag" (*Wonders of the Invisible World*, p. 159). It is probable that Hawthorne accepted Upham's view of Mather: "The famous Cotton Mather . . . combined an almost incredible amount of vanity and credulity, with a high degree of cunning and policy; an inordinate love of temporal power and distinction, with every outward manifestation of piety and Christian humility; and a proneness to fanaticism and superstition with amazing acquisitions of knowledge" (*Lectures on Witchcraft*, p. 103).

27 As Chadwick Hansen has shown, the nineteenth-century view of the witch trials is fundamentally wrong. At least three of the presumably innocent martyrs had in fact practiced witchcraft. The behavior of the afflicted girls suggests medical hysteria rather than imposture. Cotton Mather published his reservations about the use of spectral evidence before, during, and after the trials. The people did not check the witch-hunting of the clergy; the clergy

checked the witch-hunting of the magistrates, whose preliminary examinations and trials were supported by the popular opinion through the autumn of 1692. ("Preface" to *Witchcraft at Salem* [New York: Braziller, 1969], pp. ix–xvi and passim.)

28 Hawthorne, "Main-Street," p. 72.

29 Hawthorne, "The Man of Adamant," in *The Snow-Image*, p. 162.

30 Hawthorne, "Main-Street," pp. 67–8.

31 Hawthorne, "Roger Malvin's Burial," in *Twice-Told Tales*, pp. 352, 351. Here I am indebted to Frederick Crews, *Sins of the Fathers*, pp. 80–95.

32 See Hubert H. Hoeltje, "The Writing of *The Scarlet Letter*," *New England Quarterly*, 27 (1954), pp. 326–46; and Arlin Turner, *Nathaniel Hawthorne: A Biography* (New York: Oxford University Press, 1980), pp. 200–10. Although reliable information about Hawthorne's feelings toward his return to Salem is lacking, we may presume that his family's prompt desire to move to new lodgings was motivated by a desire for greater elegance as well as independence. In the fall of 1846, Hawthorne's family moved from Charter Street to small quarters on Chestnut Street where Hawthorne found it difficult to write. On December 20 Sophia wrote Horatio Bridge, "We are residing in the most stately street in Salem, but our house is much too small for our necessities" (Horatio Bridge, *Personal Recollections of Nathaniel Hawthorne* [New York: Harper & Bros., 1893], pp. 187–8). For a time after his dismissal from the Custom House and completion of *The Scarlet Letter*, Hawthorne's attitude toward the Salem community was to become almost as scornful and reclusive as Young Goodman Brown's. He declared to Horatio Bridge, "I detest this town so much that I hate to go into the streets, or to have the people see me" (ibid., pp. 208–9).

33 Earlier in the tale, the showman has explained, somewhat sardonically, "During this little interruption, you perceive that the Anglo-Saxon energy – as the phrase now goes – has been at work in the spectacle before us" (p. 57). Hawthorne's reference to the "sturdy footsteps" of Anglo-Saxon energy resembles O'Sullivan's phrase, "The Anglo-Saxon foot is already on its [California's] borders" ("Annexation," *United States Magazine and Democratic Review*, 17 [1846], p. 9). Assertions of Anglo-Saxon virtue, a commonplace among American historians of the era, are discussed in chap. 4 of David Levin's *History as Romantic Art* (Stanford, Calif.: Stanford University Press, 1959).

34 Michael Colacurcio describes Hawthorne's comparison of Hester to Anne Hutchinson as "a trap for D. H. Lawrence or other romantic (later, feminist) readers." Colacurcio asserts that "obviously we are being offered a saint's legend in which Hawthorne expects no reader literally to believe" ("Footsteps of Anne Hutchinson: The Context of *The Scarlet Letter*," *ELH*, 39 [1972], p. 460). The irony of Hawthorne's trap is, regrettably, still not obvious to all.

35 *The Scarlet Letter*, pp. 77, 83, 84, 108, 182, 184, 246, 247. Although Hawthorne's attitude toward Hester's adultery lies beyond my concerns, it is significant that the narrator of the novel applies the term "sin" to Hester's act in eight different passages (pp. 56, 83, 84, 85, 159, 189, 246, 247).

36 *The Scarlet Letter*, p. 176. Karl Wentersdorf remarks that "Hester, like other normal and sensible persons in her age, takes the existence of the Black Man

for granted and is convinced that the activities of his followers are real enough to constitute a serious problem for the community" ("The Element of Witchcraft in *The Scarlet Letter*," *Folklore*, 83 [1972], p. 149).

37 "What is most exciting about Hester is her emotional openness to all the varieties of experience – intellectual, imaginative, emotional – that the continuing emergency of her life brings to her" (Richard Brodhead, *Hawthorne, Melville and the Novel* [Chicago: University of Chicago Press, 1976], p. 63).

38 Hawthorne says of Hester's return to Boston, "Here had been her sin; here, her sorrow; and here was yet to be her penitence" (p. 246). In the forest Dimmesdale tells Hester, "Of penance I have had enough! Of penitence there has been none!" (p. 182). If Dimmesdale's public confession and last speech show his final and true penitence, must we not then credit his dying belief that Hester cannot join him in the afterlife because he is no longer "lost" (p. 241)? When the presumption of salvation ends in such harshness, a compassionate reader might prefer to be damned.

3. THE PURITAN REVOLUTION OF 1775?

1 *The Works of Daniel Webster* (Boston: Little, Brown, 1853), I, p. 58; Edward Everett, "Oration Delivered at Concord, April 19, 1825," in *Orations and Speeches* (Boston: American Stationers, 1836), p. 78.

2 Daniel Webster, "The Bunker Hill Monument," in *Works*, I, p. 73.

3 Ibid., pp. 72–3; Michael Kammen, *A Season of Youth: The American Revolution and the Historical Imagination* (New York: Oxford University Press, 1978), chap. 6.

4 Everett, "Oration Delivered at Concord," p. 81; Cooper, *Lionel Lincoln* (New York: W. A. Townsend, 1861), pp. 222–3.

5 Mason L. Weems, *The Life of Washington*, ed. M. Cunliffe (1809; reprint, Cambridge, Mass.: Harvard University Press, 1962), pp. 128, 187–202; George Bancroft, *The History of the United States of America*, 5th ed. (Boston: Little, Brown, 1861), VII, pp. 294–6, 384–403.

6 Bancroft, *History*, 5th ed., VII, p. 23; ibid., 4th ed. (1838), p. 322.

7 Sacvan Bercovitch, "Typology of America's Mission," *American Quarterly*, 30 (1978), pp. 135–55.

8 Webster, "The Bunker Hill Monument," p. 57; Emerson, *Nature*, in *Selections from Ralph Waldo Emerson*, ed. S. E. Whicher (Boston: Houghton Mifflin, 1957), p. 21.

9 Hawthorne, "John Adams," in *Hawthorne as Editor*, ed. Arlin Turner (Baton Rouge: Louisiana State University Press, 1941), p. 43; Hawthorne, "A Book of Autographs," in *The Snow-Image and Uncollected Tales*, ed. J. D. Crowley, vol. XI of the Centenary Edition (Columbus: Ohio State University Press, 1974), p. 372.

10 See Turner, *Hawthorne as Editor*, pp. 20, 23, 97.

11 Hawthorne, "A Book of Autographs," p. 373.

12 These arguments may be found, in order, in the Declaration of Independence, Adams's "Novanglus" letters, Barlow's *Advice to the Privileged Orders*, Paine's "Common Sense," and Burke's "Speech on . . . Conciliation with the Colonies."

13 Webster, "The Bunker Hill Monument," pp. 73–7.

14 Hawthorne, *The Whole History of Grandfather's Chair*, in *True Stories from History and Biography*, ed. R. H. Pearce, vol. VI of the Centenary Edition (Columbus: Ohio State University Press, 1972), p. 5. The word "authentic," even when applied to the historicism of all of Hawthorne's Revolutionary writings, seems a characteristically modest claim. Between 1828 and 1840 Hawthorne withdrew the following books from the Salem Athenaeum: five volumes of Franklin's *Works*, three volumes of Hamilton's *Works*, two volumes of Jefferson's *Memoirs*, Sparks's *Life of Washington*, Tucker's *Life of Jefferson*, Hutchinson's *History of the Colony and Province of Massachusetts Bay*, and various State Department papers on the Revolutionary era. See Marion K. Kesselring, *Hawthorne's Reading: 1828–1850* (1949; reprint, New York: Folcroft, 1969), pp. 43–64.

15 Only in *Grandfather's Chair* does Hawthorne claim that the Patriots were motivated by a struggle for democracy. Perhaps this is his one concession to his audience.

16 Hawthorne, "Old News," in *The Snow-Image*, p. 136.

17 When the old Tory exclaims, "What a fleet of privateers – pirates, say we – are fitting out for new ravages, with rebellion in their very names" (p. 156), Hawthorne surely must be thinking of his grandfather Daniel.

18 Leo Levy has argued persuasively that Hawthorne was never able to confine himself to one consistent theory of history ("Time's Portraiture: Hawthorne's Theory of History," *Nathaniel Hawthorne Journal*, 2 [1971], pp. 192–200).

19 Hawthorne, "Legends of the Province-House," in *Twice-Told Tales*, ed. J. D. Crowley, vol. IX of the Centenary Edition (Columbus: Ohio State University Press, 1974), p. 291.

20 Joliffe is not a wholly fictional character. On three occasions Hutchinson mentions John Joyliffe, a selectman of Boston who had defied Andros in 1689, had served as a member of the ad hoc "Council for Safety of the People," and had died in 1702. (Thomas Hutchinson, *The History of the Colony and Province of Massachusetts Bay*, ed. L. S. Mayo [1764; reprint, Cambridge, Mass.: Harvard University Press, 1936], I, 318, 324, II, 53). By selecting the name Joliffe, postdating Joliffe's existence seventy years, and giving him as much fictive significance as Howe, Hawthorne again links the Charter Rebellion of 1689 to the taxation rebellions of the 1770s.

21 These parallels have been noted by Julian Smith, "Hawthorne's 'Legends of the Province House,' " *Nineteenth Century Fiction*, 24 (1969), pp. 31–44.

22 Hawthorne, "A Book of Autographs," p. 367; Hawthorne, *Grandfather's Chair*, p. 174.

23 Q. D. Leavis, "Hawthorne as Poet," *Sewanee Review*, 59 (1951), p. 200.

24 Kammen, *Season of Youth*, pp. 198–200.

25 Leavis, "Hawthorne as Poet," pp. 200–5. The following comments illustrate the persistence of Leavis's interpretation. Daniel Hoffman: "Robin has cast off the remaining dependence of his immaturity" (*Form and Fable in American Fiction* [New York: Norton, 1973], p. 122); Richard Chase, The story is "the legend of a youth who achieves manhood through searching for a spiritual father" ("The Progressive Hawthorne," *Partisan Review*, 16 [1949], p. 98);

Roy Male: "Robin's coming of age . . . applies to the awakening of our national consciousness . . . Robin becomes a symbol of young Colonial America beginning to break free from its provincial Puritanism and its dependence upon the wealth of England" (*Hawthorne's Tragic Vision* [Austin: University of Texas Press, 1957], p. 52); Julian Smith: Both Robin and Ben Franklin "out of their humiliation learn the lesson of self-reliance" ("Coming of Age in America: Young Ben Franklin and Robin Molineux," *American Quarterly*, 17 [1965], p. 551). See also the articles by Seymour Gross, "Hawthorne's 'My Kinsman, Major Molineux,' " *Nineteenth Century Fiction*, 12 (1957), pp. 97–109, and by A. W. Allison, "The Literary Contexts of 'My Kinsman, Major Molineux,' " *Nineteenth Century Fiction*, 23 (1968), pp. 304–11. For a challenge to those views see two essays by Roy Harvey Pearce: "Robin Molineux on the Analyst's Couch," *Criticism*, 1 (1959), pp. 83–90; and "Hawthorne and the Sense of the Past; or, The Immortality of Major Molineux," *ELH*, 31 (1954), pp. 327–49. Only very recently has the accuracy of Hawthorne's historical details been shown. See Robert C. Grayson, "The New England Sources of 'My Kinsman, Major Molineux,' " *American Literature*, 54 (1982), pp. 545–59.

26 Hawthorne, "My Kinsman, Major Molineux," in *The Snow-Image*, pp. 208–9.

27 Hawthorne, *Septimius Felton*, in *The Elixir of Life Manuscripts*, ed. William Charvat and Roy H. Pearce, vol. XIII of the Centenary Edition (Columbus: Ohio State University Press, 1977), pp. 43, 158.

28 Hawthorne, "The Old Manse," in *Mosses from an Old Manse*, ed. William Charvat, R. H. Pearce, and Claude Simpson, vol. X of the Centenary Edition (Columbus: Ohio State University Press, 1974), p. 8.

29 Webster, "The Bunker Hill Monument," p. 73.

30 Hawthorne, *Grandfather's Chair*, p. 72.

4. A DIMINISHED THING

1 For discussion of the canon of "The Story-Teller" see Nelson Adkins, "The Early Projected Works of Nathaniel Hawthorne," *Papers of the Bibliographic Society of America*, 39 (1945), pp. 119–55; and Nina Baym, *The Shape of Hawthorne's Career* (Ithaca, N.Y.: Cornell University Press, 1976), pp. 40–52.

2 Hawthorne, "Passages from a Relinquished Work," in *Mosses from an Old Manse*, ed. William Charvat, R. H. Pearce, and Claude Simpson, vol. X of the Centenary Edition (Columbus: Ohio State University Press, 1974), p. 406.

3 Ibid., pp. 410, 411.

4 Ibid., p. 409.

5 Hawthorne, "The Journal of a Solitary Man," in *The Snow-Image and Uncollected Tales*, ed. J. D. Crowley, vol. XI of the Centenary Edition (Columbus: Ohio State University Press, 1974), pp. 326–7.

6 Hawthorne, "Passages from a Relinquished Work," pp. 406, 421.

7 Hawthorne, "Journal of a Solitary Man," p. 314.

8 Hawthorne, *The American Notebooks*, ed. Claude M. Simpson, vol. VIII of the Centenary Edition (Columbus: Ohio State University Press, 1972), p. 181.

9 The Gardiner House (ibid., pp. 41–4), the Knox Mansion (pp. 66–8), the Browne House (pp. 159–62, 274–8), and the Pepperell Mansion (pp. 268–9). Hawthorne once planned to write "a sketch – the devouring of old country residences by the overgrown monster of a city" (ibid., p. 239).

10 Hawthorne, "The Canal-Boat," from "Sketches from Memory," in *Mosses from an Old Manse*, p. 430.

11 Tocqueville, *Democracy in America*, trans. Henry Reeve, ed. Phillips Bradley (New York: Random House, 1945), II, 78.

12 In the only essay yet to suggest the quality and importance of "The Canal-Boat," Leo Levy concludes that the story provides "an analytically cold rejection of the highest product of . . . society – the American girl" ("Hawthorne's 'The Canal-Boat': An Experiment in Landscape," *American Quarterly*, 16 [1964], p. 214).

13 Hawthorne, "The Old Apple-Dealer," in *Mosses from an Old Manse*, pp. 440, 441.

14 Ibid., pp. 405–6. Hawthorne developed this juxtaposition of cultural symbols from an almost wholly descriptive passage: "This old man, wearing out dismal day after dismal day, over his little stock of apples and candy – imagine him sitting in the Station house, in the very midst of the bustle and movement of the world, where all our go-ahead stream of population rushes and roars along beside him" (*American Notebooks*, p. 226).

15 Hawthorne, "Sunday at Home," in *Twice-Told Tales*, ed. J. D. Crowley, vol. IX of the Centenary Edition (Columbus: Ohio State University Press, 1974), p. 23; Hawthorne, *American Notebooks*, pp. 352, 339.

16 Hawthorne, "The Custom-House," in *The Scarlet Letter*, intro. by Larzer Ziff, reprint of the Centenary Edition (Indianapolis: Bobbs-Merrill, 1963), pp. 3, 10.

17 Hawthorne, *Mosses from an Old Manse*, pp. 323, 335, 336.

18 Hawthorne, "The Procession of Life," in ibid., p. 216.

19 Hawthorne, "Earth's Holocaust," in *Mosses from an Old Manse*, p. 403.

20 Hawthorne, "John Inglefield's Thanksgiving," in *The Snow-Image*, pp. 184, 185.

21 Hawthorne, *Life of Franklin Pierce*, in *The Complete Works of Nathaniel Hawthorne*, ed. G. P. Lathrop (Cambridge, Mass., 1883), XII, p. 354.

22 Hawthorne, "The Great Stone Face" (1850), in *The Snow-Image*, pp. 27, 28.

23 Hawthorne, "The Old Manse," in *Mosses from an Old Manse*, p. 5.

24 Hawthorne, "Ethan Brand," in *The Snow-Image*, p. 88.

25 Brother Joseph FSC, "Art and Event in 'Ethan Brand,'" *Nineteenth Century Fiction*, 15 (1960), pp. 249–57.

26 Because Ethan's contemporaries have no sense of religious community, Sharon Cameron rightly insists: "Since the Unpardonable Sin is dislodged from any context but that of the human heart, sin and the heart also come into an unspecified equivalence" (*The Corporeal Self: Allegories of the Body in Melville and Hawthorne* [Baltimore: Johns Hopkins University Press, 1981], p. 93).

27 Tocqueville, *Democracy in America*, II, p. 106.
28 Ibid., p. 82.
29 Hawthorne, "Monsieur du Miroir," in *Mosses from an Old Manse*, pp. 160, 165. Despite Malcolm Cowley's suggestive comments on this sketch, its implications for Hawthorne's processes of characterization have not been fully considered ("Hawthorne in the Looking Glass," *Sewanee Review*, 56 [1948], pp. 545–63).

5. BROKEN LINES

1 In the face of all the words spoken and written about the Puritan tradition during the first half of the nineteenth century, James Russell Lowell praised *The House of the Seven Gables* as "the most valuable contribution to New England history that has been made" (letter to Hawthorne, April 1851). Jonathan Arac suggests the reason why Lowell could read Hawthorne's romance as a work of historical understanding: "The enduring physical establishment of the house forms an interface between the family and history, just as the established institution of the family joins the individual and society" (*Commissioned Spirits: The Shaping of Social Motion in Dickens, Carlyle, Melville and Hawthorne* [New Brunswick, N.J.: Rutgers University Press, 1979], p. 98).
2 Hawthorne, *The House of the Seven Gables*, ed. William Charvat, vol. II of the Centenary Edition (Columbus: Ohio State University Press, 1965), p. 119.
3 Thomas Hooker, "A True Sight of Sin," in *The Puritans*, ed. P. Miller and T. Johnson (New York: Harper & Row, 1963), I, pp. 298–9.
4 After assuring Hawthorne that he could not be removed from the Salem Custom House because of the Whig victory in the 1848 elections, Upham sent a petition to Washington charging Hawthorne with writing political articles in Democratic newspapers. After two trips to Washington to lobby for Hawthorne's removal, Upham succeeded. See Stephen Nissenbaum, "The Firing of Nathaniel Hawthorne," *Essex Institute Historical Collections*, 114 (1978), pp. 57–86. With regard to the vexed question of Upham's resemblance to the judge, Nissenbaum asserts only that "an Upham-like personage did appear in 1852 as Judge Jaffrey Pyncheon" (p. 71).
5 See Paul John Eakins, *The New England Girl: Cultural Ideals in Hawthorne, Stowe, Howells and James* (Athens: University of Georgia Press, 1976). Eakins shrewdly observes that "fair Phoebe makes her show of strength in the absence of any competition from Hawthorne's dark alternative, the doubting, even unbelieving woman" (p. 74).
6 "The heroine of sentimental literature . . . cannot be a mere parishioner, a mere party-member, a cog. The reader seldom knows her exact affiliation . . . Her chosen philanthropic arena is the home, whether someone else's or her own. Furthermore, she never attacks poverty or prostitution as social phenomena. That would in itself presuppose a degree of abstraction which she would find abhorrent and irrelevant. Her attempt . . . is always to improve conditions to the greatest possible extent by improving character" (Ann Douglas, *The Feminization of American Culture* [New York: Knopf, 1977], pp. 157–8).

7 See Alfred H. Marks, "Who Killed Judge Pyncheon? The Role of the Imagination in *The House of the Seven Gables*," *PMLA*, 71 (1956), pp. 355–69.

8 F. O. Matthiessen, *American Renaissance* (New York: Oxford University Press, 1941), p. 332. Defending Hawthorne's ending, Brook Thomas argues that "Holgrave's abandonment of his bachelor's quest to be a self-contained original author of reform is a fall into history and community" ("*The House of the Seven Gables*: Reading the Romance of America," *PMLA*, 97 [1982], p. 209).

9 Hawthorne, "The Journal of a Solitary Man," in *The Snow-Image and Uncollected Tales*, ed. J. D. Crowley, vol. XI of the Centenary Edition (Columbus: Ohio State University Press, 1974), p. 314.

10 Hyatt H. Waggoner, *Hawthorne: A Critical Study* (Cambridge, Mass.: Harvard University Press, 1955), pp. 176–87; Maurice Beebe, "The Fall of the House of Pyncheon," *Nineteenth Century Fiction*, 11 (1956), pp. 3–22.

11 Hawthorne, *The Blithedale Romance*, ed. William Charvat et al., vol. III of the Centenary Edition (Columbus: Ohio State University Press, 1964), p. 196.

12 Surely Hawthorne chose his narrator's name not only for the implications of the surname, but also as a test of the reader's ability to perceive ironic historical contrasts. After publishing the first English Bible in 1535, Miles Coverdale became a Marian exile and was almost surely involved in the preparation of the Geneva Bible. Like others who would emerge as Puritans, he had attended Cambridge, opposed heard confession, and decried the worship of images. His fictional counterpart never completes his book, loves confessions, and delights in making icons of people.

13 Compare Hawthorne's first letter to Sophia Peabody from Brook Farm, April 13, 1841: "Here is thy poor husband in a polar Paradise! I know not how to interpret this aspect of Nature – whether it be of good or evil omen to our enterprise. But I reflect that the Plymouth pilgrims arrived in the midst of storm and stept ashore upon mountain snow drifts" (*Love Letters of Nathaniel Hawthorne* [Chicago: Dofobs, 1907], II, p. 3). Hawthorne's next comment, "Nevertheless they prospered, and became a great people – and doubtless it will be the same with us," seems wholly sincere.

14 For a contrasting view of the parallels between Blithedale and the Puritans see A. N. Kaul, *The American Vision* (New Haven, Conn.: Yale University Press, 1970), pp. 196–213.

15 Compare Francis Grund's wording: "The Genius of Liberty . . . is the bond of union, the confession, the religion, the life of Americans" (*The Americans in Their Moral, Social and Political Relations* [Boston: Marsh, Capen & Lyon, 1837], p. 107).

16 "Behind the aloofness, behind the witty and abrasive language, stands the man of good will who insists that the ideal represented by Blithedale is one to which he once genuinely subscribed" (James Justus, "Hawthorne's Coverdale: Character and Art in *The Blithedale Romance*," *American Literature*, 47 [1975], p. 33).

17 The various claims offered for Albert Brisbane, Orestes Brownson, or even George Ripley as models for Hollingsworth all ignore Hawthorne's refusal

to suggest any of these identities. His absurdly inappropriate comparison of Priscilla to Margaret Fuller should warn us against reading the book as a *roman à clef.*

18 "*The Blithedale Romance* is a daring book because in it Hawthorne tried for once to face directly the almost metaphysical anxiety that the practice of his art seemed to arouse in him" (Taylor Stoehr, "Art vs. Utopia: The Case of Nathaniel Hawthorne and Brook Farm," *Antioch Review*, 36 [1978], p. 102).

19 Howard Kerr has assembled persuasive evidence to show that "Coverdale's harangue resulted from an associative overflow of Hawthorne's own irritated and fearful feelings about trafficking with spirits, whether mesmeric or scientific" (*Mediums, and Spirit-Rappers and Roaring Radicals* [Urbana: University of Illinois Press, 1972], p. 59).

20 "The account of Westervelt's spiritualism reveals how fully, in the nineteenth century America of *The Blithedale Romance*, even the antiformal impulse of spiritual regeneration has become a species of formal, mechanical artifice" (Michael Bell, *The Development of American Romance* [Chicago: University of Chicago Press, 1980], p. 186).

21 Hawthorne, *The Marble Faun*, ed. William Charvat et al., vol. IV of the Centenary Edition (Columbus: Ohio State University Press, 1968), p. 3.

22 I am here indebted to Terence Martin's informative essay "Hawthorne's Public Decade and the Values of Home," *American Literature*, 46 (1974), pp. 142–52.

23 Hawthorne, *Our Old Home*, ed. W. Charvat, R. H. Pearce, C. Simpson, and M. Bruccoli, vol. V of the Centenary Edition (Columbus: Ohio State University Press, 1970), p. 334.

24 Hawthorne, *The English Notebooks*, ed. R. Stewart (New York: Russell & Russell, 1962), p. 23.

25 Probably written in 1862, quoted in E. H. Davidson, *Hawthorne's Last Phase* (New Haven, Conn.: Yale University Press, 1949), p. 77.

6. DISTRUST IN CONFIDENCE

1 Melville, *White-Jacket; or, The World in a Man-of-War*, ed. Harrison Hayford, Hershel Parker, and Thomas Tanselle (Chicago: Northwestern–Newberry, 1970), p. 151.

2 Melville, *Redburn: His First Voyage*, ed. Harrison Hayford, Hershel Parker, and Thomas Tanselle (Chicago: Northwestern–Newberry, 1969), p. 169. An informative study of Melville's upbringing in the Calvinistic tenets of the Dutch Reformed Church may be found in T. Walter Herbert's *Moby-Dick and Calvinism* (New Brunswick, N.J.: Rutgers University Press, 1977), pp. 20–44. Orthodox ministers like the Melvilles' Jacob Broadhead staunchly resisted the millennialism implicit in the Second Great Awakening.

3 Melville, *Redburn*, p. 169.

4 Carlyle had endowed Anacharsis Clootz with many of the qualities Melville was to ascribe to his ideal American: "He has wandered over this terraqueous Planet; seeking, one may say, the Paradise we lost long ago . . . A dashing man, beloved at Patriotic dinner-tables; with gaiety, nay with humour; headlong, trenchant, of free purse; in suitable costume; though what mortal ever more despised costumes? Under all costumes Anacharsis seeks the man." Among

Clootz's pilgrims are "long-flowing turbaned Ishmaelites" (*The French Revolution: A History* [New York: Random House, 1934], pp. 248, 269).

5 Melville, *Moby-Dick; or, The Whale*, ed. Charles Feidelson (New York: Bobbs-Merrill, 1964), p. 166.

6 Ibid., p. 114; Emerson, "Circles," from *Essays, First Series*, in *Complete Works of Ralph Waldo Emerson*, ed. E. W. Emerson (Boston: Houghton Mifflin, 1903–4), II, p. 301.

7 Melville, *White-Jacket*, p. 150.

8 *The Letters of Herman Melville*, ed. Merrell Davis and William Gilman (New Haven, Conn.: Yale University Press, 1965), p. 31.

9 E. H. Miller, *Melville* (New York: Braziller, 1975), pp. 21, 179.

10 Melville, *Moby-Dick*, p. 152; Melville, *Israel Potter: His Fifty Years of Exile*, ed. Harrison Hayford, Hershel Parker, and Thomas Tanselle (Evanston, Ill.: Northwestern University Press, 1982), pp. 9, 5.

11 Emerson, "Experience," in *Selections from Ralph Waldo Emerson*, ed. S. E. Whicher (Boston: Houghton Mifflin, 1960), p. 267.

12 Melville, *Moby-Dick*, p. 257, italics mine.

13 Ibid., p. 362.

14 Melville, review of *The California and Oregon Trail*, *Literary World*, 4 (1849), p. 292; *The Battle-Pieces of Herman Melville*, ed. Hennig Cohen (New York: Thomas Yoseloff, 1963), p. 52.

15 *Letters of Herman Melville*, p. 80; Melville, *Journal Up the Straits*, ed. Raymond Weaver (New York: Colophon, 1935), p. 149; Melville, "On the Photograph of a Corps Commander," in *Battle-Pieces*, p. 104.

16 Melville, *Moby-Dick*, p. 364; *Literary World*, 4 (1849), p. 291.

17 Melville, *Typee: A Peep at Polynesian Life*, ed. Harrison Hayford, Hershel Parker, and Thomas Tanselle (Chicago: Northwestern-Newberry, 1968), pp. 200, 201.

18 Ibid., p. 204.

19 Ibid., pp. 201–2.

20 Chap. 27 of *Typee*, in which this passage appears, was a late addition to the manuscript. See Leon Howard's "Historical Note" to *Typee*, p. 279.

21 Melville, *Israel Potter*, pp. 142, 148. See John McWilliams, "The Faces of Ethan Allen," *New England Quarterly*, 49 (1976), pp. 257–82.

22 *The Narrative of Colonel Ethan Allen* (New York: Corinth, 1961), p. 44.

23 Ibid., p. 78.

24 Melville, *Israel Potter*, p. 144.

25 *Walt Whitman's Leaves of Grass: The First (1855) Edition*, ed. Malcolm Cowley (New York: Viking, 1961), pp. 48, 69, 70.

26 Melville, *Journal of a Visit to London and the Continent (1849–1850)*, ed. Eleanor Melville Metcalf (Cambridge, Mass.: Harvard University Press, 1948), pp. 42, 66, 45, 72.

27 Melville, "Hawthorne and His Mosses," in *Herman Melville: Representative Selections*, ed. Willard Thorp (New York: American Book Co., 1938), p. 339.

28 Ibid., p. 339.

29 Ibid., pp. 337, 335–6, 338. After the excursion to the top of Monument Mountain in August of 1850, Duyckinck noted in his diary that Melville had "vigorously attacked" Holmes for declaring the superiority of the English (Perry Miller, *The Raven and the Whale* [New York: Harcourt, Brace & World, 1956], p. 284).

30 Melville, *Mardi: And a Voyage Thither*, ed. Harrison Hayford, Hershel Parker, and Thomas Tanselle (Chicago: Northwestern-Newberry, 1970), p. 557. See also Merrell R. Davis, *Melville's Mardi: A Chartless Voyage* (New Haven: Yale University Press, 1952).

31 Augusta Melville to Peter Gansevoort, April 7, 1857, quoted in Eleanor Melville Metcalf, *Herman Melville: Cycle and Epicycle* (Cambridge, Mass.: Harvard University Press, 1963), p. 165.

32 Melville describes Allen as "a tall, gaunt warrior, ferociously tatooed, with a beak like a buzzard" (p. 516). Such images invert Allen's public role as the subduer of savages. Allen had been one of the loudest proponents of All Mexico, had opposed the Wilmot Proviso, and had been proposing sponsor of the 1848 congressional resolution welcoming the French to the fold of revolutionary civilization (Frederick Merk, *Manifest Destiny and Mission in American History: A Reinterpretation* [New York: Random House, 1966], pp. 149, 175, 196–8).

33 A few years later, Melville's view that the 1848 revolutions would return the old order seemed historically confirmed. In "The Piazza" he wrote: "So Charlemagne, he carried it. It was not long after 1848; and, somehow, about that time, all round the world, these kings, they had the casting vote, and voted for themselves" (*The Piazza Tales* [London: Constable, 1923], p. 4).

34 Melville, *Moby-Dick*, pp. 4, 468.

35 Melville, *Redburn*, p. 202.

36 Merrell Davis suggests that this scene may reflect Melville's reaction to the Free Soil convention held in Buffalo in June 1848. Davis notes that Melville had written "a scroll containing ideas which a Free-Soil Convention would violently oppose" (*Melville's Mardi*, p. 90).

37 Alan Heimert, "*Moby-Dick* and American Political Symbolism," *American Quarterly* 4 (1963), p. 504.

38 Melville, "Hawthorne and His Mosses," p. 323.

39 Richard Chase, *Herman Melville: A Critical Study* (New York: Macmillan, 1949), p. 32.

40 Melville, *Redburn*, p. 188.

41 Melville, *Mardi*, p. 547. Compare Hawthorne's ridicule of Judge Pyncheon for pursuing "the big, heavy, solid unrealities, such as gold" (*The House of the Seven Gables*, ed. William Charvat, vol. II of the Centenary Edition [Columbus: Ohio State University Press, 1965], p. 229).

42 *Collected Poems of Herman Melville*, ed. Howard P. Vincent (Chicago: Hendricks House, 1947), p. 389.

43 Tocqueville, *Democracy in America*, trans. Henry Reeve, ed. Phillips Bradley (New York: Random House, 1945), II, pp. 62–3.

44 Heimert, "*Moby-Dick* and American Political Symbolism," pp. 498–501.

7. MIRROR MEN

1 *The Letters of Herman Melville*, ed. Merrell Davis and William Gilman (New Haven, Conn.: Yale University Press, 1965), pp. 123–5, 129.

2 Ibid., pp. 142, 125.

3 Ibid., p. 125.

4 Melville, "Hawthorne and His Mosses," in *Herman Melville: Representative Selections*, ed. Willard Thorp (New York: American Book Co., 1938), p. 332; Hawthorne, "Monsieur du Miroir," in *Mosses from an Old Manse*, ed. William Charvat, R. H. Pearce, and Claude Simpson, vol. X of the Centenary Edition (Columbus: Ohio State University Press, 1974), p. 170.

5 Thomas Philbrick, *James Fenimore Cooper and the Development of American Sea Fiction* (Cambridge, Mass.: Harvard University Press, 1961), pp. 40–1, 49; Edwin Fussell, *Frontier: American Literature and the American West* (Princeton, N.J.: Princeton University Press, 1965), pp. 12–18.

6 Melville, *Moby-Dick; or, The Whale*, ed. Charles Feidelson (New York: Bobbs-Merrill, 1964), p. 17.

7 The famous published version of the sailors' legend suggests the same need. See J. N. Reynolds, "Mocha Dick," *Knickerbocker Magazine*, 13 (1839), pp. 377–92.

8 Melville, *Mardi: And a Voyage Thither*, ed. Harrison Hayford, Hershel Parker, and Thomas Tanselle (Chicago: Northwestern-Newberry, 1970), p. 512.

9 Compare the conclusion of Reynolds's "Mocha Dick." To Reynolds, the killing of Mocha Dick and the growth of the American whaling fleet merely confirm the virtues of the American people and of their republican polity: "The varied records of the commercial world can furnish no precedent, can present no comparison, to the intrepidity, skill, and fortitude, which seem the peculiar prerogatives of this branch of our marine. These characteristics are not the growth of forced exertion; they are incompatible with it. They are the natural result of the ardor of a free people; of a spirit of fearless independence, generated by free institutions. Under such institutions alone, can the human mind attain its fullest expression, in the various departments of science, and the multiform pursuits of busy life" (p. 392).

10 Henry Nash Smith, "The Image of Society in *Moby-Dick*," in *Moby-Dick Centennial Essays*, ed. Tyrus Hillway and Luther Mansfield (Dallas: Southern Methodist University Press, 1953), p. 65.

11 *Letters of Herman Melville*, pp. 126–7.

12 Melville, "Hawthorne and His Mosses," p. 339.

13 Tocqueville, *Democracy in America*, trans. George Lawrence, ed. J. P. Mayer (New York: Doubleday, 1969), p. 755.

14 Ibid., p. 761.

15 Tocqueville, *Democracy in America*, trans. Henry Reeve, ed. Phillips Bradley (New York: Random House, 1945), II, p. 3.

16 Ibid., p. 16.

17 "Over a period of time Ahab made the White Whale the focus of exasperations that had accumulated in him as a widely if not universally shared human experience. In this interpretation (which I think Melville clearly intended) the

insanity consists in a cognitive change that focuses hostility and resentment previously directed against life and the universe in general, on the single tangible and accessible adversary" (Henry Nash Smith, *Democracy and the Novel* [New York: Oxford University Press, 1978], p. 42).

18 "Ahab throughout has eyes only for darks and depths, for leviathans and sharkish thoughts – like Narcissus, he mistakes his own dark reflection for truth, 'and this is the key to it all' " (John Seelye, *Melville: The Ironic Diagram* (Evanston, Ill.: Northwestern University Press, 1970), pp. 72–3. Similar suggestions have recently been made by Sharon Cameron (*The Corporeal Self: Allegories of the Body in Melville and Hawthorne* [Baltimore: Johns Hopkins University Press, 1981], p. 49) and by Michael Rogin ("Herman Melville: State, Civil Society, and the American, 1848," *Yale Review*, 69 [1979], p. 80).

19 Marvin Meyers, *The Jacksonian Persuasion* (Stanford, Calif.: Stanford University Press, 1957), p. 39.

20 Paul Brodtkorb is surely right to conclude that Ishmael "seeks out the interestingly strange, even to the extremes of horror and dread, to replace his sense of constricted emptiness with a sense of plenitude" (*Ishmael's White World: A Phenomenological Reading of Moby-Dick* [New Haven: Yale University Press, 1965], p. 112). Ishmael's awareness of these mental traits also enables him to retain a sense of humor and refrain from any suicidal action.

21 See Edwin Haviland Miller, *Melville* (New York: Braziller, 1975), pp. 55–6.

22 Tocqueville, *Democracy in America*, trans. Reeve, II, p. 106.

23 Melville to Richard Bentley, in *Letters of Herman Melville*, p. 150.

24 Ibid.

25 Melville, *Pierre; or, The Ambiguities*, ed. Harrison Hayford, Hershel Parker, and Thomas Tanselle (Chicago: Northwestern-Newberry, 1971), p. 30.

26 Melville's grandfather, General Peter Gansevoort, also died in 1812. Melville may have chosen the name Pierre because it connoted foreign aristocracy long rooted on American soil. Henry Murray discovered that three successive generations of Pierre Van Cortlands – two of them generals – maintained a large manor on the Hudson between 1762 and 1852 ("Introduction" to *Pierre* [New York: Hendricks House, 1949], pp. 430–1).

27 Isabel's probable illegitimacy may, in turn, be based upon family history. Amy Puett Emmers has discovered a letter of Thomas Melvill, Jr., which reveals that, shortly after Allan Melvill died, a "Mrs. A.M.A." and a "Mrs. B." made claims against Allan's interest in his father's estate. Thomas Melvill, Jr., paid money to Mrs. B., and no further claim was made. Emmers surmises that Mrs. A.M.A. was probably Allan Melvill's illegitimate daughter by Mrs. B. ("Melville's Closet Skeleton: A New Letter About the Illegitimacy Incident in *Pierre*," *Studies in American Romanticism*, 1 [1977], pp. 339–43).

28 Hawthorne had used the phrase "thorough-going democrat" to describe his own political attitudes in "Legends of the Province-House." This may be another instance of Melville's absorption of phrases from his reading; surely no comparison was intended.

29 Joel Porte, "Nature as Symbol: Emerson's Noble Doubt," in *Emerson and Thoreau: Transcendentalists in Conflict* (Middletown, Conn.: Wesleyan University Press, 1965), pp. 45–67.

30 Edgar Dryden has observed that "in Pierre's almost perfect prelapsarian world the realms of art and life, like those of the ideal and the actual, the subjective and the objective, should be as one" (*Melville's Thematics of Form* [Baltimore: Johns Hopkins University Press, 1968], p. 132). Unfortunately, Pierre carries the same expectations into his postlapsarian world.

31 F. Scott Fitzgerald, *The Great Gatsby* (New York: Scribner, 1953), p. 99.

32 Walt Whitman, *Leaves of Grass*, ed. H. W. Blodgett and Sculley Bradley (New York: Norton, 1965), p. 450.

33 Melville, "Hawthorne and His Mosses," p. 342.

8. CONFIDENCE IN DISTRUST

1 Newton Arvin, *Herman Melville* (New York: William Sloane, 1950), pp. 232–4.

2 Melville, "Poor Man's Pudding," in *Billy Budd and Other Prose Pieces*, ed. R. W. Weaver (London: Constable, 1924), pp. 201–2.

3 Melville, *Redburn: His First Voyage*, ed. Harrison Hayford, Hershel Parker, and Thomas Tanselle (Chicago: Northwestern-Newberry, 1969), p. 202.

4 Melville, "Rock Rodondo," in *The Piazza Tales* (London: Constable, 1923), pp. 196, 197. R. H. Fogle interprets the sketch as "a vision of complex organic unity in its reconciliation of opposing elements" (*Melville's Shorter Tales* [Norman: University of Oklahoma Press, 1960], p. 11). Many details of the sketch do not fit so benign an interpretation. The birds are described as making a "dissonant din," the penguins are at the bottom because they have short bills and no wings, and the fish beneath them are pathetic examples of "victimized confidence" ("Rock Rodondo," pp. 196–8).

5 Melville, "Charles's Isle and the Dog-King," from "The Encantadas," in *The Piazza Tales*, pp. 213–18.

6 Melville, "Rich Man's Crumbs," in *Billy Budd and Other Prose Pieces*, p. 208.

7 Melville, "The Paradise of Bachelors and the Tartarus of Maids," in *Billy Budd and Other Prose Pieces*, p. 244. As the seedsman specifies, the passage also confirms the Lockean notion of the *tabula rasa*.

8 "His last words reveal for the final time his vision of similitude and connect the two experiences he has had: 'Oh! Paradise of Bachelors! and oh! Tartarus of Maids.' The two, he is saying are one" (William B. Dillingham, *Melville's Short Fiction: 1853–1856* [Athens: University of Georgia Press, 1977], p. 205).

9 Melville, "I and My Chimney," in *Billy Budd and Other Prose Pieces*, p. 289.

10 H. Bruce Franklin's chapter comparing "Bartleby" to "Benito Cereno" is aptly titled "Worldly Safety and Other-worldly Saviors" (*The Wake of the Gods* [Stanford, Calif.: Stanford University Press, 1963], pp. 126ff.). The religious issue common to both stories also has an important national application.

11 Melville, "Bartleby the Scrivener," in *The Piazza Tales*, p. 20.

12 Leo Marx, who has interpreted the tale as "a compassionate rebuke to the self-absorption of the artist," observed that "only Bartleby faces the stark problem of perception presented by the walls" ("Melville's Parable of the Walls," *Sewanee Review*, 61 [1953], pp. 627, 607).

13 Tocqueville, *Democracy in America*, trans. Henry Reeve, ed. Phillips Bradley (New York: Random House, 1945), II, p. 135.

14 "If there is something saintly about Bartleby's other-worldliness, there is something loathesome about it too" (John Seelye, *Melville: The Ironic Diagram* [Evanston, Ill.: Northwestern University Press, 1970], p. 98).

15 Melville, "Benito Cereno," in *The Piazza Tales*, p. 67.

16 Melville, *Moby-Dick; or, The Whale*, ed. Charles Feidelson (New York: Bobbs-Merrill, 1964), p. 510.

17 Melville, "The Apple-Tree Table," in *Billy Budd and Other Prose Pieces*, p. 312.

18 *Letters of Herman Melville*, p. 170.

19 Warner Berthoff argues that *Israel Potter* "seems to have been undertaken as a piece of job work" and that it is "impromptu to the point of negligence in its narrative sequence and correspondingly erratic in emphasis and detail" (*The Example of Melville* [Princeton, N.J.: Princeton University Press, 1962], pp. 69–70). Perhaps the episodic, disconnected structure of this picaresque work is exactly appropriate to Melville's sense of the discontinuity in national history.

20 Melville, *Israel Potter: His Fifty Years of Exile*, ed. Harrison Hayford, Hershel Parker, and Thomas Tanselle (Evanston, Ill.: Northwestern University Press, 1982), p. 4.

21 Edwin Fussell, *Frontier: American Literature and the American West* (Princeton, N.J.: Princeton University Press, 1965), pp. 297–9.

22 Linking *Israel Potter* to *Pierre*, Carolyn Karcher argues that "Melville had by now come to see . . . the chief outcomes of the American Revolution [as] the enslavement of the white working class to the native American overlords who had replaced the British" (*Shadow over the Promised Land: Slavery, Race and Violence in Melville's America* [Baton Rouge: Louisiana State University Press, 1980], p. 108).

23 *Life and Remarkable Adventures of Israel R. Potter* (New York: Corinth, 1962), p. 51. For a detailed study of Melville's reworking of his source see the "Historical Note" to his *Israel Potter*, pp. 184–205.

24 Melville, *The Confidence-Man: His Masquerade*, ed. Hershel Parker (New York: Norton, 1971), p. 6.

25 Melville, *Israel Potter*, p. 148.

26 The comparison of Westerners to Tartars was not unique to Melville. Describing the political outlook of Easterners, Harriet Martineau wrote, "One fears the influence of the national councils of the Tartar population of the west, observing that men retrograde in civilization when thinly settled in a fruitful country" (*Society in America* [New York: Saunders & Oatley, 1837], I, p. 21).

27 Quotations are from Robert R. Allen's transcription of "The River" in *The Confidence-Man*, pp. 222–3.

28 Melville, "The 'Gees,'" in *Billy Budd and Other Prose Pieces*, p. 274.

29 Constance Rourke, *American Humor* (New York: Doubleday, 1953), pp. 86–90, 119, 231–6.

30 Tocqueville, *Democracy in America*, II, p. 17, I, p. 412, p. 443, I, pp. 223–4, II, p. 18.

31 Ibid., II, p. 74. In discussing Melville's novel, Warwick Wadlington observes that "the Trickster tricks because everything – whether law, proposition, or

role – is immaterial to him as an end and completely credible to him as a means" (*The Confidence Game in American Literature* [Princeton, N.J.: Princeton University Press, 1975], p. 159).

32 Melville, "Hawthorne and His Mosses," in *Herman Melville: Representative Selections*, ed. Willard Thorp (New York: American Book Co., 1938), pp. 335–6.

33 "Melville had led himself into a maze of nondramatizable speculation to which none of the traditions he could make use of were fitted to give adequate form . . . He attempts allegory without a superstructure of belief, and dialectic without the possibility of resolution" (Daniel Hoffman, *Form and Fable in American Fiction* [New York: Norton, 1973], p. 310). This is a puzzling conclusion to a splendid essay. Surely each of the conversational interchanges in *The Confidence-Man* is highly dramatic. Moreover, although Melville is working within a tradition of allegorical pilgrimage narrative (including "The Celestial Railroad" as well as Bunyan), none of his characters, except possibly the old man in the last chapter, seems to have an allegorical referent.

34 I am indebted here to Edgar Dryden's fine chapter on *The Confidence-Man* in *Melville's Thematics of Form* (Baltimore: Johns Hopkins University Press, 1968), especially pp. 151–2. For a careful and convincing account of the art with which *The Confidence-Man* was fashioned, see Watson G. Branch, "The Genesis, Composition, and Structure of *The Confidence-Man*," *Nineteenth Century Fiction*, 27 (1973), pp. 424–8.

35 See Hugh W. Hetherington, *Melville's Reviewers* (Chapel Hill: University of North Carolina Press, 1961), pp. 209, 218, 231, 233, 237, 242, 246; and G. Watson Branch, ed., *Melville: The Critical Heritage* (London: Routledge & Kegan Paul, 1974), pp. 272, 290, 295, 310, 317, 341.

36 Reprinted in *The Confidence-Man*, p. 278.

37 See G. Dekker & J. McWilliams, eds., *James Fenimore Cooper: The Critical Heritage* (London: Routledge & Kegan Paul, 1973), pp. 1–27. At the time Melville was beginning *Pierre*, he wrote the following self-prophetic sentence in his letter to the Cooper Memorial Committee: "It always much pained me, that for any reason, in his later years, [Cooper's] fame at home should have apparently received a slight, temporary clouding, from some very paltry accidents, incident, more or less, to the general career of letters" (*Letters of Herman Melville*, p. 145).

38 Melville, "Hawthorne and His Mosses," in *Herman Melville: Representative Selections*, ed. Willard Thorp (New York: American Book Co., 1938), p. 338; Melville, *Israel Potter*, p. 120.

9. TRUE BRIDGE OF SIGHS

1 Deborah P. Clifford, *Mine Eyes Have Seen the Glory: A Biography of Julia Ward Howe* (Boston: Little, Brown, 1978), pp. 138–47.

2 Letters quoted in Daniel Aaron's *The Unwritten War: American Writers and the Civil War* (London: Oxford University Press, 1973), pp. 42–55. Although Aaron does not discuss "Mine Eyes Have Seen the Glory" or Lowell's "Ode," my sense of the place of *Battle-Pieces* in literature about the Civil War is greatly indebted to his work.

3 Hawthorne to Henry Bright, 1863, in Aaron, *The Unwritten War*, p. 48.
4 Hawthorne, "Chiefly about War Matters," in *Tales, Sketches and Other Papers*, vol. XII of the Riverside Edition (Cambridge, Mass.: Houghton Mifflin, 1883), pp. 309–11.
5 Lowell, "Ode Recited at the Harvard Commemoration," July 21, 1865, in *The Complete Poetical Works of James Russell Lowell* (Cambridge, Mass.: Riverside Press, 1925), pp. 340–7.
6 *The Battle-Pieces of Herman Melville*, ed. Hennig Cohen (New York: Thomas Yoseloff, 1973), p. 37.
7 Melville, *White-Jacket; or, The World in a Man-of-War*, ed. Harrison Hayford, Hershel Parker, and Thomas Tanselle (Chicago: Northwestern-Newberry, 1970), p. 151.
8 Henry James, *Notes of a Son and Brother* (New York: Scribner, 1914), p. 430.
9 Melville, *Clarel: A Poem and Pilgrimage in the Holy Land*, ed. W. E. Bezanson (New York: Hendricks House, 1960), p. 422.
10 W. E. Bezanson, notes to *Clarel*, p. 543.
11 *The Letters of Herman Melville*, ed. Merrell Davis and William Gilman (New Haven, Conn.: Yale University Press, 1965), p. 277.
12 Jay Leyda, *The Melville Log* (New York: Harcourt, Brace and World, 1951), II, p. 714; Merton M. Sealts, Jr., *Melville as Lecturer* (Cambridge, Mass.: Harvard University Press, 1957), pp. 134–5.
13 *Collected Poems of Herman Melville*, ed. Howard P. Vincent (Chicago: Hendricks House, 1947), pp. 235–6.
14 Edward Gibbon, *The Decline and Fall of the Roman Empire* (New York: Random House, 1932), pp. 52–73.
15 George Bancroft, "An Oration Delivered before the Adelphi Society of Williamstown College, 1835," in *Literary and Historical Miscellanies* (New York: Harper & Bros., 1855), p. 433.
16 See Merton M. Sealts, "Melville's Burgundy Club Sketches," *Harvard Library Bulletin*, 12 (1958), pp. 253–67. The sketches are titled "Portrait of a Gentleman," "To Major John Gentian, Dean of the Burgundy Club," "Jack Gentian (Omitted from the Final Sketch of Him)," and "Major Gentian and Colonel J. Bunkum," in *Billy Budd and Other Prose Pieces*, ed. R. W. Weaver (London: Constable, 1924), pp. 353–77.
17 Melville, *Redburn: His First Voyage*, ed. Harrison Hayford, Hershel Parker, and Thomas Tanselle (Chicago: Northwestern-Newberry, 1969), p. 169.
18 Melville, *Billy Budd, Sailor (An Inside Narrative)*, ed. Harrison Hayford and Merton M. Sealts (Chicago: University of Chicago Press, 1962), p. 108.

CONCLUSION

1 Hawthorne, *The Blithedale Romance*, ed. William Charvat et al., vol. III of the Centenary Edition (Columbus: Ohio State University Press, 1964), p. 70; Melville, *Pierre; or, The Ambiguities*, ed. Harrison Hayford, Hershel Parker, and Thomas Tanselle (Chicago: Northwestern-Newberry, 1971), p. 284; Melville, "Hawthorne and His Mosses," in *Herman Melville: Representative Selections*, ed. Willard Thorp (New York: American Book Co., 1938), p. 332.

2 Henry Adams, *History of the United States of America during the Administrations of Jefferson and Madison* (New York: Scribner, 1909), IX, pp. 226, 240, 241, italics mine. The small yield of Adams's conclusion confirms an assertion made in his first volume: "Of all historical problems, the nature of a national character is the most difficult and the most important" (I, p. 176).

3 David M. Potter, "The Quest for the National Character," in *The Reconstruction of American History*, ed. John Higham (New York: Harper & Row, 1962), pp. 197, 207.

4 Emerson, *Journals and Miscellaneous Notebooks of Ralph Waldo Emerson*, ed. A. W. Plumstead and Harrison Hayford (Cambridge, Mass.: Harvard University Press, 1969), VII (1840), p. 525.

5 Ibid., X (1847), pp. 95–6.

INDEX